Daniel Mann

"The smell of Ujamaa is still there"

WÜRZBURGER GEOGRAPHISCHE ARBEITEN

Herausgegeben vom Institut für Geographie und Geologie der Universität
Würzburg in Verbindung mit der Geographischen Gesellschaft Würzburg

Herausgeber
R. Baumhauer, B. Hahn, H. Job, H. Paeth, J. Rauh, B. Terhorst

Schriftleitung
R. Klein

Band 121

Die Schriftenreihe Würzburger Geographische Arbeiten wird vom Institut für
Geographie und Geologie zusammen mit der Geographischen Gesellschaft
herausgegeben. Die Beiträge umfassen mit wirtschafts-, sozial- und naturwis-
senschaftlichen Forschungsperspektiven die gesamte thematische Bandbreite
der Geographie. Der erste Band der Reihe erschien 1953.

Daniel Mann

"The smell of Ujamaa is still there"

Tanzania's Path of Development between
Grassroots Socialism and Central State Control
in Ruvuma

Würzburg
University Press

Dissertation, Julius-Maximilians-Universität Würzburg
Philosophische Fakultät, 2017
Gutachter: Prof. Dr. Hubert Job, Prof. Dr. Barbara Sponholz

Impressum

Julius-Maximilians-Universität Würzburg
Würzburg University Press
Universitätsbibliothek Würzburg
Am Hubland
D-97074 Würzburg
www.wup.uni-wuerzburg.de

© 2017 Würzburg University Press
Print on Demand

ISSN 0510-9833 (print)
ISSN 2194-3656 (online)
ISBN 978-3-95826-066-5 (print)
ISBN 978-3-95826-067-2 (online)
urn:nbn:de:bvb:20-opus-154079

Acknowledgements

The following PhD thesis would not have been possible without the financial and institutional support of Friedrich-Ebert-Stiftung and their scholarship program. In particular, my deepest gratitude goes to Dr. Ursula Bitzegeio and Simone Stöhr for their continued encouragement throughout the entire research process. The successful conclusion of this dissertation would not have been feasible without the endorsement of a number of people, to all of whom I would like to express my appreciation at this point.

First of all, I have to thank my supervisor, Prof. Dr. Hubert Job. Not only for his constant scientific advice and constructive exchange throughout this PhD study, but first and foremost for giving me the great opportunity to partake in his extensive knowledge and deep compassion for Sub-Saharan Africa – ever since my first visit to Kenya on a field trip back in 2009.

I would also like to take the opportunity to thank Prof. Dr. Barbara Sponholz for her offer to act as the secondary assessor for this thesis.

Furthermore, I am obliged to my colleagues and friends at the Chair for Geography and Regional Studies at the University of Würzburg, Manuel Woltering, Johannes Schamel, Cornelius Merlin, Anu Lama, and Manuel Engelbauer, for their valuable inspiration and constructive suggestions throughout my years at the Institute for Geography. In particular, I would like to thank Ferdinand Paesler for his inestimable insights into the development discourse and the countless inspiring discussions on the progress of Africa.

Additionally, I would like to express my gratitude to Winfried Weber, for the preparation of the cartographic features of this thesis and his continued support in the creation of graphics and figures.

For a research like this, it goes without mentioning that the entire project would not have been possible without the support and the cooperation of the people of Ruvuma, and especially the inhabitants of Litowa, Matetereka and Mbingamharule. I will forever be obliged to their openness to this study and their engagement in its progression. Special thanks have to go to Lukas Mayemba for his hospitality during my stay in his village, and all the other wazee who offered their wisdom for the fruition of this thesis.

Above all else, I have to thank the St. Augustine University at Mwanza and the Archbishop James University College at Songea for their institutional support, without which the groundwork in Ruvuma would have been impossible. Especially, I would like to extend my deepest appreciation to my friends Noel Joram and Dennis Mpazagade, without whom I would never have gotten the access necessary for this study. Furthermore, I would like to thank Lena Dörsch for her support during the mapping of the villages and Neil Warner for proofreading the manuscript.

Last but not least, I would like to extend my thankfulness to my family, who has always supported my scientific career, and all of my friends, who offered to me their moral encouragement. Particularly, I am obliged to my comrades Johanna, Claas and Milos, for their neverending appreciation of my work, in good and in bad times. Finally, I have to thank my friend Annika Tulke for her invaluable support and friendship throughout the whole process. Without her advice, this thesis would never have been possible.

Würzburg, May 2017   Daniel Mann

Content

List of Figures

List of Tables

List of Maps

Abbreviations

ASP	Afro-Shirazi Party
CC	Central Committee
CCM	Chama cha Mapinduzi (Party of the Revolution)
FRG	Federal Republic of Germany
GDP	Gross Domestic Product
GDR	German Democratic Republic
HDI	Human Development Index
IDS	Institute for Development Studies
IfS	Institut für Sozialforschung (Institute for Social Research)
IMF	International Monetary Fund
MVIWATA	Mitandao wa Vikundi vya Wakulima Tanzania (Tanzanian Network of Farmers' Groups)
NBS	National Bureau of Statistics
NGO	Non-government Organization
NUTA	National Union of Tanganyikan Workers
PADI	Tanzania Mission to the Poor and Disabled
PRA	Participatory Rural Appraisal
RDA	Ruvuma Development Association
RRA	Rapid Rural Appraisal
RUCODIA	Ruvuma Commercialization and Diversification of Agriculture
SAGCOT	Southern Agricultural Growth Corridor of Tanzania
SDC	Songea District Council
SNC	Songea Network Center
SnP	Soya ni Pesa (Soya is Money)
TAA	Tanganyika African Association
TANU	Tanganyika African National Union
TFL	Tanganyika Federation of Labour
TSh	Tanzanian Shilling
TMMTF	Tanzania Mineral Mining Trust Fund
UK	United Kingdom
URT	United Republic of Tanzania
USAid	United States Agency for International Development
USD	United States Dollar
USDA	United States Department of Agriculture

Glossary of Kiswahili terms used in this thesis

Chama	a (political) party; an association
Fundi	a craftsman
Jembe	a hand hoe, the most commonly used tool in agriculture
Karanga	groundnut (Arachis hypogea)
Kikundi, pl. vikundi	literally: any kind of group; in the case of this study, a farmers' group
Kilimo	agriculture
Kipato	income
Kujitegemea	self-reliance
Maharage	common bean (Phaseolus vulgaris)
Mahindi	maize (Zea mays)
Mashine (ya kusaga)	a milling machine, usually just called "mashine" by local farmers
Mbegu	seed(s)
Mbolea	fertilizer
Mchama, pl. wanachama	(party) member; also, used for members of => *vikundi*
Mgomba, pl. migomba	plantain
Mjamaa, pl. wajamaa	a socialist
Mkulima, pl. wakulima	a farmer
Mnyonyaji, pl. wanyonyaji	literally: a sucker, a parasite; commonly used as term for exploiters
Mtaji, pl. mitaji	capital
Mtendaji	(village) manager
Mvuvi, pl. wavuvi	a lazy person
Mwalimu	literally: teacher; honorary form of addressing J.K. Nyerere, the first President and "teacher of the nation"
Mwenyekiti	(village) chairperson
Mzee, pl. wazee	an elder
Ndizi	banana
Pembejeo	(farm) inputs
Pesa	money
Shamba	a field
Soko	market
Tangawizi	ginger (Zingiber officinale)
Uchumi	economy
Ufuta	sesame (Sesamum indicum)
Ujamaa	literally: Familyhood; established as the general term for socialism in Kiswahili by J.K. Nyerere
Ujamaa vijijini	literally: => Ujamaa in the village; the commonly used term for the post-Arusha policy of "socialism and rural development"
Uhuru	freedom; independence

Umaskini	poverty
Umoja	unity
Ushirika	a cooperative
Wananchi	common people; common citizens

Abstract

In the 1960s, when most African nations gained their independence after the age of colonialism, several theories and strategies emerged with the goal of "developing" these apparently "underdeveloped" territories. One of the most influential approaches for this task was represented in Julius K. Nyerere's idea of Ujamaa, the Tanzanian version of African socialism.

Even before the Arusha Declaration established Ujamaa as a national development strategy in 1967, several groups of politicized young farmers took to the empty countryside of Tanzania to implement their own version of cooperative development. From one of these attempts emerged the Ruvuma Development Association (RDA), which organized up to 18 villages in southwestern Tanzania. The RDA became the inspiration for Nyerere's concretization of Ujamaa and its implementation on national level. Yet, the central state could not replicate the success of the peasants, which was based on voluntariness and intrinsic motivation.

In 2015, this exploratory study has revisited the Region of Ruvuma. Through a case study approach, relying mostly on qualitative methods, new insights into the local history of Ujamaa and its perception have been gathered. In particular, narrative interviews with contemporary witnesses and group interviews with the present-day farmers' groups have been conducted. Furthermore, NGOs active within the region, as well as regional and local government institutions were among the key stakeholders identified to concretize the local narrative of Ujamaa development. All interviews were analyzed according to the principles of qualitative content analysis. Additionally, individual villager questionnaires were used to achieve a more holistic picture of the local perception of development, challenges and the Ujamaa era. None of the original Ujamaa groups of the times of the RDA was still operational at the time of research and no case of village-wide organization of collective agriculture could be observed. Nevertheless, in all of the three case study villages, several farmers' groups (vikundi) were active in organizing development activities for their members. Furthermore, the perception of the Ujamaa era was generally positive throughout all of the case study sites. Yet, there have been significant differences in this perception, based on the village, age, gender and field size of the recipients. Overall, the period of Ujamaa was seen as an inspiration for present-day group activities, and the idea of such activities as a remedy for the developmental challenges of these villages was common among all stakeholders.

This thesis concludes that the positive perception of group activities as a vehicle for village development and the perception of Ujamaa history as a positive asset for the inception and organization of farmers' groups would be highly beneficial to further attempts to support such development activities. However, the limitations in market access and capital availability for these highly-motivated group members have to be addressed by public and private development institutions. Otherwise, "the smell of Ujamaa" will be of little use for the progress of these villages.

Zusammenfassung

In den 1960er Jahren, als die meisten Nationen Afrikas ihre Unabhängigkeit erlangten, entstanden etliche Strategien und Theorien, welche die „Entwicklung" dieser „unterentwickelten" Territorien zum Ziel hatten. Einer der einflussreichsten Ansätze für dieses Ziel war Julius K. Nyereres Idee von Ujamaa, der tansanischen Variante des afrikanischen Sozialismus.

Noch bevor die Arusha Deklaration Ujamaa 1967 als nationale Entwicklungsstrategie verankerte, versuchten sich verschiedene Gruppen junger, politisierter Bauern an ihrer eigenen Version der kooperativen Entwicklung im dünn besiedelten ländlichen Raum Tansanias. Aus einem dieser Versuche ging die Ruvuma Development Association (RDA) hervor, welche bis zu 18 Dörfer im Südwesten des Landes organisierte. Die RDA wurde die Inspiration für Nyereres Konkretisierung von Ujamaa, sowie dessen Umsetzung auf nationaler Ebene. Allerdings war der Zentralstaat nicht in der Lage, den auf Freiwilligkeit und intrinsischer Motivation beruhenden Erfolg dieser einfachen Bauern zu reproduzieren.

Die vorliegende explorative Studie wurde 2015 in der Region Ruvuma durchgeführt und konnte durch einen, im wesentlich auf qualitativen Methoden beruhenden, Case-Study Ansatz neue Einblicke in die lokale Ujamaa-Geschichte sowie deren Wahrnehmung sammeln. Insbesondere wurden narrative Zeitzeugeninterviews und Gruppeninterviews mit heutigen Bauerngruppen durchgeführt. Zur Konkretisierung des lokalen Narratives der Ujamaa Entwicklung wurden zudem in der Region aktive NGOs sowie Regional- und Kommunalverwaltung befragt. Alle Interviews wurden mittels qualitativer Inhaltsanalyse ausgewertet. Zusätzlich dienten an individuelle Dorfbewohner gerichtete Fragebögen zur Herausarbeitung eines umfassenden Bildes der lokalen Wahrnehmung von Entwicklung, Herausforderungen und der Ujamaa Ära an sich.

Keine der ursprünglichen Ujamaa Gruppen war zum Zeitpunkt der Erhebung noch aktiv. Ebenso konnte kein Fall einer das ganze Dorf umfassenden kollektiven Landwirtschaft beobachtet werden – kleinere Bauerngruppen (vikundi) kristallisierten sich dagegen als rezente Form kooperativer Entwicklungsmodelle heraus. Darüber hinaus war die Wahrnehmung der Ujamaa Ära in allen untersuchten Dörfern überwiegend positiv. Jedoch zeigten sich signifikante Unterschiede dieser Wahrnehmung bezüglich des Wohnortes, des Alters, des Geschlechts und der Größe des Feldes der Befragten. Insgesamt wurde die Zeit von Ujamaa als eine Inspiration für heutige gruppenbasierte Entwicklungsaktivitäten gesehen, welche wiederum von allen Akteuren als Möglichkeit zur Überwindung der Entwicklungsprobleme dieser Dörfer gesehen wurden.

Diese Dissertation kommt zu dem Schluss, dass die positive Wahrnehmung von Gruppenaktivitäten als ein Instrument zur kommunalen Entwicklung und die Wahrnehmung der Ujamaa Ära als ein positives „Asset" für die Gründung und Organisation von vikundi sehr vorteilhafte Voraussetzungen für weitere Entwicklungsaktivitäten bieten. Allerdings fehlen diesen Gruppen Kapital und Marktzugang. Dies muss von staatlichen wie nichtstaatlichen Entwicklungsorganisationen angegangen werden, andernfalls wird der „smell of Ujamaa" wenig zum Fortschritt in diesen Dörfern beitragen.

For Mzee Lukas Mayemba
and the Peasants of Ruvuma

May their spirit of solidarity forever overcome the hardships of life and
be an inspiration for the generations to come.

Umoja ni Nguvu

–

In unity, there is strength

1 Introduction:
The Tanzanian path of development

"Different are the lives of modern Africans from those of our grandparents, still we and our ancestors are linked together indissolubly. Our present day attitudes and reactions cannot be properly understood without reference to the economy, social organization, and religious basis of the society of fifty years ago; and so on back through time. But equally, I believe that great light can be thrown at the recent past, and then backwards, by an understanding of the aspirations and attitudes of present day Africa."

J.K. NYERERE, *Opening speech to the International Congress on African History*, 26th of September 1965 (NYERERE 1968c: 81)

Five decades ago, the newly independent Nation of Tanganyika embarked on a journey to develop the vast, rural areas of its territory and to transform the colonial order into a self-reliant, socialist society. From the eve of independence, Julius Kambarage NYERERE (1922-1999), the first President of Tanganyika and leader of the Tanganyika African National Union (TANU), tried to establish his idea of development, based on the values of the "traditional African" society and the vision of a future which would be free from the exploitation of men by men. In his understanding, one had to know one's own history, in order to build one's future. As becomes evident from his statement cited above, the new birth of free African nations necessitated the re-education of its citizens on their own history – a history which was supposed to act as a guiding idea in the development of the postcolonial society (NYERERE 1962b: 5).

At a time in which the Western world discussed ROSTOW's stages of capitalist development (ROSTOW 1956, 1959) and African intellectuals scrutinized the colonial "underdevelopment" of their continent and the influence of (neo-)imperialism on its societies (RODNEY 2012; FANON 1966, 1972; CABRAL 1968, 1970; MBOYA 1972; NKRUMAH 1963, 1965), Nyerere shared the common idea of many leaders of Africa's national liberation movements – that modernization and industrial development in the capitalist sense was not the exclusive model for the progress of their peoples (BHENGU 2011: 30).

In the years following Tanganyika's independence in 1961, and the unification with Zanzibar in 1964, Nyerere's powerful vision for a self-reliant Tanzania became one of the most discussed African development concepts of its era: Ujamaa – the Tanzanian version of socialism (SCHICHO 2009: 180). Building on an "attitude of mind" (NYERERE 1962b: 1) that would oppose individual accumulation of wealth and instead emphasize the values of equality and mutual solidarity that were thought to be represented in the extended family of the precolonial era (NYERERE 1968f: 106), it also emphasized the need for modernization in a society which was not yet able to produce enough wealth to escape poverty (NYERERE 1968g: 102p.).

Nyerere's call for building a nation based on the "traditional" values of African communitarism, was not only heard in the metropolis of those times. His words also reached the peripheral region of Ruvuma, in the very South of Tanganyika. There, a small group of enthusiastic TANU Youth league members would start their own interpretation of rural socialism in a village, which would soon become the role model for Ujamaa in the whole country: Litowa (IBBOTT 2014: 57–68). It has been their story and their ideas which inspired this research on Tanzania's path of development, as much as the thinking of Nyerere. And it will be the history of Tanzania's first Ujamaa village, and the grassroots association emerging from it, that will form the center-piece of this thesis.

Just as the late Nyerere sought to find the proper path to national development and independence in the past of his society, this thesis will attempt to learn from the experiences made by the people of Tanzania in the last five decades, in order to understand the challenges, they have faced and the insights they have gathered – and to appreciate which lessons this may hold for the future.

Ujamaa villages and policies for rural development

The Ujamaa ideology, as described by President NYERERE, called for a policy of development and self-reliance, based on communal work and the agricultural resources of Tanzania (NYERERE 1968b). While acknowledging the principles of European-style socialism, NYERERE emphasized that African socialism was to refer to different historical roots: Instead of class struggle and revolution after a period of capitalistic exploitation, Ujamaa was based on the principle of the extended family and the communalist traditions of Africa (NYERERE 1962b: 8).

While a coherent approach for rural development in the form of Ujamaa villages was not implemented before the Arusha Declaration of 1967, some local initiatives such as the Ruvuma Development Association (RDA), and several other communal villages organized by TANU Youth League members across the country, were engaging in cooperative agriculture since independence (EDWARDS 1998; PRATT 1978; IBBOTT 2014). On the side of the central state, it was the so-called settlement schemes that represented most of the rural development efforts before the declaration. These schemes were widely characterized as modernizing elements, but not as true communal efforts (IFS 1970; RODNEY & BOTCHWERY 1976).

After the Arusha Declaration (NYERERE 1967b), the Ujamaa village became the centerpiece of Tanzania's rural development strategies, being based on the principles of mutual solidarity, communal organization of work and communal ownership of social services, like healthcare and schools (HUIZER 1973; WEAVER & KRONEMER 1981). The pace of expansion of Ujamaa policy was tremendous by quantitative standards: While in 1968, there had been 180 villages with around 58,500 inhabitants (ELLMAN 1970: 5p.), by December 1972, over 2 million people were living in over 5,000 Ujamaa villages (JUMA 1976: 37).

Generally, three types of Ujamaa villages could be distinguished: Firstly, villages put up by enthusiastic supporters of the policy as a sort of "grassroots" movement. Secondly, new villages centrally planned by the national government, often in remote and formerly unsettled areas. And lastly, existing settlements that were allowed to "brand" themselves as Ujamaa villages, after introducing some forms of communal labour and ownership (KÜRSCHNER 1975; RAUCH & ALFF 1997; WEAVER & KRONEMER 1981).

During the rapid progress in the creation of "new" Ujamaa villages, however, less and less emphasis was given on the principles of communal work, local self-reliance and governance. Instead, the aspect of relocation and, later on, "villagization" became paramount, while the reorganisation of agricultural work became neglected. This "frontal approach" (RAIKES 1975: 46) might have led to the rapid increase in village numbers (CEDILLO 1973), but it also laid one basis for the subsequent development crisis of the mid-1970s to 80s, which eventually marked the end of Ujamaa policy (BRIGGS 1979; O'NEILL & MUSTAFA 1990; SAMOFF 1981). Nevertheless, some remarkable results in the provision of social services could be achieved through the creation of the Ujamaa village principle: The literacy rate reached an all-time high of around 90 % in the 1980s and up to 60 % of the population had access to medical services and clean water (MBELLE et al. 2002a).

It is the goal of this study to shed light into how these different stages of Ujamaa's rural development policy affected the life of the villagers on the ground. Specifically, the local history of the first grassroots movements represented by the villages of the RDA and its perception among the present-day inhabitants of those villages will be of key interest for this purpose.

The failure of Ujamaa in contemporary and recent analysis

LAL argues that analyzing the development of Ujamaa in theory and practice has to be done over different scales of analysis: From the global, to the national, to the regional, to the local. Rather than seeing these spatial scales as clearly separated into a respective inside and outside, however, the author argues that a more valuable understanding of the development of Ujamaa can be achieved by seeing these scales as mutually interlinked in various ways. The global backdrop of the postcolonial, cold war world cannot be seen as separated from the national development of Tanzania, and much less so the village scale as connected to the national policy in a linear fashion from top to bottom only. On the contrary, the local understanding of the Ujamaa policy, in many ways, shaped the national development policies. Specifically, LAL urges more scrutiny to the translocality of local communities even in early postcolonial times. Those villages should not be seen as isolated settlements, only receiving information from the outside world in the form of central state directives, but as entities connected to various levels through a variety of personal and institutional linkages (LAL 2015: 234–236).

The apparent difficulties in inducing agricultural growth and economic progress through Ujamaa policy and the subsequent abandoning of the socialist development paradigm have been the source of a vivid scientific debate from both "left" and "conservative" perspectives throughout the 1970s and 80s. Some disagreement could already be noticed on NYERERE's construction of an communal African past: While authors like IBHAWOH and DIBUA (2003) and TREUHEIT (1971) have clarified that there has been historical evidence for these classless African societies in the pre-colonial era, several analyses show that even before the colonization of Tanzania, there were signs of class hierarchy (BUGENGO et al. 1976; COULSON 1976). During the colonial period, the higher ranked members of the colonial bureaucracy could acquire the necessary education and resources for constituting a "petit bourgeoisie" at the break of independence – thus making the way "back" to a classless society even more difficult (COULSON 1976). Apart from this "cultural" approach, other authors have criticised Tanzania's failure to "disconnect" from its structural dependence on the former colonizing powers (RODNEY & BOTCHWERY 1976).

On a more technical and local scale, a large amount of critique has been directed at the work of agricultural extension workers and the development bureaucracy in general, for being too elitist and showing a considerably low esteem of local knowledge and the culture of the peasants (FREYHOLD 1975; OLIECH 1975). The most striking example for this indifference of the bureaucratic, urban based "petit bourgeoisie" (FREYHOLD 1979) towards the realities of rural livelihoods was possibly the complete neglect of pastoral communities even during the times of highest interest in rural development in Tanzania (MUSTAFA 1990).

The general attitude of Ujamaa's approach to rural development could therefore be characterized as underestimating the capacities of peasants and pastoralists alike, while trying to implement agricultural "modernization" from above (BOESEN et al. 1977) – in stark contrast to the basic-democratic principles of the Ujamaa-ideology. Indeed, a growing gap appears between the early idea of (local) self-reliance of the peasants and the fear of the central bureaucracy to "lose control" over its citizens, should they try to emerge on their own vision of Ujamaa (ERGAS 1980). Elaborating on this discrepancy, some authors – such as SHIVJI (1973, 1976) and HIRJI (1976), have accused the urban elite of the colonial era of acting as the new "ruling class" in post-colonial Tanzania.

In any case, there was a lack in qualified personnel for implementing agricultural change and providing assistance to the farmers, and a lack in the material prerequisites such as fertilizers and the like, leading to the disillusion of the peasants (NGEZE 1975). Furthermore, while the newly created villages had little to offer to potential new inhabitants in the form of material gains, there was still no shortage of arable land in Tanzania in the 1960s, which meant that land-reform and land shortage could not be used as incentives towards the peasantry (MABELE 1975; FREYHOLD 1979). It may have been this lack of incentives which induced the coercive policy of "villagization", rather than trusting in the ideological mobilization of the peasantry – another pivotal deviation from Ujamaa's principles and certainly the most critical aspect of NYERERE's political legacy (SCHNEIDER 2004).

More recent research on the history of Ujamaa has focused on the interrelations between foreign aid and national development policy (RUGUMAMU 1997), as well as on the particular role of NGOs within the practical implementation of Tanzania's rural development approach (JENNINGS 2002, 2008). The "class conflict" between the bureaucratic elite and the peasant population, which became highly debated during the 1970s and 80s (SHIVJI 1973, 1976, 1982; NABUDERE 1982; MEYNS 1982; MAMDANI & BHAGAT 1982) has also continued to be discussed against the concept of participatory development (SCHNEIDER 2014; LAL 2015).

After the end of socialist policy in Tanzania in 1985, and the general decline in interest in socialist development ideas after the fall of the Soviet Union, there has been considerably less scientific interest in the failure of Ujamaa and the implications for rural livelihoods. However, the renewed interest in natural resource management has led to the discussion of the issue of local ecological consciousness and consequences, as exemplified by SHERIDAN (2004) or LAWI (2007). Furthermore, the political legacy of "Mwalimu" Nyerere (MBELLE et al. 2002b), the perception of Tanzania's political history (KAMAT 2008) and the ongoing debate on state sovereignty in a globalized world still lead to new viewpoints on Tanzania's post-independence policies (BJERK 2010; LAL 2012).

In this regard, this thesis will try to elaborate the local perception of the failure of Ujamaa, as well as the local understanding of contributing factors on different scales.

Neoliberal development and its effects on the Tanzanian countryside

The ongoing economic crises of the 1980s – fuelled by rising oil prices and the war with Uganda – finally led the Tanzanian government to accept some of the "structural adjustments" advocated by the International Monetary Fund (IMF) in 1982, and the end of the Nyerere Presidency 1985. In this political environment, the demand for multi-party democracy, supported by various civic groups, questioned the viability of the former one-party system and eventually led to the creation of different opposition parties (MPANGALA 2004).

Even if socialism and the Ujamaa ideology were never officially abandoned, this led to a policy of deregulation and a drive towards lower state expenditure (MAIR 1996; SHIVJI 2006). Communal production and Ujamaa villages were no longer seen as a feasible way to increase agricultural produce and spark economic development. Instead, private investment and ownership became the strategy of rural development. Yet, many authors have criticized this neoliberal strategy for not delivering the economic growth and social development it promised: LIMBU and MASHINDANO (2002), for instance, have described the results of the rapid decrease of state intervention in rural areas as a vacuum, leaving these areas without social services and threatening the achievements of the Nyerere era. KOPOKA (2002) similarly points out the severe cuts in health care and education. On the side of agricultural production, authors like SKARSTEIN (2010) have described how neoliberal policy failed to increase the output, especially of food crops, in Tanzania. Even compared to the crisis years of 1979-1984, productivity and production remained stagnant. The free market, according to this view, was not the right incentive to inspire progress in a still smallholder dominated sector. On the contrary, a return into subsistence farming could be noticed in many areas of the country.

However, while market liberalization in Tanzania could generally not be characterized as improving rural lives from a material perspective, it created opportunities for the few wealthier peasants to expand their base of production through the expansion of private land property. More often than not, laws meant for restitution of "traditionally" owned land that was expropriated during colonial rule or early independence, were used by the more affluent members of society to enrich themselves by claiming traditional land rights (SHIVJI 1998). The question of how the transformation to multi-party democracy and the shift to free-market development strategies have influenced the opportunities and livelihoods of the rural population is still an open debate (SHIVJI 2009).

The question of how these changes after the end of Ujamaa affected the farmers of Tanzania on the village scale, and which strategies they have employed to adapt, will be another area of interest for this research.

Research questions

Within this context of Tanzanian development policies and strategies, this study aims to answer the following research questions:

On a direct analytical level, the aim of this thesis is to create a better understanding of the local perceptions, as well as the local understanding of development, with a specific focus on the influence of the Ujamaa period in this understanding. In particular, the following questions have been guiding the empirical research of this study:

1. How was the period of Ujamaa perceived on different levels, especially at the level of the villages?

2. How did contemporary witnesses experience the different phases of Ujamaa after independence and the subsequent changes after the end of the Ujamaa policy?

3. How do actors concerned with rural development today evaluate the period of Ujamaa? Are their views similar or different from those of contemporary witnesses and common villagers?

4. Does the period of Ujamaa still affect the present-day life at the village level? And if so, how does it affect it in the perception of different actors?

5. Does the perception and evaluation of Ujamaa on the village level shed new light into the discussion of why Ujamaa failed as a national development policy in Tanzania?

Secondly, the thesis aims to present an enhanced picture of how these local perceptions and actions interlinked with the national and international political sphere and, therefore, contributed to the shaping of the Ujamaa policy itself. Last but not least, the findings of this study have to be discussed regarding their importance for the present discourse on local development.

Structure of the thesis

Following this overall introduction into the Tanzanian framework of development policies and strategies, the thesis will present a short overview into the main concepts of development, in order to illustrate the background of ideas that influenced the Tanzanian history of development (chapter 2). As the core of this study has been the analysis of the Ujamaa era, most attention in that chapter will be given to the socialist perspective of development, especially the "original" Marxian understanding and the theories of Imperialism spearheaded by Lenin – both of which are considered to provide a valuable background into the history of political thought that eventually led to the blooming of various types of African Socialism in the early independence period. The conclusion of chapter 2 will be an in-depth analysis of one of the most contested elements of the Ujamaa ideology itself – the understanding of class structure in the Tanzanian context. Finally, the role of the party in the creation of this ideology will be scrutinized.

After this presentation of the relevant aspects of political history, chapter 3 will describe and analyze the different development strategies in Tanzania, which have been the result of the changes of political thought presented in the preceding chapter. Again, the focus will be on the different phases of development strategies after independence, with particular interest for the period of Ujamaa. In particular, the influence of the RDA on the practical implementation of Ujamaa's development policy will be discussed. The shifts after the end of Ujamaa and the most recent developments will be presented as well, in order to give a coherent background to the developments on the local level, which were the center of empirical research.

Subsequently, Chapter 4 will present the methods used for field research, while chapter 5 will present the case study area of Ruvuma, as well as the villages in which the research took place. Afterwards, the findings will be presented throughout chapter 6, before being discussed against the wider background of the Ujamaa discourse in chapter 7.

Limitations of research

While the development of Ujamaa ideology and its practical implementation will be discussed on the national level, and the general effects of the Ujamaa era and the subsequent changes after its disbandment will be illustrated for Tanzania in general, the local perceptions of these effects could only be analyzed for a limited area of case study villages, all within the Region of Ruvuma. Therefore, although the influence of these particular villages on the development of Ujamaa as a whole was considerable, the results of the empirical research cannot be considered to be representative for other regions of the country, which have a different local history and a different involvement in national policy making.

Furthermore, most of the data gathered from those case studies were derived from qualitative inquiries with different groups of stakeholders. As such, they are considered to provide a valuable addition to the understanding of local perceptions of development. However, as the restricted timescale and the general design of this research limited the collection of quantitative data on the village scale, the informative value with regards to issues like the concrete economic development on the village scale might appear to be less significant. In this sense, the thesis will adhere to the interpretation of those qualitative perceptions, which in itself are considered to be of valuable interest to the understanding of Tanzania's path of development.

2 Concepts of Development

"The purpose of development is man. It is the creation of conditions, both material and spiritual, which enable man the individual, and man the species, to become his best."

J.K. Nyerere, *The Church and Society* (Nyerere 1974b: 84)

Before we can start to have a look into the concrete development of the research area, it is necessary to consider the different ideas and concepts of development, which acted as an environment of thought during and after the Ujamaa period in Tanzania. Therefore, the following chapter is meant to give a short introduction into the major streams of ideas, also known as the "grand theories" of development, which were particularly influential during the early independence period of Tanzania and other African countries in the 1960s (Scholz 2004: 74p.). Although both sides of the big theoretical debate of this era are predated by the Marxian understanding of development (and were influenced by it in different ways), both the modernization and the dependency paradigm will be presented at the opening of this chapter. Afterwards, a longer consideration on Marxian and other socialist concepts of development will follow, leading up to the detailed discussion of Tanzania's Ujamaa ideology.

2.1 Terms, Definitions and "Grand theories"

The issue of wording

It appears to be worthwhile to address some definitory issues first: The term "development" as such has been an area of constant debate, at least since the second half of the 20th century, and several different understandings have emerged since then. First of all, the development of a society can be understood as a movement towards a status of being developed, i.e. one where basic needs like food and shelter are catered for, or one which would also include social participation by the members of society. Secondly, development could encompass a continuous process of change, both socially and economically. Thirdly, and more recently, the question whether there is one kind of development which is "good" for all societies has also gained ground (Chant & McIlwaine 2009: 12–14).

Bebbington, for instance, suggests that development might have two distinct meanings: On one hand, development as the expansion of the global capitalist system, integrating more and more people into the world market economy and therefore intentionally and unintentionally affecting livelihoods on various scales. On the other hand, development as the different interventions to develop the South (or the Third World after the Second World War), as an intentional process. Both aspects of development should be taken into consideration in geographic research of development (Bebbington 2005: 16–18).

Regardless of these "philosophical" foundations, however, the assumption of a process of development as such has led to different ideas on how to measure development, and thereby compare the status of development for different societies. While in the 1950s, development was mainly seen as synonymous with economic development, and the measurement of a nation's GDP was basically seen as sufficient for defining its development status, more holistic concepts have since been created. One of the more common examples is the Human Development Index (HDI), which also includes social indicators like health and education to measure the state of development (CHANT & MCILWAINE 2009: 14–18).

Coming with these ideas of measuring development was the difficulty of how to categorize different nations according to their "level" of development. While in the mid-20th century, expressions like "backward" or "underdeveloped" nations were common, the world system of the cold war led to the emergence of the term "Third World". Actually, this term was derived from the alignment or non-alignment of countries according to the blocs of this era, with the First World consisting of the capitalist West, the Second World of the real existing socialist East, and the Third World of the non-aligned countries. As the Third World was mainly made up of newly independent, hence "less-developed" nations, it later became strongly associated with being the "poorer" part of the world. The Brandt Report of 1980 established the term Global South as an alternative. In this understanding, South described the nations disadvantaged by a global economy, which was dominated by and profited almost exclusively the industrialized Global North (DICKENSON et al. 1995: 2–4).

With the end of the cold war, the term Third World has become increasingly criticized and is hardly used in the development debate of the 21st century. The main points of critique were that the three-world model oversimplified the complex situation of global economic relations, and implied a uniformity of Third World nations that was neither a political nor an economic reality. Even newer alternatives, like "developing world" or "developing countries" face the same weaknesses. In general, all of the terms, which attempt to subsume a wide range of nations, bear the difficulty of underestimating the internal differences both between and within those nations (CHANT & MCILWAINE 2009: 8–12).

Within this thesis, on the other hand, a closer look into the development of one nation (Tanzania) and the internal differences of its development will be taken. The place of Tanzania within the aforementioned categories is, therefore, of lesser concern. However, the thesis will use the term Third World in its original, political meaning, i.e. as a self-defined description of the non-aligned nations during the cold war era. It was the term that Julius Nyerere himself repeatedly used when evoking the spirit of a common struggle of these nations for the one world free of poverty (see, for instance, NYERERE 1970, 1977b).

Development Theory

The inaugural address of Hary S Truman at the beginning of his second term as president of the United States in 1949 is often considered to represent the advent of the "Age of Development". Throughout this period, the issue of global development became not only a political battleground between the two sides of the cold war, but also the center of a theoretical debate in development research (PAESLER 2015: 30p.).

One of the most influential approaches to the observation of differing economic development on a global scale has become subsumed under the label of "modernization theory". The origins of its understanding of the economic development of societies can be traced back to two concepts of thought. The first one was the application of Darwin's concept of evolution on human societies, represented by 19th century philosophers like Max Weber and Emile Durkheim. Within this understanding, there would not only be a continuous process of evolution in nature, but also an evolutionary succession of stages of social development. Hence, there would be a unilinear direction from "traditional" to more "advanced" societies. The second theoretical background consisted of diffusionist economic theories, based on the works of Adam Smith and David Riccardo, which proclaimed that growth would start in poles of growth or innovative centers, and then spread out to change the more backward periphery (CHANT & MCILWAINE 2009: 27–30).

One of the most well known and most illustrative examples of modernization theory is represented by the works of W.W. ROSTOW in the 1950s, which will act as an example for the basic elements of this stream of thought. As the level of examination by Rostow was the Nation State, he took a closer look at the macroeconomic data (production per capita, specifically) of different "developed" and "less developed" nations. Development in this context is understood as the level of production of a national economy. Rostow was particularly interested in the phase of rapid increase of GDP per capita, which he observed during the phase of industrialization of the major developed nations, a phase which he then dubbed the "Take-off". This Take-off would be preceded by a long phase of relatively slow economic development and then a phase of rapid technological advancements which would signify the "preconditions for the take-off" (ROSTOW 1956: 27).

Coming from this observation of historical economic development, he later proclaimed five distinct phases of economic development for each national economy: First, the "traditional society", characterized by traditional economic relations among producers and consumers, as well as common people and authorities. In this phase, the incentives for economic innovation would have been low and economic progress very slow. After this long phase, another phase would begin, which sets the preconditions for take-off. As already mentioned, this would be a phase of rapid technological advancement, but also political change – from the medieval feudal society to the liberal bourgeois one in Europe, for instance. This phase would therefore induce economic entrepreneurship and further technological development and lead up to the actual phase of the take-off, in which the observed rapid increase in economic growth took place in the European societies. This phase would also be accompanied by progress in other fields, especially health care, and lead to increased life spans and dropping birth rates. Afterwards, a "drive to maturity" would lead to the final stage of the age of mass consumption, as Rostow observed to be achieved in the Western countries of his era. He also theorized an additional stage "beyond consumption", as he observed tendencies in the United States of the 1950s to diverge some of the productive gains in higher birth-rates again, instead in increasing mass consumption. Nations and societies, according to this model, can be categorized along these stages, according to their level of production (ROSTOW 1959: 4–14).

Actually, Rostow's ideas underlined the necessity for short-term, "revolutionary" changes in the "methods of production" as well as of a "society's economic organization and its effective scale of values" (Rostow 1956: 47), rather than a long term economic growth in order for any society to develop from one stage to the next higher one. Rostow himself essentially was very aware of the similarities of his understanding of development to the Marxian idea of development (see below): A process of stages differentiated by rapid and revolutionary changes between those stages. However, he claimed that while Marx would only have seen the movement between stages as a product of the needs of the economy itself, he would include the human ability to decide between alternatives presented by technological process (Rostow 1959: 14–16).

This might be called quite an oversimplification of Marx's understanding of human development, especially since the element of human decision to change an existing system is, in fact, the cornerstone of Marxian historical dialectic (see chapter 2.2.1). Rather than adding a new element to Marxian thinking, Rostow appears to have just left out the role of economic development in shaping a society altogether, having thus presented a theory of development stages just as the Marxists – but without class struggle. This, of course, may explain the popularity of his works during the cold war era, where a "non-communist" theory of development was highly needed. This notion of his earlier works has been enshrined in the title of his standard monograph "The stages of economic growth. A non-communist manifesto", first published in 1960 (Rostow 1971).

Based on this understanding of development as a succession of stages which can be reached through technological progress and social modernization, most development strategies of the 1960s and 70s followed this concept of development in which the lower developed countries (i.e. the newly independent states of Africa, for example) ought to repeat the steps which the industrialized nations had taken to achieve their stage of development. Derived from Rostow's look at the Nation State as the basic unit of development, any obstacles to this repetition of development were seen as inherent to the traditional elements of these societies and the lack of entrepreneurship within their economies. In spite of increasing criticism by representatives of dependency approaches (see below), the modernization paradigm of big technological investment and social modernization remained the staple of international development intervention throughout the 1980s (Scholz 2004: 74p.).

From a more radical point of view, the whole idea of "development" has repeatedly been under attack for its underlying notion that there would be a state of being underdeveloped and a state of being developed, and that development would enable a society to move from the former to the latter. Instead, development and underdevelopment can be seen as two sides of the same ongoing process. The one side is developing through exploiting and thereby underdeveloping the other (Blaut 1977: 310).

Based on the philosophical and theoretical basis of Marxist thinking, various neo-Marxist theories of development emerged from the 1960s. In this stream of thought, the universality of the European way of economic development was challenged from different angles. Specifically, these theories questioned the idea that the economic development of Europe, and later the United States, which Rostow and others had observed, was based entirely on endogenous factors within these societies. On the contrary, these scholars saw the exploitation of the non-capitalist, "traditional societies" during the ages of mercantilism and imperialism as one of the actual reasons for this economic development during industrialization (see also chapter 2.2.2) (Scholz 2004: 81–86).

Dependency theory became one of the most powerful of these approaches. It was based on a historical materialistic understanding of colonialism, i.e. that the development of Europe and the United States was inherently based on the domination and the active underdevelopment of the non-European world. Teontonio Dos Santos (1970) described the geographical structure of this underdevelopment and observed that in the world system of the 20th century, only a few economically advanced nations (the centers or metropolis) could achieve independent development, while all other nations and regions could only develop dependent on the former. Accordingly, their economies were geared towards the (colonial) centers and surplus was extracted by the ruling class of those centers, while a local class of collaborators (compradors) exercised the power in the dependent nations on behalf of the centers.

Two main schools of thought influenced the creation of dependency theory. Firstly, the *Monthly Review* (a U.S. based socialist journal) school of monopoly capitalism, which regarded the economic stagnation of most Third World countries as an irrational form of dependency, as it contradicted the development of industrialized countries, which had overcome stagnation through fostering general consumption (through the creation of the Military-Industrial complex, in their view) and the emergence of a consumerist society. Only through eradicating dependence on those industrialized countries, could economic development of the Third World be achieved (Baran & Sweezy 1968).

Secondly, the *dependencia* school of thought emerged in Latin America, analyzing the economic dependence and stagnation in this region (Sunkel 1972; Furtado 1968; Dos Santos 1970). The latter was made popular in the Anglophone world by the works of Andre Gunder Frank, a leading critic of modernization theory. In his analysis of the economic development of Latin America, he emphasized the continuing extraction of surplus value out of the periphery into the capitalist centers, even after the political independence of those countries. Only the leading metropolis would be able to extract all the surplus value, while regional centers would themselves be satellites to the main metropolis and could control only their direct, regional periphery. In his account, trade and connection to the world economy did not foster development (as in modernization theory), but on the contrary intensified the ongoing underdevelopment of the periphery, by constantly removing the surplus created in it (and thereby the base for capitalist accumulation inside its own society). Only the disconnection from world economy could therefore induce development in the periphery. In conclusion, it was not the perseverance of old traditions and outdated social relations that hampered development in the Third World, but its economic connection to advanced capitalist societies (Frank 1966, 1979). One shortcoming in Frank's theory has been described as the lack of characterization of the exact mode of surplus extraction, which partly led to the notion of emphasizing the relations of countries and regions and neglecting the relations of classes inside and across different societies. Cardoso (1982) was one of the dependency theorists who was more interested in the specific nature of (under-)development in different societies and found Frank's approach too generalizing. Overall, however, dependency theory retained a holistic and global approach and often equated dependency with under-development (PEET & HARTWICK 2009: 166–172).

Despite their differences, representatives of the dependency school of thought actually agreed with the modernization paradigm, in a sense that the less developed nations should be enabled to achieve the higher development stage of industrialized nations. The main difference therefore lay in the diametrically different concepts which either theory presented as the strategy for this goal: While modernization the-orists suggested the rapid and full integration into the global market economy, in or-der to enable technological progress through foreign investment, and social change through globalization, dependency theorists recommended (partial) disconnection from the world economy, in order to enable those nations to develop a self-sustain-ing economy in the first place, before having to compete on the international level (SCHOLZ 2004: 86p.).

Accompanied by the structural changes of global economy in the 1980s, the big theoretical debate between modernization and dependency slowly petered out and was replaced by a new "realism" in development thinking. A plethora of new devel-opment theories of small and middle range emerged in this time, which refrained from trying to address the big structural issues of underdevelopment on a global scale, and instead tried to concentrate on the creation of ideas and strategies that could actually be tested "on the ground". Such theories include vulnerability and livelihood approaches, participatory and communal development, to name just a few. On global scale, the 1980s have often been described as the lost decade for de-velopment, due to the prevalence of structural adjustment programs and economic downturn in many less developed countries. Partly as a reaction to this observation, the new common idea of sustainable development has emerged since the 1990s and is supposed to lead the strategy of international development cooperation (SCHOLZ 2004: 86–89).

An interesting overview on some of the most influential concepts of development from a geographical perspective, as well as the implications of the recent post-devel-opment discourse within this context, has been presented by PAESLER (2015: 60–73).

2.2   Socialist Development Theories

"First, and most central of all, is that under socialism Man is the purpose of all social activity. The service of man, the furtherance of his human development, is in fact the purpose of society itself. There is no other purpose above this; no glorification of 'na-tion', no increase in production – nothing is more central to a socialist society than an acceptance that Man is its justification for existence."

J.K. NYERERE, *Freedom and Socialism* (NYERERE 1968d: 4)

After this short introduction into some of the most well-known views on develop-ment, the question arises, how the different thinkers of socialism approached the theme of human development. Therefore, this study will take a closer look into the original Marxian understanding of the topic. After these considerations, the basic elements of the theories of imperialism, which were developed by Lenin and other (alleged) followers of the Marxist tradition will be illustrated. Both chapters are seen as a theoretical background for the analysis of Tanzania's own version of socialist development ideology, which will be presented in chapter 2.3.

2.2.1 Classical Marxian understanding of development

In order to understand the Marxist conception of human development, one first has to understand the concept of historical materialism, which was developed as an antithesis to radical Hegelian idealism. In HEGEL's understanding of human history, he would state that ideas and philosophies direct the path of human history. Those ideas and philosophies would be developed in a dialectic manner through a chain of thesis, antithesis and synthesis, thus step by step arriving at a new leading idea for human societies. The role of philosophy and sciences would, therefore, be the synthesis of practical arts and spiritual beliefs, creating an "absolute" or "objective" spirit, which would entail this leading idea for each epoch of human history (HEGEL 2014: 367–388). For instance, in the times of European Enlightenment, the belief that God's will shaped the form of society was replaced by the idea of human rationality as a leading idea. Human history would, therefore, be more than a repetition of the same ideas and the same sorts of societies, but would have a progressive direction, ultimately arriving at the ideal form of society (PEET & HARTWICK 2009: 143–145).

In HEGEL's concept however, all these ideas would already exist in a transcendental entity dubbed the World Spirit, sometimes described as a modern concept of God, sometimes as the collective conscience of humankind. In a sort of dialectic repetition, ideas and philosophies would pass between human rationality and the World Spirit eternally, creating advancement in human societies (HEGEL 2013a: 224p.).[1] While both, Karl MARX (1818-1883) and Friedrich ENGELS (1820-1895), were followers of this sort of radical German idealism during their youth, they ultimately rejected the idea of a transcendental World Spirit, simultaneously based everywhere and nowhere. They insisted that all human thinking, including human rationality, was created by physical human beings. Human beings, in their view, would base their thinking on their experience of nature and society, on the material base of their livelihood. Therefore, they created the idea of historic materialism to replace Hegel's concept of a World Spirit, in order to describe the external factors of human thinking that shaped the world in which individuals would develop their ideas. This world, of course, was in itself the result of ideas developed by human beings, thus human history remained a dialectic process (PEET & HARTWICK 2009: 143–145).

The most useful starting point for a wider view of the Marxist understanding of human behavior and human development, therefore, is the basic concept of labor

---

1 For a deeper understanding of Hegel's concept of the "spirit" and the interaction between philosophy and human history, see, for instance, HEGEL (2013b: 226–349) and HEGEL (2013c: 6–49).

that underlies all of MARX's analysis of economic as well as social development. In accordance with his scientific view on human evolution, MARX defines labor as an interaction between human beings and nature itself. In the beginning of human evolution, humans used their natural means, their hands and minds, to interact with nature and to fulfill their needs for food, shelter, and so on. However, by transforming nature through labor, humanity also changed its own nature, developing the hidden potentials of natural resources, gaining higher forms of productivity and therefore transforming nature more efficiently. By developing the efficiency of labor, humankind changed from being just another species relying purely on nature, to one shaping nature itself to satisfy its needs and wants (MARX 1972b: 192).

For them, there was no transcendental, independent or eternal "human nature". For both, MARX and ENGELS, humans were just a distinct form of social, albeit conscious animal, a result of evolution. As any other animal, humans were bound by their internal metabolism to depend on nature for addressing their needs to survive. As such, human consciousness and society were shaped by the (external) natural environment. However, in contrast to any other animal, humans started to consciously and intentionally transform nature to fulfill their needs and create their subsistence. The unique part of human evolution was not only the use, but also the constant development of new tools and techniques to transform the environment. Humankind therefore produced its own subsistence. By constantly developing more and more efficient tools and forms of labor, humans were able to extend the power of these productive forces for the transformation of nature and thereby reduce the time of labor required for fulfilling the metabolic needs of their bodies. Thus, they created the opportunity to advance the material standard of living and create time available for the advancement of ideas, concepts, science – and the creation of more and better tools. In Marxist thinking, the forces of human development consist of human labor, physical tools and the mental capability to invent conceptions, plans and intentions – these forces are described as productive forces. The development of its productive forces therefore enabled humankind to gain independence from the pure dependence on nature and a life only consisting of survival (PEET & HARTWICK 2009: 147p.).

By putting the spiritual belief of Hegelian idealism back on its feet, MARX and ENGELS insisted that human consciousness was the product, rather than the cause of the material base. In his critique on the Hegelian philosophy (MARX 1964: 378p.), MARX exemplified this materialist view on human beliefs by depicting religion as a man-made structure for organizing and controlling human societies. While, in this sense, the critique of religion would be the first sort of critique necessary to change society, MARX does not stop there: Human consciousness does not come out of nowhere, but is a representation of the real (hence material) conditions in which human beings are living at a given time. Therefore, philosophy cannot refrain itself in analyzing the leading ideas of a society (like Idealism would), but has to include the material basis of the respective society as well (MARX 1964: 383–385; see also MARX & ENGELS 1962: 17–50).

However, consciousness and matter are seen as being in a dialectic relationship, meaning that human development was a product of inner and outer contradictions. The environment shapes the social system and vice versa. Inner relationships are binding societies together like parts of a body, but there are also contradictions between different parts of any society. Furthermore, there are outer relations, meaning that different societies influence one another – both in the way of ideas and physical (spatial) connections. In any case, rapid human development (i.e. the step from one dominant order of society to another) can only occur, if the contradictions (be they internal or external) reach a breaking point (PEET & HARTWICK 2009: 146).

The classical example for this process would be the transition from the feudal to the bourgeois organization of society during the French Revolution, which replaced the feudal ownership of the means of production with the bourgeois one (MARX & ENGELS 1960a: 475). In Marxist terms, this was caused by the overwhelming contradictions between the emergent capitalist production and the persistence of the old, aristocratic system of governance. The craftsman was replaced by the factory worker, the invention of the steam engine powered the industrial revolution, which needed the free, proletarian worker – and not the small farmer tied to his feudal lord for eternity. It needed the world market and the liberal government – not absolute aristocrats ruling over tiny pieces of land (MARX & ENGELS 1960a: 462–465).

Having defined the intentionality of production as the first transformative historical moment in human development, MARX sees the second transformative historical event in the moment when the means of production came under the control of a ruling elite. Since this moment is seen in the area of five to six thousand years before the present, it was mostly (fertile) land which could be considered to be a means of production. From this time onward, the individual working on this land did not only have to spend labor for the subsistence of him or herself, but also for the subsistence of the landlord (MARX 1982: 383–386).

This unwarranted surplus labor is the definition of exploitation. To explain why people were attending surplus labor not for their own benefit, but for the benefit of someone else, is the main reason for Marx's interest in the social relations of production. Since the application of the productive forces is essential to human existence, control over these productive forces is power in its pure form, as it means the power to control the future of existence. Again, social relations are not seen as something static or eternal, but as a dialectic interplay between various actors, aiming at controlling the productive forces of a given society (PEET & HARTWICK 2009: 148p.).

As the control over the means of production represented the most basic and powerful social relation between individuals and groups in the Marxian understanding, the economic order had profound effects on the social organization and the political life of a society. MARX and ENGELS argued that the development of the productive forces (i.e. the stage of development of human ability to transform nature to suit its needs) determined the shape of a society in cultural and political terms (MARX & ENGELS 1962: 69p.).

That is not to say, however, that the economic development determined the social structure in an absolute manner. Rather, it laid the economic foundations on which the social structure would develop. Indeed, MARX himself observed the apparent anachronism of the German situation after the failed revolution of 1848: Even in an industrializing society, it was possible to reestablish elements of feudalism and absolutism, illustrating the non-linear relation between the development of productive forces and the organization of society (MARX 1964: 381–383).

On the other hand, the development of productive forces determines the level of exploitation of surplus labor in any society: In a society with low productive forces, the margins of labor that can be exploited are very narrow, as taking away labor time or produce from a peasant can be a matter of life and death, since he or she hardly produces enough for his or her family. When the productive forces are higher, more commodities are produced, and the material base for exploitation increases. Yet, societies with a higher material development necessitate higher specialization, and therefore a more complex organization of society – especially when the ruling class wants to legitimize extracting surplus labor. Thus, in historical terms, the rule of the clan leader was replaced by that of the church and the nobility, and then by the liberal democracy, which represents the bourgeois state. In Marx's understanding, any state will always be the vehicle of the ruling class. However, since the economy does not determine the political superstructure in a unidirectional way, the exact nature of economic order, social formation and political system can only be understood through specific empirical analysis. The whole complex of the dialectic inter-linkage between natural environment, the forces and the relations of production, as well as ideology, culture, state and politics are understood as the *mode of production* (see Figure 1) (Peet & Hartwick 2009: 154–156).

Figure 1: The Mode of Production

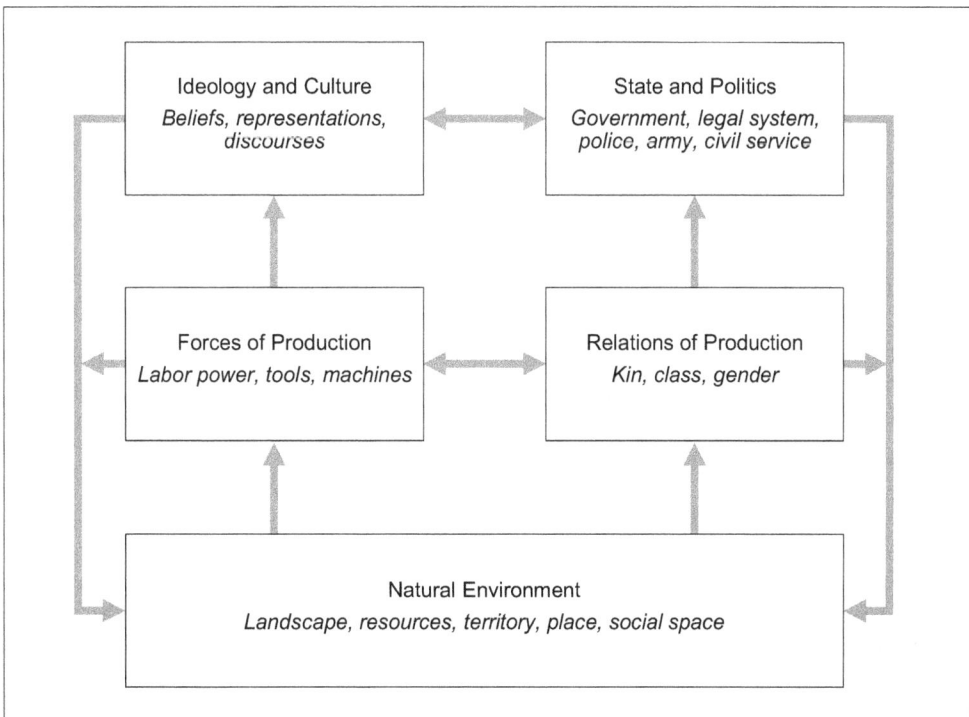

Source: Peet & Hartwick (2009: 156)

In the Marxian view, economic development necessitates the development of more productive tools, machinery, etc. to increase the average amount of production in a given time of labor. Some of these material benefits can be distributed inside the capitalist society by means like unionizing, strike, etc. Generally, however, a social transformation would mean a shift from one mode of production to another, i.e. from one with lower to one with higher productive forces. As any historical mode of production had its inner contradictions, MARX and ENGELS see these revolutions – the qualitative shift from one mode of production to another – as a result of those contradictions becoming too big to be contained inside the old mode of production. The revolution would be preceded by the ideas and concepts of the new mode of production emerging under the old system, but materializing itself under the new one: While the ruling class is able to subjugate the whole society in order to sustain its material base (in the case of the bourgeoisie this would be the global establishment of capitalism), the material base of all the subjugated classes would diminish to a point where they themselves have to break the power of the ruling class in order to survive, and become the new ruling class themselves. The ideas and concepts that were created during the time of oppression (in the case of the bourgeoisie, individual freedom) would then become the new ruling ideas of the society (MARX & ENGELS 1960a: 471p.).

However, these "laws of transformation" cannot be seen as a sort of fixed, functionalist law of history, which would imply that these changes have to occur at a certain moment of time. Rather, they are an example of MARX's dialectical view on human history. In his lifetime, Marx only analyzed one specific mode of production in a detailed manner – the capitalist one – and his views on other modes (like the "Asiatic" one) suffer from the colonial nature of his information (PEET & HARTWICK 2009: 156–159). Nevertheless, according to the posthumous *Grundrisse*, he appears to have acknowledged at least four historic modes of production (plus the envisioned socialist and communist mode of production). These were primitive communist hunter-gatherer societies, kin-ordered tribal agricultural societies, tributary or state societies (feudalism) and finally capitalism (MARX 1982: 383–421).

While some of their earlier works suggest that MARX and ENGELS saw these stages of the mode of production in a linear manner (see, for instance, their understanding of history in *Die deutsche Ideologie* (MARX & ENGELS 1962: 50–71), first published in 1845), meaning that each society would run through each stage through its development, later comments imply that MARX was starting to see the economic and social development of societies as a more complex issue. Different modes of production can occur simultaneously in different countries, and even coexist inside one country, while some societies may skip some stages on their development. The same is true for the nature of accumulation, which may show different characters in different societies, may happen at different stages in history, and may have a different order of phases. MARX himself saw the "classical form" of the history of the modes of production only to be true for the case of England, which he used as his main field of analysis (MARX 1972b: 744). Furthermore, the combinations and interactions between different societies – its articulations – imply that the uneven development among societies leads to the dominance or subordination of one society over or under another. Therefore, each of these articulations bears the potential of developing the more powerful (by exploiting the subordinated) and underdeveloping the less-powerful society (PEET & HARTWICK 2009: 156–159).

Although the majority of Marx's work is based on his analysis of British industrialization and the British proletariat (see LINDNER 2011, for instance, for a discussion on Marx's eurocentrism), his writings on British rule in India and colonialism in general give an impression on his view of the connection between capitalism, colonialism and development. Most of these writings were published in 1853 in the *New-York Daily Tribune* (MARX & ENGELS 1960b).

In MARX's view, British rule in India did not differ from the style of rule applied by other foreign powers, and was in many ways replicating its mode of exploitation. Yet, the colonial rule over India brought more atrocities to the Indian people than centuries of foreign rule by the Moguls. All wars, conquests and invasions before colonialism had only touched the surface of the Indian society, while the rule of the British meant that the whole society was affected by the new mode of exploitation. MARX argues that the European colonizers treated their new subjects even worse than the slave owners of the old time, as those slave owners had paid for their "property", while the Europeans developed a whole new level of despotism and oppression to extract any available surplus from their colony. On the other hand, the British did not care to establish a new society or a new development idea in place of the old Indian world, which they had so thoroughly destroyed (MARX 1960a: 128p.).

MARX sees two important traditional elements of Asian societies, which had been destroyed by the British: Firstly, Asian agriculture would by and large depend on irrigation, and the organization and maintenance of the irrigation infrastructure was the main task of the administrative class. All Asian governments therefore had the main economic function of organizing these public works. Thus, agricultural production was heavily dependent on the quality of the respective governments. While the British took over the financial and military functions of the old governments, they neglected this task of public work organization and thereby induced agricultural decline and stagnation. Secondly, MARX sees the village as the basic economic unit in the Indian context, which he describes as a largely self-sufficient unit (except for the centrally organized irrigation), characterized by the integration of agricultural and craft-making activities, especially weaving and textile production. By the introduction of industrialized textiles from the British motherland and the destruction of the traditional production methods in India, the colonizers thus destroyed the economic base of this village economy. The social formation of the Indian village was therefore on its way to disappearance, not so much by the military rule of force, but by the introduction of British steam power and British free trade (MARX 1960a: 129–132).

While emphasizing the purely egoistic reasons of the British for the colonization of India, MARX strongly argues against the idealization of the idyllic traditional village society. In his view, the old society of India (and all of Asia for that matter) had been a bulwark of despotism and social stagnation, characterized by the caste system and slavery. The destruction of the traditional Indian society by the colonizers had therefore been the first social revolution ever occurring in Asia. By disconnecting the craftsman and the farmer from his means of production and his piece of land, the British thoroughly destroyed the old social order. Even given the atrocities of British rule, MARX therefore asks if mankind could fulfill its destiny without the radical revolution of the social conditions in Asia. This radical revolution he sees as being brought about by the British colonization in India, which therefore might be playing an (unintended) part on the way to a socialist future (MARX 1960a: 132p.).

In his second writing about India – this time titled "The future results of British rule in India" (MARX 1960b), – MARX emphasizes this modernizing power of the British colonialism. Firstly, he describes India as a land without history, in which no history would be that of its people, but that of the respective foreign invaders, who brought India under their control in the past. Therefore, the British rule would not be anything novel in the Indian case. However, in contrast to the Arab, Turkish or other foreign rulers who actually adapted to the Indian culture, the British would be the first "superior" culture to rule over India, and therefore be able to transform the Indian society on all levels. MARX assigns two "historic" tasks to the English invaders: To destroy the old "Asian" society, and to lay the foundation of a "Western" society for the future. While in his point of view, the signs of destruction would overwhelm any signs of future development for the moment, they are nevertheless evident in the new social formations and economic structures emerging in colonized India: The (forced) political unity, the building of infrastructure, the emergence of free press and a local, urban class of educated administrators, and last but not least the Indian army would eventually enable the Indian people to break the chains of foreign domination decisively (MARX 1960b: 220–222).

Amilcar CABRAL, one of the most outspoken representatives of Marxism during the independence period of Africa, later shared the idea that class struggle, in the Marxist sense, is the dominating force of history. However, as he adheres to the idea that the creation of new classes and the struggle between those classes is dependent on the development of the productive forces and the ownership of the means of production, he asks the question if there would be history before the emergence of classes – or, for that matter, after the end of classes, i.e. in classless socialist societies. In his view, the emergence of classes does not happen simultaneously in all corners of the world and is by no means free of external influences, which might accelerate or decelerate the formation of classes. However, if there was no history before the creation of classes and class struggle, that would mean robbing the peoples of the Third World of their history, and pronouncing them to be history-less creatures. Without mentioning it, he is thereby referring to Marx's observation on India (MARX 1960a, 1960b). Yet, as in CABRAL's view class struggle and class formation are in themselves results of the development of productive forces and the ownership of the means of production, this would assure that history in this sense existed before the emergence of class struggle, and therefore negate the image of peoples without history in the colonies (CABRAL 1968: 21–24).

It has to be added, that CABRAL is implicitly only referring to class struggle as the struggle between proletariat and capital in the era of capitalism. Thus, his attempted critique of MARX is in some ways misinterpreting MARX's and ENGEL's basic statement made in the Communist Manifesto, that history itself is the history of class struggle. In MARX's original statement on that matter, it becomes quite clear that class struggle does not only mean the one between proletariat and capital, but also earlier class struggles in earlier eras, like that between feudal power and the bourgeoisie (MARX & ENGELS 1960a: 462).

In this context, it is important to emphasize that MARX does not intend to defend colonialism or imply any kind of benevolent desire to develop the colonies on the side of the British (or any other colonial power, for that matter). While colonialism was born from the aristocrat desire to rule and possess, capitalist production and exploitation cannot work in a territory of isolated villages without (then) modern infrastructure like railways and telegraph networks. The colonizers did not present India with a railway system as a gift to the Indian people, but because capitalist demand for profit implied the building of efficient transport infrastructure. As soon as one builds railways however, MARX continues, one cannot rely on importing the machinery from the motherland and therefore has to induce the process of industrialization inside the colony. This process of induced industrialization will decisively destroy the old social order and free the Indian society of the chains of tradition and the outdated mode of production. This character of capitalist modernization, however, will not bring any kind of freedom or social development to the colonized people, unless they themselves appropriate the productive forces which colonial capitalism has developed. In this sense, capitalism and the bourgeoisie would fulfill the same historic task in the colonies as they did in Europe: To free the productive forces from its feudal chains and to prepare the material base for the social revolution. Nothing more has ever been done by the bourgeoisie, argues MARX, and never has it fulfilled this task without bringing misery, oppression and devastation to whole peoples. The only ways for the Indian people to cherish the modern elements of society bought by the British, would therefore be either the industrial proletariat coming to power in England and replacing the ruling class in charge of colonialism, or the Indian people itself becoming strong enough to end British rule by themselves (MARX 1960b: 222–224).

MARX concludes his remarks on India by emphasizing the cynicism of bourgeois rule. It is in the colonies that he urges the reader to see the true face of bourgeois "civilization", to see the endless cases of misery and suffering brought upon by the absolute rule of capital that defines the capitalist mode of production. The necessity of the concentration of capital, which is existential to its independent power, leads to the destructive nature of world markets. These world markets, however, would only demonstrate the inherent political economic laws of capitalism, which is unable to develop the power of its productive forces without subjugating the working masses under the rule of capital itself. The bourgeois system of industry and commerce is developing the global material base for a new world order. But only if a major social revolution of the most advanced peoples would be able to appropriate the modern forces of production and the global market, would human progress be possible without the oppression and exploitation of colonized peoples (MARX 1960b: 225p.).

2.2.2 Theories of Imperialism

As we have seen, in a Marxist understanding, capitalism is a social form of develop-ment, based on the extraction of surplus value generated by the workers by a ruling elite. This extraction can take internal and external forms. While the internal forms (especially in England) were the historical basis of Marx's analysis of capitalism itself, the external forms of surplus extraction are described in different theories of imperialism. Again, from the Marxist perspective, one has to distinguish between mercantile imperialism, which was prevalent from the 15th throughout the 19th cen-tury and led to the colonization of the Americas and most of Asia on the one hand, and the second phase of classical imperialism on the other, which emerged from the end of the 19th century and brought almost the entire planet under the control of the big imperial powers. Mercantile imperialism can be characterized as a phase of resource and labor extraction from the colonies through direct intervention and strict regulation by the colonizing states, for instance by the extraction of gold and silver from Latin America or the abduction of slaves from Africa for work on Amer-ican plantations. As mercantilist theory stressed the importance of the accumulation of gold and silver as determinant for a country's development, colonizing nations sought to maximize imports and minimize exports – a goal that could most efficient-ly be achieved through direct colonial control over new territories (Peet & Hartwick 2009: 161p.).

In Marx's view, this mode of colonial extraction allowed the so-called primitive accumulation in the most advanced mercantile nations of this era to go beyond the appropriation of peasant land by feudal landlords and create the modern industrial capitalist. The exploitation of the colonies, in his view, enabled those nations to enter the era of a credit system based on large state debts, and thereby further the transfor-mation of money into capital (Marx 1972b: 777–788).

Mercantile imperialism was marked by exploitation, violent conquest and the subjugation of large territories – and it spanned around four centuries. The indepen-dence of the United States is widely seen as the end of this phase of imperialism. By contrast, the phase of classical imperialism from the middle of the 19th century on-wards saw an unprecedented rise in the speed of colonization, becoming a scramble for the last unclaimed territories of the Earth, with the additional influence of rising industrial powers like Germany and Japan challenging the old colonial powers of France and Britain (Peet & Hartwick 2009: 162p.).

Authors like Schumpeter sought the explanation for this phenomenon in the aggressivity of human nature, a sort of leftover from more animalist days, which reappears from time to time, but would actually be an atavism in modern civiliza-tion (Schumpeter 1919: 18). Indeed, from his perspective, the aggressiveness and violence that characterized the phase of imperialism would be a contradiction to his observation of capitalist development, which would actually mean progress, peace and civilized manners. A purely capitalist society, therefore, would be no base for imperialist aggression. Rather, aggressivity, nationalism and militarism are rem-nants of the pre-capitalist societies, which continue to exist under capitalism, but are no new phenomenon, let alone an inevitable result of capitalist development (Schumpeter 1919: 48–76).

In contrast, Marxists have always seen imperialism as connected to the maturation of capitalism inside the main imperialist nations. John Hobson (1858-1940) saw a direct connection between the capitalist stagnation, caused by the limited purchasing power of underpaid workers, and the need for continued capitalist growth, which in this understanding could only be achieved through the export of capital. However, according to his figures on English imperialism (the center of his study), he concluded that the trade with the colonies actually made up only a negligible amount of the total size of the British economy and that only few specific sectors were the beneficiaries and the main driving force behind the extension of the Empire (Hobson 1902: 30–45, 1902: 51–68).

Rudolf Hilferding (1877-1941) was one of the first Marxists to analyze the monopolist tendencies of capitalism not only for industrial capital, but also for the banking system (Hilferding 1955). In his understanding of this new phase of financial capitalism, it was this concentrated financial capital, which demanded a strong state who could enable a steadily growing export of over-accumulated capital by means of subjugating more and more territories under imperial control. This is a notion which was later elaborated by Lenin (1972) in his theory of imperialism as the highest form of capitalism (Peet & Hartwick 2009: 164).

On the other hand, Rosa Luxemburg (1871-1919) concentrated her analysis more on the side of commodity production and stagnant consumption in her understanding of imperialism. Within this concept, capitalist overproduction of commodities needed new markets, as the underpaid workers inside the imperialist nations could not create a viable demand to sustain capitalist growth (Luxemburg 1921: 337). Since the creation of new markets necessitated the destruction of the existing economic system in the new colonies, this implied the use of force and violence, as no society would voluntarily relinquish its existing mode of production. Furthermore, the imperialist nations also had to fight among themselves to establish new colonies in the first place (Luxemburg 1921: 423p.).

Founded on the principles of the Marxist understanding of capitalism as an economic system based on the exploitation of labor and the competition between capitalists with the inherent goal of achieving monopoly, V. I. Lenin developed his theory of imperialism as a distinct phase of capitalist accumulation. This theory, which would become one of the most influential and controversial descriptions of the era of colonialism, understands imperialism as the highest (and last) stadium of capitalism (Lenin 1972).

Derived from his observation of the fight between colonial powers for hegemony and new spheres of influence, which culminated in the First World War, Lenin tried to apply the principles of the Marxist description of capitalist competition on the competition between nation states. Published in 1917, at the eve of the Russian Revolution, this competition is seen as the result of capitalist expansion coming to its limits within the developed nation states. Lenin sees the phase of imperialism, which emerged out of laws of capitalist accumulation, described by Marx (1972b: 640–740) not only as a specific phase of capitalist accumulation, but as the highest stadium of capitalism – the stadium of monopolism (Lenin 1972: 270p.).

LENIN starts with a description of the economic situation in Germany and the United States in order to underline his hypothesis that capitalism had entered the stage of monopolist capitalism at the turn of the 20th century. Specifically, he emphasizes that while big companies would make up less than 1% of all companies in these two countries, they would employ 10 % of the workforce in Germany and over 30% in the U.S.A. Even more strikingly, those companies would use more than two thirds of steam engines and produce the majority of the two nations' GDP. It has to be taken into account that LENIN considers all companies employing more than 50 workers as big companies. In addition to this observed concentration of workforce and production, LENIN notes the increasing vertical and horizontal integration of the big companies, who thereby take firm control over the chain of production and impede smaller competitors from challenging their position. All these observations led LENIN to support MARX's theory of the inherent tendency of free competition to lead to concentration of production, which in turn leads to the creation of monopolies. Differences in national economic policy, like the prevalence of protective tariffs in Germany vs. open market approaches like in the UK would only lead to differences in the time and the nature of the appearance of those monopolies, but not hinder its emergence. From LENIN's point of view, the capitalist nations of Europe had entered the stage of monopoly capitalism at the beginning of the 20th century (LENIN 1972: 200–205).

LENIN continues with his description of the emerging monopoly capitalism by characterizing the economy of cartels and trusts in Germany and the United States. By controlling all parts of the chain of production – starting with raw material and continuing with their own sections for the buying and development of patents and technical innovations – these big corporations are able to control large sections of industrial sectors. By all means available, these monopolists will continue to integrate new competitors into their arrangement or make their economic survival impossible in the case of noncompliance. By bringing more and more companies under their control, these monopolies would actually socialize the production – through integrating ever bigger masses of workers and resources into smaller numbers of corporations – while the property of the means of production would be concentrated in the hands of fewer and fewer private individuals. LENIN argues that even "bourgeois" economists would observe that the productive gains achieved by this concentration of production would increasingly be appropriated by speculators and financial entrepreneurs, not by the knowledgeable factory owner of the old type of free competition capitalism. Alas, those economists would dream of a way back to those old times of "honest" and "peaceful" competition. Indeed, while cyclical crises of the capitalist economy nurtured the emergence of cartels and trusts, those forms of monopolist capitalism would by no means make future crises less likely: Through marginalizing other industrial sectors and fostering technological advancements, the big monopolies would actually increase the chaotic tendencies of capitalist development and exacerbate the emergence of economic crises (LENIN 1972: 206–214).

If this view is applied to the imperialist scramble for Africa in the late 19th century, the Marxist laws of accumulation of capital, which lead to monopolies (MARX 1972b: 640–740), and the tendency of falling rates of profit, which leads to the export of capital (MARX 1972a: 221–277), led to the need for capitalists to extend their base of production and integrate new territories into the capitalist mode of production. Therefore, led by the ruling class of capitalist monopolists, the big European nations sought and managed to get territorial control over the last part of the globe available: Africa (MEYNS 1977: 9p.).

In order to understand the reasons for the imperialist nations to engage on such a costly endeavor, Rosa LUXEMBURG delivers an in-depth theoretical analysis of MARX's concept of extended reproduction as a basis for the continuing accumulation of capital. She concludes that MARX indeed does not solve the contradiction of eternal and steady growth of capital and accumulation based on the transformation of surplus value into capital. As this surplus value is the representation of surplus production of commodities, these commodities need a market to be produced for, and in the setting of *The Capital*, this market is only consisting of capitalists and workers. Accordingly, profit could be used for consumption or the accumulation of capital, but as it is a closed system, it could not produce more and more commodities and extend the market to eternity. But without production, there is no such thing as surplus value, let alone accumulation of capital. Therefore, capitalism could not sustain itself (LUXEMBURG 1921: 299–317).

As MARX's original analysis in the Second and Third Volume of *The Capital* (MARX 1972c, 1972a) was based on the abstract construction of a purely capitalist society, i.e. a world, in which capitalism is the only existing mode of production, LUXEMBURG sees this apparent contradiction as stemming from the abstract nature of the model: Indeed, capitalism cannot sustain itself, but it does not have to do so in the real world. It is surrounded by other modes of production: Feudalism and rural economy in Europe, even more "primitive" modes of production in non-capitalist societies outside Europe. In LUXEMBURG's conclusion, accumulation of capital is only possible through the exploitation, appropriation and ultimately destruction of non-capitalist societies by capitalist ones. Therefore, capitalism has to conquer non-capitalist societies, but it also has to transform their mode of production into a capitalist one, in order to appropriate its resources, its productive forces, and its labor. In this sense, colonialism and imperialism are the solution for the inability of the capitalist mode of production to sustain continued accumulation. However, by the destruction and conversion of the conquered non-capitalist societies, capitalism will eventually run out of new regions to conquer and new societies to transform and thereby limit its own ability to survive as a global mode of production (LUXEMBURG 1921: 318–339).

LENIN, on the other hand, takes a less theoretical approach to illustrate the inherent logic of imperialist expansion: After analyzing the domination of financial capital over other forms of capital as a result of concentration in the industry and the banking sector, as well as the emergence of a financial oligarchy by the mutual inter-linkages and institutional connections between industrial and financial monopolies, he turns his attention to the regional concentration of these oligarchies. Derived from the overall value of emission and worth of securities, stocks and bonds from 1871 to 1910, he concludes that the four countries of England, France, U.S.A. and Germany control almost 80 % of all global financial capital. In other words, two "old" colonial powers and two "new" emerging capitalist powers with rapid economic and technological development would host almost all of the world's financial oligarchies and thereby relegate any other nation to the role of debtors to those four dominating capitalist powers (LENIN 1972: 243p.).

By the use of several examples from various industrial sectors, LENIN describes the increasing subdivision of the world under the respective monopolists in these sectors. While this description itself shows the different ways of achieving an arrangement of spheres of interests and access to different markets, LENIN insists that the appearance of these competitions between monopolists does not alter its inherent logic. The interlinkages between private and state monopoly are numerous and the conflicts over global arrangements between the capitalists may show various forms from peaceful negotiation to open war. However, overall, in the monopolist stage of capitalism, capitalists do not subdivide the world because of evil intentions, but because the stage of concentration achieved under this form of capitalism necessitates them to seek international arrangements in order to be able to maintain profits (LENIN 1972: 250–258).

In conclusion, LENIN sees capitalist imperialism as a new (and higher) stage of capitalism. He criticizes "bourgeois authors" – first and foremost KAUTSKY (1914) – for defining imperialism as a mere phase of policy of capitalist, industrialized nations. For LENIN, imperialism is the direct result of the advanced stage of certain capitalist economies, which have reached a phase of monopoly capitalism. This type of capitalism would have replaced the old capitalism of free competition, with a new one dominated by industrial monopolists and financial capital. This new stage of capitalism would be synonymous with the stage of imperialism. Therefore, imperialism would be more than a phase of national policy, but rather a new stage of capitalism itself. In this sense, the reduction of imperialism to its political element – the urge to subjugate new territories – would neglect its economic base, which – in LENIN's view – is financial capitalism. Specifically, imperialism would not only seek new agrarian territories – as KAUTSKY suggested – but strive for any territory available, especially already industrialized ones, to fulfill the monopolies' demand for new spaces for profit (LENIN 1972: 269–273).

However, competition and monopoly are mutually reflexive: the goal of capitalist competition is monopoly, while monopoly hinders competition. Yet, in order for a monopoly to make profit and reproduce itself, it has to enter new competition, constantly. In the theory of imperialism, LENIN (1972: 269–280) predicted the same observations to be true for the competition between the big capitalist nations: The world had been divided completely, but it would be irrational to think that this status quo would be kept for eternity. Technological advancements and higher productivity in one country may lead to the need for capitalists to find new markets, and thus the possibility of new conflicts over spheres of influence. The ambitions of previously less important countries, like Germany and Japan, for territorial expansion can be taken as an example of such disruptions of the imperialist order. Therefore, in Leninist terms, imperialism would not enable the capitalist system to stabilize itself, but on the contrary, intensify its inherent contradictions.

According to the Leninist view on imperialism, the monopolist tendencies of capitalism, which led to the phase of imperialism, will also be one reason for the demise of the capitalist mode of production. While the bourgeois revolution against the feudalist system set free the enormous productive forces formerly chained to the feudal economy, the stage of monopolist capital now constrains those same forces. Therefore, in the Leninist theory of imperialism, this stage is the dying stage of an ill capitalism, which needs evermore territories and peoples to exploit. Fewer and fewer capitalists hold more and more capital in this stage, and the size of the exploited proletariat rises globally in this stage of capitalist expansion. It is also the phase of the upcoming socialist revolution, which would overthrow this obsolete system of production. However, it is necessary to emphasize that this revolution would not come about simply by the weakness of the bourgeoisie, but needs the commitment of a strong (socialist) proletariat to lead the revolution. Since the phase of imperialism made the capitalist mode of production a global phenomenon, it would also need a world revolution, as national movements would no longer be able to change an economic system, which operates globally (MEYNS 1977: 10–12).

Two tendencies of capitalist imperialism are interpreted by LENIN as signs for the increasing stagnation and decay of capitalism itself. Firstly, capitalist monopolies are in constant and unsolvable contradiction to the capitalist principle of competition, but possess the tendency of economic stagnation, as monopolist prices and profits reduce incentives for technological progress. Similarly, the possession of profitable colonies implies the same tendency of stagnation for the colonial powers. On the other hand, the emergence of financial capitalism induced a growing social formation of rentiers, who make their living on stocks and other financial papers, but whose livelihood is increasingly disconnected from any form of production. By the same process, the economy of the colonial powers is increasingly dependent on the exploitation of foreign territories and peoples under its control. Not only individual persons, but whole nations would practically live on the parasitic exploitation of labor in its oversee territories. Therefore, the world would increasingly be divided in lenders and debtors. All social formations are affected by these economic changes, and in LENIN's view, the proletariat itself becomes divided into a lower stratum of workers and a small stratum of wealthier workers, who are vulnerable to tokenism or who follow the lead of self-proclaimed proletarian leaders, who are in fact bourgeois or payed by the bourgeoisie. LENIN is specifically hard in his criticism of these imperialist tendencies in parts of the workers' movement, especially in social democratic parties and trade unions. These "opportunist" tendencies, which would legitimize imperialism as beneficial for the proletariat of the capitalist countries, would have to be overcome immediately in his view, as this support of imperialism would be inherently opposed to the interests of the proletariat (LENIN 1972: 280–290).

At the same time, the need for increasing exploitation in the colonies, in order to compete with the other imperialist powers striving for monopoly, would strengthen the resistance of the dominated people and further the emergence of liberation movements in the colonies. In this process, again, the imperialist struggle for hegemony weakens the imperialist system itself. The October Revolution in Russia would be seen as "the price" the imperialist powers had to pay for their conflict, with a social revolution ending the influence of imperialism in this territory. Indeed, MEYNS sees the development of global power relations since LENIN's analysis as a proof for this theory (MEYNS 1977: 12–14).

The expansion of imperialism coincided with the rise of capitalist production in countries like England and other European nations. Although the peoples of America, Africa and Asia had long been subjugated to colonial modes of exploitation (and the colonization of America is probably the best example), the expansion of capitalism now led to an accelerating need for new territory, new workers and new markets. Old traditional industries and political and social systems were thoroughly destroyed, and the colonies were made to be cheap producers of raw materials. With the increased competition between a smaller number of imperialist powers, the export of capital became more important, in order to establish capitalist markets in the colonies. The subjugation of peoples under colonial rule, however, led to movements against this oppression. And as the First World War had already strengthened those movements, the Second World War and the subsequent downturn of old colonial powers like England, The Netherlands or Belgium led to the victory of anticolonial movements all over Africa. But, as Kwame Nkrumah (1963: 57–65, 1965) already observed after the groundbreaking independence of his country, the old colonial powers, as well as the new super-powers, sought ways to continue economic and social control, wherever direct colonial rule was not possible anymore. Hence, through economic ties and neocolonial policies, the newly gained independence was already under pressure (Meyns 1977: 14–16).

Imperialist rule and anti-imperialist struggle

Regardless of their stress on capital or commodity export, all these views on imperialism saw imperialist expansion as being caused by the internal contradictions of the most advanced capitalist societies, enabling capitalism to grow without solving those inner contradictions. Even after most of the oppressed peoples of the world gained political independence after The Second World War, many radical authors have stated that the imperial system of surplus extraction continues to this day, albeit by indirect means. This concept of neo-imperialism or neocolonialism remains a highly debated issue in the development discourse, and implies the question whether imperialism is a phenomenon of the past, or if the same structures and mechanisms continue in today's world system (Peet & Hartwick 2009: 164p.).

In his characterization of imperialism, Cabral sees two major forms of imperialist rule: Classic colonialism and neo-colonialism. While these two forms would differ in the nature of control, the defining commonality is that both forms of domination deny the subjugated peoples of their right to a free development of their own history. It is important to mention, that Cabral does see historic development mainly based on the development of the productive forces in each society. Imperialist disruption therefore had denied the oppressed peoples of their own free development of those productive forces inside their societies and thus also disrupted their social development. While the times for national liberation might have seemed positive in the 1960s, Cabral emphasizes that national liberation, and therefore the true return to independent historic development, can only be achieved if all forms of dominance from the outside are broken. In this sense, he sees the struggle against neocolonial domination as the most important one, as national independence alone cannot break the domination of the former colonies' economy by foreign capital. In his remarks about imperialism and the anti-imperial struggle, CABRAL does attribute a "historical personality" to nations, which in his view can only be retained by victory over imperialist oppression (CABRAL 1968: 27–32).

CABRAL characterizes three basic phases of the mode of production: First the primitive, elementary mode of production with low productive forces and a horizontal order of society, without a state. Secondly, the beginning of private ownership of the means of production and the increasing specialization of production, combined with the rapid development of the productive forces. This phase would be represented by a vertical organization of society, first through the feudal and then through the bourgeois state. The third phase would be that of socialism or communism, with collective ownership of the means of production. In CABRAL's view, this last phase would be represented by the socialist and communist states (he does not differentiate between the two concepts like in MARX's original theorem). Again, CABRAL argues that on a global scale, two or three phases of the mode of production can exist at the same time. However, in the era of imperialism, all societies that had been conquered, were exposed to violent disruption of their historic development. In the struggle against imperialism – which CABRAL describes as the last phase of capitalism, in accordance with LENIN – the subjugated peoples of the world would find the possibility to transform their status of exploitation into a higher form of social order (CABRAL 1968: 24–27).

In his critique of imperialism, LENIN concludes that there is no way of reconciling the inherent contradictions of imperialism by going back to the old order of free competition. As imperialism, itself, was the result of the old capitalism of free competition, this approach of bourgeois critique of the imperialist era would be a contradiction in itself. Furthermore, as the development of imperialism is inherently uneven, it would be impossible to imagine the peaceful unification of the world under the rule of one monopolist entity, as in KAUTSKY's (1914: 921p.) idea of an ultra-imperialism. Periods of peaceful arrangements between the big imperialist powers would, therefore, only be interludes between violent ways of solving these discrepancies of capitalist development, i.e. wars between those same powers. In addition, the era of imperialism would not only bring a new level of exploitation and inequality into the controlled territories and colonies, but also increase the inequalities between classes inside the colonial powers themselves. Therefore, the development of imperialism would also foster the emergence of forces opposing imperialism, both in the colonies and inside the imperialist nations (LENIN 1972: 290–303).

In the eyes of the followers of these theories of imperialism, the proponents of neocolonial dependency (i.e. the imperialist powers) have continued their domination over the former colonies through their integration into the world market economy. While prices for raw materials and agricultural produce remain low with a tendency to decline, the prices for industrial goods tend to rise. This price differential is aggravated through the monopolistic market position of many former colonies in relation to the imperial centers. Inside the underdeveloped countries, a small ruling class – privileged through their access to higher education and well-paid government positions – has emerged, which increases the market for (luxury) products from the industrialized countries. However, this market is not connected to the productive forces in the underdeveloped countries. Indeed, the agriculture of many African countries remained mostly subsistence based and traditional due to lack of capital, in spite of the prevalence of individual production for the world market. Through both ways, surplus value and labor created in the former colonies is mostly exported to the imperialist centers. In fact, the nationalization of the few industries and export agriculture after independence put those means of production in the hands of the bureaucratic ruling class and increased the process of capital import (through foreign investment and loans) and surplus export (through the export of undervalued agricultural produce) (MEYNS 1977: 17–22).

While these observations led to the creation of *dependencia* theories as a counter measure to the seemingly unbreakable process of neocolonial underdevelopment, MEYNS insists that these theories remain too structuralist and undervalue the importance of the social effects of this system of neocolonial exploitation. In the sense of MARX's (1960a) comments on the British Rule in India, he implies that the continuation of such imperialist practices also creates the foundations for class struggle and revolution, in which case the imperialist exploitation would lay the foundations of its own demise. While the author acknowledges the analytical input of structuralist approaches to the system of world economy, he therefore argues that *dependencia* arguments remain too economistic and thereby undervalue the revolutionary power that latently lies in the exploited masses of the underdeveloped countries (MEYNS 1977: 17–22).

For Samir AMIN, the different phases of capitalist accumulation represent distinct phases of exploitation, and the understanding of the nature of the regime of accumulation at any given time would lead to the understanding of the main struggle for social transformation on a global scale. In the beginning 21st century, he sees this main struggle to be between continued globalized imperialism and the global pauperization of the peasantry (AMIN 2015: 60p.).

2.2.3 Towards a geographic understanding of socialist development concepts

Considering the concept of development brought forward by MARX and ENGELS, as well as its interpretation by the proponents of theories of imperialism, it becomes clear that the socialist approach to human development bears some distinct geographic features. While MARX's image of human history as a history of class struggles might at first seem to lack a spatial component, the further elaborations of this understanding, as presented in the preceding chapters, illustrate the spatial aspects within this history of thought – or, to express it with the words of David HARVEY: "The accumulation of capital has always been a profoundly geographical affair." (HARVEY 1998: 49).

As had already been concluded by the likes of LENIN and LUXEMBURG (see above), the capitalist mode of production was not capable of producing the continual economic growth it needed for its own survival, without the spatial expansion of its markets and its base of resources and labor. However, this "spatial fix" of expanding capitalism beyond the borders of the own nation state, did not solve the inner contradictions of capitalism, it just exported the system and its contradictions to new territories. In some ways, the expansion of the capitalist system of production did reduce the importance of geographic space on a superficial level: Technological progress and economic globalization reduced the importance of distance and national boarders, at least for the movement of capital and commodities. On the other hand, it became all too obvious that capitalism did not develop all regions of the world in the same manner. While prosperity and growth continued at the central places of the world economy (by and large, the industrialized nations), the majority of (former) colonies were not able to experience the same sort of benefits. Therefore, the concept of socialist development cannot be analyzed without looking at the geographical structure of global class relations (HARVEY 1998: 49–60).

Indeed, one may find Marxist categories of analysis at all different scales of geographic space. And, more often than not, the interrelations between these different scales will be of utmost interest for the understanding of phenomena like poverty, exploitation and alienation (SANTOS 1974: 2). This way of analyzing the spatial relations of global inequality and the spatial conditions of power and economic development from a political economy perspective has been the focal point of radical geography approaches (REUBER 2012: 108–113).

More specifically, representatives of this area of geographic research have argued that the usual understanding of political geography would be dominated by conservative approaches, which concentrated their efforts on the illustration of different political systems in different spaces, without considering their economic base or analyzing possibilities for change (TAYLOR 2003: 47–49). Hence, they would see the need for a radical political geography, which "investigates spatial power within a holistic political economy." (TAYLOR 2003: 50).

One of the attempts to characterize the postcolonial situation of economy, politics, and power from a spatial perspective is the World System Theory, which shares the dependency school's interest in the relation between center and periphery. Furthermore, it has roots in the French *Annales* school of thought, which was created by a group of historians around Lucien Febvre and Marc Bloch. This school had set itself the goal of introducing the comparative method into historical sciences, by comparing historical developments in different societies over long timeframes and between different geographic regions. French human geographer Vidal de la Blache was also connected to this school of historical research. Ferdnand Braudel and other second generation scholars of the *Annales* school were particularly interested in the long term development of Third World countries and the radical changes implied by their contact with the First World during colonialism (PEET & HARTWICK 2009: 172p.).

From a geographic perspective, it was Immanuel WALLERSTEIN's characterization of the World System (WALLERSTEIN 1974, 1980, 1988), which proved to be the most appealing version of this theory. This can mostly be attributed to his conceptualization of the World System as being comprised of three hierarchically arranged layers: The core, the semi-periphery and the periphery – a pattern that was intrinsically geographic in nature (FLINT & SHELLEY 1996: 497).

In WALLERSTEIN's observation, the core was comprised of the economically powerful and politically well-organized nations, who dominated the whole system. These states were able to implement their economic interest on a global scale and were the beneficiaries of the world market. Peripheral states, on the other hand, were marginalized countries, who depended on the will of the center and showed a very weak internal organization. The semi-periphery shared some properties of both other categories, and would be in an intermediary position (PEET & HARTWICK 2009: 173p.). With regards to the more recent characterization of the World System, "the basic spatiality is a world-economy with a core-periphery pattern." (TAYLOR 2003: 52).

Within this view on the spatial characterization of the global system, the peripheral states cannot develop themselves by repeating the steps of the developed ones, without overcoming this global hierarchy in the first place (FLINT & SHELLEY 1996: 497). On the contrary, development of the core and underdevelopment of the periphery are dialectically connected to each other, i.e. the core continues to grow economically by exploiting and thereby actively underdeveloping the global periphery.

However, this understanding should by no means imply that the nation state is the only level of analysis. On the contrary, it is the inquiry into the spatial relations of political economy within peripheral states, which might hold the most interesting aspects for a geographic understanding of socialist development strategies like Ujamaa (DATOO 1977: 70). After all, it is geography's ability to discover the relations between the global and the local scale which represents its biggest possible contribution to social science in general and to the scientific evaluation of different development approaches in particular (FLINT & SHELLEY 1996: 506).

In this sense, this study will try to analyze the emergence of Ujamaa in Tanzania from a core-periphery perspective which is informed by the background of the Marxian understanding of development as such, as well as by the theories of imperialism. It will try to focus on the relations between the different levels of space within Tanzania, without forgetting about the international environment in which this ideology was created. It is the understanding of the author, that this unique concept of development can only be understood when looking at all of these levels, since there have been enough studies on the emergence and failure of Ujamaa which equated this concept with the thinking of Nyerere alone (see OKOKO (1987: 24–26), for example), but failed to look at the interrelations of (national) core and periphery in the creation of the concept in the first place. Rather, this thesis will try to look at the internal differentiations from the local to the national level which have shaped its creation and implementation (LAL 2015: 175p.).

2.3 Ujamaa: Background and Ideology of Tanzania's development paradigm

"Socialism – like Democracy – is an attitude of mind. In a socialist society it is the socialist attitude of mind, and not the rigid adherence to a standard political pattern, which is needed to ensure that people care for each other's welfare."

J.K. NYERERE, *Ujamaa. The Basis of African Socialism* (NYERERE 1962b: 1)

It is without a doubt in these words, where the idea of Ujamaa as a genuine own "brand" of socialism is most strikingly defined by its inventor, the first president of Tanzania: Lacking the strictly economic definition of class and power of its European counterparts, but instead advancing the thought of a transition to socialists practices first and foremost by a change of attitude and state of mind (NYERERE 1962b). As already evident in this short introductory statement of NYERERE, the Tanzanian version of socialist ideology did not necessarily lead to only one possible development strategy or political praxis. While there have been attempts both by NYERERE and other political leaders in Tanzania to clarify and structure this ideology (for instance by the Arusha Declaration; NYERERE 1967b), it remained in many ways different from European socialism. Both the self-definition of Ujamaa and other African Socialisms will be the focus of the following chapters – thereby trying to create a deeper understanding of the ideological background of Tanzanian development policies and practice.

2.3.1 Basic Elements of the Ujamaa ideology

Between independence in 1961 and the Arusha Declaration in 1967, the new state and ideology were shaped by the thinking of Nyerere, while the economy would carry on in its former way. Indeed, NYERERE himself made it clear that the purpose of his first writing on Ujamaa was not to define how socialism could be brought about in a modern society. Rather, he wanted to discuss this attitude of mind, which he saw as the basic difference between socialist and non-socialist behavior – both on the level of the individual and on the level of a society as a whole (NYERERE 1962b: 1p.).

This reflects the fact that the Ujamaa ideology of Nyerere was arguing more from a moral than a material point of view: Evoking the image of the "noble African" and of mutual cooperation and fair distribution much more than a Soviet type of ideology based on material growth and industrial development. Indeed, Ujamaa was more closely related to Chinese ideas on rural development, and at least before 1973, it not only outspokenly opposed Stalinist notions of forced development, but also practically emphasized voluntarism and mass support. Nevertheless, Ujamaa implied a top down perspective on social change, not at least because Nyerere deemed the prospective of a class struggle or even guerilla style revolution to be unnecessary in the African setting (HEDLUND & LUNDAHL 1989: 18–20). And while the concept of exploitation and capitalism as such was seen as thoroughly un-African, he acknowledged that during colonialism, such ideas of individual wealth and power had reached some of his fellow compatriots. Accordingly, immediate action had to be taken to impede the further spread of the capitalist attitude of mind:

> "Our first step, therefore, must be to re-educate ourselves; to regain our former attitude of mind. In our traditional African society we were individuals within a community. We took care of the community, and the community took care of us. We neither needed nor wished to exploit our fellow men.

And in rejecting the capitalist attitude of mind which colonialism brought into Africa, we must reject also the capitalist methods which go with it. One of these is the individual ownership of land. To us in Africa, land was always recognized as belonging to the community. Each individual within our society had a right to the use of land, because otherwise he could not earn his living and one cannot have the right to life without also having the right to some means of maintaining life. But the African's right to land was simply the right to use it; nor he had other right to it, nor did it occur to him to try and claim one." (NYERERE 1962b: 5)

The underlying concept of socialism in Tanzania, which became the guideline for development in the Arusha Declaration, is the idea of a society which thrives without the exploitation of men by men (or one class by another). According to the post-Arusha strategy, social development is given the priority over economic development, and the latter is given a new impetus: Rather than continuing on the classical modernization agenda of many postcolonial states in Africa, the new path of economic development is seen in the concept of communal agriculture. BIENEN, therefore, sees the Arusha Declaration as a significant shift towards an independent African development strategy. At the same time, the declaration would allow TANU to legitimize its leading role in the country's policy and unify the different development concepts still prevalent in the Tanzanian elite (BIENEN 1972: 178p.).

Many ideological positions have claimed Ujamaa as proof of their theoretical approach to either socialism or development as such. MEYNS gives the examples of representatives of third way theories of non-capitalist development as well as the church. However, those reports would mostly pick the part of Ujamaa that would support their view, and leave out others, such as its class characteristics. Furthermore, such analyses of Ujamaa would neglect the context of national liberation and colonial influences, which in MEYNS' view is crucial to an understanding of the Tanzanian ideology (MEYNS 1977: 93).

Ujamaa by far exceeded the scope of many other African socialisms. Although it stemmed at least from Nyerere's Edinburgh time, most of his ideology only became public in the 1960s and the practical model of Ujamaa was introduced in the late 1960s, when others like Nkrumah and Senghor had long abandoned their models. Furthermore, Ujamaa differed from the other socialisms by being directed to a rural Tanzanian citizen much more than at the intellectual (and international) elite (SCHICHO 2009: 180).

Specifically, it appealed to a traditional construction of society, which afforded dignity and security to the individual, by a sort of mutual help and "universal charity" while emphasizing age-proven codes of conduct of communal living (BHENGU 2011: 34). Overall, three principles of Ujamaa would be derived from the perception of the pre-colonial situation: "...mutual respect, common ownership, and everyone's obligation to work" (MAPOLU 1973: 56).

In his writing on *Socialism and Rural Development*, NYERERE (1968f: 107p.) elaborated on these three basic principles, which he assumed to be the foundation of the traditional form of Ujamaa of peasant communities: First of all, all members of the extended family – i.e. the basic unit of production – were related to each other by bonds of affection and respect. This mutual interrelation was based on each individual's role within the extended family, and as long as each member was fulfilling this role, he or she would receive the respect of all the other family members. This form of respect nurtured the coherence of the extended family as a unit, rather than as a group of individuals with competing interests.

Secondly, all goods and all means of production (i.e. the land and the farm tools), were seen as a common property of the extended family, and not as individually owned items. While NYERERE acknowledges the fact that some family members could own more property than others through their hard work, he insists that this could only occur if all the basic needs of all members of the extended family were catered for: No member would have been able to appropriate the fruits of his labor for his own consumption, while another member would have gone hungry, for instance. Furthermore, if a more affluent member of the family would die, the property would be divided between a large number of family members, keeping the accumulation of wealth socially moderated.

Third of all, every member of the traditional extended family would have the moral and social obligation to work to the best of his or her abilities. Even guests would have to work if they were staying for an extended period of time. Therefore, nobody would have to fear that his or her work was exploited by idlers doing nothing, according to Nyerere's view (NYERERE 1968f: 107p.).

Therefore, Nyerere's socialism is based on the attitude of mind, but also on the principles of equality, the right to labor and the obligation to work. He thereby draws connections to African traditions as well as Pope Leo XIII's Social Encyclica. On the other hand, the communal ownership of the means of production, as well as land, opposes the papal point of view and relates Nyerere more closely to the Communist Manifesto (SCHICHO 2009: 181).

Nyerere's concept of socialism was in many aspects stressing the importance of the individual and his or her moral choice to engage in communal work and the common good, instead of a "Western" pursuit of individual wealth. Contrary to Marxian analyses of society, which would usually emphasize on the structure of society and production, Nyerere's Ujamaa was relying on individual commitment and behavioral change to achieve the goal of overcoming the capitalist society:

> "In the individual, as in the society, it is an attitude of mind which distinguishes the socialist from the non-socialist. It has nothing to do with the possession or non-possession of wealth. Destitute people can be potential capitalists – exploiters of their fellow human beings. A millionaire can equally well be a socialist; he may value his wealth only because it can be used in the service of his fellow men. But the man who uses wealth for the purpose of dominating any of his fellows is a capitalist. So is the man who would if he could!"   (NYERERE 1962b: 1)

Nyerere did see the influence of the social and economic structure on this attitude of mind, as well as on the wealth of individuals. For instance, he understood socialism as a system based on the idea of distribution, not individual accumulation – making it very unlikely for a socialist society to produce millionaires in the first place (NYERERE 1962b: 1–3). Nevertheless, his key to eradicate exploitation and to create such a socialist society remained the attitude of mind, the commitment to the community and the recreation the pre-colonial spirit of cooperation:

> "Our first step, therefore, must be to re-educate ourselves; to regain our former attitude of mind. In our traditional African society we were individuals within a community, and the community took care of us. We neither needed nor wished to exploit our fellow men." (NYERERE 1962b: 5)

Therefore, Nyerere's concept of socialism was in rhetoric and political practice relying on the recreation of an African mindset and the African traditional system of land tenure, in which no farmer should be able to possess land he or she did not cultivate him- or herself. In convincing the individual to join Nyerere's socialist vision, he again referred to traditional images of the pre-colonial rural community, in which the benefit of communal work was combined with the moral obligation to work (and the social sanctions by the own community if an individual would refuse to do so; HEDLUND & LUNDAHL 1989: 21–23). According to MAPOLU, Nyerere's thinking resembles that of Robert OWEN's (1817) idea of human development, that was the basis of his "cooperative village", as well as that of other early utopian socialists. As such, his ideas are both idealistic and nostalgic. MAPOLU calls this a "petty bourgeoisie socialism" (MAPOLU 1973: 55).

Due to NYERERE's emphasis on class harmony instead of class struggle and the continued attempt to establish a border between his ideology and both capitalism and (Soviet style) communism, Ujamaa might seem close to ideas of neocolonial third way proponents. However, when taking a closer look, MEYNS (1977: 93–97) insists that those are the only parallels between Nyerere's expression of Ujamaa and third way theories. In fact, he sees Nyerere as the leader of a nationalist movement, trying to establish true independence and freedom for the former colony. Given this background, the critical view on the Soviet Union's imperialist tendencies make as much sense as the critical relationship to "Western" capitalism. Indeed, the influence of the two superpowers is crucial for the insistence on self-reliance and the confidence in the country's own strength, as expressed by the Arusha Declaration and the subsequent international and domestic policy.

That is not to hide the fact that Nyerere rejected the so-called scientific socialism of the Marxist-Leninist variety. MEYNS declares that this rejection stemmed from the petit-bourgeois character of the Tanzanian leadership and the bourgeois character of the peasant movement as such – a point where he implies that LENIN's characterization of the peasantry as an inherently conservative class (LENIN 1971: 443) holds true also in the Tanzanian context. Therefore, Ujamaa would neither be a neocolonial, reactionary ideology, nor a practical implementation of scientific socialism (MEYNS 1977: 93–97). The latter was previously discussed by RODNEY (1972: 72), who emphasizes that there might very well be a lack of thorough theory in Tanzanian socialism, but that claiming that there would be an unsurmountable gap between Ujamaa and "scientific socialism" was certainly not the case.

In ECKERT's (2007: 223–227) view, the question of the idealized past is not that important to the Ujamaa discourse, because it only acted as a backdrop for an explicitly new model of society. The question of who would belong inside the new "familyhood" of Ujamaa and who would be excluded, was centered around Nyerere's work ethic and the statement that it was everyone's obligation to work. The renunciation of loiterers and idlers (Nyerere 1962b: 3p.) was almost as explicit as that of rich people and capitalists: There was no such thing as socialism without work, in Nyerere's understanding, and a society which would fail to give its members the means to work was bound to fail as a whole. However, if an individual would not be willing to work when given the tools to do so (land for instance), this person would put himself out of the society and would have to bear the consequences for his loitering. After all, "hard work" was the number one condition for development, as underlined by the Arusha Declaration (Nyerere 1967b).

The most commonly used term in Kiswahili for this unwarranted loitering was *unyonyaji* – meaning as much as the concept of sucking, which became equivalent to the English term of exploitation. *Wanyonyaji* were therefore exploiters and enemies of the new concept of Ujamaa, and the expression was used both for foreign and domestic capitalists, and for people without jobs. Two groups were specifically targeted by this rhetoric: Firstly, Asian small traders and shopkeepers, who became the personification of *Wanyonyaji* as opposed to the *wananchi* – the regular, African child of the Nation, a hard-working peasant. Secondly, urban migrant workers and unemployed people, who were denounced as useless and lazy persons (*wavuvi*), and who were exploiting the working people committed to Ujamaa. This rhetoric led to tangible effects in discrimination against the Asian citizens of Tanzania and several police raids against "jobless" urban dwellers, including their incarceration or forced removal from Dar es Salaam. Even identity papers stating the occupation of the holder were introduced as a prerequisite for legal residence in Dar es Salaam. Thus, internally, the big family of all Tanzanians, which Ujamaa attempted to create, did not look exactly harmonic from the inside (Eckert 2007: 223–227).

Like any utopian ideology, Ujamaa had to contend with the material reality as well as the diverse mindset about development both within and outside the Tanzanian society. As Lal argues, it is important to understand the contradictions of Ujamaa ideology and practice not only from a Western viewpoint of developmentalism, but also from the point of view of the various local actors involved in policy making and implementation. Administration, party official, as well as institutions like the TANU Youth League and the People's Militia had roots back in the late colonial period, and had to face the material realities of a post-colonial society, which influenced the reality of Ujamaa policy. In this sense, the unfolding of Tanzania's Ujamaa project should be seen with a dialectic approach (Lal 2015: 76p.).

2.3.2 The Image of Traditional Communitarism in Africa and its relevance for Ujamaa

The understanding of many African politicians and thinkers of the early independence era, regarding the precolonial times of their societies, has been thoroughly influenced by a communal understanding of the individual person. Within this system of thought, the individual human being is not imaginable as being separated from the society they are born into. In contrast to a libertarian understanding of the individual, in this concept, a person is always defined by their role within the family, the clan or other kinship connections. As such, this "African" understanding of a communal theory of the human person has resemblances to Aristotle's understanding of humans as social beings. Most representatives of African Nationalist Movements, and especially African Socialism, have furthermore relied on a philosophical concept of a radical or unrestricted communitarian idea, i.e. that the physical and material wellbeing of any individual person is equally unimaginable without the wellbeing of their social group, extended family or clan. All prominent examples of African Socialist thinking, including Nyerere, Nkrumah and Senghor, emphasized heavily the image of a largely communitarian precolonial past, ruled by moral and ethical obligations of the individual to society, in contrast to the colonial concept of individualistic competition and individual rights against the society. As such, the roots of communitarian Africa were not only presented as an objective view on history, but rather were used as a key element in cultural reconstruction during the struggle for national liberation and society building after independence. The Ujamaa ideology of Nyerere, specifically, emphasized the importance of the radical communitarian past as the foundation of his vision of African socialism (Obioha 2014: 14–18). In "Ujamaa – The Basis of African Socialism" he states:

"In traditional African society everybody was a worker. There was no other way of earning a living for the community. Even the Elder, who appeared to be enjoying himself without doing any work and for whom everybody else appeared to be working, had, in fact, worked hard all his younger days. The wealth he now appeared to possess was not his, personally; it was only 'his' as the Elder of the group which had produced it. He was its guardian. The wealth itself gave him neither power nor prestige. The respect paid to him by the young was his because he was older than they, and had served his community longer; and the 'poor' Elder enjoyed as much respect in our society as the 'rich' elder."   (Nyerere 1962b: 3)

Later on, he derived his three basic principles of traditional Ujamaa from this depiction of the pre-colonial situation in Tanzania (see above). The "traditional African family" was the core of this image of a communitarian past:

"The traditional African family lived according to the basic principles of ujamaa. Its members did this unconsciously, and without any conception of what they were doing in political terms. They lived together and worked together because that was how they understood life, and how they reinforced each other against the difficulties they had to contend with – the uncertainties of weather and sickness, the depredations of wild animals (and sometimes human enemies), and the cycle of life and death. The results of their joint effort were divided unequally between them, but according to well understood customs."   (Nyerere 1968f: 106)

The accuracy of this simplified view of Tanzania's past, as a territory of exclusively communitarian societies, has repeatedly been questioned by scholars, as had its tangible influence on the implementation of Ujamaa policy in practice. A major point of critique regarding Nyerere's basic principles was brought forward by MAPOLU (1973: 58): In his view, Nyerere would have eschewed to define the space and the time in which these principles were supposed to have been a reality. Therefore, one would have to conclude that the existence of this "traditional past" was assumed to be true for all of Africa at all times before colonialism.

Some early observers, like TREUHEIT (1971: 79p.), noted this utilization of an idealized African past within Nyerere's concept of socialism, and attested that, while this idea of a generally classless subsistence-based society could certainly be found among the history of several Bantu tribes in what would later become Tanzania, this was certainly not true for all of the original ethnic groups and clans in precolonial times. For example, there had also been Hamitic prestige systems and other forms of hierarchical societies within the territory. Nevertheless, while certainly oversimplifying the precolonial situation, Nyerere's idea of communitarian Africa did indeed have a real background in Tanzania's history.

According to other authors, however, these idealized societies never existed and could no longer exist after colonialism. Furthermore, the traditional principles which Nyerere saw in his construction of the Tanzanian past were inadequate for a modern socialist society (WATZAL 1982: 8). In this view, the work ethic of Nyerere was anything but traditional: In the past people worked to survive, not because of moral obligation. Help was given, but not as a means to promote equality. The family was the core unit of production, not the village, and poverty was seen mostly as an individual fault. Therefore, Nyerere's socialism had hardly any base in traditional rural society (WATZAL 1982: 12–14).

This critique could be even more pronounced in areas with a feudal history of agriculture, like Bukoba. In such areas, people farmed mostly on individual plots and communal activities were almost entirely clan based, rather than involving the whole village. Most cases of communal work were based on the principle of reciprocity and limited to seeding or harvesting activities on the individual plots, the building of houses, or emergencies, such as unexpected sickness. Activities like common meals and the like were not known with the exception of procedural beer drinking, weddings or funerals, in which the whole clan was supposed to take part, pay the bride price, etc. There was also a sharp division in the roles between men and women, with women doing most of agricultural work, including the cultivation of virgin land (rweya) (BAKULA 1971: 16p.).

SPALDING (1996: 104–105) concludes that Nyerere's decision to project the history of some areas in precolonial Tanzania (including his own Zanaki home region) onto all parts of the country, led to Ujamaa's underestimation of the individualistic tendencies within the peasantry: Because – in the mindset of Ujamaa – there was a concrete socialist past in Tanzania, people just had to relearn this traditional way of life and shake off colonial individualism in order to succeed in building an independent socialist nation. This underestimation of individualism and overestimation of communitarian idealism, in her view, explained the difficulties of the Tanzanian leadership in dealing with the peasantry's reluctance to join collective agriculture in Ujamaa villages later on and impeded a deeper understanding of the real problems for socialist transition on the national level.

That being said, NYERERE himself was well aware that his vision of a socialist society based on the values of traditional Ujamaa implied more than just going back to the precolonial organization of society. For example, he saw the role of women as one of the major inadequacies in the traditional organization of the extended family, as women would have had a role that was in many ways inferior to that of their male counterparts. Furthermore, the inequalities which they suffered in the traditional system would not have been the result of their contribution to work: On the contrary, while their work was often harder than that of men, they would be deprived of some of the fruits of their labor simply by virtue of their gender. Therefore, Nyerere saw the equality of women in social and economic terms as one of the major points in which modern Ujamaa would have to overcome the limitations of the traditional extended family system (NYERERE 1968f: 108p.).

Additionally, he was very reflective on both the advantages and the limitations which he saw in his depiction of the peasant communities at the time of independence. In NYERERE's observation, there was still a very low level of exploitation in the peasant agriculture of Tanzania in this period. However, the small scale of productive units (i.e. the family) also led to a very low level of productivity when compared to the capitalist organization of agriculture in the more advanced nations. Under the capitalist system, more people would work together for a common goal, which made their work more effective. Yet, as this common goal in capitalism is the profit of the owner, it leads to the exploitation of the workers. In his view, the challenge for economic development for Tanzania after the Arusha Declaration lay in inducing higher productivity in this sector by increased cooperation among the peasants, thereby creating the same economies of scale as under the capitalist system, but without inducing the exploitation of the many by the few (NYERERE 1968g: 102p.).

The equality which he saw in the traditional communities of the past therefore reached limitations in scale, with respect to both economic viability and the political organization:

> "In traditional African life the people were equal, they co-operated together, and they participated in all the decisions which affected their lives. But the equality was an equality of poverty; the co-operation was on small things; and their government was only a government of their own family unit, and of their clan, or at most of their tribe. Our task, therefore, is to modernize the traditional structure so as to make it meet our new aspirations for a higher standard of living." (NYERERE 1968a: 171)

Following this logic also led to the question of the system of ownership intended for the modern, socialist Tanzania of Nyerere's persuasion. Nyerere's basic assumption is that for a society made up of equals, every individual has to have control over the tools necessary for his or her livelihood. In the traditional Tanzanian society, this sort of direct control over the own means of production was a basic feature of the peasant society. Only in a few parts of the country, feudal systems had already begun to change this direct ownership before the advent of colonialism. However, after independence, there would be no use in simply going back to the old system of ownership, based on the family and the clan, as modern life had become too complicated and technologically advanced. In this stage, even if the small farmer had direct control over his means of production, i.e. the land and the hand hoe, he would still depend on other members of society for his livelihood. If this interdependency is not supposed to lead to the exploitation of some members of the society by others, the ownership over the means of production has to be organized not individually, but based on a group or a cooperative. In Nyerere's view, this is the only possible way of organizing a modern society which does not increase inequality and competition between its individual members (Nyerere 1968h: 81–84).

In conclusion, then, Nyerere himself gives a comprehensive picture of the connections between his understanding of the traditional, family based African communities, and the modern elements which had to be added in order for his idea of Ujamaa to succeed:

> "The principles upon which the traditional extended family was based must be reactivated. We can start with extended family villages, but they will not remain family communities, and they must certainly be larger communities than was traditionally the case. Also, modern knowledge must be applied by these communities and to them; and the barriers which previously existed between different groups must be broken down, so that they co-operate in the achievement of major tasks. But the basis of rural life in Tanzania must be the practice of co-operation in its widest sense – in living, in working, and in distribution, and all with an acceptance of the absolute equality of all men and women."
> (Nyerere 1968f: 120)

2.3.3 The ideological development of African Socialism

This glimpse into Nyerere's construction of a "communitarian African past" as the basis of Ujamaa, leads to the question of the wider ideological context of African socialism in this era. The composition of African socialist ideologies and programs is at least as diverse and differentiated as the continent itself. The development of those ideologies, which became very popular in many newly independent African states from the 1950s up until the collapse of the Portuguese colonies in the 1970s, can only be understood when taking into account the background of those politicians and parties promoting African Socialism as national liberation movements.

In many ways, there was not much new in the new states of Africa. Only flags, but still the old colonial administration – export oriented, not caring about the people – while politicians were promising a completely new world, often based on socialism. After independence, the struggle against the external colonizer became obsolete. Thus, the rhetoric of fighting against the oppressors was replaced by the rhetoric of development. The developmental state or developmentalism became paramount for the new African elite. African Socialism was highly prestigious during the 1950s and

60s. First of all, the term "African" allowed its proponents to exclude "the others" from the possibility of defining it (i.e. the European socialists). Secondly, the term Socialism allowed the distancing of oneself from the old colonial and western model of exploitation, while still not braking completely with western ties. The ideological base often seems erratic, combining elements of African traditions, mythology, Christianity and Marxism. Instead of orthodox Marxist (or Leninist) ideology, African socialism would be defined by the two core elements of being "people centred" and "developmentalist" (SCHICHO 2009: 175–178).

Idealist approaches to African socialism pointed out the emancipatory power which would be enshrined in "those proven codes of conduct in the African societies which have, over the ages, conferred dignity on our people and afforded them security regardless of their station in life." (MBOYA 1963: 17), and which would be able to lead the way to progress and independence. On the side of the leaders of national independence, however, two additional motivations were seen for the use of the socialist theme: Firstly, it encompassed national unity, as opposed to the "traditionally" fragmented tribal society. Secondly, it enabled them to promote rapid economic growth and modernization of their "underdeveloped" nations. Furthermore, the use of the African socialist rhetoric also aided those leaders to perpetuate the image of an external enemy (like under colonialism), thereby reducing the threat of internal opposition to their leadership (MOHAN 1966: 220p.).

The situation of former colonies almost invariably led to a nationalist discourse, which was populist, but not necessarily socialist or progressive (LOPES 1988: 9p.). Indeed, the nationalist background and the emphasis on national liberation and self-determination meant that the term "socialism" was sometimes used very vaguely by African leaders, and the core rhetoric frequently changed if circumstances demanded it. As TORDOFF and MAZRUI (1972: 428p.) observed, French speaking representatives of African Socialism were more likely than the Anglophone ones to adhere to some degree of Marxist terminology. Yet, hardly any of the new leaders would develop their own consistent ideology or stress the paramountcy of class struggle or other key elements of Marxist thinking. In terms of local varieties – besides Ujamaa – African Socialism became emblematic through such different approaches as the "Arabic-Islamic socialism" of Muammar Ghadaffi in Libya or the "Mobutoism" of Mobuto sese Seko in Zaire, "Nkrumahism" in Ghana or the "vague amalgam of Marxism, Christian socialism, humanitarism and 'negritude' of Léopold Senghor of Senegal" (BHENGU 2011: 33). Furthermore, there was the humanism-based approach of Kenneth Kaunda in Zambia and a sort of "scientific socialism" put forward by Marien N'Goubi of Kongo (Brazzaville), to name just a few.

In fact, only very few African countries did not develop their own brand of socialism at some point after independence. To speak in Marxist terms, all African liberation movements could be described as transclassist. As such, they consisted of the forces of both the petit bourgeoisie and the peasantry. However, hegemony in the anticolonial struggle always belonged to the petit bourgeoisie, never the proletariat. While some may argue that the former possessed enough revolutionary consciousness to lead that struggle in a socialist way, LOPES is less optimistic: The petit bourgeoisie followed its own interests, as the common goal for the two different classes disappeared after independence, when class contradictions became obvious (Lopes 1988: 12). At a point in history when purely capitalist models of development and state organization would have been unimaginable for the peoples who had been dominated so recently by the forces of colonial exploitation, African Socialist concepts thus represented a sort of middle-ground between capitalism and "scientific socialism (Marxist-Leninist)" (Entralgo 1986: 56; cited in Lopes 1988: 9).

Due to the background of oppression and the perceived necessity of restoring their own cultural heritage, many African leaders did not, in fact, see any reason to let outsiders teach them the best version of their own ideology. In the Tanzanian case, Nyerere made the connections between the African past, the struggle for independence, and the future of his continent very clear:

> "We, in Africa, have no more need of being 'converted' to socialism than we have of being 'taught' democracy. Both are rooted in our own past – in the traditional society which produced us. Modern African Socialism can draw from its traditional heritage the recognition of 'society' as an extension of the basic family unit. But it can no longer confine the idea of the social family within the limits of the tribe, nor, indeed, of a nation. For no true African Socialist can look at a line drawn on a map and say "The people on this side of that line are my brothers, but those who happen to live on the other side of it can have no claim on me"; every individual on this continent is his brother.
> It was in the struggle to break the grip of colonialism that we learnt the need for Unity. We came to recognize that the same socialist attitude of mind which, in the tribal days, gave to every individual the security that comes of belonging to a widely extended family, must be preserved within the still wider society of our nation. But we should not stop there. Our recognition of the family to which we all belong must be extended yet further – beyond the tribe, the community, the nation or even the continent – to embrace the whole society of mankind. This is the only logical conclusion for true Socialism."
> (Nyerere 1962b: 9)

Within the context of national liberation, there were several concepts that stressed the "classless" nature of the African past and saw "traditional collectivism" and "African humanism" as the immediate basis for a socialist future in postcolonial Africa. Apart from Nyerere's Ujamaa, Sekou Touré's "communaucratique" would be another example of the image of a classless rural society as the traditional basis for African socialism (Cohen 1972: 231).

In his vigorous call for an African socialist society, Nyerere insisted heavily on the traditional, communitarian past of rural African societies. In this attempt to adapt socialist principles to the specific historical context of postcolonial Africa, however, it remains unclear if these repeated recurrences to the precolonial past are chiefly seen as an illustrative analogy for the envisioned future social order of Africa, or if those alleged cultural peculiarities and societal roots are treated as a necessary cultural prerequisite to motivate the African peoples to join the cause of a socialist future (Saul 1972c: 180).

In any case, Cohen characterizes Nyerere's "African societies" rather as gerontocratic communities, than as classless societies in a socialist sense. Indeed, he argues that there was a lack of economic stratification, as the level of the division of labor mostly remained relatively embryonic. Therefore, such societies were able to solve the few remaining conflicts on consensus principles. "Some African leaders, notably Senghor, have however attempted to generalize the description of such societies to presignify the achievement of a continent-wide socialism." (COHEN 1972: 231)

MEYNS sees a direct connection between the anticolonial struggle and the the victory of the October Revolution in Russia: Through this revolution, the proletariat had become the deciding class in world history and the struggle of the oppressed peoples against colonialism is at the front of this world revolution. However, national liberation is not synonymous with socialist revolution. Since the (former) colonies were still chained to dependency in the imperialist system – and pre-capitalist modes of production, such as subsistence farming, persisted in large areas of the new nations – a national liberation would have to create the possibility of national independence beforehand, as a prerequisite for the transformation to socialism. In this struggle, all classes of the oppressed territory have to unite, and as peasants make up the vast majority of population in most of these nations, it will be this class who will make up the most important force in this struggle (MEYNS 1977: 22–24).

Brought up in a world of poverty and need, the individual peasant has a legitimate demand to improve his situation and that of his family, and these demands have revolutionary power in the colonial situation. However, the justified demands of the small-scale farmer for ownership of his own land are technically bourgeois in nature, and the class situation of the peasantry, in MEYNS view, cannot enable them to lead the socialist cause after the victory of national independence, or even the leading role in the liberation struggle (see also chapter 2.3.5). This role lies with the workers. This insistence on the leading role of the proletariat in the struggle against imperialism is derived from the argument that imperialism is the highest form of capitalism, and the fight against imperialism, therefore, part of the socialist-proletarian world revolution. Moreover, in MEYNS view, there is no third way between capitalism and socialism, and as the proletariat is the only class directly and diametrically opposed to the capitalist class, it has to be the proletariat to take the lead in the anticolonial struggle. Otherwise, this struggle cannot reach the only possible way of true independence, which is socialism. The alliances between all the revolutionary classes, united against colonial rule may, differ depending on the specific situation and the historical context. But if the national liberation is not led by the proletariat, it cannot attain independence in this kind of argument (MEYNS 1977: 24p.).

In his analysis of the national liberation movements of the former Portuguese colonies of Cabo Verde, Mozambique and Angola (as well as the particular case of Zimbabwe), LOPES (1988: 18) tries to summarize several observations on the transition from independence struggle to (ruling) party establishment. The main point in his conclusion is that there is no linear development (or "chain reaction", as he coins it) from a national liberation movement to a socialist party. As the objectives of liberation are basically fulfilled at the point of independence, existing class contradictions and social inequalities become apparent. At the same time, those movements did not consider the type of development or state construction envisioned after independence during their fight for freedom, as this goal overshadowed any action of the group and functioned as a glue, binding together the different social classes within the movement. In all the movements observed by Lopes, Marxist-Leninist influences and rhetoric became more prevalent after independence, regardless of official alignment with the Soviet Union and its ideology. Nevertheless, a socialist ideal which would develop answers to the unequal distribution of wealth and income, and challenge the capitalist development agenda, was increasingly absent in those parties. Hence, Marxism and Marxist development strategies have been virtually absent from policy making in those four countries in the ten years following independence, despite the continued socialist rhetoric.

While Lopes' study only looks at the four parties of the countries mentioned, his remarks could be used to describe most of the African Socialist parties and leaders that emerged from the struggle for independence: There was an alliance between petit-bourgeois leaders and peasants in their struggle for independence. Both classes were radicalized through their struggle, but the connection broke after independence, so the "chain-reaction" was broken, too (Rudenbeck 1988: 22).

Cabral used the stage of the first tricontinental meeting of liberation movements from Africa, Asia and Latin America in Havana, Cuba in 1966, to criticize this apparent lack of revolutionary theory in many liberation movements. While acknowledging the fact that national liberation cannot be exported and is necessarily a local struggle against oppression, which has to be shaped by the specific historical realities of the respective peoples, he urges the congress to spend more time on the exchange of revolutionary theory. As Cabral underlines, the lack of theory and knowledge about one's own history was one of the biggest weaknesses of the anti-imperialist movements of the 1960s (Cabral 1968: 20p.).

In general, the dependency of colonies and neocolonies within the imperialist world economy limited the emergence of a national bourgeoisie in these countries. While the involvement in the world market and the connection to international capital affords this class some luxury possibilities for economic development, they are still limited in their economic possibilities by the far more powerful foreign capitalists. Meyns underlines the ambiguous role of this class: Depending on the historical situation and its internal composition, the petit bourgeoisie can choose between joining the liberation or remaining in their limited position of power in alliance with international capital. While joining the national liberation would not necessarily make sense from their material point of view, the members of this class have experienced the same forms of discrimination and oppression as the other classes under colonialism. Therefore, although privileged in many ways compared to their fellow countrymen, the petit bourgeois elite of the colonies can be part of national liberation. Analyses, which see the petit bourgeoisie in the colony as a monolithic block in close alliance with international capital for the oppression of the peasants and workers, are thus far too structuralist in Meyns' view. Specifically, those analyses would undervalue the inner differentiation and the social situation of the petit bourgeoisie and remain too economist in their arguments. Indeed, it was this class of teachers, clerks and colonial white-collar workers, who took the lead in many African independence struggles. However, as Meyns observes, if the petit-bourgeoisie did take the lead in this struggle, it tended to take over all the positions of power in the newly independent state and, therefore, created a bourgeois rather than a socialist state (Meyns 1977: 26–28).

45

Concerning this class structure of national liberation, CABRAL sees significant differences between the fight against colonialism and neocolonialism: Under colonialism, the emergence of a national bourgeoisie was as much denied as the emergence of an industrial or rural proletariat: Therefore, the struggle for national liberation almost naturally demands a fight between a united "national class" and the colonial power. As there is virtually no proletarian class available, which is big or revolutionary enough to lead this struggle, it will have to rely on a small, active vanguard. This vanguard, however, bears the utter responsibility to keep in mind the class character of the anti-imperialist struggle and has to educate the masses, in order to gain true national independence. In the neocolonial situation, where there is usually a bigger national petit bourgeoisie, it is much more difficult and risky to rely on a national unity movement, as this national bourgeoisie has already developed its own class interests and, if given the chance, will make true independence from international capital impossible. In the latter case, there is no use in national independence, and a socialist revolution led by the emerging proletariat is the only chance for true liberation (CABRAL 1968: 32–34).

In the colonial situation, the national petit bourgeoisie is the only social group, which – in CABRAL's view – can gain a true consciousness of the nature of imperialist oppression. Through their work in administration and other state offices, its members are the only locals who have constant contact with the persons he calls agents of colonialism. That means the petit bourgeoisie enjoys some of the material benefits that are created through colonial exploitation, while it is at the same time exposed to constant (racial) discrimination and humiliation. Furthermore, the colonial system of governance and economy limits their ability to develop into a true ruling class and to create an economic base for this role. Consequently, it is the petit bourgeoisie which, in the absence of a large urban or rural proletariat, will lead the struggle for national liberation. Inside the new state, they are the only social group which can lead the state apparatus inherited from imperialist rule. In the neocolonial situation, however, which usually follows the attainment of national (political) independence, it is upon the members of the petit bourgeoisie to decide: Either, they will join the struggle for true national liberation, which would mean transferring their newly gained power over the institutions of the state to the proletariat and to cut their linkages to the international bourgeoisie. Alternatively, they will try to hold on to their political power and attempt to extend their economic base through the exploitation of their fellow compatriots and through their connections to international capital in order to become a true national bourgeoisie. This latter option would be illusionary in CABRAL's view, as the power relations between international capital and the national petit bourgeoisie would dictate that the true ruling class in this scenario would always remain the bourgeoisie of the imperialist centers. On the other hand, joining the struggle for national liberation in the neocolonial situation would mean "committing suicide as a class" for the members of the national bourgeoisie, as there would be no such class in a truly liberated (socialist) country (CABRAL 1968: 35–39).

MEYNS emphasizes that the countries of the Third World – especially in Africa – have achieved remarkable successes in the period after the Second World War in gaining political independence. He denounces the views that this independence was granted by imperialism rather than successfully fought for by the peoples of the former colonies themselves, or that only a socialist revolution done simultaneously with the fight for political independence could have the power to establish national liberation in one move. Rather, he sees the achievement of political independence as one step to national liberation (MEYNS 1977: 32p.).

On this journey, the now politically independent countries face two major challenges: Firstly, the national bourgeoisie that took over state power with independence is mostly reluctant to change the status quo of (theoretical) political independence and economic dependence, because it is beneficial to their class interests. Secondly, the emergence of the US as Western and the Soviet Union as Eastern super-powers continues the imperialist struggle for world domination and intensifies the unequal development of imperialism, with tremendous dangers for world peace and economic repercussions all over the globe. In MEYNS' view, in both areas imperialism itself is creating the resources for its own fall: On the one hand, the national bourgeoisie in the neocolonies becomes unsatisfied with the limitations implied by dependency on imperialist capital – and MEYNS sees the occurrence of coup d'états and other turmoil as a sign for these contradictions – and join the antiimperialist cause. On the other hand, the cooperation of all peoples suffering under the dominance of both super-powers enjoys an increasing number of supporters as this fight for world dominance intensifies. Therefore, the cooperation among all Third World nations is paramount, because it increases their power and opportunities for change on a global scale. In MEYNS' view, the main contradiction on this scale is that between the poor nations of the South (i.e. the Third World) and the big super powers of the North (i.e. United States and Soviet Union). In his analysis from the 1970s, the author is positive on the prospect that increased Third World cooperation and the inherent contradictions of imperialism might induce the end of global capitalism (MEYNS 1977: 33–37).

In retrospect, Samir AMIN has described the years between 1945-90 as characterized by the coexistence of social democracy in the West, "really existing" socialism in the East and the victory of National Liberation in the South. In his view, this phase of socially controlled systems made it possible to circumvent the capitalist logic of pure competition and exploitation and enabled social advancements on a global scale (AMIN 2015: 69). The historical block that was formed by the national liberation movements achieved significant social progress during the 1960s and 70s, according to AMIN's view. However, inner contradictions which emerged during this progress, as well as the outer opposition of continued global imperialism, led to the demise of this progressive role and the loss of social achievements. As a result, the peasantry of the global periphery became increasingly marginalized for the benefit of a local ruling class, keen to assert full control over the local economy (AMIN 2015: 107).

2.3.4 Influences of and differences to European Socialism and Marxism

In several parts of his writings on African socialism, NYERERE actively distances himself from the Marxist ideology and its underlying "scientific" principles. With his high regard for the traditional and – in his view – communitarian society of precolonial Africa (see above), he would often underline that Africans would not need any foreign inspiration to know what socialism was all about. After all, they had not only all been socialists by Nyerere's definition before the arrival of the colonial system of production, they would also be able to understand the basic principles of the relation between work and wealth without the help of Western scientists:

> "The production of wealth, whether by primitive or modern methods, requires three things. First, Land. God has given us the land, and it is from the land that we got the raw materials which we reshape to meet our needs. Secondly, Tools. We have found by simple experience that tools do help! So we make the hoe, the axe, or the modern factory or tractor, to help us produce wealth – the goods we need. And, thirdly, human exertion – or Labour. We don't need Karl Marx or Adam Smith to find out that neither the Land nor the Hoe actually produces Wealth. And we don't need to take degrees in Economics to know that neither the Worker nor the Landlord produces Land. Land is God's gift to Man – it is always there. But we do know, still without degrees in economics, that the axe and the plough were produced by the labourer. Some of our more sophisticated friends apparently have to undergo the most rigorous intellectual training simply to discover that stone axes were produced by that ancient gentleman 'Early Man' to make it easier for him to skin the impala he had just killed with a club, which he had also made for himself!"   (NYERERE 1962b: 3)

While SAUL sees good reasons for this strategy on a political level – given the prevalence of orthodox Marxist-Leninist movements within the socialist camp – he poses the question of whether the continued neglect of Marxist analysis and strategy within the Ujamaa agenda might lead to an oversimplification of the African social reality and induce overwhelming pragmatism when it comes to policy implementation. Specifically, Nyerere's argument that the lack of capitalism within the postcolonial context would negate the use of a Marxist analysis of class structures and class struggle raises severe doubt, as other contemporary Third World "leaders" like Mao, Ho Chi Minh or Castro did not see any contradiction between skipping the capitalist phase of development and branding themselves as Marxist (SAUL 1972c: 180p.).

Yet, NYERERE's opposition to what he calls "doctrinaire socialism" appears to go beyond a simple political tactic. In fact, he seems to have held a deep conviction that the concept of classes, exploitation and all other basic concepts of Western socialism would be as foreign to Africa as the capitalism brought by colonialism. Therefore, while acknowledging that "everybody was a worker" in traditional Africa (see above), he wanted to make sure that this term would entail a different meaning for him than it did for the "European Socialist":

> "The other use of the word "worker", in its specialist sense of "employee" as opposed to "employer", reflects a capitalist attitude of mind which was introduced into Africa with the coming of colonialism and is totally foreign to our own way of thinking. In the old days the African had never aspired to the possession of personal wealth for the purpose of dominating any of his fellows. He had never had labourers or 'factory hands' to do

his work for him. But then came the foreign capitalists. They were wealthy. They were powerful. And the African naturally started wanting to be wealthy too. There is nothing wrong in our wanting to be wealthy; nor is it a bad thing for us to want to acquire the power which wealth brings with it. But it most certainly is wrong if we want to the wealth and the power so that we can dominate somebody else. Unfortunately there are some of us who have already learnt to covet wealth for that purpose – and who would like to use the methods which the capitalist uses in acquiring it." (NYERERE 1962b: 4)

Specifically, he interpreted the Marxist understanding of history as the history of class struggles as an unnecessary glorification of violence, as well as an overestimation of the importance of capitalism. If, in his idea, the peoples of Africa had just a few generations ago lived a socialist life, how should it be necessary to endure the exploitation of capitalism followed by the horrors of class war, just to arrive again at a form of living which he thought to know from his own childhood:

"European Socialism was born of the Agrarian Revolution and the Industrial Revolution which followed it. The former created the 'landed' and 'landless' classes in society; the latter produced the modern capitalist and the industrial proletariat.
These two revolutions planted the seeds of conflict within society, and not only was European Socialism born of that conflict, but it apostles sanctified the conflict itself into a philosophy. Civil War was no longer looked upon as something evil, or something unfortunate, but as something good and necessary. As prayer is to Christianity or Islam, so Civil War (which they call "class war") is to the European version of Socialism – a means inseparable from its end. Each becomes the basis of a whole way of life. The European Socialist cannot think of his socialism without its Father – Capitalism!
Brought up in tribal socialism, I must say I find this contradiction quite intolerable. It gives capitalism a philosophical status which capitalism neither claims nor deserves. For it virtually says "Without Capitalism, and the conflict which Capitalism creates within society, there can be no Socialism"! This glorification of Capitalism by the doctrinaire European Socialists, I repeat, I find intolerable." (NYERERE 1962b: 8)

And with this understanding of European Socialism, he again underlines the basic principle of Ujamaa – his own brand of non-capitalist development envisioned for Africa:

"'UJAMAA', then, or 'Familyhood', describes our Socialism. It is opposed to Capitalism, which seeks to build a happy society on the basis of Exploitation of Man by Man; and it is equally opposed to doctrinaire Socialism which seeks to build a happy society on a philosophy of Inevitable Conflict between Man and Man." (NYERERE 1962b: 8)

Yet, NYERERE's opposition to "doctrinaire socialism" was not only based on his disregard for the idea that it had to be brought about by violent conflict following a phase of capitalist exploitation. He also frowned upon the "theology of socialism", by which he meant the tendency of some socialists to engage in lengthy discussions on the true meaning of the classic works of Marx, Lenin, or Mao. For him, all these works – as inspiring they might be – were just the work of men. And as a committed Christian he did not support the idea of treating those works with the same techniques as a theologian might treat the Bible – looking for the true will of God. In Nyerere's understanding, there was not one true socialism which might hold the solution for any problem and the way forward for any given circumstances. On the contrary, the exact shape and the exact strategies for the creation of a socialist society – i.e. one guaranteeing everyone's well-being without the exploitation of man by man – would depend on the specific historical and economic conditions of each society (NYERERE 1968h: 76p.).

From his point of view, this was especially true for the situation of the new states of Africa, as they found themselves in completely different circumstances than the industrialized nations of the West:

> "It is not possible for a country which moves to socialism from a highly developed capitalist economy, to follow the same path as one which starts from a backward peasant economy. Nor is it likely that two backward countries moving to socialism will follow exactly the same path if one starts from a feudal base and another from traditional communalism. Each state must move in a direction which is appropriate to its starting point. Although, however, each country with a socialist purpose has a different path to tread, we can still learn a great deal from each other." (NYERERE 1968h: 87)

Nevertheless, some of Nyerere's post-Arusha writings and speeches suggest that he – to some degree – revised his earlier interpretation of African socialism as an ideology equally opposed to capitalism and "doctrinaire socialism". One of the most striking examples underlining this tendency can be found in *The Rational Choice* (NYERERE 1974c), a speech originally given at a conference in Sudan in 1973. This time, he made much more punctuated statements indicating the dichotomy between capitalism and socialism – and emphasized that there was no third way between those two systems:

> "In the modern world there are two basic systems of economic and social organization – capitalism and socialism. There are variations within these broad classifications, like welfare capitalism or humanistic socialism; but the broad distinction between the two systems remains, and our first choice has to be between them." (NYERERE 1974c: 113)

As he goes on with his description of the political and economic systems which he observed during the 1970s, his analysis of capitalism becomes much closer to the ideas of Marx and Engels than had been the case in Nyerere's earlier essays on socialism:

> "Remnants of feudalism and of primitive communalism do, of course, still exist in the world; but neither of these are viable systems when challenged by the organized technology of the twentieth century. Sometimes, as in Japan, these old systems influence the organization of capitalism for a while; but the influences are subordinate to the logic of the later organization, and will eventually be completely eradicated. For in the last

resort anything which detracts from the profit of an individual capitalist enterprise will be abandoned by that enterprise; and anything which militates against the efficiency of the capitalist system will be uprooted." (Nyerere 1974c: 113)

In the Communist Manifesto, this power of capitalism, this inherent logic of uprooting all elements of society which would hinder the growth of profits and the expansion of capitalist production, was seen as one of the main results of the bourgeois revolution. In the search for increasing profit rates, the new ruling class would not only bring down the old ways of production, but also the social system organizing the relations of production. And in the pursuit of new markets and new resources, the cheap commodities produced in the industrialized countries were dubbed to be the "heavy artillery that would bring down all of the Chinese walls" which were protecting the pre-capitalist societies in one way or another (Marx & Engels 1960a: 463–467).

Indeed, Nyerere now appears to share the same analysis regarding the interaction of global capitalism with traditional communitarian societies:

"Primitive communalism is equally doomed. The moment the first enamel pot, or factory woven cloth, is imported into a self-sufficient communal society, the economic and social structure of that society receives its death blow. Afterwards it is merely a question of time, and of whether the members of that community will be participants or victims of the new economic order." (Nyerere 1974c: 113)

This new economic order, in Nyerere's understanding comprises of the social organization of production according to the needs and the will of those owning the means of production, i.e. the capitalists. The decisions about which goods are produced and in what quantity are solely depending on the need of these capitalists to increase their profit. The necessity of these commodities hence is secondary to their ability to increase profit and the needs of those actually producing the goods (the workers) are only relevant in the sense that they are able to reproduce their labor power. The power of those who own the means of production, however, is not limited to their ability to direct production and employ labor according to their needs. The wealth which they achieve by exploiting the labor of their employees also enables them to subjugate the political structures and the decisions of elected governments to their interests (Nyerere 1974c: 114p.).

Although Nyerere uses the terms of "capital" and "money" much more loosely than Marx had done in his analysis of the metamorphosis of money into capital (Marx 1972b: 161–191), his basic understanding of the social and economic organization of capitalism does not deviate much from Marx's description of the division between the use value and the exchange value of commodities, as well as the division between labor itself and the product of labor, which enabled the capitalist system of accumulation in the first place (Marx 1982: 414–419, 1972b: 741–744): While in pre-capitalist societies, the value of commodities was measured in their ability to satisfy certain needs (uses), it is now measured in their ability to be sold for profit. While before, labor was used to create the products which were needed, it is now applied according to the will of the capitalist and employed for his profit.

Furthermore, LENIN's (1972: 218, 248-249, 264-265) notions of the concentration of capital in the form of big capitalist monopolies, competing with each other for dominance and inducing the age of imperialism in the search for new markets and resources, is also very present in NYERERE's thinking, as:

> "This development is part of the dynamic of capitalism – for capitalism is very dynamic. It is a fighting system. Each capitalist enterprise survives by successfully fighting other capitalist enterprises. And the capitalist system as a whole survives by expansion, that is, by extending its area of operations and in the process eradicating all restraints upon it, and all weaker systems of society.
> Consider now what this means for the new nations of the Third World."
> (NYERERE 1974c: 115)

This statement also resembles LUXEMBURG's analysis of the need for capitalism to continuously expand its reach on the pre-capitalist societies on a global level, in order to sustain its own reproduction. Capitalism needs those societies for its own survival, but in order to appropriate their resources and their labor power, it has to destroy the old social organization of those societies (LUXEMBURG 1921: 392p.).

Once this subjugation of these societies under the capitalist system has been achieved, the formal independence of a state becomes secondary. This means, in NYERERE's view, the permanent dominance by the big capitalist nations over the newly independent states of the Third World. Under the capitalist system, the inherent logic of big enterprises getting bigger and eliminating competition would imply a continuous process of fewer and fewer capitalist corporations dominating the world economy. Even progressive governments in the capitalist centers would be unable to oppose the will of these few powerful enterprises, as they would face the threat of mass unemployment and economic crises. Therefore, true independence would be impossible to achieve for a country like Tanzania, if it adhered to the logic of capitalism (NYERERE 1974c: 119).

Therefore, the only rational choice for any nation like his own would be to try to establish a socialist order of economy and society, in order to be able to achieve full independence as a country. And while he continues to elaborate that many of the "so-called socialist countries" of his time would by no means be free of exploitation or injustice, he insists that the socialist paradigm of economy would be the only one of the two systems which can be compatible with his understanding of development, as it puts the needs of people at the center, and not the needs of a small group of capitalists to increase their profit (NYERERE 1974c: 123p.).

And, after all, he also agrees on the Marxian analysis of the capitalist formation of classes in its dialectical form:

> "...capitalism automatically brings with it the development of two classes of people: a small group whose ownership of the means of production brings them wealth, power and privilege; and a very much larger group whose work provides that wealth and privilege. The one benefits by exploiting the other, and a failure in the attempt to exploit leads to a breakdown of the whole system with a consequent end to all production! The

exploitation of the masses is, in fact, the basis on which capitalism has won the accolade for having solved the problem of production. There is no other basis on which it can operate. For if the workers ever succeeded in obtaining the full benefits of their industry, then the capitalist would receive no profit and would close down the enterprise!" (NYERERE 1974c: 121)

What can be concluded from this short selection of Nyerere's views on European socialism and Marxian thinking is that he did share the basic elements of Marxian analysis of capitalism, especially regarding the inherent logic of capitalist development and expansion. He also appears to share the basic assumption of the theories of imperialism, i.e. the tendency of capitalist concentration and the resulting domination of the peripheral countries by the imperialist centers. The main difference between his idea of socialism and the Marxist-Leninist version, and the underlying reason for his outspoken opposition to "doctrinaire socialism", seems to be based on his disregard for the idea that there can be only one way to a socialist society – and that this way would include the necessity to introduce capitalism into what he perceived to be classless society, only to overthrow it by a violent revolution afterwards.

Another contributing factor in Nyerere's apparent distance from Marxist rhetoric may be found in his skepticism on the role which the so-called socialist bloc was playing in the early independence period in Africa. In a speech called *The Second Scramble* (NYERERE 1962a: 1–3) he emphasizes that in his view, socialism will be the only possible way of development for the newly independent states. Nevertheless, he argues that this socialism has to be different from the one found in the Eastern bloc of the cold war era. In his observation, while those countries led by the Soviet Union had achieved remarkable results in material development, they would now use this wealth to dominate and subjugate poorer nations – very similar to the way the capitalist countries did. Therefore, in his perspective, the main line of conflict in that era was different from the one Marx had described:

"We, in Africa, must beware of being hypnotised by the lure of the old slogans. I have said already that Socialism arose to remedy the mistakes which Capitalism had made. Karl Marx felt there was an inevitable clash between the rich of one society and the poor of that society. In that, I believe, Karl Marx was right. But today it is the international scene which is going to have a greater impact on the lives of individuals than what is happening within Tanganyika, or within Kenya, or within Uganda. And when you look at the international scene, you must admit that the world is still divided between the 'Haves' and the 'Have-nots'. This division is not a division between Capitalists and Socialists, nor between Capitalists and Communists; this is a division between the poor countries of the world and the rich countries of the world. I believe, therefore, that the poor countries of the world should be very careful not to allow themselves to be used as the 'tools' of any of the rich countries – however much the rich countries may seek to fool them that they are on their side! And don't forget that the rich countries of the world today may be found on both sides of the division between 'Capitalist' and 'Socialist' countries." (NYERERE 1962a: 3)

This view on the global system of the cold war era was one of the main arguments for Tanzania's non-alignment policy in the 1970s (NYERERE 1970) as well as for the rejection of both, Western and Soviet military presence in Africa (NYERERE 1978). Overall, NYERERE's understanding of (neo-) imperialism appears to be closer to authors like MEYNS and CABRAL, than to LENIN, LUXEMBURG or MARX, when it comes to the analysis of global class struggle (see above).

2.3.5 The Concept of Class in the Tanzanian Situation

The discussion of national liberation and African socialism in chapter 2.3.3 has already touched some of the main streams of thought concerning the role of classes and their importance in the postcolonial situation in Africa. Since this question appears to be of great importance for a thesis concerned with the idea, development and failure of socialist development in Tanzania, it seems paramount to get a more detailed look at the issue of class in this country, in particular. Furthermore, in a study dealing with the issue of rural development, the class situation in the rural environment is of specific interest. Therefore, the following paragraphs will discuss the formation of classes in rural Tanzania, starting with the pre-colonial situation. After elaborating on the influences of colonialism on the peasantry, it will conclude with the post-independence developments and their relevance for the analysis of rural living conditions and development strategies today.

The pre-colonial situation – Classless communities or feudalism?

While acknowledging the difficulty in generalizing the description of pre-colonial societies in Tanganyika due to their heterogeneity and lack of written documents, RWEYEMAMU considers the village community to be the dominant productive system before colonization. Politically, these societies were organized in tribal groups, with relatively weak direct power represented by chiefs or elders. The main reason for this weak political organization is explained by the economic base of the village community, which was the independent peasant, working his own land for the subsistence of his family. Land tenure was secured in the way that individual ownership was dependent on the productive use of allocated land and the individual peasants' membership of their respective socio-cultural groups. Individual alienations of land were strictly prohibited in these systems, and the specific ownership of land was dependent on the use of land for agriculture. Therefore, there was no absolute individual ownership of land. As fertile land was abundant in these societies and shifting cultivation the dominant agricultural technique, there was little need for a central power to regulate or control access to land, which was virtually the only means of production. In this sense, there was no market for land, nor for labor, as the productive relations of the village community were characterized by relations of family and kinship. As independent, subsistent units, the peasants were not alienated from their work as in the Marxist understanding of the capitalist economy. In the village community, they were owners of their land (i.e. their means of production) and not laborers. Furthermore, communal work was organized in a system of social obligations (work parties, etc.). Market exchanges of agricultural or other products remained limited, as the village community operated in a mostly self-sufficient way. Due to the subsistence character and the low general productivity of this mode of production – and the low incentives it provided for innovation or increased productivity – economic differentiation was virtually non-existent. Hence, there was no emergence of classes in these societies (RWEYEMAMU 1973: 3–7).

NYERERE himself based his understanding of the classlessness of traditional African societies on this depiction of traditional agricultural production, which he saw as the dominating, if not the only, form of agriculture before colonialism. Neither an agricultural, nor an industrial revolution, had therefore laid the foundations of classes within these societies:

> "African Socialism [as opposed to European Socialism], on the other hand, did not have the 'benefit' of the Agrarian Revolution or the Industrial Revolution. It did not start from the existence of conflicting 'classes' in society. Indeed I doubt if the equivalent for the word "class" exists in any indigenous African language; for language describes the ideas of those who speak it, and the idea of "class" or "caste" was non-existent in African society.
> The foundation, and the objective, of African Socialism is the Extended Family. The true African Socialist does not look on one class of men as his brethren and another as his natural enemies. He does not form an alliance with his 'brethren' for the extermination of his 'non-brethren'. He rather regards all men as his brethren, as members of his ever extending Family."
> (NYERERE 1962b: 8)

Nevertheless, at least three other modes of production emerged in pre-colonial times, in addition to the village community. Firstly, the pastoral societies in the more arid parts of the country. Secondly, the so-called banana cultures of the Lake Victoria and Usambara regions, where the more perennial agricultural systems of banana cultivations implied more value and competition for fertile land and led to the emergence of feudal societies like the Nyarubanja system in the West Lake region (see BUGENGO et al. (1976: 1, 3-7, 10-13) for a more detailed description of this feudal system). A similar mode of production could be found the Ukerewe system of more intensive (irrigated) agriculture and the pit-cultivation of the Matengo highlands. Thirdly, there is evidence of a regional and long-distance trade in agricultural as well as artisan products in the pre-colonial period (e.g. in iron products among the Yao and Nyamwezi), which implies the existence of artisan and trader societies. Generally, RWEYEMAMU characterizes the precolonial society of Tanganyika as a complex and differentiated system of various modes of production, yet he emphasizes that this system was in fact economically viable as a whole (RWEYEMAMU 1973: 7–9).

COULSON (1976: 20), acknowledges this differentiated understanding of the precolonial situation of Tanzania, but categorizes these social systems into two main variants: On the one hand, he sees the "traditional Ujamaa" societies of Nyerere's understanding, on the other hand feudal systems based on chiefdoms. Down to the present day, however, the commemoration of those highly developed agricultural societies – like those of the Haya of the West Lake Region and the Chagga of the

Kilimajaro area – remains hardly tapped, even by the country's "Cultural Tourism Programme", while the "traditional society" of Tanzania is mostly represented by the image of pastoral cultures like those of the Maasai (JOB 2017: 129).

Going further in the level of abstraction, BERNSTEIN (1981: 5p.) considers the dominating form of social organization in precolonial Africa to be based on "natural economies", i.e. economic systems in which the production of use values was prevalent. While he does not consider this abstraction to give a historically accurate picture of the precolonial situation, he emphasizes that it represents a valid starting point for the analysis of the "capitalist penetration" into these societies. This penetration of capitalism into the natural economies, however, would have begun even before the epoch of large scale colonialism in Africa – with the slave trade having the most significant consequences for the social structures of these societies. Both the precolonial and the colonial period could therefore – in the terms of Rosa LUXEMBURG (1921: 339–359) – be considered as an example of the fight between capitalist expansion and the natural economy.

With the large-scale introduction of clove plantation in Zanzibar under the rule of Seyyid Said in the first half of the 19th century, the demand for slave labor from mainland Tanganyika grew steadily. As labor power was also the main determinant of the traditional agricultural societies on the mainland, the intensified abduction and enslavement of able-bodied Africans implied severe negative effects on general productivity and the economic viability of the traditional economy. In many cases, traditional patriarchal democracies were replaced by warrior monarchies, while famines became increasingly common due to the reduced productivity of mainland agriculture. In Zanzibar, the clove plantation economy led to the emergence of a hierarchically organized class society, with an Arabian ruling class owning the plantations, a mostly Indian class of traders and clerks, and an undifferentiated majority class of African slaves (RWEYEMAMU 1973: 9–11).

The Colonial formation of Classes – The role of the peasantry

While the coastal slave trade and early trade relations with Europeans influenced some of the traditional societies on the Tanzanian coastline, it was the systematic colonization of Tanganyika by the Germans and British that intensified traditional class differences and brought the widespread formation of classes. Economic and social differentiation was implied by the introduction of cash crop production, the administrative technique of indirect rule and the colonial educational system (RWEYEMAMU 1973: 25p.). The most significant effect of this colonial influence on the social organization of these societies in the context of rural development has been described as the transformation of the rural smallholder population into peasants (SAUL & WOODS 1969: 1251p.).

BOESEN et al. describe this peasantry as a social formation, whose ultimate livelihood depends on the access to land and the labor force of the (extended) family. It is therefore a household-based mode of production which depends on land as the main physical means of production. As such, it has no inherent drive for economic growth, although the natural growth of a family or clan over generations may imply a certain level of either productive or areal expansion. Social and trade relations do exist to non-peasant sections of the society. While not necessarily opposing social or technological changes, the family-farm cycle that defines the peasant economy will head towards an equilibrium in which expansion of farming area or the introduction of new crops will only occur if population growth necessitates it, or if those changes implicate an immediate benefit and do not represent a threat to the economic and social system based on family security. If changes in agrarian production or social structure are supposed to be implemented from the outside, those changes will often be met with implicit or open opposition by the peasantry (BOESEN et al. 1977: 27–29).

Together with the different rural development approaches emerging at the end of colonialism and the early postcolonial period in Africa, a scientific and political discussion on the characteristics of the African peasantry as a social class unfolded. The key point of this debate was represented in Goran HYDÉN's (1980) monograph on the uncaptured peasantry. African peasants, according to HYDÉN, have their own mode of production, which he characterized by a "domestic orientation" of the economy in small, cellular household units, which operate more or less independently and sustain themselves. It would be based on mostly rudimentary agricultural techniques and low mechanization, and thus has a low capitalization. Farm labor is therefore the main means of production. In this setting, the peasantry can reproduce itself without the help or intervention of the "superimposed" state (HYDÉN 1980: 12–18). This would mean that the peasants in Tanzania would have survived the era of colonialism more or less untouched and were equally reluctant to join new development projects of the independent state.

HYDÉN describes the peasantry of sub-Saharan Africa (except Zimbabwe and South Africa) as being uniquely different from the picture seen in Asia or Latin America. According to him, small scale production still contributes a large part of GDP, farmers operate independently from state intervention and income difference is not so much caused by land size but by skill. The farm size is still limited due to the limited technological resources and the farmer societies are less integrated into market economy than anywhere else. As he suggests, this is partly because the creation of the peasantry as a social class only started in Africa with colonization about a century ago and that this class formation was still not finished in 1980. The state thus is not so much relevant to the peasant as the peasant is for the state, since the former can survive by his own means while the latter needs the peasant agriculture to transform, in order to achieve its developmental agenda (HYDÉN 1980: 10–12).

However, this thesis of an African peasantry uncaptured by the forces of colonialism and market integration has come under criticism from different sides. Firstly, the implied homogeneity of the Tanzanian peasantry has been questioned in various accounts: COULSON (1976: 22p.) sees the peasant economy rising during colonialism, motivated by the smallholders' will to keep independence as farmers, but at the cost of selling cash crops at very low prices. Asian trades were acting as middlemen and introducing manufacturing production from Europe through their shops. A small class of richer farmers (Kulaks) and small capitalist farmers were rising by using profits from coffee and cotton production.

LYIMO (2012: 32p.) describes a stratification of farmers through the introduction of cash-crop production in colonial times. As a result, the pre-colonial situation of homogenous small-scale farmers was differentiated into strata of rich farmers, middle and poor peasants, and rural (migrant) wage laborers. He does still see a common (class) interest of all African farmers and traders against the (mostly) Asian middleman. FREYHOLD (1979: 63) also observes the rise of a new class of Kulaks, who – in her view – gained their starting capital from paid work on farms, as well as in bureaucracy or other paid work. These Kulaks would be structurally different from middle and marginal peasants: employing labor, running small businesses, and engaging in trade – as opposed to the classical description of a self-sustaining peasantry.

This class differentiation, however, did not take place in a uniform manner, but had strong regional differentiations. The emergence of cash-crop production led to the creation of a fairly prosperous peasantry in climatically favorable areas with sufficient rainfall, fertile land and good transport connections. Cash-crop production in these areas was mostly reliant on only one or two crops. It was areas such as Lake Victoria and Kilimanjaro that class formation was most significant. As the agricultural techniques remained mostly the same during the whole colonial era, increase in production meant increase in acreage, which in turn led to increasing scarcity of arable land. In the regions most affected by cash-crop production, a new class of landless rural population emerged, as young men could not hope to get ownership to their own piece of land before the death of their fathers. With the increase of land scarcity, communal land tenure and social relations based on family and kinship gave way to a system where land was treated as a commodity in private ownership. At the same time, the traditional village economy gave way to commercial agriculture, as well as a new class of African traders (who, however, remained economically weak compared to the Asian trading class, because of the racist regulations in this sector). The reinforcement or invention of chiefdoms as a measure of indirect rule by the colonial administration intensified the formation of classes, as these local elites were the first to profit from the emerging cash-crop economy and extended their economic and political power, especially in feudal systems like Narubanya in the West Lake area (RWEYEMAMU 1973: 26–30).

On the other hand, in less favorable areas with limited rainfalls and lack of transport and market connections, the peasant economy was hardly changed, since cash-crop production was not viable in these regions. WOODS (1975: 41–44) has described this phase as the emergence of "area based peasantries", as the differentiation of the respective rural societies was mainly determined by the natural conditions of the area in which they were based.

In a study of the peasantry of Kagera District (Bukoba, in colonial times), SMITH (1989), puts HYDÉN's thesis to the test. Specifically, he is critical of the notion of HYDÉN that the peasantry of Africa does not need other classes to produce or reproduce. While SMITH agrees that there is a certain level of self-sufficiency – especially food security through the subsistence nature of peasant agriculture –, he argues that HYDÉN overlooks the influence of consumer goods and other needs for living that changed the live of the peasants since the 1920s and led to a growing integration of the peasant mode of production into the wider (capitalist) macro economy (SMITH 1989: 5p.).

First of all, the traditional economy was destroyed by the introduction of non-indigenous diseases with the arrival of the Germans. Secondly, the introduction of the Hut Tax implied that the formerly independent smallholders now had to engage in either cash-crop production (mostly coffee, in this region) or wage labor, in order to get the money to pay the tax. Regarding food security, the old system of using the tribute that had to be paid to the king as a food reserve in case of drought, was also destroyed. Overall, the total production of food crops declined dramatically in the early colonial period. While relief measures were taken by the colonial administration, this also meant that the traditional, tribute based food reserve system was replaced by one relying on money and therefore market production. Lastly, the introduction of "luxury items" like cigarettes, beer or meat meant that the money necessary to take part in the now changed pattern of socially necessary consumption implied that the smallholders had to divert some of their agricultural activities to cash earning. The combined effects of those colonial influences led to a change in the economic (agricultural) activities of the Haya farmers, for instance, with the substitution of banana trees with coffee cultivation. Therefore, the peasants of Bukoba were "not proletarianized, but the natural economy[2] (…) had been transformed."(p.10) (SMITH 1989: 7–10).

The survival of the peasantry as a class in spite of their integration into the colonial capitalist economy is mainly explained by the character of this integration. It took place in the form of a trade economy, where, instead of changing the peasant mode of production completely, the establishment and control of trade links with peasants as cash-crop producers was seen as more efficient by the colonizers. The peasantry itself became divided into different strata, and while most of the rural population would be considered simple peasants, BOESEN et al. identify at least three specific deviations in their study of West Lake Region. The first one would be landless rural laborers from Rwanda and Burundi. The second group they call "peasantry-cum-lumpenproletariat" (BOESEN et al. 1977: 162), which is characterized by peasants who have access to their own land, but whose land is too small to produce enough to sustain the family. Therefore, members will be engaged in paid farm labor or non-farm small-scale enterprises like shoemaking, carpentry or any other "fundi" businesses. Some will be able to use the income derived from these activities to invest in their agriculture and become "normal" peasants again, some peasants will move to this social formation because of diminishing incomes from farm activities. Overall, this social group has the highest fluctuation inside the peasantry, and most peasants will be part of this group at some point in their lives. The last deviation would be peasants, who are rich enough to hold more than one farm at once, usually because they derived income from positions in the bureaucracy. Farm activity is not a necessity in their daily life, as they are able to employ laborers. Since their economic base does not lie in their own agriculture, it is questionable whether this group can be seen as belonging to the peasantry, at all. However, their farms are not only seen as an investment opportunity, but are mainly kept as subsistence base

---

2 The term "natural economy" is used with refrence to LUXEMBURG's (1921: 339–359) understanding of an economic organization preceding the capitalist mode of production.

for the extended family and are thus part of the family-farm cycle. Generally, the composition of the aforementioned groups is highly fluid and shows high upward and downward social mobility (BOESEN et al. 1977: 160–163).

By the example of the expansion of coffee cultivation, SMITH (1989: 11–13) describes the changes of smallholder relations of production among the Haya farmers. While in precolonial times, coffee would only be cultivated in very low numbers under the Kings' monopoly, the introduction of the Arabica variety and new plantation cultivation meant a significant change in smallholder organization of labor and production. The harvest of the coffee beans, which would now all be ripe at almost the same time took up almost all of the available work force of the family for a period of about two months. Processing of the beans would be shifted away from individual farms to centralized production plants.

As the male population controlled this new cash crop enterprise, women would take over more and more of the food crop production over longer periods, thus also changing the gender relations of agricultural production in the region (see also DON-NER-REICHLE 1988). Overall, the introduction and expansion of coffee cultivation in Bukoba would severely change the pattern of peasant agriculture. Therefore, SMITH negates HYDÉN's thesis that the production cycles of cash crops were "not in conflict with the demands of existing production cycles" (HYDÉN 1980: 48).

While DONNER-REICHLE (1988) agrees with much of HYDÉN's observation of the African peasantry and their mode of production, she sees some crucial shortcomings in his analysis and the resulting hypothesis: In her view, HYDÉN does not analyze the core unit of African rural economy – which is the household – in a manner that is differentiated enough. Through his Eurocentric (and male – one could say gender blind) point of view, he omits the inner differentiations of this household unit, which leads to a wrong view of the character of subsistence production. According to DONNER-REICHLE, what is left of African subsistence farming can be characterized more as a residual economy of those who have no other choice. In this view, the remaining peasant production is not an act of independence actively pursued by small producers, but an economy of need. As men have been favored by the marketization and the formalization of agricultural ownership since colonial times, it is also they who take the opportunities of new employment in other fields. Women are left behind – not only with household work as HYDÉN might suggest, but also with the farm work to sustain that family. Generally, HYDÉN's European concept of the male breadwinner would not fit in the African rural context. With the deterioration of rural conditions for production, it is the women who are left with this residual subsistence economy, while the men try to leave the countryside for better employment opportunities elsewhere. After all, the African peasantry is more integrated into the market economy as HYDÉN might suggest (DONNER-REICHLE 1988: 34–40).

The influx of wage labor on farms since colonization, often done by migrant workers employed on a seasonal basis, would also leave its mark in the peasant mode of production. Richer peasants could afford more wage labor and steadily increased their production and profit. They emerged as a petit bourgeois class, who increasingly derived additional income from non-farming activities, as well, such as acting as middlemen for Asian traders, working in the administration or as teachers.

In many ways, this new class of rich peasants or "Kulaks" was different from the old royalty who employed the Nyarubanja system to exploit their tenants: Basing their profit on the exploitation of wage labor, their new wealth was not spent for luxury, but invested in increases of land or (sometimes at least) in the modernization of their agriculture. The creation of this class of Kulaks, on the other hand, increased the fragmentation of land and reduced the overall size of land available to middle and small farmers. It also intensified the work on the usual smallholding (SMITH 1989: 23p.).

Actually, neither the migrant labor system nor the peasant economy had to pay living wages, because they were subsidized – in a way – by the subsistence production of the laborer's wife and family (COULSON 1976: 22). This subsistence production of peasants enabled overseas buyers to lower prices beneath the actual value of labor, while the instability of markets kept investment by peasants in cash crops to a minimum. The peasants were therefore isolated and kept from technological innovations (FREYHOLD 1979: 5). On the other hand, HYDÉN (1980: 18p.) would argue that the peasant mode of production was low on investments and innovation for more endogenous reasons: The "economy of affection", which he sees prevailing among the African peasantry, would be based on relations of kinship and tradition, not on the market economy and the influx or shortage of capital.

The question of land and access to land is another contested point of debate in the description of the peasantry in Tanzania. Most authors agree that even by the end of colonial rule, there was no shortage of land, no landlessness or unequal distribution of land in Tanzania. Only 10 of 63 districts could be characterized by land shortage in 1967 (FREYHOLD 1979: 3). This would support HYDÉN's image of the African peasant economy, in which land, i.e. the essential mean of production, was virtually available for free.

On the other hand, regions such as Kilimanjaro and Tanga, which were affected by settler activities, and areas like Bukoba, with preexisting feudal structures, showed a more differentiated picture. Land in Bukoba could be communally owned by the clan or privately acquired, given the land was outside the clan land. Within the clan land system, there was personal responsibility for the land, usually inherited by the sons from the father. Through to the further subdivision of land by fathers giving land to their sons before they died in order to enable them to raise their own family, the plots became smaller and there was a definite pressure to move and cultivate more land. As opposed to other areas like Ruvuma, there was a shortage of land in the Bukoba area (BAKULA 1971: 17–19). Pastoral land was also prone to alienation and destocking, as exemplified in Bagamoyo by MUSTAFA (1990: 110p.).

In general, MASSARO (1998: 284) sees four basic types of regions emerging from the colonial organization of agriculture in Tanganyika: First, areas of peasant-based cash-crop production, secondly areas with large scale plantations and thirdly areas which acted as a reserve for migrant farm labor. The fourth category would be represented by areas with a very remote location, which demoted them to a completely peripheral role within this system. Accordingly, the rural population would have been "selectively articulated into European capitalism" or "deliberately dearticulated" according to the requirements of the colonial economy.

In one way or the other, however, all but the fourth category of areas within the territory were penetrated by colonial capitalism, either by cash-crop production or by the (out-)migration of laborers (Lᴙɪᴍᴏ 2012: 31). The differing nature of connection to the (colonial) center, on the other hand, induced a spatial differentiation of the emerging class structure. Peripheral areas became dependent on cash crop producing ones, which were themselves dependent on the colonial motherland to sell their produce, resulting in a geographically uneven development across the territory. Furthermore, as both production and consumption within the colony were dependent on the external interest of the motherland, no inductive effects could be expected for the economy of the colony itself, while an economic downturn in the capitalist center would be directly felt in the dependent peasant economy (Dᴀᴛᴏᴏ 1977: 74p.).

In addition to these changes in the rural areas, the penetration of capitalism had significant effects to the social formations in the whole territory. It induced the creation of a small national bourgeoisie, based on trade and incipient industrialization (Bᴏᴇsᴇɴ et al. 1977: 162p.), while the needs of the colonial administration for qualified personnel created a new class of educated African clerks, teachers, and bureaucrats, who occupied paid positions within the colonial system (Rᴡᴇʏᴇᴍᴀᴍᴜ 1973: 30). Apart from the economic differentiation between wage earners and subsistence farmers, the colonial nature of the (missionary) education system also "facilitated the separation of the African from his traditional society for absorption into the colonial socio-economic system." (Hɪʀᴊɪ 1976: 41).

All in all, however, the formation of classes remained embryonic during the colonial period, and the class differences between the European ruling class, the Asian class of traders and the African majority remained much greater than the economic differentiation within the African population. This may have been one reason why class differences were not very visible during the African struggle for independence, as the common interest in self-governance overwhelmed any competing economic interests within the African population. The economic and regional differentiation brought about by the capitalist penetration during colonialism, however, was big enough – at least in Rᴡᴇʏᴇᴍᴀᴍᴜ's view – to induce the heterogeneity of TANU party branches and the relatively weak central structure of the party after independence (Rᴡᴇʏᴇᴍᴀᴍᴜ 1973: 30–32).

Postcolonial Development and "The Debate"

In the eyes of the post-War colonial policy, the African bureaucracy was supposed to act as a stabilizer of colonial rule in Tanganyika. However, this small group of well-educated Africans took the lessons in humanism and liberalism they had enjoyed at European universities serious. Very quickly, the apparent contradiction between reform rhetoric and authoritarian administration in the colonies became a spark to ignite the struggle for political independence. The very idea of colonialism as a school for democracy for the Africans was exposed as a contradiction in itself. These African bureaucrats were no longer willing to be seen as children or treated as inferior by their colonial masters. They saw themselves as citizens and wanted to construct a modern state of their own. While they were introduced to European modernism and philosophy through their education, they began to learn and appreciate African history and disregarded the image of Africa as a primitive continent without history. However, their belief in modernism was converted into a latent feeling of supremacy compared with their fellow African countrymen, an attitude that would result in some of the paternalistic tendencies of this same African bureaucratic elite which would emerge after independence (ECKERT 2007: 215).

Indeed, while the colonial education system put the petit bourgeoisie in a more favorable economic situation than the majority of the African population, the failure of the colonial system to satisfy its further advancement meant that "the petty-bourgeoisie acquired a consciousness of themselves as a class much more readily than any other oppressed class in the society." (HIRJI 1976: 42). However, after independence, this meant that the leadership of Tanzania and many other African nations was not so much defined by the political conviction of an individual, but by his position within the preceding colonial system of administration and education. Therefore, the class consciousness of this new leadership did not necessarily enable them to act on behalf of the interests of the majority of rural peasants or the small urban proletariat (SAUL 1972b: 119–122).

When NYERERE (1962b) explained his vision of Ujamaa as the Basis of African Socialism, he made it very clear that he did not want to pursue the European way of socialism, because this would mean creating a fight between classes that – in his opinion – did not exist in Tanganyika. Only the colonizers had brought the system of capitalism and exploitation and, therefore, there would be no classes – neither proletarians nor capitalists – inside the country after independence. The same opinion was brought forward time and again by scholars following a Marxist-Leninist understanding of class formation and class struggle in the (former) colonies (NABUDERE 1982; MEYNS 1982; MAMDANI & BHAGAT 1982): Even after independence, the capitalist exploiters – the owners of the means of production – would be the foreign investors or the former colonials masters. The only representatives of this international capital on the ground would come in the form of local administrators, but no endogenous ruling class could have been developed under the rule of the colonial system. Hence, those scholars adhered to the Theory of "Imperialism as the highest form of Capitalism" (LENIN 1972: 269p.).

However, given the ongoing struggles within the Tanzanian political and economic system, representatives of a new stream of Neo-Marxist students and scholars at the University of Dar es Salaam began to challenge this view (NURSEY-BRAY 1980: 55). Both key concepts of Nyerere's understanding came under scrutiny: The classlessness of Tanzania before independence, and the claim that the ruling class – i.e. the capitalist exploiters – would still be sitting outside the country, in the former mother countries of the colonies.

Issa SHIVJI became one of the most cited and critiqued representatives of this line of thought, when he coined the term "bureaucratic bourgeoisie" (SHIVJI 1976: 86) to describe the special sort of class formation he was observing in Tanzania after independence: At the time of independence, there was indeed only a small class of "commercial bourgeoisie" in Tanzania, mostly made up of Asian traders and an equally small class of petit bourgeois clerks, teachers, and the like. However, after the external ruling class of the colonizers left after *Uhuru* (independence), the new state was ruled by the leaders of the national liberation movement and the African bureaucrats that used to work within the colonial administration before. While this situation could be easily described as a form of local representation of foreign capital, SHIVJI argues that this class of administrators and politicians took over not only the political power, but also the economic power in Tanzania. Through the policy of nationalization of industry (and later agriculture), the state apparatus took over the control over the economic base of the country, hence this bureaucratic bourgeoisie became the new ruling class of Tanzania.

After independence, this bureaucratic class challenged the small national petit bourgeoisie as the new ruling class of the country. In the view of BOESEN et al., the bureaucratic class took control over the national economy by nationalization and established a new cooperation with international capital under a system of neo-colonialism. Therefore, the main division inside Tanzanian society is still seen between the peasants as agricultural producers and non-agricultural sectors (BOESEN et al. 1977: 163).

With the help of a new form of bureaucratic capitalism, this class would actually use the necessary stage of nationalization of the means of production for their own class interests. In Shivji's view, this form of nationalization cannot be automatically considered to be a socialization of the means of production, as a true transformation to socialism would require (SHIVJI 1973: 308–310). On the contrary, in his observation, the political development of Tanzania after independence would be an example of a new type of dependent state capitalism – and underline the country's status as a neo-colony in the world system of the 1970s (SHIVJI 1973: 310–312).

SAUL (1973b: 354p.) was one of the first scholars to underline the importance of SHIVJI's critical view on the issue of nationalization and its implications for the emerging class structure of newly independent nations like Tanzania. COULSON (1976: 25) argues in the same direction, when he describes the fact that the leading positions in government and economy – formerly held by the colonial administration – were now taken over by African bureaucrats. This emerging bureaucratic class was yet lacking a substantial economic basis, but could get hold of some of the surplus of the national economy in the process of nationalization of industry. Together with the petit bourgeoisie comprising of teachers, clerks and some advanced farmers, they would, in his eyes, build the new ruling class of the country.

Several other authors supported SHIVJI's characterization of the class formation in independent Tanzania (TANDON 1982b; HIRJI 1982; COULSON 1976) that sparked an argument among the academia in Dar es Salaam that became known as "The Debate". Many different viewpoints on the issue of class, state and imperialism can be found in TANDON's (1982a) comprehensive collection of essays and argumentative papers. Many of these arguments revolved not only around the specific class formation of post-colonial societies, but also the overall idea of the role of the state within the development process. As this role was generally seen as very important and very direct with regards to the economic and social organization of countries like Tanzania, the question of whether it was better to "Smash the post-colonial state or use it?" (SAUL 1974: 367), became a central one for many of the new politically engaged scholars of the University of Dar es Salaam, who tried to contribute to a more radical understanding of socialism than Nyerere's writings might have implied (SAUL 1973a).

Authors like FREYHOLD underlined their analysis that the emerging state economy of Tanzania did by no means serve the interest of the majority of its population. On the contrary, the nationalization effort in the years following independence would mainly have followed the interest of the bureaucratic class of the country to extend its control of the economic base and to attract the influx of "metropolitan capital" into what she conceived to be a "peripheral sate capitalism" (FREYHOLD 1979: 119). In her understanding "the myth of kinship" (FREYHOLD 1979: 66), which was so prominently represented in Ujamaa's idea of the extended family, actually "disguised" the increasing contradictions between the village farmers and the bureaucratic elite who took control over the postcolonial state and its economy.

Coming back to the relation between the state and the peasantry in this scenario, HYDÉN sees the state as an integral part of the production system in the modern age, regardless of whether it defines itself as socialist or capitalist. However, and this is the main argument of his thesis of the uncaptured peasantry, the prevalence of the peasant mode of production and its associated social formations significantly limits the extent of state power in Africa. Given that the peasantry is a self-sustaining and independently reproducing class, transformations of the state-independent social and economic relations of this class cannot be made unless the mode of production itself is changed. As long as the peasants control their own means of production (which is labor and land), all state interventions depend on the willingness of the peasantry. HYDÉN gives several examples of (failed) strategies of the state to capture the peasantry and to integrate this class in the prevailing economic system, be it colonialist, capitalist or socialist. Taxation has been used as a means for transformation of the countryside since the introduction of hut taxes by the colonial administration; however, as soon as enough cash-crop production was established by the peasantry to pay the taxes, taxation lost its transformatory potential. In the case of price incentives for certain crops, the limitation of production by the restricted availability of family labor under the peasant system led to the phenomenon that only richer peasants would transform their situation through expanding production and employing labor, while the majority of peasants would continue with their traditional form of production. State farms and village resettlements had similarly limited effects on rural transformation, in HYDÉN's view. As opposed to industrialized societies, of both capitalist and socialist character, where the author observes a plural superstructure and a solidified economic base, agrarian African societies would therefore have a fragmented economic base. This is seen as one reason for the creation of unified and mainly authoritarian political superstructures in Africa (HYDÉN 1980: 23–29).

Given the ambiguous position and the small size of national bourgeoisie and the dependence of the neocolonies as a whole within the imperialist system, MEYNS asks which contradiction would be the main contradiction at which stage of national liberation, and which fight would therefore be the main fight to be led. He argues that this question of the main contradiction – and the according revolutionary tactic – has to be asked at each stage in the struggle for national liberation. On the one hand, if the pure formal independence of a nation was seen as enough to gain true independence for its people, this would neglect the class character of the state. In his view, the state is a vehicle of class power, therefore the question of which class holds that power is of utmost importance. If state power is held by the national petit bourgeoisie, the state will be a vehicle of its class interests and will be a bourgeois state. Therefore, the state as such will not be a vehicle for socialist transformation unless a revolutionary class (the proletariat, in his view) holds state power. On the other hand, one cannot start the struggle against the national petit bourgeoisie in this stage of history, in which the contradictions between the imperialist countries and the colonies and neocolonies as a whole are much greater than the contradictions between the small national bourgeoisie and the other classes. Even after formal independence, as MEYNS argues, this international contradiction remains more powerful than the national class contradictions. As long as the national bourgeoisie is joining the fight against international imperialism, this fight therefore remains the most important one and the contradiction of imperialism has to define the class struggle in the neocolonies (MEYNS 1977: 28–32).

On the other hand, HYDÉN criticizes the one-sided view of dependency theorists and Marxists alike, who in his view tend to see all negative features in the development of Africa coming from the outside and relying on imperialist trade connections. Furthermore, those arguments would neglect the unique African situation of the peasantry and only focus on the destructive effects of colonial capitalism on the traditional economic and social systems. While not fully agreeing with the opposite notion – that capitalist penetration into the peasantry might have been not too strong but too little to result in the developmentary aspects of capitalist transformation – he is obviously closer to this side of the debate. Indeed, HYDÉN emphasizes the issues created for capitalist expansion represented by the prevalence of pre-capitalist modes of production, like the peasant economy. He therefore doubts the capitalist interest could have been in keeping on with these modes of productions as sources of primitive accumulation. Rather, he underlines that the capitalist logic of growth would require a rapid transformation of agricultural production and sees the question of why this has not happened in the African context as a result of more complicate interactions between capitalist and peasant modes of production (HYDÉN 1980: 19–23).

In HYDÉN's view, the discussion about whether the petit bourgeoisie in the former colonies is already a ruling class or merely a governing class dependent on the international capital underestimates the autonomy of the African peasantry. In his view, neither the international nor the national bourgeoisie in Africa was yet able to extend command over the African peasants in a way that would warrant the term ruling class. This relative autonomy of the peasantry again is derived from its control over the means of subsistence production, i.e. land and family labor. Furthermore, class analyses stemming from imperialist theories underestimated the class contradictions between the national petit bourgeoisie and the international capitalists, since the latter limits the former's potential for economic growth. Therefore, the national bourgeoisie is interested in extending its production base, be it through collective or private ownership over the means of production. Since the national petit bourgeoisie has the same social background as the peasantry, it might forge alliances in this economy of affection. In conclusion, it is too short sighted to suggest that the national bourgeoisie would always prefer the expansion of capitalism over the persistence of the traditional economy of affection (HYDÉN 1980: 28–31).

Summary – The different views on classes and its influence on Ujamaa

While such a lengthy debate on the different views on class in Tanzania might seem like a purely academic discussion with no direct connection to the development of Ujamaa in the country, one has to bear in mind that it has been discussions like this which actually shaped much of the development strategies that were derived from

Figure 2: The postcolonial Class Structure of Tanzania, according to Nyerere

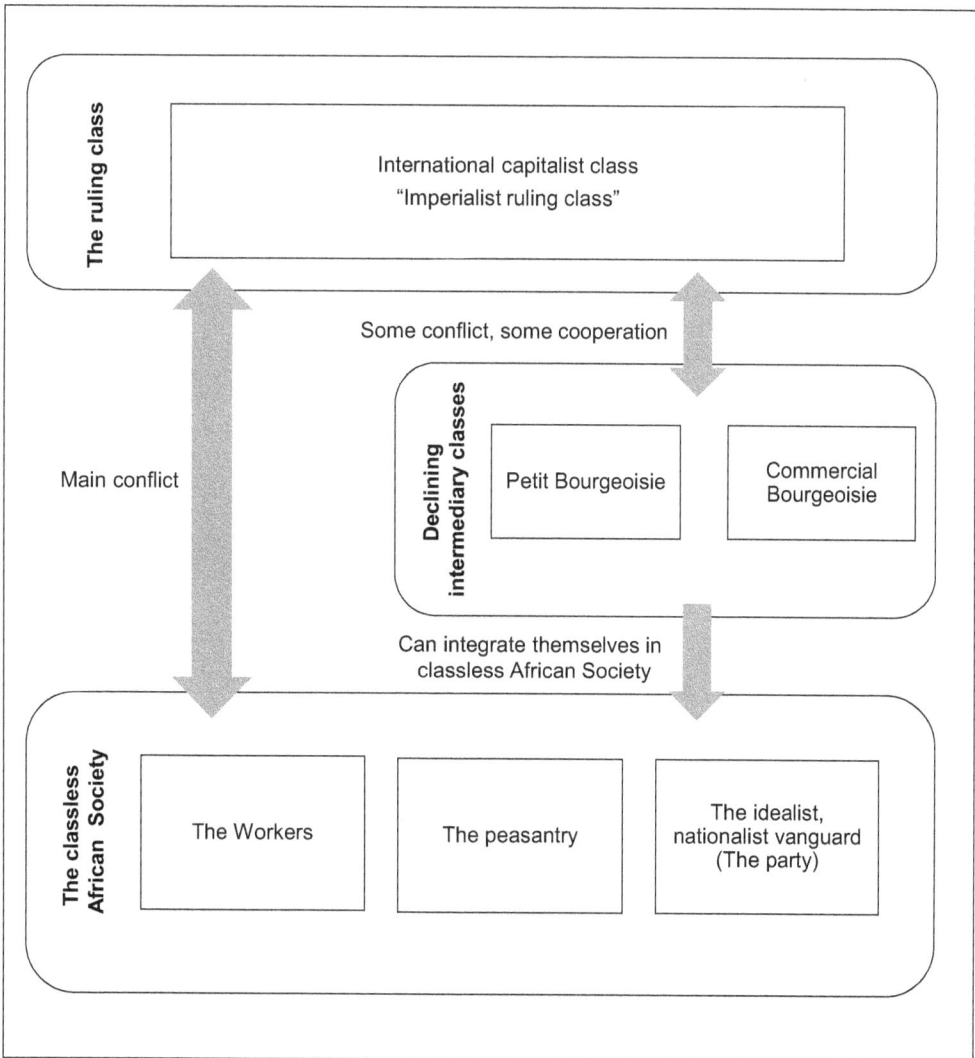

Source: own interpretation

Figure 3: The postcolonial Class Structure of Tanzania, according to thesis of the bureaucratic bourgeoisie

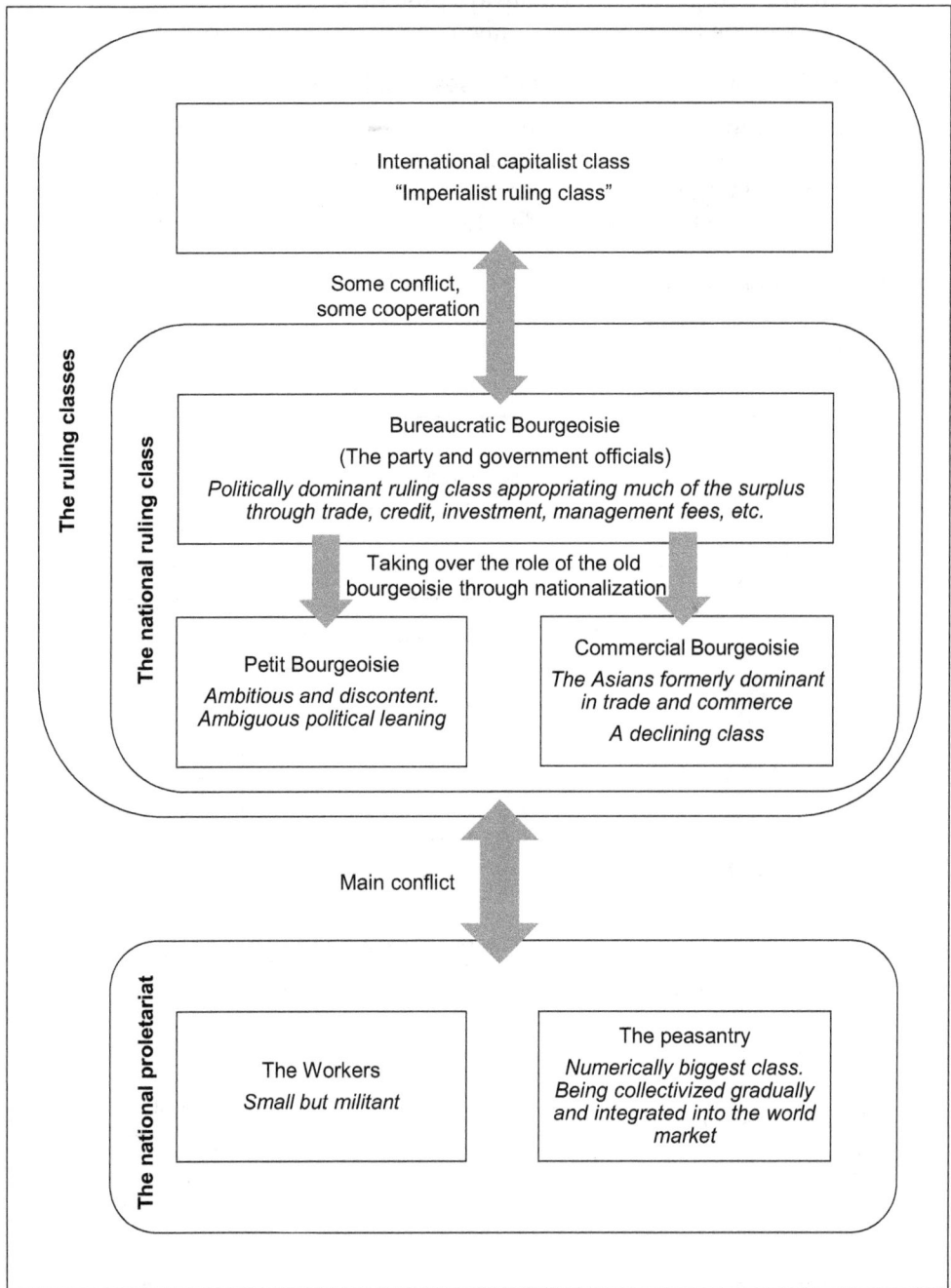

The ruling classes

The national ruling class

International capitalist class
"Imperialist ruling class"

Some conflict,
some cooperation

Bureaucratic Bourgeoisie
(The party and government officials)
*Politically dominant ruling class appropriating much of the surplus
through trade, credit, investment, management fees, etc.*

Taking over the role of the old
bourgeoisie through nationalization

Petit Bourgeoisie
*Ambitious and discontent.
Ambiguous political leaning*

Commercial Bourgeoisie
*The Asians formerly dominant
in trade and commerce*
A declining class

Main conflict

The national proletariat

The Workers
Small but militant

The peasantry
*Numerically biggest class.
Being collectivized gradually
and integrated into the world
market*

Source: own interpretation, inspired by Hɪʀᴊɪ (1976: 45)

the Ujamaa ideology (see chapter 3). Therefore, it appears to be useful to summarize the different views on this issue before engaging in the detailed description of Ujamaa's ideology.

First of all, there was the dominant understanding of Nyerere and parts of the national and international academia, that in the postcolonial situation, there would still be no classes amongst the African population, save for some very limited numbers of traders (the commercial bourgeoisie) and public servants (the petit bourgeoisie). These classes, however, were seen to be declining after the end of colonialism, and would either leave the country or align themselves to the majority of the population, which was the classless African society of Nyerere's vision. Here, the small class of workers, the large class of the peasantry and the vanguard of national liberation, i.e. the party, were each fighting the same enemy: The international ruling class of capitalists, who had ceased being colonial masters, but were still in contradiction to national independence. A simplified scheme of this understanding of the postcolonial class formation of Tanzania is presented in Fig. 2.

While this idea of a common, classless African society opposing the forces of (neo-)imperialism went mostly uncontested in the first years after independence, the group of young scholars around Shivji (1973, 1976) and Hirji (1976, 1982) began to observe a different form of development within their country: Instead of leading the presumably classless African society to true independence, members of the nationalist elite were nationalizing the old colonial possessions for their own interest. Thereby, they would not only control the political power of the new state, but also its economy. Hence, they would form a new ruling class (the bureaucratic bourgeoisie), dominating the national proletariat and at times collaborating with international capital. A simplified version of their view is presented in Fig. 3.

The implications of these different views are far reaching: If, like in the understanding of Nyerere and much of the national leadership of TANU, the main conflict on the way to socialism lies in the conflict between the Tanzanian people as a whole and the international capital, then all kinds of international cooperation become highly suspicious – especially if they are not controlled by the national leadership. As we will see in the following chapters, this fear of international influence on the local scale became decisive for the future development of Ujamaa in practice. On the other hand, if the main conflict for the Tanzanian proletariat (workers and peasants) is actually the conflict with the national bureaucratic bourgeoisie, then those groups would actually have to organize themselves against their national leadership. In both cases, however, an autocratic approach by the national leadership would be a logical consequence, since in the first case, it is their role to lead the national struggle for independence, and in the second case, it would be detrimental to their own class interests to let the proletariat organize itself.

2.3.6 The role of the Party

So, with these considerations on the ideological development of Ujamaa made, the last theme to be analyzed remains the role of the party within this context.

The formative period of TANU

The Tanganyika African Union (TANU) was officially established as a political movement in July 1954. Compared to its predecessor, the Tanganyika African Association (TAA), it was a political party and not a semi-political, semi-cultural organization like TAA. From the beginning, the party was open for all Africans in Tanganyika to join and was led by Nyerere, who had been elected president of TAA one year before. A school master at a catholic school near Dar Es Salaam, Nyerere had studied both in Makerere and Edinburgh and had come to know the country of the colonial masters first hand. It was he, who drafted the constitution of TANU, giving emphasis on the liberation struggle, fighting tribalism and promoting the unity of all Africans. TANU also supported workers' rights and the establishment of trade unions. The immediate issues tackled by TANU were the education of Africans in Tanganyika, several taxes and de-stocking regulations affecting African farmers and pastoralists, as well as the status of Tanganyika as a trusteeship, which the party pushed to be more clearly shown by the British administration. From the start, TANU was quite successful in mobilizing the African population for the independence movement, while Nyerere was travelling to the UK to start negotiations on the international scene. Inside Tanganyika, one of the major aspects in educating the Africans for the struggle was TANU's stance on a non-armed struggle in a world used to violent means of establishing power – both in the colonial history of Tanganyika and in post-war Europe (Kaniki 1974: 1–5).

Based on the roots of TAA's structure, TANU was mostly organized locally in its early years of existence. And while the common struggle for independence and the charismatic leadership of Nyerere provided some coherence in the local branches' actions, most of the party's work on the ground was highly influenced by the local nature of political conflict. This also induced a differentiated base of party activists, which meant that in some regions, TANU was mainly formed by educated public servants, while in others some few, more affluent, farmers dominated the party branch, as they were the only group with vested economic interest in challenging the colonial rule. In all settings, however, TANU was able to successfully channel the conflict of the rural population with the colonial system and to integrate their interests into the struggle for independence (Cliffe 1971: 123p.).

Naturally, the colonial administration was suspicious of TANU's activities: Even when the Union was finally registered as an organization on 30th October 1954, this did not automatically entail the registration of the local branches. During the following years, TANU branches had most problems with the administration in the Usambara and Tanga areas, where there was a stronger presence of white settlers. But even if the party was banned in several provinces (the longest in Usambara province, until 1959), TANU continued to operate underground (Kaniki 1974: 6–8).

In contrast to other national liberation movements across Africa, TANU was able to integrate almost all political groups fighting for independence into its own party structures. While this integration was based on the sole common goal of national independence, members of all different interest groups or tribal organizations were willing to align themselves with the party organization. This meant that TANU emerged from the struggle for independence as a unified – albeit diverse – mass party (CLIFFE 1967b: 1–4).

Relying on the infrastructure and leadership experience built by the TAA, TANU was quick to evolve as the biggest voice for Tanganyika's independence. The use of Kiswahili enabled the leaders on all levels to connect to almost every African in the territory, while TANU evaded the dangers of ethnic tensions and power struggles, which had harmed so many political movements of Africa. At the same time, it built a strong alliance with other movements, especially the trade unions, through common struggles and personal linkages. All in all, TANU was able to affect and organize very successfully almost all groups sufferering from the colonial regime. The establishment of the Youth Wing and the Women's section by 1956 helped the party to organize those groups and include even more fellow Africans into the struggle for independence. Ghana's independence in 1957 gave another boost to TANU's activities. The (racially segregated) elections of 1958 became a sweep victory for TANU, who not only won the "African" seats, but also managed to get TANU supported candidates winning all seats of the other "races". This put TANU in a formidable position of power to negotiate the incumbent independence of the country, and the victory in the next elections of 1960, where TANU won 70 out of 71 seats, made the way clear for constitutional conferences and the independence of Tanganyika on the 9th of December, 1961 (KANIKI 1974: 12–17).

As a result of the integrative approach which TANU and its leadership had taken during the independence period and its confederal organization, the party put emphasis on a consensus style of politics, the creation of national unity, and the maintenance of a widespread support from all parts of the population. As a self-defined national liberation movement "open for all", TANU took its time to formulate its own ideology and strategy for the time following independence (CLIFFE 1971: 126p.).

Nevertheless, the "early" TANU shared elements of both Pan African and an internationalist ideology, stressing the conviction that the true independence of any one African nation could only be achieved through the liberation of the whole continent. Therefore, while pursuing a foreign policy of non-alignment, TANU and the Tanganyikan government supported several national liberation movements in Africa, as well as breaking relationships with the UK over the one sided independence of Rhodesia in 1965 (KANIKI 1974: 17p.).

The establishment of the one-party state

By the 1960s there was as a matter of fact only one political party in Mainland Tanzania, which was TANU. Partly due to the weakness of opposition parties throughout the 1958 and 1960 elections, only one independent candidate was elected in 1960, who was himself a TANU member. So, in the view of KANIKI, when the government drafted the concept of "one-party democracy" in 1964, it was merely acknowledging an existing situation. Under the new concept, TANU would be the only legal political party, while at the same time parliamentary seats and offices at all levels would from now on be contested by at least two candidates of this party. This was supposed to give the electorate a better chance to choose their representative than before, when the sole TANU candidate could expect overwhelming support no matter what. According to the author, the fact that in the subsequent elections in 1965 and 1970, several MPs and even some ministers lost their seats, illustrates that while there was only one party in the country, there was still democracy (KANIKI 1974: 18p.).

A first statement arguing for the idea of establishing a one-party state was made by President Nyerere in January 1963. His main concern in this matter was the impression that a true democracy would not be possible to be established with the dominance of TANU compared to any of the opposing parties. Rather than adhering to the idea of multi-partyism, a direct choice of candidates by the electorate under the roof of TANU would imply a better representation of the will of the population (CLIFFE 1972: 244).

By 1964, a presidential commission had come up with recommendations for the practical implementation of this idea of one-party democracy (PRESIDENTIAL COMMISSION 1967). The basic element of this system was the idea that contested elections for parliamentary seats and other representative offices would be held between at least two candidates which were to be chosen by the respective TANU party branches. The candidates were then supposed to present themselves to the electorate at public conventions organized by the party. This proposal by the presidential commission became the framework for the first one-party elections of 1965 (CLIFFE 1967b: 15p.).

At the same time, TANU established the ten-cell system of party organization in 1964. Under this new structure, every ten households (ten-cells) of party members would elect their own ten-cell party leader, who was supposed to act as both a representative of the local interests of his or her cell and as an intermediary for the mediation of central party ideas and strategies on the ground. This move was also supposed to increase the ideological commitment of ordinary party members and the organization of local branches in terms of administrative capacity (LEVINE 1972: 329–334).

As a result of the new setup, the structure of the party became even more interlinked with the government and administrative apparatus. TANU District Chairmen became ex-officio chairmen of District authorities, and the same was true for government positions on the village level, which were automatically taken over by the respective TANU leaders. At the same time, the party was seen as the true instrument of people's power. However, this approach, based on its understanding as an integrative mass party and vehicle for the creation of a national consensus, conflicted with TANU's increasing tendency to strengthen its socialist ideology (see below). The party would have to decide whether it was to remain a nationalist mass party or to become a vanguard party for the transformation to socialism after the 1965 elections (CLIFFE 1967a: 109–113).

Indeed, a survey on the voters' perception of these elections showed that the electorate considered the party itself as more relevant to their daily lives than the parliament. TANU was seen as the main vehicle for expressing their concerns and making their demands heard. Voters at this time had a high confidence in the party as a reliable agent for the mediation of their interests with government authorities and administration. So, at least for this period, the image of the single party as the voice of the people appears to have been more than mere self-proclamation (PREWITT & HYDÉN 1967: 77–81).

ECKERT, on the other hand, has a more critical view on Tanzania's supposed one-party democracy. While he does see elements of competition for the one-seat constituencies through TANU's introduction of several candidates per constituency, overall the author describes Tanzania's political system as becoming continuously more authoritarian and less pluralistic from the 1960s through the 1970s. Hardly any newspaper would print opinions or reader contributions critical to TANU's policy, and political arrests and trials of supposed opposition members were abundant. The public discussion on the necessity of an opposition party virtually ended in the 1960s and the political discourse became increasingly monopolized by TANU. Specifically, the Army Mutiny of 1964 – which was hardly present in public discussion afterwards – increased the leaders' fear of forces opposing the government's decisions and led to a crackdown on union members, the disbandment of the preexisting TFL and the creation of the unified National Union of Tanganyikan Workers (NUTA) under the control of the party (ECKERT 2007: 227–230).

The ideological development of TANU after independence

Rather than the Leninist model of an elitist or vanguard party, TANU strived to reflect Nyerere's goal of mass support for socialist transformation by perceiving itself to be a mass party, open to all classes. At the same time, TANU underlined the necessity of a long-haul approach to development, in which the party would take the role of a teacher; leading the way, but also re-educating the African population to come back to their communal core and turn down the colonial influence that led to the pursuit of individual wealth instead of cooperative "African" living. However, the party would not be very successful to establish legitimacy on the grounds of its ideology, at least until 1967 (HEDLUND & LUNDAHL 1989: 20–22).

In spite of occasional socialist statements, TANU was basically a national liberation movement with no distinct political ideology up until the end of 1966. In 1962, NYERERE had published *Ujamaa – The basis of African Socialism* and was advocating for the adoption of a socialist program within the party. Finally, the Arusha Declaration of 1967 transformed TANU into a socialist party and laid the way for socialist development in Tanzania. Inside the party, the leadership code, wherein no party or government leader might own a company, rent out houses or receive more than one salary, led in some ways to TANU changing from being a mass party to perceiving itself as a vanguard party of workers and peasants. In fact, KANIKI sees the code as an admission of Nyerere to the fact that socialism is not only an attitude of mind, but that this attitude is deeply shaped by the material conditions an individual is living in. Hence, the emphasis that leaders of party and country had to be real socialists implied the introduction of this leadership code to impede "exploiters" or would-be capitalists from becoming leaders under TANU (KANIKI 1974: 20–23).

From 1967 onwards, the self-definition as a socialist party and the requirements of the leadership code were meant to put a hold on the advancement of the many bureaucrats, who did not share Nyerere's conviction for Ujamaa, within party and government ranks. From now on, the furthering Ujamaa ideology became the ideology of TANU itself and socialist rhetoric was no longer supposed to suffice for making a career within this system, if it was not followed up by practice (CLIFFE 1971: 128p.).

With the ideological foundation set in the Arusha Declaration, Nyerere was able to establish the party as the most important institution of policy-making in Tanzania. The constitutions of 1965 and 1975 established the one-party system for good and shifted a considerable part of national decision-making from the parliament itself to the National Executive Committee and the National Congress of the party (Morse 2013: 658–660).

In concordance with the ideological development of TANU between the 1965 and 1970 elections, its self-proclaimed role moved from one with an emphasis on national integration and a relatively open ideological background, to one with a more focused approach. Increasingly, TANU was seen by Nyerere and the other leaders as an institution which should lead the country's development in a socialist direction. Hence, its new understanding was coming closer to being the vanguard of social change, rather than a mass movement for national liberation (Saul 1972a: 282–286).

The Chama cha Mapinduzi

This post-Arusha trend manifested itself after the unification of TANU and the Zanzibarian Afro Shirazi Party (ASP) on 5th of February 1977. The new party was called *Chama cha Mapinduzi* (CCM; Party of the Revolution), and considered itself to be a revolutionary mass party. In this term alone, some of the ambiguity of the Tanzanian party development becomes clear. Members of both old parties directly became members of the new CCM, unless they wished otherwise. In this, Gama sees one reason for the persistence of "bourgeois" members and thinking within the new party, citing director positions in capitalist enterprises, the permanence of double income and other "old behaviors" as cases in point (Gama 1989: 60–63).

On the other hand, CCM was defined by its 1981 guidelines as a cadre party: Every Tanzanian could become member of the party, given that he or she is a worker or farmer and does not partake in capitalist activities. To apply for party membership, one had to accept the principles of the party and had to present three party members of the local branch who acted as bondsmen. After this, the candidate had to take part in a basic training seminar, in which his or her ability to become a member would be investigated based on the ideological principles of CCM. Only afterwards, the local executive committee would give its impression of the case to the district executive committee, which would then decide on the new membership. Membership could be terminated for violations against the party principles, readmission to the party will take a waiting time of five years and an application to the national executive committee. However, as Gama points out, the fact that all members of TANU and ASP were admitted as members of CCM in 1977 still led to the fact that there were CCM members who would not have been admitted to join the party in the first place if the rules of 1981 would have been applied (Gama 1989: 70–72).

The direction of the CCM would become increasingly authoritarian after unification, as it became a vehicle for the more and more direct control of the central state over the rural countryside. In particular, a continuous stream of guidelines and directives was facilitated through the party structures in a top-down manner (Mueller 1980: 212p.).

In fact, this intertwining of party and government policy implementation, as well as the strong organizational base of CCM, is seen as one of the contributing factors to CCM's continued electoral success after the end of the one-party state. At the same time, despite the increasing commitment to Ujamaa socialism after the Arusha declaration, the party was quick to adapt itself to the new political environment of the 1980s (see below) and remained ideologically flexible (MORSE 2013: 660p.).

After the structural changes following the end of Nyerere's presidency in 1985, the image of him as father of the nation was still used by the party to underline its claim to continue with his legacy. Especially after his death in 2000, the competition over who would be the candidate of *Mwalimu* became one of the leading themes in the selection of CCM's candidate for presidency (FOUÉRÉ 2014: 11–13).

3　History of development policies and strategies in Tanzania

The history of development policies, projects, and failure in Tanzania might have been just the same story as that of any other African post-colonial country: The unsuccessful attempt to compel "backward peasants" into becoming modern farmers by means of convincing or coercing – whatever might be necessary. As in other newly independent countries, the colonial image of the stubborn peasant dictated much of the early (pre-Arusha) actions and projects of the new African bureaucracy. In any case, the emerging developmental state had the same conviction as the late colonial one: Modernizing the people and the countryside in particular, teaching the peasants, by persuasion or by force. There would not have been many novel items for research, had it not been for the particular success of the RDA, whose grassroots, communal cooperative villages became the new way forward for Tanzania. This was not least due to the enthusiasm of Nyerere, who promoted the RDA's way of organizing and developing far beyond Ruvuma and made it – theoretically at least – a state policy in *Ujamaa vijijini* (SCHNEIDER 2014: 21–25).

Chapter 3 will attempt to give an overview of the different development policies and strategies in Tanzania before, during and after the Ujamaa era, in order to give a comprehensive background for the understanding of the local perceptions which were gathered in the empirical part of this study.

3.1　Pre-colonial situation and colonial "development"

As has been discussed in chapter 2.3.2, COULSON (1976: 20) identifies two different modes of production in pre-colonial Tanzania: On the one hand a sort of traditional, cooperative form of small-scale peasant agriculture, which he calls the "primitive ujamaa mode of production", and on the other hand feudalist structures of power and production.

In the sense of BERNSTEIN's (1981: 5p.) understanding of precolonial development, these systems can be considered as "natural economies", as the organization of their productive forces, as well as the shape of their social structures were mostly influenced by the natural environment. In MARX's understanding of human development (see chapter 2.2.1), this does not mean that there was no development at all before the arrival of European colonialism. However, any of the social formations described in chapter 2.3.2 would be considered as a formation predating the capitalist mode of production (MARX 1982: 383–421). It is only in the limited understanding of development as guided by (nationwide) development strategies and policies, that this chapter will focus on the colonial development in Tanganyika.

The actual colonization of Tanganyika (and other parts of Africa, for that matter) was preceded by the phase of European exploration of the African mainland, which saw its first peak in the middle of the 19ᵗʰ century. In the case of the Tanzanian mainland, the first journeys by Europeans were undertaken by Christian missionaries like L. Krapf and J. Rebmann, who were also the first Europeans to catch a view of Mount Kilimanjaro in 1848. In the following decades, scientific interest in geographic discoveries, as well as nationalist sentiments of competition between the European powers stimulated the further exploration of the hitherto unknown East African inland. Already, this era was characterized by an increasing rivalry between German and British interests within the region (Butzmann et al. 2008: 55). The sociological and political continuities and discontinuities between the age of exploration and the age of colonization would suffice for at least one thesis of its own, but an interesting impression on the topic can be found in Pesek (2005: 102–160).

The colonization of Tanganyika itself started in 1884 with Carl Peters' contracts guaranteeing German "protection" for some local chiefs. Only on his return to Germany in 1885, the emperor's government retroactively granted its support for his "acquisitions". In the same year, the German East African Company (Deutsch-Ostafrikanische Gesellschaft; DOAG) was founded to organize the colonization of the territory (Sippel 1995: 466–470). The "adventures" of Peters sparked some conflict with the British interests in East Africa. Nevertheless, German administration over Mainland Tanzania was established in 1891, after the conflict with the British was settled in the Helgoland-Zanzibar agreement (Engelhard 1994: 29).

In the early colonial period, development would be defined in its most basic terms as economic growth and growing production and income for the colonial motherland. While certain infrastructural projects were carried out by the government itself, those measures were mostly seen as enabling the more efficient use of the territory's natural resources. The organization of production within the colony itself, however, was meant to be organized by private investors, sparing the state from large scale investments (Jennings 2007: 73p.).

Apart from this economic imperative, two other factors contributed to the colonial concept of development. First of all, once the colonial structure had been established, some form of revenue had to be created in order for the operations to be able to sustain themselves. Secondly, the notion of development of the colony became a strong ideological component for the justification of German colonialism itself. Largely entwined with racialist conceptions, the development of the new subjects according to European concepts was seen as legitimizing the violent conquest of these parts of the globe (Koponen 1995: 176p.). In any case, however, colonial development remained an instrument to enable the exploitation of the colonized territory in the interest of the colonizers, and never of the colonized (Koponen 1995: 543).

As with other colonial powers, the German administration of Tanganyika saw the colony first and foremost as a producer of raw materials, or more specific, tropical commodities. Other possible roles for the colony, for instance as a market for German commodities or as a territory for German migration were of far less importance. The chief interest in raw materials, however, was not so much determined by the natural possibilities of the colony itself, but by the interest of the colonial motherland in gaining an independent source of tropical resources, whose supply had hitherto been controlled by other nations. With the possession of Tanganyika, the

German administration now sought to increase the production of those materials for exclusive use by the German industry (RWEYEMAMU 1973: 14p.).

Four main products became the focus of the colonial administration: Rubber and cotton, which were seen as important raw materials for German industry, as well as sisal, whose cultivation was aided by the beneficial natural environment of the territory. In addition, coffee cultivation was introduced to meet the high consumer demand for this commodity. The organization of production was envisioned in two distinct forms: Small-scale production by so called "indigenous cultures" and large-scale production on plantations employing local wage laborers under the control of European settlers. While in the early years of the colony, agricultural production had been dominated by private initiative in this sector, the colonial administration became increasingly involved in the direct control of this system from the turn of the 20th century onwards (TETZLAFF 1970: 117). A comprehensive overview on the system of agricultural production and its results can be found in the same source (TETZLAFF 1970: 117–155).

Overall, production of these cash crops by the African smallholder economy remained below expectations, and only with the arrival of German settlers and the introduction of the plantation system, could production numbers be increased. African peasants were driven out of the most fertile agricultural areas like the Usambaras and the Kilimanjaro region, in order for the European plantations to be created. Yet, the planters faced several issues in meeting the demand for African wage labor on their plantations. Firstly, the level of wages paid to the plantation laborers remained too low to be seen as an incentive to give up subsistence farming by the African peasants. Two reasons can be mentioned for the low wage levels: On the one hand, racist prejudices about the African work mentality and the underestimation of the social and economic security provided by the peasant economy led to the underestimation of the subsistence wage level by the Europeans. On the other hand, the prime interest of European settlers lay in the short-term profits of their plantation. In an environment of high elasticity of demand for labor and low elasticity of supply, raising wages to a level required to attract more African wage laborers would have reduced the short-term profit of the planters. Secondly, the production of cash crops within the traditional African smallholder economy allowed the African peasants to meet their demand for cash income without forfeiting the security of the peasant economy (RWEYEMAMU 1973: 16–20).

The early colonial era was not met without resistance by the local population, and several uprisings culminated in the Maji Maji Rebellion between 1905 and 1907, in which – for the first time – the battle against the colonizers was fought on a large scale that went beyond ethnic divisions (SCHÖNBORN 1973: 5). This upraising later became a heroic tale on the unity of the African population in their struggle against the oppressors and as such an important part of postcolonial nation building in Tanzania (LAURIEN 1995: 350–353). Without underestimating the significance of Maji Maji in this context, LAURIEN also points out that the famed "tribal unity" only lasted for the first month of the rebellion and that the remainder of the war throughout the territory was mostly fought based on the old ethnic alignments. The rebels themselves often did not know about the developments in areas other than their own – as interviews with contemporary witnesses would have shown. Therefore, the unity that enabled the uprising was soon lost during the war (LAURIEN 1995: 356–363).

After the idea of forcing Africans to work on the plantations became increasingly unpopular with the German administration, especially after the Maji Maji uprising, two political measures remained to increase wage labor on the plantations without raising the wages: With the taxation ordinance of 1897 (re-enacted by the British in 1922), the hut tax became the chief tactic to force Africans to accept the money economy and work on the plantations in order to be able to pay their taxes. However, as smallholder cash-crop production enabled Africans to create cash income without opting for wage labor, preferential tariffs for European planters and monopoly for certain cash crops were introduced later on, in order to reduce the income opportunities for independent African smallholders (RWEYEMAMU 1973: 21p.).

This era, following the definite victory of the colonial power over the indigenous resistance, has been characterized as the "age of improvement" (ILIFFE 1969a: 166–200). In ILIFFE's understanding, this term did not so much describe the efforts of the colonial administration to improve the development of the territory, but the new tendency of the African population to seek individual improvement under the now established circumstances of external rule. Classic examples of the development strategy of this era are the growth of a local class of clerks, teachers and administrators, who were receiving European style education – mostly through missionary schools. The period also saw the increase of cash crop production by African farmers, albeit in some conflict with the interests of European plantation owners. With regards to the social formation of the African population, the result of this era – which would continue under British mandate until the 1940s – was its economic and social stratification, which emerged from one individual's ability to "improve" him- or herself under these conditions, as well as from the differing usefulness of certain areas for colonial exploitation (see also ILIFFE 1969b).

Nevertheless, the new style of colonial development struggled to meet the labor demand of the plantations. Moreover, the system attracted mostly a migratory type of wage labor, i.e. Africans working on the plantations on a seasonal basis while retaining their links (of kinship at least) to their original peasant economy as a social and economic security. They were not alienated from their labor like pure wage laborers in a capitalist society, because they remained in possession of their means of production – in this case, their family's shamba. Therefore, the plantation system failed to proletarianize the majority of the peasantry and to create a market of free labor in the sense of a capitalist mode of production. Nonetheless, the introduction of cash-crop production into the peasant economy had significant effects on the class formation of Tanzanian society (RWEYEMAMU 1973: 22p.).

In 1918, the Germans had to give up control over Tanganyika as a result of their loss in the War, and the British took over their colony. Their claim was legitimized in 1922, when the League of Nations mandated them with the administration of Tanganyika as a protectorate (ENGELHARD 1994: 33).

The strategy of indirect rule employed by the British in Tanganyika between the First and Second World War was in large parts a result of the negative experiences of direct colonial rule in India, as well as other African colonies, specifically Northern Nigeria. The concept aimed to avoid the creation of a national capitalist class and well-educated locals, who would challenge the colonial rulers for power. Rather, being aware of the small numbers of White settlers and colonial personnel, the new tactic sought to maintain domination based on a cultural concept of the gentlemen-like supremacy in character attributed to the European colonizers. This image of morality and character was also accredited in some respects to the local "chiefs", who were supposed to impose the British rule upon the locals. However, the inherent differences which the colonizers saw between Europeans and Africans, were openly displayed at any level of indirect rule, down to the appearance of clothing for the African administration officials. Thus, the deemed supremacy of the White people and the subsequent power differential inside the colonial administration should be clearly visible even in the design of the uniforms. While the collaboration of the African colonial bureaucracy enabled its members to get some share of power and material benefits, it also estranged them from the majority of their fellow Africans. At the same time, career options for African officials remained limited. Overall, the strategy of indirect rule sought to develop territorially limited and ethnically "homogenous" chiefdoms in an autarkic manner. This approach was seen as limiting the threat of a united African population rising against colonial domination. On the other hand, this style of political and economic development limited the efficiency of economic exploitation of the colonial territory. Thus the concept of indirect rule contradicted one of the main goals of colonial rule itself: The effective use of the economic potentials of the colony (ECKERT 2007: 94p.).

The 1940s saw a shift in British colonial policies, which led to a stronger engagement of the colonial rulers in the economic and political development of Tanganyika. One main reason for this shift can be seen in the economic and financial difficulties of the British motherland after the Second World War, and the incumbent loss of the British colonial empire in Asia. These factors implied a strengthened interest in the economic resources of "colonial backwaters" like Tanganyika and Africa in general. Secondly, the educational metaphor was gaining momentum in the colonial discourse, and the development of political and administrative capabilities of the African population was seen as both a justification for the colonial cause and as beneficial for the decolonization process – the latter envisioned to happen at some non-specific point in future. If decolonization was to happen, it appeared to be a good idea to "educate" the forthcoming rulers of Africa in a European way. Therefore, new possibilities emerged for the local elite, including the possibility to get education at British universities and engage in limited international and Pan African exchange. On the other hand, this new colonial development strategy meant a tighter direct control of the local economy and the local population. Several large-scale economic development projects were designed during this period. However, implementation remained erratic and there was no common understanding on how and when certain development goals were to be reached. Consequently, there was no clear benchmark or timeframe at which Africans would be "educated" or "developed" enough to manage their independence. Simultaneously with strengthening the urban elite through industrialization, the old system of cooperation with "traditional chiefs" was continued, adding to the contradictory nature of British colonial policy in Tanganyika until the 1960s (ECKERT 2007: 165p.).

According to JENNINGS (2007: 74p.), independent Tanganyika would inherit two main elements of the colonial development policy: First of all, the central role of the state had been established in any matters concerning development. Secondly, colonial experiences with attempts to transform smallholder agriculture had illustrated the dangers which unpopular policies might imply for the government itself. This contributed to the interest of the new independent government in perpetuating central state control, while at the same time ensuring popular mass support for its policies.

3.2   Early post-independence strategy

When becoming independent, the new state did not have a good economic base to start from. What became even more limiting was the shortage of highly educated and trained personnel. Therefore, the new nationalist government had to rely heavily on the former colonial administration, as well as to try to reconnect with the higher educated Asian citizens. Furthermore, the trained (colonial) administrative staff usually had no experiences in areas like trade or manufacturing. At the same time, the colonial educational institutions did not provide for higher, let alone critical, education, and practically all higher learning institutions had to be built from scratch (RUGUMAMU 1997: 106–110).

Additionally, there were no natural resources or geopolitical importance to attract the super powers, a very rural economy and population, and only a small petit bourgeois class after independence, based on the first cooperatives (e.g. Kilimanjaro Native Planters Association est. 1925). The bureaucratic elite was based on careers in TANU, and also very rural (SCHICHO 2009: 178–180).

In the early years, Tanganyika more or less followed a development policy which was similar to that of neighboring Kenya. It was based on both the transformation and the progressive farmer approach. Transformation would emphasize the investment in new farming techniques and the progressive farmer concept would dictate that the available resources would be spent in "advanced areas" where the application of new technology was expected to produce the highest profit. This development strategy was mainly taken over from late colonial times and under the tutelage of the World Bank and other international advisors, the resulting settlement schemes and other high capital investments in agriculture took up most of the sparse financial resources. Furthermore, this strategy of rural development in many ways contradicted the ideas of Ujamaa and implied a separation between state ideology and practical policy for a period of five years (HEDLUND & LUNDAHL 1989: 23p.).

Immediately after independence, the Tanganyikan government under Nyerere set out to launch a massive program of investment in agricultural transformation, education and industrialization. Those development strategies were mostly developed by western consultants (WATZAL 1982: 5p.). In many ways, the first development plans resembled a majoritarian trend in the development discourse of the 1960s, which RODNEY and BOTCHWERY (1976: 30) have characterized as relying heavily on foreign investment and promoting the concentration on agricultural export with increases in cash-crop production. Industrialization would focus on light industries producing consumer goods for import substitution. Furthermore, there was an increase of commercial linkages with foreign, mainly capitalist countries, with less focus on socialist countries and intra-African trade. According to the authors, this would be the definition of what a "bourgeois social scientist" would label "development as modernization". Indeed, they saw a rise of an African petit bourgeoisie under the label of Africanization during that period.

As the limited capacities and the challenging political tasks of building a nation out of the former colony took up most of the work of the new government, there was a big influence of foreign advisors on the first Three-Year plan (1961-64) and the following Five-Year Plan for economic development. Relying heavily on foreign investment (both as aid and as private investment), it followed a path which RUGUMAMU calls a "conventional development theory": "Improvement" and "transformation" in agriculture, big capital and technological investments and an industrial policy aimed at import substitution. Since capital was difficult to come by in Tanzania, the government adopted several policies aimed at attracting foreign direct investors, protecting their investments and profits. The World Bank, as well as USAid, played a crucial role in the development of those policies, as did the UK. An ambitioned investment plan in education services was also part of the strategy. However, both the village settlement schemes and the industrialization projects depended heavily on foreign investment and aid, and protective tariffs. Overall, the development projects did not produce the ambitious results envisioned in the plan. Only four big infrastructure projects took up around 20% of all investment 1965-75 (RUGUMAMU 1997: 111–117).

The projects implied by the Five-Year Development Plan of 1964 amounted to roughly 700 Million USD, half of which had to be generated through foreign sources. Given the strong reliance on these sources and the memories of the dependence on British troops to secure the state in 1965, Tanzania's desire to diversify its foreign relations became all the more reasonable. Liberation struggles in Mozambique and Kongo also contributed to the attempt to take a neutralist position in foreign relations. Given the background of the cold war, Tanzania's assumed entanglement with the East raised suspicions in Western (donor) countries about a socialist shift in the country and made the reliance on foreign money for its own development plans all the more precarious. On the other hand, the opening up to China and the Soviet Union potentially meant an increase of possible donor countries (CLIFFE 1965: 221p.).

In general, its pronounced statement on sovereignty and non-alignment allowed Tanzania to diversify both its foreign trade and its sources of foreign aid away from the UK and the Western world and to get more donors from the East, in particular. However, certain conflicts illustrated the limitation of independence through aid reliance: In 1965, for instance, the dispute on Rhodesian independence led to the break-off of Tanzania's diplomatic relations with the UK, while in the case of the US, the alleged undermining of the Zanzibari revolution by US agents led to serious tensions (RUGUMAMU 1997: 117–122).

Furthermore, the Union of Zanzibar and Tanganyika in 1964 led to some repercussions in diplomatic affairs with the two German states. As West Germany's Hallstein doctrine suggested, Tanzania would have to choose between keeping diplomatic relations (and considerable financial support) with the FRG, or whether it would continue to have an embassy of the GDR, which had been in close relations with Zanzibar after the revolution, had their embassy on the Islands and was also giving substantial financial contributions to the revolutionary government. While some observers interpreted Nyerere's slow response to both governments' demands for "exclusivity" as a weakness of leadership in the new union setup, CLIFFE points out that the President's pragmatic approach proved successful in the end: He insisted that this was entirely a German issue and had to be sorted out by those two states, accordingly. Indeed, after unraveling the quarrels, Tanzania became the first country after the Soviet Union to host diplomatic representations of both the FRG and the GDR on its territory, and kept diplomatic and economic relations with both German states (CLIFFE 1965: 222p.).

The moderate form of socialism made Tanzania a favorite partner for Western development engagement. In the person of Nyerere, Western politicians saw an intellectual of their own kind, and in spite of the increasing authoritarian tendencies in the 1970s, the continued support for Tanzania could also be seen as counterbalancing the West's cooperation with numerous right-wing regimes and military dictators during the cold war era. Even after the aforementioned diplomatic disruptions, Tanzania did not go down the path of integration into the Eastern bloc, but rather sought to emphasize its neutrality and strengthen the Non-Aligned Movement. With the beginning of the Social Democrat-Liberal coalition in Bonn in 1969, relations between Tanzania and West Germany became very cordial again. Under the tutelage of the Social Democratic secretary for development cooperation, Erhard Eppler, Tanzania became the most important partner country of West German development cooperation (ECKERT 2007: 217–221).

Nevertheless, the conflict had already led to the interruption of West Germany's aid flows towards Tanzania in 1964/65. All these cases taught the Tanzanian government, according to RUGUMAMU (1997: 117–122), that there was no such thing as aid without conditions, and that heavy reliance on aid and foreign investment for its development ambitions invariably meant a limitation to national sovereignty and independent foreign policy. That was one of the reasons for the new development approach represented by the Arusha Declaration in 1967.

The global power relations of the 1960s also contributed to this new attempt at independent development: At the time of Tanzania's independence, the world was divided into the two opposing camps of the cold war. Most former colonies had – like Tanzania – a past as a Western colony and therefore usually aligned with the West, at least initially. While the formal introduction of the non-aligned movement in 1961 gave some room to a foreign policy independent from these blocks, RUGUMAMU (1997: 93–95) argues that Tanzania was virtually powerless on the international scale. Since the power of nations would depend on either their economic or military strength, or both, Tanzania could never really make a difference on the global level. Therefore, even if Tanzania was one of the strongest proponents of non-alignment, it could not achieve independence from the mightier nations in this sense. In this line of thought, it would make even more sense for the country to embrace a development strategy of self-reliance in order to regain sovereignty regarding its international policy.

3.3   The period of Ujamaa

"This is the objective of socialism in Tanzania. To build a society in which all members have equal rights and equal opportunities; in which all can live at peace with their neighbours without suffering or imposing injustice, being exploited, or exploiting; and in which all have a gradually increasing basic level of material welfare before any individual lives in luxury."

J.K. NYERERE, *Socialism and Rural Development* (NYERERE 1968f: 110)

When Nyerere reiterated this overall goal of Tanzanian socialism, it had already become clear that the strategy of the early independence era had not delivered the results expected. The President and the party had agreed in the Arusha Declaration to rethink the implementation of Ujamaa and to attempt to create national development based on self-reliance (NYERERE 1967b). In fact, this new approach had already been pioneered on the ground by some initiatives by local farmers, who had developed their own understanding of Ujamaa. The most influential one would become known as the Ruvuma Development Association (FREYHOLD 1979: 73).

Therefore, this chapter will begin with the detailed presentation of the RDA and its development concept, before analyzing the different phases of national Ujamaa implementation from the Arusha Declaration until the practical end of Ujamaa in the 1980s. After giving a short overview on the neoliberal changes of the latter period, the chapter will conclude by presenting an impression of the most recent cornerstones of national development policy in Tanzania.

3.3.1 The rise and disbanding of the Ruvuma Development Association (RDA)

In almost every aspect of this thesis, the Ruvuma Development Association plays a central role. Not only has it been an integral part of the history of the case study villages analyzed in the following chapters, but throughout its short lifespan, its ideology, its development strategy and its internal organization have also been influential in the creation of Ujamaa as a nationwide strategy. Furthermore, RDA's practices of community development have also become an inspiration for modern day concepts of participatory development and community engagement by the international donor community and NGOs worldwide. In this chapter, a short organizational history of the RDA will be provided, as well as an overview of its internal structure, the causes for its success, and the reasons for its disbandment.

The establishment of the RDA

In fact, the RDA was neither the first nor the only grassroots attempt at rural development in the early days of independence in what was then Tanganyika. Many peasants and political youth felt compelled by the new opportunities and the encouraging speeches of Nyerere and made it to the uncultivated countryside to try their own ideas of national development (MAGHIMBI 1995: 43). Even before independence, TANU was advocating for a rural development based on farmers engaging in communal production, who were to be motivated to settle in nucleated settlements, with the aim of nourishing political and economic development (MASSARO 1998: 288).

One man who would become decisive for the future history of the RDA and, in fact, of the whole endeavor of Ujamaa was Ntimbanjayo Millinga: He was the leader of the TANU Youth League in the Peramiho Branch and had been working as a nurse in the hospital of the Benedictine Mission in the same village. Inspired by Nyerere's appeal to create cooperative agricultural production in new villages to develop the soon-to-be independent state, he was eager to put the spirit of a new beginning into practice (SCHICHO 2009: 183). After listening to one of his radio speeches, which was directly addressed to the youth, Millinga gathered his comrades to develop a plan to put Nyerere's words into practice (IBBOTT 2014: 57).

Together with around fifteen fellow members of the Youth League, he undertook a first attempt at settling in November 1960, on a ridge around 15 km from Peramiho, near the Litowa River. However, poor preparation and the lack of resources meant that the group would be out of food before any harvest could be brought in at the new settlement. Therefore, in February 1961, they had to give up and the whole project appeared set to take the way of many unsuccessful grassroots settlements of the time. Yet, instead of giving up, Millinga and one other comrade from this first attempt were able to mobilize a new group of potential settlers, as well as more institutional and material support, and started another time in June 1961. This time, their efforts would be rewarded, and the village of Litowa would become the base for one of the most impressive grassroots development projects of the time (SCHNEIDER 2014: 25; COULSON 1982: 263).

In other accounts, there were only five Youth League Members, involved in both attempts (WENNER 1970: 28–30), but in any case, it was Millinga's vision and leadership which provided much of the motivation to push it through. He was born as John Millinga in a small village located near Lake Nyasa, and had went to Peramiho to join the primary school, going from there to join the seminary to become a priest, eventually, in the 1950s. In his time at the seminary, he met Ado Mgimba and John Ngairo, who would later be part of the community at Litowa. All three of them were more interested in politics than in the church sermon, and left the seminary to find paying jobs (Millinga, as mentioned, at the missionary hospital). Their main interest in 1960 lay in the independence of their country and so they all joined the TANU Youth League. Arguably, such revolutionary ideas did not fit well into an institution like the Peramiho mission, which was still praising its German colonial heritage, and Millinga lost his job there because of his political involvement. After the foundation of Litowa, Millinga became one of the first students at the Kivukoni college in Dar es

Salaam, where he met Ibbott. In 1965, he became a Member of Parliament (WENNER 1970: 195–197).

MEYNS sees the experience of the colonial style of exploitation, which the founders of Litowa experienced as nurses and workers at the Peramiho mission, as one of the major motivations of these settlers to seek a new form of development and living for themselves. In the vast empty areas of bush in Ruvuma, where no shortage of land could hinder them, they found the possibility to escape the colonial economy and pursue their own vision of a cooperative future (MEYNS 1977: 160p.).

Apart from Millinga's charismatic leadership, another person would prove to be of utter importance for the success of the settlers and the connection the RDA would provide among several villages with a similar history in Ruvuma. Ralph Ibbott, an Englishmen who had lived in Rhodesia before and had tried to establish communal farming projects with Africans and Europeans there. Ibbott had been deported from Rhodesia after he came into conflict with the apartheid administration of that country. At the same time, the grassroots settlers of Ruvuma were looking for an adviser on how to organize their work and expand their agriculture. Brought into contact with Millinga through a Tanzanian Member of Parliament, Ibbott was willing to move to Litowa with his whole family to engage as a fulltime adviser to the farmers (BRAIN 1977: 239p.).

In the early days of Litowa, there appear to have been good connections to the local and regional TANU branches. One of the most striking examples of the local commitment to the practical implementation of Ujamaa on the ground emerged from this cooperation, when the Ruvuma Ujamaa Committee (which included the regional party leader, as well as Ibbott and Millinga) came up with its own plan for the establishment of African Socialism within the region (IBBOTT 2014: 76p.). Many of the principles established by this committee later became the daily praxis of development among the RDA member villages. The full text of these outlines can be found in the same source (IBBOTT 2014: 82–92).

Soon, the settlers at Litowa started to cooperate with other new villages in the area. The first meeting between villages took place in 1963, when settlers from Liweta visited Litowa in order to learn more about the organization of communal farming. Representatives from regional development authorities also participated in the meeting (IBBOTT 2014: 80p.). Later in the same year, the Songea Development Association was created, formalizing the cooperation between the villages of Litowa, Liweta and Njoomlole. The spirit of self-help and the success of the cooperation soon attracted other villages, and when the organization was formally renamed into Ruvuma Development Association in 1964, it already counted eight member villages (JENNINGS 2002: 518p.).

The internal organization and the development strategies of the RDA

During the years of 1963 and 1964, the RDA not only expanded its number of member villages, it also established its own constitution and management structures. The main facility to discuss the proceedings of the organization was the General Meeting, to which two representatives of each village were delegated. This institution controlled the work of an executive committee comprising of eight elected members, who had the task to oversee the day to day activities of the Association (JENNINGS 2002: 518–520).

In an attempt to characterize the activities of the RDA concerning their understanding of development, SCHMIED (1989: 94) has framed it as "a mixture of the improvement (…) and the transformation approach." According to her, the villagers were aware that development would be a time-consuming process in which core values of the old society could be conserved (like the spirit of communality), while at the same time modernization of agricultural techniques and the gathering of modern knowledge was appreciated and actively promoted by the association.

In spreading this development approach in all member villages, the Social and Economic Revolutionary Army (SERA) took a central role. Consisting of highly motivated and politicized villagers, its members would spread all over the RDA and share the knowledge of a certain agricultural practice or the efficient installation of water supply when called upon by any member village (COULSON 1982: 265). Most of SERA's members had enjoyed secondary education and were specialists of sorts in one or more aspects of village live and organization. Therefore, whenever a new village was founded that wanted to join the RDA, a man or woman of the group would assist the new villagers and stay with them until the basic institutions of the new village were running. Regular visits afterwards ensured some degree of sustainability in creating new villages (BRAIN 1977: 240).

Through the SERA, each member village of the RDA benefited from the knowledge of all the villages combined. IBBOTT (2014: 162–166) himself remembered it as one of the most important institutions for the development of the RDA, and emphasized the open and mutually beneficial relation of SERA's activists with the villages. If issues regarding the implementation of certain projects arose, they would be discussed in a constructive manner until the best solution for the respective village was found. Work with SERA was never remunerated, and this might have contributed to the on-par atmosphere between those experts and the common villagers. This, together with the efficient management of the Association and the ability to access external assistance from various NGOs, meant that each village was able to increase production and strengthen its organizational capacities during the existence of the RDA (MEYNS 1977: 163p.).

What made the RDA special, according to SCHNEIDER, was not that it had an alternative concept of development or that it opposed the state or nationalism: On the contrary, the politicized members of the RDA saw themselves as part of a countrywide effort in nation-building and national development and were active members of the ruling party. What made RDA special was its radically democratic approach to village and organizational governance: Membership was a voluntary (and reversible) act of choice, the members were involved in all areas of decision-making at practically all times and accountability was key to all areas of delegating power or positions (SCHNEIDER 2014: 29p.).

All decisions regarding village life would be made consensual at village meetings that usually took place at least two times a week. All adults in the village took part in these meetings. Once a year, a leadership team would be elected that took care of the daily proceedings of the village, the creation of work plans and so on.

Leadership positions were unpaid, honorary offices, and in cases of misconduct, the village assembly could expel those elected leaders. Potential new members, who wanted to join a village, would be invited for a visit of a few days, and then, if they were still interested, they could stay for a probation period of several months (e.g. six months in Liweta). If they proved themselves to be accepting of the rules of village life and were happy with the situation inside the community, the assembly then officially accepted them as full members of the village (SCHMIED 1989: 94p.). During the probation, the candidate would be accommodated in a guest room of one of the existing houses and hosted by the family residing there. After acceptance, the new member was given a site for his house and a field for the personal crops. He would then continue to build his own house on that site in the following months (BRAIN 1977: 242).

The RDA's own primary school – An example for self-organized socialist development

The extent to which the farmers of the association were motivated to create their own, independent development, is possibly best characterized by the school established in Litowa from 1964 onwards. Students from all member villages were admitted at the school, if their parents were living in other villages, the children would stay at Litowa as boarding students. The RDA school was first and foremost the villagers' own project, with the goal of educating the students in the ways necessary for its communal development agenda. Class activities included technical training and farming techniques as well as work on the communal shambas. Its approach to education in self-reliance was reflective of the Ujamaa ideology and a far cry from the colonial system of education practiced in missionary schools like Peramiho. In the later years of the Association, a plan emerged to establish a technical secondary school as well, as the need for better education was clearly seen in the member villages and only few students from the RDA school could get a place at the sparsely established technical schools that were already existing in the country (MEYNS 1977: 165p.).

The RDA school was founded by Ado Mgimba, mainly because the RDA could not afford the school fees of the existing primary schools. Later on, they got the school registered with the ministry of education, which from thereon provided for some of the school's funding. Millinga became the director and a woman called Ms. Chips the head teacher. Even under the state's acknowledgement, the school was able to introduce its own curriculum, which focused on the practical education of the children as prospective farmers and members of the Ujamaa villages of the RDA. The idea of the school's setup was inspired by those of the Israeli Kibbutz schools, as Ralph Ibbott recalled during a conversation with Kate Wenner upon her arrival in Litowa (WENNER 1970: 46–48).

Upon the publication of Nyerere's proclamation on Education and Self-Reliance (NYERERE 1967a), Samuel TOROKA, who was by then the new Headmaster of Litowa's RDA School, delivered his short descriptions of the RDA's school concept. Indeed, TOROKA saw the curriculum and the teaching techniques at Litowa as a practical example for the future concept of education in Tanzania, whose overall impetus was to educate the pupils on the principles of Ujamaa and to prepare them for a life as productive members of the Ujamaa communities. On the ground, the RDA school therefore attempted to create viable school projects, which were completely integrated with the general village life. At the time of writing in 1969, the school had fifteen acres of school shamba planted, eight pupils working in the RDA Wool Industry Project and a further two working at the village dispensary, with the extension of nursery training envisioned. Generally, TOROKA emphasized the paramount necessity of true community integration and tangible benefits for the pupils in order for school projects to be more than pure showpieces without sustainable results (TOROKA 1973: 264p.).

It was not by coincidence that the founders of RDA decided to start their own school in Litowa, rather than sending their children to existing schools in the area. From the beginning, the school was supposed to be part of the village community. This was seen as the only way to teach children the practical aspects of village life and prepare them for the future of the Ujamaa idea. In contrast to the disconnected islands of education that were seen in the old, colonially influenced state schools, the RDA school was supposed to educate its pupils as self-confident but also practically trained members of the village community – without neglecting the benefits of "higher education". One tactic to encourage their communal spirit was to send them to other RDA villages during school holidays – not as a vacation, but as a hands-on way of getting to know the other communities of the project and to learn to respect other people not because of their formal education, but because of their hard work for the RDA project – a project which would become theirs in the near future (TOROKA 1973: 266).

Among the staff of the RDA school, the idea that Ujamaa was not a utopian future, but a historic reality, was enthusiastically accepted. Therefore, it was not the old people who had to be taught about the new concept of Ujamaa, but the children, who had only heard the word and not yet seen the reality. With this mindset, it becomes clear why the school at Litowa placed emphasis on the practical teaching of communal work, as they thought it was not possible to understand and embrace the idea without participating in its reality. Therefore, all projects – especially the school shamba – were seen as projects of all the pupils. The idea of having different – or even competing – school groups was seen as foreign to the Ujamaa idea, just as the concept of block farms that was applied in some non-RDA villages at that time (TOROKA 1973: 266p.).

As committed as the wajamaa of Litowa were to their idea of Ujamaa, as innovative and participative were many of the teaching techniques at the RDA school: The technique first mentioned by TOROKA is practical work (dubbed "Practical Ujamaa", p. 267), i.e. the work of pupils on the school shamba or in the different school projects – an emphasis consistent with the overall goal of seeing pupils as part of the village community throughout their education. As farming was seen as the foundation of all life in the villages, all pupils took part in these activities. The second column was lectures on Ujamaa, which included the teaching of Tanzanian national heroes, Ujamaa readings and communal economy. The third and maybe the most innovative part of Ujamaa teaching in Litowa can be seen in the organization of the student body, which is made up of a detailed system of executive and managerial parts and is supremely governed by *the pupils' own Ujamaa assembly*, where all students met and elected their own leaders, discussed the work plans on their communal shamba and the use of the income from the students' projects. It appears that these student bodies even had influence on the curriculum and the way of teaching at the RDA school – a truly revolutionary approach in this time and in the environment of colonial and missionary education. The deeply-felt commitment to create a new education for a new society and to embrace the students not as recipients of knowledge but as capable individuals with a responsibility for their own education and their own community can be felt throughout Toroka's contribution and gives a lively impression of the communal spirit at Litowa and other RDA villages in 1969 (Toroka 1973: 267–271).

The social life of socialist villagers

What added to the spirit of community and mutual responsibility within the RDA was certainly the high importance given to social activities that strengthened the feeling of togetherness: Village meetings would be accompanied by a communal dinner, and sometimes singing or other group activities that kept the villagers together as a kind of big family (IfS 1970: 76). Particularly in such events, the RDA villages manifested themselves as the purest form of utopian Ujamaa in Tanzania (Freyhold 1979: 77), evoking the spirit of Nyerere (1962b), who had envisioned this sense of familyhood to be the basis of African socialism.

And as in a real family, there were obviously some levels of hierarchy involved in its daily live. The RDA certainly was no authority-free zone and the villagers submitted themselves to quite a large number of rules regarding work etc., but the crucial difference between authority and leadership in RDA – as opposed to the later villagization – was that RDA interpreted leadership as something empowering that was literally leading other people to more self-consciousness, more abilities and more development. Much of this had to do with the systems of self-control and accountability present in the RDA villages, but also with the character of the most important leaders and experts like Millinga and Ibbott. While they most certainly were not neutral to the actions the villager would take (why would they be?), they were very much concerned to take a kind of pedagogical approach in the development of the village and its people. From being praised as a deliverer from poverty in the beginning, Ibbott for instance tried to take a back seat when it came to village policy and act more as an adviser in the background. First and foremost, the whole population of villages like Litowa, Liweta and Matetereka lived in a culture of critical authority and equality among leaders and villagers (Schneider 2014: 29–34).

Therefore, while the structure of village administration and labor organization might have seemed similar to that of the early settlement schemes in other parts of Tanzania in formal terms, the RDA villages and the association itself were completely different. Managers, leaders and other persons with prominent positions were truly a part of the village and – most importantly – peasants themselves. Inside the settlement schemes, the types of leadership positions were virtually identical, but those leaders were paid representatives of the government. As overseers of the developmental state, they were not part of the local communities. Authors like MEYNS hence see the settlement scheme type of organization as the emergence of a class society with class contradictions implicated between the settlers and the government officials. The RDA villages, on the other hand, were free of such contradictions (MEYNS 1977: 161p.).

Indeed, the local control and democratic decision-making that characterized both the RDA and its member villages was paramount to the creation of commitment to communal work and cooperation. It contributed to the building of confidence in their own strength and knowledge – items which would be referred to as "social capital" in the recent development discourse (SCHNEIDER 2004: 351).

Production at the RDA villages

In their endeavor to create a rural community on basic democratic principles, all of the RDA villages were based on the goal establishing collective agricultural production. The newsletters published by Ibbott and Millinga in the first years of the Association from 1964 to 1966 give a good impression of the early organization of production in Litowa, as well as the other villages that had founded the RDA. After their first planting season 1963/64 they assessed that the crops "had all done very well", although the clearing of the virgin farmland meant long and hard working-hours for all members. In Litowa, cultivation started with maize and groundnuts, while fire-cured tobacco was planted as a source of cash revenue for the settlers. The latter was sold through the Ngomat Cooperative Union. Despite being happy with the results of the first growing season, Ibbott and Millinga observed that the villagers lacked experience in the preparation and cultivation of fields larger than the usual family shamba – a phenomenon which they partly attributed to the destruction of cooperative knowledge in the country during the colonial period (IBBOTT & MILLINGA 1964a).

With the first harvest brought in, the villagers of Litowa focused their attention on the sharing of knowledge with the inhabitants of other villages, who had been attracted by the success of collective farming and wanted to attempt similar production methods (IBBOTT & MILLINGA 1964b). In time for the preparations for the 1964/65 season, the increased membership within the villages and the experiences of the first year made collective work easier. Furthermore, association members had begun to enhance the connection between the villages, for instance by preparing a direct road link between Litowa and Liweta – enabling better cooperation and eliminating the necessity of taking the long detour via Songea. For this season, more villages were opting for cultivation on collective fields, inspired by Litowa's success (IBBOTT & MILLINGA 1964c).

However, private plots existed in most of the RDA villages. LEWIN, for instance, sees a problem with the persistence of too much individual agriculture in Matetereka, but insists that the change of the mode of production would take its time, and that those changes cannot come by compulsion. Therefore, the issue of private plots in Ujamaa villages would have to be addressed in a long term approach with democratic decision-making (LEWIN 1973: 193).

Indeed, each of the RDA villages had a different extent of communal farming, which depended mostly on the background of the farmers. Liweta, for instance, started as a village of individual farmers, who wanted to engage in communal agriculture. Therefore, each farmer had an individual block of two acres. In Matetereka, it was one acre. MEYNS sees this persistence of individual agriculture in collective villages as a class contradiction, but agrees with LEWIN that changes in the mode of production may take some time, since peasants in the RDA villages are not isolated from the rest of the (capitalist) society. However, as long as the work on the communal shambas would be the core of village economy and activity, MEYNS does not see a contradiction with the goal of building a truly classless society in these villages (MEYNS 1977: 162p.).

In any case, the RDA members themselves were under the impression of creating their own collective society step by step. For the second season, the farmers at Litowa were cultivating 75 acres collectively, and the management committee had set the goal of doubling the acreage for the upcoming season. Although rains were late in 1964/65, the crops looked promising in the beginning of 1965 (IBBOTT & MILLINGA 1965b). Indeed, the season would produce satisfying yields, and with their achievements in collective crop production ensuring enough food for all their villagers, communal activities during the dry season no longer had to be limited to bush clearing operations. Instead, further collective activities like brick production for improved housing were initiated. By that time in 1965, the success of Litowa, in particular, began to attract more visitors from central government authorities, who were eager to learn how these farmers were able develop their own communities (IBBOTT & MILLINGA 1965a).

In retrospect, the villages of the RDA have been seen as "Tanzania's most successful collective villages" (PUTTERMAN 1985: 176), not only on the level of voluntary political organization, but also on the level of agricultural production. And certainly, it was in large parts their material success in creating tangible development results with low capital input, which led to their role as an inspiration for Nyerere's subsequent policies on rural development in Tanzania as a whole (WEAVER & KRONEMER 1981: 843).

The last newsletter of the RDA which could be found at the library of Dar es Salaam University dates from March 1966. Both Ibbott and Millinga share an optimistic outlook on the future of Litowa village and the Association as a whole. They were in the process of acquiring the milling business in Songea and had just received the first tractor of RDA – a gift by Oxfam. The number of villages which wanted to join RDA's concept of collective agriculture and democratic organization of work was increasing steadily and the harvests in all villages appear to have been more than satisfying again (IBBOTT & MILLINGA 1966).

Of course, the RDA villages did not exist or develop without interaction with the outside world. At least until 1969, this interaction was mostly fruitful and mutually beneficial. SCHNEIDER (2014: 35–37) gives many examples in which both financial involvement and technical expertise from international organizations could be attracted by the villagers (first and foremost Oxfam, see JENNINGS 2002).

The RDA villages soon became much more successful than the state settlement schemes, such as Mlale in their immediate vicinity. While both approaches certainly relied on (financial) help from national and international sources, the RDA way of self-help and learning while practicing participatory and democratic organization proved to be much more sustainable, both regarding the economic outlook of the villages and the capacity building that took place among the villagers. This successful way of doing things at RDA would become the inspiration to Nyerere to create the concept of *Ujamaa vijijini* (SCHNEIDER 2014: 24).

The "opening" for the RDA approach as a national policy

The RDA's importance can be exemplified by two elements: First of all, it was started by local peasants in a free association of their own motivation. As such, it was a movement from below, completely opposed to the project of creating Ujamaa villages from above, as it would become prominent in state policy after the Arusha Declaration. Secondly, its concept of cooperative development was based on the hard work and voluntary communal action of its members, in contrast to the capital and technology-intensive development strategies that were the centerpiece of Tanzania's rural development approach in the early 1960s. HEDLUND and LUNDAHL share no doubt that the RDA's success became a major point of inspiration for *Ujamaa vijijini* (HEDLUND & LUNDAHL 1989: 34p.).

The opening for the RDA model to become the national model of rural development was not least made possible by the failure of the heavily capitalized settlement schemes. Not only were these schemes completely overshooting the predicted investment costs by 1965/66, they also had problems with attracting potential villagers or earning anywhere near cost, and suffered heavily from a "fetish" for machinery. On the other hand, the RDA was able to produce tangible results and much more incentives for its members by far less investment. Apart from these technocratic incentives to "try out" the RDAs way, there was a split opinion as to whether the model could deliver nationwide. While some saw the reason for the better results exactly in RDA's radically democratic and somewhat decentralized structure, others were more skeptical about the implied loss of central authority over the development process. In any case, since Tanzania simply lacked the financial and personell resources to continue with "professionally managed" settlement schemes, the self-organizing path of RDA seemed much more attractive (SCHNEIDER 2014: 37–40).

The results of RDA's development approach were clearly visible. However, in economic terms, the progress was slow. Only a few villages were able to pay their members a dividend from communal cash-crop production (Litowa 50 TSh and Liweta 70 TSh, for instance, for each member in 1968). Most villages could not pay their members any shared profit from the communal activities. Development was more clearly felt in the sector of education, were the RDA school in Litowa was establishing a new model of formation, different from colonial times – and in the spirit of communality and involvement in a project created by the peasants by themselves and for themselves (MEYNS 1977: 164p.).

The "Nationalization" of RDA

So, seemingly at the high point of RDA, its strategy was made into national policy with the Arusha Declaration (see the following chapters). However, it was not only the ideology and the development strategy, which would be nationalized; it would turn out to be the Association and its assets itself: Meyns (1977: 168p.) underlines that the disbandment of the RDA in 1969 – at a time when its approach to participatory communal development became a national policy – is no coincidence. Indeed, the development strategy became the model for *Ujamaa vijijini* and the state ideology of TANU. However, as a basic democratic movement with a reluctance to accept external authority, the RDA necessarily had to be in contradiction with TANU's idea of a central, developmentalist state. Meyns characterizes RDA's ideology as partly populist, in the sense of a petit bourgeois small farmer socialism.

That, in fact, would not be in contradiction with Ujamaa, as Nyerere's ideology is literarily based on the same principles of radical democracy and voluntary involvement of the peasants in the national development agenda. Had TANU and the president adhered to these principles, a centralized move like *Ujamaa vijijini* would have been a contradiction in itself. However, the urge of the postcolonial development state to achieve rapid development on a national scale prevailed, and the RDA fell victim to this overwhelming goal. In a way, the association had shown both the possibilities and the limitations of the strict use of Ujamaa principles: Participatory communal development on voluntary basis was indeed achievable. Yet, the speed of this development appeared too slow and the task of inducing behavioral change in the peasantry by persuasion seemed too great for the state leadership to be considered as the way forward. Therefore, as a matter of power relations, the state bourgeoisie defeated the spontaneous movement of peasants in Tanzania, which was best represented in the RDA (Meyns 1977: 169p.).

When the Arusha Declaration established Ujamaa as a national policy, it shifted the attention of national development to the rural areas and the advancement of agriculture. In his post-Arusha writings *Socialism and Rural Development (Ujamaa vijijini* (Nyerere 1968f), first published 1967) and *Freedom and Development* (Nyerere 1974a, first published 1968) Nyerere laid down his vision of how this kind of rural development ought to be organized: In basically the same way that had worked so favorably for the RDA villages, radically democratic and self-organized. While "theorizing" the practice of RDA, Nyerere thereby switched the core reason for why people should live in centralized villages at all: Before, it had been for the sake of easier provision of social services by the state and the increase of agricultural production by economies of scale and mechanization. Since especially the latter failed to materialize and was simply deemed too expensive, the new key motive was to enable people to live together and create their own community; trying to create the space for the communal endeavor of Ujamaa. And the president had a very clear idea on what exactly the government's role was supposed to be in this process:

> "The Government's role is to help people to make a success of their work and their decisions. (...) The Ministry of Local Government and Rural Development, too, must be active in these villages; their field workers should be available to help the people to organize themselves, to advise them on how to be eligible for advances for seed, or for small loans for farm equipment. It would be this Ministry, too, which should draw up a model constitution for the villages at different stages, although it must be stressed that no one model should be imposed on any village. Any model which is drawn up should

just be a guide which draws the attention of the people to the decisions which have to be made by them; each village community must be able to make its own decisions. Nonetheless, the experience of existing ujamaa villages, such as those now operating within the Ruvuma Development Association, could be helpful, and the Ministry of Local Government and Rural Development should make this experience available to people from different parts." (NYERERE 1968f: 142p.)

Not only was RDA explicitly taken as an inspiration for these plans, the villages were the location for a large amount of training and teaching people (especially state officials) on how Ujamaa should look on the ground. In 1968, the Department of *Ujamaa vijijini* at the TANU headquarters was established, and Millinga was made the head of this institution. Under his leadership, Nyerere was hoping to familiarize the cadres with his vision and expand the RDA model all over Tanzania (SCHNEIDER 2014: 40–45).

From the mid of 1968 onwards, Nyerere initiated institutional and procedural changes to establish *Ujamaa vijijini* nationwide. Among other measures, the members of TANU's Central Committee (CC) attended seminars in Handeni and were then sent to spend several weeks at Litowa, Liweta and Matetereka in 1969. When they came back to report their experiences in the Central Committee meeting on September 20, 1969, it was announced that from now on the party would take the lead in *Ujamaa vijijini*, as well as in the RDA villages. Development Minister Peter Kisumu was the head of a delegation to Ruvuma to announce to the villagers that the RDA was to be disbanded and the assets to be transferred to state control (SCHNEIDER 2014: 46p.).

What is reported about this crucial meeting of the Central Committee is symptomized by EDWARDS' accounts of an interview with Millinga in 1998. After failing to convince Nyerere that the RDA was a subversive organization working against the interests of party and state, they accused the villagers of having tried to kill the committee members on their visit to Litowa:

"(…) apparently they tried to make a tree fall on top of one member while he was witnessing a demonstration of how to fell trees with a winch. Similarly they had apparently tried to roll a large rock onto another member while he was inspecting the village water supply construction project. A third attempt to kill the visitors involved a hostile bull." (EDWARDS 1998: 16)

In the same account, Millinga, who was himself a Central Committee member in 1969, reported that President Nyerere was outraged at the way the opponents of RDA reported and accused them of stupidity for claiming to be attacked in such a way. Nevertheless, the committee members had made up their mind on ending the Association and stuck to their stories. The discussion went on for some more time, but in the end Millinga reports:

"After further argument, Mwalimu had only one supporter – the oldest member of the Committee (over 70 years old), Mr. Selemani Mhigiri. Mhigiri said, "This is very strange. These people are making progress for themselves, for the pride of this nation. It makes me disbelieve these stories. Let them live in peace." There was an uproar. Mwalimu said, "I think you people want to disband the RDA without any reason. But because you are 'the power', then let us disband it. But I want this kind of development for the country. If necessary, then, we will make TANU the controllers and implementers of this." He said to me, "What is your feeling about this decision?" I said, "When we started the RDA we were simply following Party policy. The Party encouraged us to do this kind of development, so we did it. Today we will follow Party policy again. We are being told to stop, so we will stop." Even this was not enough [for the anti-ujamaa Committee members]." (EDWARDS 1998: 17)

This direct account of the meeting gives rise to the argument that Nyerere – himself an outspoken supporter of the RDA – might have allowed the disbandment of the RDA because he saw sacrificing the association as the only way to achieve the implementation of *Ujamaa vijijini* in the whole country. Oxfam – a strong supporter of RDA – might have come to terms with the disbandment out of the same reasons. The greater good was the establishment of RDA policy in the whole country, and some might even have seen TANU central leadership as necessary and beneficial to this goal (SCHNEIDER 2014: 54).

According to SCHNEIDER (2014: 48p.), the quick disbandment of the RDA had not so much to do with conflicts over the surplus created (i.e. that the bureaucratic bourgeoisie might have felt threatened by farmers working communally for themselves and not for the state; see, for instance, MUSTI DE GENNARO 1981: 129-130), but with the break away from traditions of authority and leadership which were the core of the postcolonial developmental state. Personal rivalries (like the one between Millinga and Kisumu) and the clash of culture apparent in the CC's visit to the RDA villages might have sparked the quick move by the party establishment.

As SCHNEIDER points out, the issue of surplus appropriation by the state through the seizure of RDA's assets might be overestimated even on the regional scene. While there was some quarrel regarding the RDA's saw mill or the general topic of tobacco production (Ruvuma's main cash crop, which was regarded as much more valuable by regional officials than by the RDA members), SCHNEIDER see's the regional conflict much more as one of power relations. Personified by the difficult relationship between Millinga (who became MP in 1965) and Barongo, the Regional Commissioner, who was an appointed official directly responsible to the president, those tensions became obvious during Nyerere's visit to the Region in 1966, when he quite openly supported the villagers against the commissioner's accusations of neglecting tobacco production. In the bigger picture, this occurrence might be seen as indicating the level of threat that the successful villagers posed to regional and local officials like Barongo. If those RDA villages were more successful than the officials' development programs, much more cost effective and much more in favor of the president's plans, than it posed an immediate danger not only to the officials' power, but also to their livelihood as paid development "experts" (SCHNEIDER 2014: 49–52).

The aftermath and the reasons

According to SCHNEIDER, most of the assets confiscated on the disbandment of the RDA were quite quickly returned to the ownership of the individual villages: At least two of the tractors seem to have continued operating at Litowa and Matetereka, while the sawmill was returned to Litowa. He argues that placing several vehicles under the office of the regional commissioner was a temporary measure to facilitate the transfer to village authorities and cannot be used to demonstrate that the disbandment was about the appropriation of surplus by the state (SCHNEIDER 2014: 49).

When looking at the Central Committee that sealed the fate of the RDA, one has to take into account that the composition of the committee was changed in 1969 compared to the previous structure. From now on, representatives elected by the regional party branches on TANU would make up the majority of the committee (COULSON 1982: 270p.). This restructuring might have increased the importance of regional rivalries for the decisions of the committee – and the RDA certainly had its share of arguments with local and regional party big shots.

However, SCHNEIDER (2014: 52–58) points out, that the conflict between the CC members and the RDA was probably more determining for the fate of the association than the regional quarrels. The RDA's way of doing things threatened the CC in different ways: Obviously, the members had to be afraid of "rising stars" like Millinga, who had the ear of president and was one indication for them that they might have to fight to keep their positions of power. Much more relevant to SCHNEIDER, however, is the "clash of culture" specifically that of the culture of authority between the RDA and the CC members: as became apparent from various stories surrounding the ill-fated CC visits to the RDA villages (EDWARDS 1998: 15–18; IBBOTT 2014: 147–152), the members could no digest the villagers down to earth approach to authority. They felt offended and disrespected, when villagers worked on the fields instead of holding a welcoming ceremony, they could not process the way pupils at the Litowa School were taught to be critical and ask questions to authority, which they found appalling. Overall, it was the way authority and leadership was constructed at RDA that truly threatened to turn the elite's world upside down. They might have thought they could reduplicate RDA's success with classical authority but probably neglected how much the RDA style of authority was essential to the association's success.

The insistence with which CC members claimed TANU's supremacy in authority and agenda setting has to be understood in the historical and cultural setting: First of all, TANU was by self-definition a nationalist liberation movement, organizing all Tanzanians against colonial oppression. This led to the first de-facto and then de-jure one party state. Opposition to this rule (even if it was not about ideology, since RDA was at least as socialist as TANU itself) therefore had to raise suspicion. The frequent support by foreign donors and the presence of foreigners (especially those coming from NATO member nations, given the context of Mozambique's armed struggle) added to the almost paranoid fear of neo-colonial forces being on the move in Tanzania. At the very least, it gave those CC members, who were opposing RDA's independence, more than enough ammunition to attack the association. Culturally, RDA's radically democratic constitution and way of life was in stark contrast to the gerontocratic society of post-independence Tanzania: The seemingly "un-respectful" behavior of Litowa's students, for instance, therefore represented more than a nuisance. The CC members perceived themselves as the elders of society in many ways, and in the society which they lived in, elders were not to be questioned by students. Again, RDA thus represented to them an open attack to the society and the state they were living in (SCHNEIDER 2014: 58–63).

The RDA's ways of doing things in a self-organized and pragmatic manner raised opposition from the state bureaucracy and other authorities like the Peramiho mission, because it challenged the centralized and paternalist manner of organizing development that were in charge since the era of colonialism (MEYNS 1977: 165).

Apart from the issue of authority prevailing inside the association, it seems that the kind of development that RDA was achieving was not only denounced by officials out strategic interests. They more often than not simply could neither understand nor appreciate the initiative based approach used by the RDA villages. Officials were used to 3-5-year plans, big "operations", production targets and large-scale investment schemes. The association's seemingly day-to-day attitude to planning, therefore, did not fit into a development model where the agency to bring progress lay firmly in the hands of party officials, experts and "scientific" methods. Around the time of RDA's disbandment, Kisumu and other CC members thus promoted schemes like Mlale and Njoomlole[3] as the way forward. Development, in their eyes, could only be brought by modernizing the backward peasantry, not by the peasantry organizing themselves and finding their own solutions (SCHNEIDER 2014: 63–66).

After RDA's disbandment, villages like Litowa and Liweta fell into a kind of shock that resembled a collective depression. Newer, less established villages often folded all together. While most of the material resources returned to the villages and the government launched a massive investment campaign in the former RDA villages, the loss of the expatriates and far more the loss of ownership in the own project led to serious demotivation among the villagers. Relations with the state experts that came in were difficult and reinforced a top-down hierarchy, which the peasants did not support. Finally, the massive influx of new settlers from 1974 onwards destroyed what was left of the old RDA way of doing things. As SCHNEIDER cites EDWARDS (1998), Matetereka due to its remote setting was able to keep most of its original institutions going after the disbandment, but own research in 2015 showed that the last remaining cooperative stemming from RDA times folded there in 2000 (SCHNEIDER 2014: 66–68).

Under different circumstances, the RDA could have become a regional organization as part of a national peasant movement – a role that the old cooperatives from colonial times could not play. In any case, MEYNS underlines the limitations of such spontaneous farmer movements and emphasizes the need for a national coordination and leadership for socialist development on a broader scale. However, the bourgeois nature of Tanzania's ruling class made it impossible for them to keep the positive experiences of RDA in organizing communal development and collective agriculture and transport them to a higher – national – level. After all, the needs

---

3 Njoomlole originally was one of the first villages to engage in the mutual cooperation of the Songea Development Association (see above) and a founding village of RDA. However, its villagers came into conflict with the other members of the Association very soon and Njoomlole consequently left the Association. It later became the site of a government funded development schemed, which is reffered to here. For further information, see IBBOTT (2014: 247–251).

and wishes of the local peasantry depend on the question of the power in the state, since according to his view, only a different constitution of the state power would have enabled the villagers way of development to truly becoming a national policy (MEYNS 1977: 170).

The end of the RDA – and similar villages started in Tanga Region by TANU Youth League members – signified the end of Ujamaa from below. Despite his earlier ideological and practical support of the RDA against regional politicians, Nyerere underlined the importance of central state and party leadership for the Ujamaa village program. However, the effort to reproduce this type of voluntary cooperative economy and basic democratic political organization proved to be difficult on national scale. HEDLUND and LUNDAHL evoke a similar experience with the Israeli kibbutz, in the sense that while the kibbutzim were very successful in engaging their membership and producing tangible economic results, these cooperative villages never represented the majority of the Israeli population. The RDA villages, which were the only communal project resembling the kibbutz idea in Tanzania, found similar limitations on a larger scale: The model was not inherently attractive to the majority of the peasantry, and material incentives had to be provided by the state to convince the farmers to move into the new villages. In many cases where these incentives worked between 1971 and 1973, a patron-client relationship emerged between the villagers and the regional or local authorities, in which compliance by the peasants was bought by material benefits for the village in question. Even this approach, however, led to stagnating numbers of new village foundations by 1973 (HEDLUND & LUNDAHL 1989: 38–40).

Summary – The line of conflict between RDA and the standard way of development

With all this information on the history of the RDA collected, it seems worthwhile to take a comprehensive look at the line of conflict between the Association and other actors in Tanzania. As we have seen, it was both the development planning and the implementation of such plans that differed significantly between the RDA's villages and the standard way of doing things at this time in Tanzania. The author therefore proposes the following illustration of the line of conflict, which can be seen in Figure 4. On the right side of the figure, the common or "standard" way of development planning and implementation is shown as follows: The national leadership, i.e. the Central Committee of TANU and President Nyerere are the actors deciding on the outlook of national (development) policy. This policy is then enshrined in national (usually five-year) development plans and handed down to the Prime Minister's Office for implementation. From there it goes down to the Regional Commissioners, who are heading the Regional Development committees and from there on to the wards and villages. While even in those times, villagers were electing their own leadership, their role in the whole process was the implementation of those centrally arranged development plans, which they received from the higher-ranking institutions. Although in theory at least, there would also be a bottom-up stream on this side of the chart for the creation of the next national development plan (see

Figure 4: The conflict between the RDA and the standard way of development in Tanzania

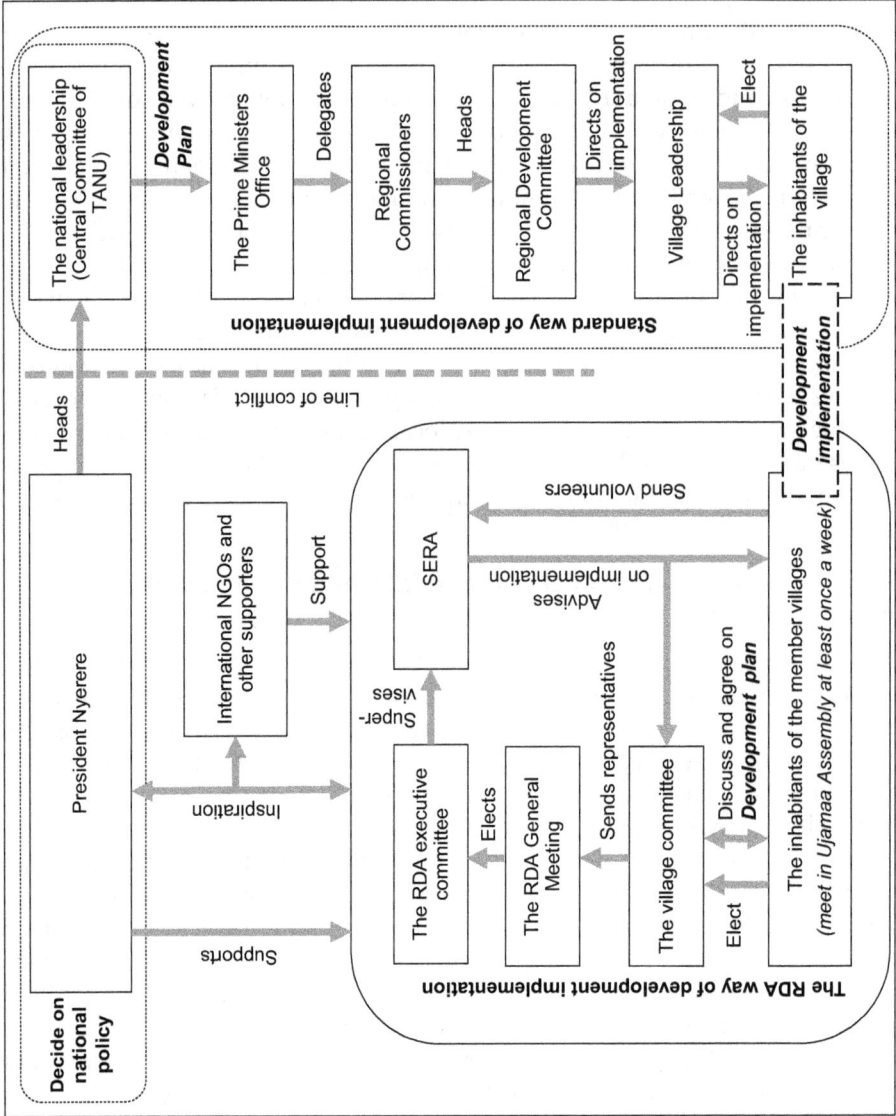

Source: own interpretation based on IBBOTT 2014; SCHNEIDER 2014; EDWARDS 1998; BRAIN 1977; MEYNS 1977; ABRAHAM & ROBINSON 1974

ABRAHAM & ROBINSON 1974: Appendix, p. 6), the general idea was that the central government (and party) institutions would develop the plans for the whole nation from the top down.

On the other hand, one can see a simplified version of the RDA's approach to development planning and implementation on the left side of the graphic. Here, the villagers and their elected leadership would discuss any development plan during the Ujamaa assembly and agree on how to implement it. Even issues as small in scale as the introduction of a new crop would be discussed by the whole village – and discussed again during implementation to organize the work plans, for instance. All higher structures of the RDA (the General Meeting, the Executive Committee and SERA) were mainly thought to have an advisory role in this model and would not direct the shape of development for each member village. This sort of independence was made possible through direct support from international NGOs, who provided capital and farm tools, as well as through direct endorsement from President Nyerere, to whom the RDA provided a great deal of inspiration for the further conceptualization of Ujamaa, as has been shown above.

So, while in both cases the task of actually implementing any (rural) development plans lay with the general village population, it becomes clear that their involvement in the planning of this development was much more direct within the RDA model. While Nyerere supported this approach, and wanted to implement it for the whole nation, the rest of the national leadership, and especially the regional officialdom, was on the other side of the line of conflict: These actors were not willing to accept the RDA's independence from their system of a developmental state, and in 1969 the conflict was ultimately solved in their favor.

3.3.2 Establishment of Ujamaa as a nationwide strategy

While the early post-independence policy on development in Tanzania has been widely categorized as "orthodox" continuation of colonial development models, the "real story" of Tanzanian development – at least according to the conventional narrative – would begin with the adoption of the Arusha Declaration in 1967 (JENNINGS 2003: 163). Therefore, it is imperative to this thesis to have a closer look at this policy paper, which tried to reframe development in Tanzania and to establish Ujamaa as a nationwide strategy.

The Arusha Declaration

The Arusha Declaration of 1967 (NYERERE 1967b) marked a remarkable shift in Tanzania's development strategies. It reunited the intended policy with the Ujamaa ideology, identified foreign dependence as one of the key threats to national independence and development, and switched the focus of development from industrialization in urban areas to rural development. As industrialization was seen as only possible with heavy reliance on foreign aid and investment, agriculture would be the new way forward. Since financial resources for the modernization of this sector were scarce – and the technological-heavy approach of the settlement schemes of the early 1960s had failed – hard work of the people was seen as the only resource available for development:

"A Poor Man does not use Money as a Weapon.
But it is obvious that in the past we have chosen the wrong weapon for our struggle, because we chose money as our weapon. We are trying to overcome our economic weakness by using the weapons of the economically strong – weapons which in fact we do not possess. By our thoughts, words and actions it appears as if we have come to the conclusion that without money we cannot bring about the revolution we are aiming at. It is as if we have said, 'Money is the basis of development. Without money there can be no development.' (…)
The development of a country is brought about by people, not by money. Money, and the wealth it represents, is the result and not the basis of development. (…)
A great part of Tanzania's land is fertile and gets sufficient rain. Our country can produce various crops for home consumption and for export. (…)
All of our farmers are in areas which can produce two or three or even more of the food and cash crops enumerated above, and each farmer could increase his production so as to get more food or more money. And because the main aim of development is to get more food, and more money for our other needs our purpose must be to increase production of these agricultural crops. This is in fact the only road through which we can develop our country – in other words, only by increasing our production of these things can we get more food and more money for every Tanzanian." (NYERERE 1967b)

Therefore, this willingness to work had to be mobilized: as developed in *Ujamaa – The Basis of African Socialism* (NYERERE 1962b), the Declaration would again emphasize the moral obligation to work and the individual motivation to contribute to national development. The Declaration stressed the importance of voluntarism, but also made it very clear that party and government would expect all citizens of Tanzania to take part in the new strategy. This inherent conflict between voluntary, individual decision and the necessity of comprehensive engagement in the collective task of developing the country would become obvious in the villagization of the 1970s (HEDLUND & LUNDAHL 1989: 24–28).

Indeed, early observers of the Declaration and its policies argued that it provided a much clearer definition of the kind of socialism implied by Nyerere's earlier writings on Ujamaa. Furthermore, it supplied a concrete vision of the policies necessary to attain the goal of socialism in Tanzania (MOHIDDIN 1972: 175). Instead of stressing the importance of the industrial sector for development, as virtually all economist and developmental approaches did beforehand, the Arusha Declaration sought the source of development for Tanzania in the agricultural sector. As a result of the problems concerning the pre-Arusha development policy, through the Declaration and subsequent policy papers, President NYERERE (1968a, 1968e, 1968f, 1968g, 1968h, 1975, 1977a) tried to increase the influence of the state in predefined core industries, as well as to employ stricter policies for receiving foreign aid and investment. Especially, the issue of foreign debt and negative capital flows in the previous five-year period was of concern for future international cooperation. On the other hand, investor protection was still granted, as the government did not see the possibility of raising domestically all the resources needed for development. While the stricter guidelines on the individual scale were a positive development, according to Rugumamu, the lack of a coherent state investment strategy or development plan undermined the Declaration's goals in regard to the nation's self-reliance (Rugumamu 1997: 124–129).

With the Arusha Declaration, the inspiration taken from the success of communal peasant-founded projects was transformed into a policy. On the ideological side, the new policy should rely on traditional values like the obligation to work and the collective ownership of arable land. Instead of continuing on a way of material incentives in order to capture and transform the peasantry and to integrate them into the national development effort, moral exhortation was now the approach to rural transformation. From the economic perspective, the capital-intensive strategies of the early post-independence era were to be replaced by moral obligation and ideological motivation. Considering the fact that this type of transformation would be a slow process, Nyerere himself repeatedly emphasized the need of patience and the paramountcy of voluntariness, adhering to Lenin's warning on the of use force to capture the peasantry. A three-step process was envisioned for this strategy of rural development: First, people should move together into villages, then they should start building their own houses and establishing private plots. After this, a communal shamba was to be established and finally, when the cooperative way of agriculture was fully working, those villages should be registered as multi-purpose producer cooperatives (Hedlund & Lundahl 1989: 35–37).

Arusha's approach to the peasant population

What arises from Schneider's discussion of paternalism in the Tanzanian development debate, is the question of who has the power to define development. Even if Nyerere was ahead of his time in many ways when it came to participation of the peasantry and the self-organized development of the rural poor, it was he who defined that this idea of basic democratic communal living was the way to develop. So, when the peasants showed reluctance in self-organizing themselves in this fashion, they were, in his eyes and the eyes of the developmental state, not executing their right to self-organize, but instead showing their backwardness and stubbornness, thereby defying their benevolent patron, which was the head of the whole Tanzanian development effort. In other words, the concept of rural self-organizing and rural self-sufficiency remained a central concept and project, not a peripheral one. Neither Nyerere, nor the state were willing or prepared to give the peasantry the authority to self-define their development. Ergo, if they could not be convinced by the state to move to Ujamaa villages and work together, they had to be coerced to do so for their own good. Thus, Tanzania remained a benevolent authoritarian (paternalistic) developmental state, in spite of the decentralising, participatory and radically democratic notions of the Ujamaa concept (Schneider 2004: 359–363).

McHenry described three basic concepts for achieving the kind of behavioral change in the peasant population, which the post-Arusha conception of Ujamaa aimed at. In his view, they would be the prerequisite to achieving any kind of development (i.e. a change of existing conditions) in rural areas: Persuasion, Inducement and Compulsion. Even under the colonial administration, change in the agrarian society of Tanzania was one main goal. Apart from integrating small-scale farmers into (colonial) market economy, concentrating peasants into permanent settlements was one of the main targets of this policy. When inducement (in form of wage labor on farms and plantations, for instance) failed to produce the expected results, compulsory resettlement was often employed. Given this background, the focus of Ujamaa policy on persuasion and inducement makes even more sense. However, the new policy still relied on the envisaged benefits of concentrating the rural population. While migration was traditional to many rural societies in Tanzania, permanent settlement was not. The attempt to persuade the peasants of the new ways of Ujamaa was only partly successful and the party, in particular, proved to be more useful in policy formulation than implementation. The latter task was mainly placed in the hands of government officials, often replicating the bureaucratic and non-participative approaches to resettlement known from colonial times (McHENRY 1979: 205–207).

ECKERT (2007: 259p.) sees many continuities in the behavior of the bureaucratic elite of Tanzania stemming from colonial influence. While this elite was by no means homogenous and while many leading personalities (first and foremost Nyerere himself) were convinced of their new ideology and saw themselves as acting on the principles of the humanistic ideal, the paternalistic view on the rest of the population was ubiquitous. Therefore, discontent with the government's plans and strategies was frowned upon, and independent organizations were more and more centralized under the leadership of TANU. It was their old role as "cultural brokers", which they had internalized as colonial bureaucrats that was now interpreted as an obligation to bring backward peasants to modernity and rid urban entrepreneurs off their individualistic tendencies. Fear of loss of control implied the tightening grip of the bureaucracy on all aspects of life and the wish of the new ruling class to control all measures of development. In a way, the Ujamaa ideology of rural development reflected the European view, in which the right place of a true African was in the countryside. In this context, the construction of Dodoma as new capital is seen as an example for the self-perception of a new African ruling class, which would build lush cities for themselves and rural villages for the rest of the population.

COLLIER et al. argue that many of Tanzania's agricultural policies can be explained by the fear of the emergence of a class of Kulaks. These policies include the limitation of landholdings, monopolization of market networks and the introduction of communal production. However, all of these measures turned the terms of trade against the normal peasant and did not in any way foster their productivity or improve the economic situation of the rural population. In the view of the authors, if a Kulak is defined as a farmer who cultivates significantly more agricultural area than would be possible by the family's labor through the use of hired labor, then there would be a negligible number of Kulaks present in Tanzania, even in 1986. The main reason for this is seen of the abundance of land in Tanzania, which hindered the emergence of a Kulak class in the first place. By limiting the legal trade links however, the Tanzanian policy did not favor the normal peasant, but those few farmers who were able to establish connections to the black market and increase their economic base not through increased field sizes, but through profit from trade. This effect actually increased rural inequality (COLLIER et al. 1986: 130–134).

When looking at the local political economy of Ujamaa villages, PUTTERMAN found that it was usually the (slightly) wealthier and better educated peasants that held leadership positions at the village level. At the same time, there was a level of distrust in leadership qualities and especially in the correctness of collective work records – aggravated by the fact that many villagers were illiterate and therefore could not ensure that the village officers noted down their work effort in a correct manner. This, together with the poor managerial skills that led to poor results in collective farming, might have contributed to the observation that small-scale individual farmers found it easier and more attractive to adapt to a hierarchically organized enterprise like a plantation as a wage laborer, than to engage in a collective village enterprise. At least in a hierarchical company, wages were paid and management was perceived to know what they were doing. In villages where the leadership was perceived as good and trustworthy by the inhabitants, the share of collective production was significantly higher (PUTTERMAN 1986: 238–243).

The bureaucratization of Ujamaa

At its core, the Ujamaa ideology is of revolutionary nature. In fact, the transformation of the whole society based on communal control of production and cooperative organization of the producers would also have implied a complete change in trade relations and the overcoming of exploitative relations between peasants and buyers. However, the concrete Ujamaa failed to do so. Even more decisively, the omission to establish clear policy guidelines for the implementation of Ujamaa villages and rural producer cooperatives left the responsibility for creating those strategies to the local and rural bureaucracy. This led to a bureaucratization of the whole Ujamaa policy, in such a way that bureaucrats could more or less freely decide how to interpret the items of motivating and educating the peasantry. Consequently, the set-up of the villages was more concerned with the presentation of number of people moved or communal area established, than with enabling peasants to create viable producer cooperatives. Due to this bureaucratic approach to rural transformation, Ujamaa fell short at even trying to change the peasant agriculture and transform the rural economy on a cooperative basis. The patron-client relationship typical of this period of Ujamaa development added to the difficulties (BOESEN et al. 1977: 164–166).

Overall, it was seen as easier to switch to an approach of "Ujamaa by projects" (see also PUTTERMAN 1986: 234–236), in which non-agricultural enterprises could be presented to the authorities as working cooperatives. These Ujamaa projects, in fact, did deliver some additional income to the peasantry, but they were usually operating in sectors which the "peasantry-cum-lumpenproletariat" had engaged in before in an informal way. Therefore, they also represented an attempt by the bureaucracy to extend their control over additional spheres of the peasants' livelihoods. Overall, in its failure to address the existing power relations and social formations in the areas it attempted to change, the Ujamaa policy fostered its own bureaucratization. This bureaucratization tightened the state's grip on the peasantry, rather than empowering them to develop their own future under the possibilities of Ujamaa (Bo-ESEN et al. 1977: 166–169).

In his conclusions on the colonial influence on the African bureaucrats and the leaders of the newly independent Tanzania, ECKERT does not see much proof for individuals having inner conflicts between tradition and modernity. According to the author, most of the Africans employed and educated by the colonial administration were very prudent navigators in the nexus between the two worlds they were exposed to. Accordingly, the apparent dichotomy between modernity and tradition would be more of a European concept not experienced by the African bureaucrats. However, when the small African elite took over the state after independence, the contradiction between the strong, interventionist welfare state they envisioned and the comparatively weak, yet authoritarian state they inherited from the colonizers became visible. While the new leaders of Tanganyika were used to the colonial practice of giving orders and directives, the peasantry, which made up the majority of the population, was used to reacting to authoritarian directives with reluctance and to circumnavigating officials. Neither group had much experience in basic democratic organization of development. Overall, ECKERT does not see too much reason to debate whether the colonial heritage or the incapability of the new leaders after independence is to blame for the failure of postcolonial development. Yet, he argues that the specific development of the Tanzanian state after independence cannot be analyzed without analyzing the colonial influence on its development strategies and the behavior of the people who tried to implement them (ECKERT 2007: 263–266).

The discourse on Ujamaa and Nyerere himself – especially in his more idealistic writings like *Freedom and Development* – precedes a large amount of thinking on participatory issues in the development debate. While concepts like participatory development and community development only came into vogue in the 1990s, the policy of *Ujamaa vijijini* underlines the importance of voluntarism and involvement of the peasants in the creation and development of the rural ujamaa communities. As much of the literature suggests, this idealistic approach by Nyerere was not taken seriously by the Tanzanian officialdom, thus promoting the idea of Nyerere as mostly uninvolved in the coercive turn of Ujamaa in the 1970s. However, SCHNEIDER suggests that a lot of the "self-defeating"-turn from voluntary persuasion to forced resettlement did indeed stem from Nyerere himself. Apart from the question of the President's involvement in this policy shift, SCHNEIDER poses the wider question of the nature of the conflict between intended participatory rural development and factual state authority over both the definition and the practice of rural development in Tanzania (SCHNEIDER 2004: 344–347).

3.3.3 Villagization

Probably the best known and certainly the most controversial practical implication of the Arusha Declaration was the concept that the entire rural population should move from scattered settlements – which were still prevalent in 1967 throughout Tanzania – into nucleated villages that should subsequently be transformed into multi-purpose producer cooperatives. While the concept of the village as the base of rural and national development was already enshrined in the Declaration itself (NYERERE 1967b), the practical implementation of the villagization policy can roughly be divided into three phases:

The first phase between 1967 and 1970 was characterized by an emphasis on voluntariness of the peasants and attempted to motivate their movement mainly through moral exhortation and their presumed commitment to the building of the nation. Three steps were planned to create these cooperative villages: First, the farmers had to be motivated to move to the new villages, secondly some of them were to be convinced to start cooperative farming on a communal shamba, and finally the expected success of this communal farming should persuade all the farmers that all activities were better done communally. Indeed, there were a total of 531,200 people moving to 1,965 Ujamaa villages within these three years – mainly in the economically weaker regions of Southern Tanzania, such as Lindi, Mtwara, Ruvuma and Iringa. In economically stronger regions such as Tanga, Kilimanjaro, Arusha or Lake Victoria, however, only 1% of the population moved to Ujamaa villages. Furthermore, the number of peasants moving began to decline after the first rush of highly motivated farmers (WATZAL 1982: 8, 10).

However, the progress of creating Ujamaa villages based on the voluntary involvement of farmers went slowly, and production on the communal fields remained below expectations – and below the level of production on the private plots. In spite of the expressed commitment to a long-term process, the state became increasingly reluctant to wait for tangible results of villagization at the beginning of the 1970s (HEDLUND & LUNDAHL 1989: 37p.).

Contemporary literature describes the issues that came with the uneven distribution of population within Tanzania. In order to establish working Ujamaa villages, people could no longer live in sparsely populated settlements. On the other hand, people would have to be moved from densely populated areas like Kilimanjaro to the empty plains, which posed a whole new set of issues, concerning the location of the new village sites and their environmental conditions. Consequently, farmers without ideological background were hesitant to move. There were various concepts on how to move them anyway. But some of these, like making unrealistic promises to the peasants, proved to have detrimental effect. If people were promised a lot of services, they tended to become passive and would wait for the services to arrive. If they didn't, people would become uncooperative towards further development projects. Even worse was the use of force, according to DARAJA: No village established by forced movement had ever been successful. Generally, those villages where local leaders consulted experts on the preconditions of the chosen site (soil, water, etc.) had a much higher success rate than those villages established in unsuitable natural environs (DARAJA 1971: 48–50).

Nevertheless, the increased use of force would signify the beginning of the second phase of villagization from 1970 to 1973. In the end, 2,028,164 people, or 15% of the total population of the country, would live in 5,628 villages. Even this progress was seen as being too slow, however, and in September 1973, the TANU conference decided that all the population had be organized in villages by the end of 1976. This third phase of villagization resulted in the (mostly coercive) movement of 2.5 million people in 1974 alone; and by the end of 1975, 9 million people lived in Ujamaa villages. Villagization, especially in the 3ʳᵈ phase, was poorly organized. Many farmers were to be moved at the height of the growing season, which led to the loss of almost all the harvest on their old fields, while none of them could manage to grow a substantial harvest on the new fields before the next dry season (WATZAL 1982: 10p.).

Over these three phases, the concept of "working together" in cooperative villages appeared to become less and less important, while the concept of "living together" in nucleated settlements became the core of almost any action concerning villagization. Thus, the plan to collectivize the agriculture and establish Ujamaa villages as producer cooperatives became secondary to the movement of people (JUMA 1976: 36p.). The deemphasizing of communal work increased from 1972 onwards and staff-villager relations became ever more bureaucratic. The concentration of rural development policy would henceforth lie on the creation of villages with controllable layout, not the (change of the) mode of production (FREYHOLD 1979: 57p.).

In this regard, McHENRY (1979: 208–210) observed that the component of living together, i.e. moving people to villages, went from a persuasion to an inducement to a compulsion phase, while the element of working together did so much less. He cites several reasons for this observation: Moving together was seen as a prerequisite for working together, not the other way around. The political costs for the central and regional government officials in charge of the compulsory movement were much lower than they would have been for local government to force people to work together. The same could be said about the resources for inducing people by material gains. Secondly, forced resettlement took place out of "pragmatic" reasons like the aftermath of the flooding in Rufiji, long before Nyerere set a deadline for resettlement in 1973, so compulsory means were seen as successful when it came to numbers.

Thirdly, there were doubts about the effectiveness of communal farming, and with the food shortage of 1974-76, food production on the private plots became paramount over the (small) additional income an individual farmer could make on the communal plots. McHENRY also cites the low participation of women (responsible for the families' food supply) as one indicator of this phenomenon. When communal work took place, by and large it was non-agricultural work like the construction of communal buildings or the creation of community shops. This kind of work happened in almost all villages and was seen as more effective. Overall, McHENRY underlines the fact that communal living was seen as much more important by the administration and therefore much more (and harder) means were used to get people to move than to get them to work together (McHENRY 1979: 208–210). Basically, this is a great example of how NYERERE's (1974a: 28) famous words "you can drive a donkey to water, but you cannot make it drink.", proved to be prophetic.

While Nyerere is best known for his idealistic writings on participation and voluntarism in rural development, his role in the coercive turn of Ujamaa and Villagization should not be underestimated. After all, he never got out of his role as a benevolent teacher of his people, leading the way to development. That meant that although he preached the freedom of people as a prerequisite for development, he would not accept his people (or students, in that case) disregarding his vision of a modern Tanzania by "stubbornly" ignoring the guidance of the state and the party. Furthermore, Nyerere himself grew increasingly impatient with the slow progress of villagization, a policy which was developed by himself as a cornerstone of any rural development. So, under the impression of "the window of opportunity" for socialist transition closing, he supported Operation Rufiji and other, even bigger, mass resettlements. At the same time, Nyerere's impatience increased the pressure on local and regional officials to produce tangible results in Ujamaa implementation. With the number of villages founded and people moved being the most-tangible outcomes, coercive measures were adopted more and more regularly. Ideally, the lower officials would do the "dirty work" of compulsory movement without too much publicity, while Nyerere could go on preaching the importance of freedom and voluntarism. However, at least according to SCHNEIDER, Nyerere was very much responsible for the forced villagization campaigns, both by direct endorsement (as in Rufiji) and by the implicated results of his demand for quicker results on the ground (SCHNEIDER 2004: 366–371).

Although Nyerere was very clear in his writings on *Socialism and Rural Development* (NYERERE 1968f: 130–132) that persuasion was the method to be used to get people to move to villages, the slow progress in this process led to the increased use of inducement in the form of aid or social services. Finally, the technical separation between "village" and "ujamaa village" from the mid-1970s made it feasible for the administration to use compulsion to get people to villages before they became ujamaa villages (MCHENRY 1979: 208).

In their postscript to the study of Ujamaa villages in the West Lake Region, BoESEN et al. express their concern with the switch to large scale villagization in 1973. The main explanation for this change in policy is seen as government's concern regarding food security implied by the economic crises of 1973/74. Specifically, the authors deliver a stern warning that the new policy of Operation vijiji would signify that new village sites would now be chosen only based on infrastructural requirements, like road access, and not on agricultural suitability like under *Ujamaa vijijini*. The organization of agriculture through cooperative farming was no longer put on the agenda as well. Therefore, the new policy would run at the risk of actually endangering the productive capacity of the Tanzanian agriculture and therefore worsening the food security situation of the country (BOESEN et al. 1977: 170–172).

ECKERT sees some structural continuities in Tanzania's policy of village development and the style of indirect rule under the British. Instead of the ethnic or clanwise arrangement of self-sufficient economic territories, the new concept of Ujamaa villages implied the cooperative village as basic unit for self-reliance. Compared to other rural resettlement projects and forced collectivization, e.g. in the Soviet Union or South Africa, the villagization campaign had a definite social engineering and welfare impetus. Nevertheless, Ujamaa's vision of a better world would rely on forced resettlements, if the "backward" peasants couldn't be convinced to voluntarily join the biggest relocation program in Sub-Saharan Africa. ECKERT is not very clear in differentiating between pre- and post-Arusha policies, and criticizes the settlement schemes of the early post-independence period and the later Ujamaa village concept on the same grounds of inefficiency in planning and neglect for the ecological properties of the centrally chosen settlement sites. Overall, the dichotomy between an urban based political elite and a reluctant peasant population would lead to the centralization of modernization attempts and the paternalistic behavior of politicians and bureaucrats towards the peasantry (ECKERT 2007: 253–256).

Faced with the slow progress of resettlement by persuasion or inducement and a severe drought hitting the country from 1973, it was decided to accelerate the villagization of the entire rural population with the help of force. Furthermore, the state ran short on material resources that could be used for intensifying inducement. Without any discussion with the people affected by this decision, the new program was started in September 1973. Making use of the armed militia and later the military itself, people were loaded on trucks and resettled against their will. On many occassions, the old settlements were burned down, in order to impede any possibility of moving back. With the help of these atrocities, the state reached its goal of relocating the rural population by 1975. However, while the first stage of Ujamaa development (moving together) could be fulfilled in this manner, the use of compulsion (mostly in the form of fines) to coerce people to work together as planned in the second stage of *Ujamaa vijijini* proved to be virtually impossible. Apart from those impediments, HEDLUND and LUNDAHL see an even more crucial problem with the state led version of Ujamaa development: An approach based on voluntary involvement of the peasantry in cooperative agriculture could only work in small groups of motivated individuals. This intrinsic motivation of the group made any discussion on material gains secondary. Even if the motivation of one individual might not be enough on a given day, peer pressure by the group would it make impossible to stay in the community as a "free rider" for an extended period. The use of material inducement as documented for the early phases of centralized Ujamaa policy, however, creates a contradiction between the material benefit used to encourage people to move and the motivation to work cooperatively, which would have been needed to achieve Ujamaa's development goals. The use of force from 1973 onwards aggravated this dichotomy. Furthermore, the new settlements created by these measures were much bigger than the successful villages of the RDA (above 250 compared to around 40 families), which created a significant free rider problem not known from the early cooperative villages. In conclusion, the authors acknowledge that the idea of Ujamaa could only be successful in practice in RDA type settlements, but doubt that there would have been enough peasants who would have been intrinsically motivated to join such village to make the model work on a national scale (HEDLUND & LUNDAHL 1989: 41–44).

The switch to compulsory resettlement in 1973 was accompanied by a switch of focus away from communal farming towards increased production: The Iringa Declaration of 1972 put emphasis on the mechanization of agriculture and the creation of larger farms, not collective agriculture. By-laws reintroducing compulsory cultivation in 1974 underlined this change in approach to rural development. The Ujamaa Village and Village Act of 1975 further differentiated between Ujamaa villages as collective producer cooperatives and villages simply as places for people to live together. Henceforth, Tanzania's rural development policy focused on numbers of production and people moved, not on the way in which people lived or worked together (JENNINGS 2002: 511p.).

With the introduction of compulsory villagization in 1973, the will of the Tanzanian state to establish control over the peasantry became clearly visible. As the new village sites were now almost exclusively chosen according to infrastructural requirements and accessibility, the aim of resettling the rural population into controllable nucleated settlements was decisively demonstrated as the top priority of development policy. The second goal of increasing agricultural production became increasingly eclipsed by this logic of state control. Much like in colonial times, state control over the peasantry was seen as a prerequisite to implement the state's modernization and development agenda – and this control could not be executed with a population living in scattered hamlets. Economic policy in the new villages reflected this urge for state supervision, as paid government officials increasingly took over the planning of agricultural production on the village level, while big state controlled cooperatives were established as the only available trade link for the farmers. Accordingly, the idea of administration became synonymous with control during the 1970s (ECKERT 2007: 256–258).

Concerning the objective of using the nucleated Ujamaa villages as vehicles for development, the results have been mixed. Generally, the provision of health services and education facilities is mentioned as a success of the villagization program, since these kinds of social infrastructures could not have been established with the same efficiency without the idea of "moving together". The same goes, to a lesser extent, for the construction of access roads and village water supply, which was made easier by virtue of a more concentrated population, but could not be completed everywhere by the mid-1980s. On the other hand, the environmental situation of many new villages appeared to be precarious, partly due to errors in planning, partly due to negligence by agricultural officers and the persistence of agricultural practices not suitable for the now higher concentration of population in a smaller area (PUTTERMAN 1986: 268–270).

When it came to establishing villages as agricultural producer cooperatives, the results were mostly negative, although many of the impediments in this endeavor appear to be derived from the badly functioning cooperative commerce system on the national level, especially concerning the large parastatals. Cooperative enterprises in non-agricultural sectors, however, had been established in various ways on the village level, and many of these enterprises produced tangible results as income generating activities for the village. Yet, there were tendencies in the management of these enterprises to work more hierarchically than the village constitution would dictate, and some of them were seen more as private enterprises by a few villagers, than as a communal enterprise owned and operated by the whole village community (PUTTERMAN 1986: 270–274).

Overall, however, the prospects for communal development in Tanzania would have depended more on the political economy of the nation, than on the level of village organization. PUTTERMAN therefore emphasizes the need to reorient the agricultural policy on the national scale in a way that actually supports cooperative organization on the village level, for instance regarding crop prices and market opportunities for cooperative produce. The setting of the 1980s, in which farmers had to rely on illegal black markets to sustain their families, fostered a behavior of individualism and competition among the peasants, which was certainly counter-productive for the emergence of a well-functioning collective sector in the villages (PUTTERMAN 1986: 274).

3.3.4 Economic difficulties and the end of Ujamaa

LAL describes the different phases of analyzing the Ujamaa project in different times and emphasizes the need for the recognition of different views over time. While many of contemporary Ujamaa analyses from the 1960s and 70s concentrated on the weaknesses and failures of the Ujamaa ideology and much more of its practice, these scholars usually showed a compassion towards the project in a way which suggests that the main interest was on how Ujamaa could have worked. In this endeavor, they often simplified the different influences and power relations, especially concerning the capitalist-socialist or imperialist-third world dichotomy. After relative silence throughout the 1980s, a new stream of research focused on the failure of Ujamaa, albeit with an implicit or explicit backdrop of neoliberal thinking, in which state intervention as such was almost vilified and Ujamaa was mostly presented as a classic example of why such state led development projects were bound to fail. Contrary to the earlier stream of thought, those scholars usually oversimplified the contradictions inside the Tanzanian society, as well as the contradictions on a global scale, which had all contributed to the apparent failure of the Ujamaa project. Finally, as LAL argues, in the early 21st century emerged a new wave of research on Ujamaa and the postcolonial period of development, which tries to analyze this period in a broader manner. However, even this school is often characterized by a consent on the impossibility of alternative development and an almost relenting view on the big, sometimes utopian development policies of the postcolonial era. Yet, LAL emphasizes that the problems on the ground have not changed that much compared to the period of early independence and that the prevalence of poverty for the majority of the rural population in Tanzania should warrant the emergence of a new compassion for seeking alternatives for global capitalist development, especially at the level of the state (LAL 2015: 236–239).

Conceptual flaws of the Arusha Development Model and its consequences

In his reflections on the ten years following Arusha, NYERERE (1977a) presents a picture of a policy that, despite the best intentions and efforts, failed to deliver: It came in time to stop the nascent capitalism after independence, but it could not achieve enough ideological compassion or compulsory compliance to make it work. Neither were the party leaders and other authorities adhering to their own principles like the leadership code, nor were the peasants motivated enough by the incentives to create the envisioned progress in agriculture. For HEDLUND and LUNDAHL, Ujamaa was not able to elicit enough true participation by the people. Only the movement into nucleated villages could be counted as successful, but that was also made possible by the use of force (HEDLUND & LUNDAHL 1989: 29–31).

Buntzel makes several criticisms of the key concepts for the practical implementation of the Ujamaa policy (or lack thereof). Overall, he underlines the rudimentary idea of collectivization and the reliance of the Ujamaa ideology on traditional values of communal agriculture, which were supposed to be sufficient to mobilize peasants to move together and form collective villages at a large scale. Ujamaa takes a clear stand on the conviction that the agricultural transformation has to be supported by the peasantry and that the implied development has to be implemented according to their needs and decisions (NYERERE 1968f: 127–132). However, there was no clear concept on how this voluntary mobilization was to take place, apart from minimal material incentives that could be provided by the state. Thereby, Ujamaa relied heavily upon the construction of a communitarian pre-colonial society, engraved in the traditions of tribal society – much like the Russian Narodnik movement (BUNTZEL 1976: 330–333).

LAL sees the inherent contradictions of Ujamaa as coherent within the context of the global developmental discourse and international power relations. As such, the internal contradictions of Ujamaa (between state authority and basic democracy, participatory development and central development projects, for instance) are reflective of these contradictions on a bigger scale. This is one reason why so many scholars of different developmental schools found what they sought in the Ujamaa project. Rather than seeing these contradictions as mutually exclusive however, LAL suggests treating the inner dialectics of Ujamaa as representative of the dialectics of the postcolonial developmental discourse. In her view, Ujamaa was neither a purely African concept opposed to the Western concept of a developmental state, nor a pure "African rhetoric" justifying neocolonial modernization from the outside. The struggles with the outside world and within the post-independence Tanzanian society were reflective of existing and changing power relations on different scales and resulted in the differing threads of Ujamaa in ideology and practice (LAL 2015: 231–234).

Economic development after villagization and its connection to agricultural collectivization

Up until 1972, crop production remained stable under *Ujamaa vijijini*, but the drought from 1974 and the fast rush to create more Ujamaa villages from 1976 deteriorated the situation. While the Asian and Indian middlemen were abandoned, old trade cooperatives were also abolished. However, the new centralized State Trading Cooperation and the Ujamaa shops on village level were not up to the task. Both the inefficiency of these new institutions and the stronger pressure from the central state led many peasants to abandon state production and retreat to subsistence farming instead (SCHICHO 2009: 183p.).

In a widely criticized paper, LOFCHIE (1978: 470–474) identified the internal opposition of the peasantry as the main cause for the unsatisfying economic results of villagization. As largely independent crop producers, they did not see benefits in joining the new villages, which explained the amount of force necessary to move the whole rural population to the villages. Yet, LOFCHIE did not discriminate between the effects of the forced movement of millions of farmers on the one hand and collective agriculture as such on the other, arriving at the conclusion that the idea of collective socialist agriculture was the reason for the supply crisis per se.

Other authors, like WATZAL (1982: 9p.) are critical of LOFCHIE's thesis of "too much socialism" as the root of the crises, since a agricultural growth rate of 2.3% annually from 1967 to 1973 showed that socialist rural development could indeed match the population growth and produce what the people needed. The supply crisis of 1974-76, however, would directly relate to the 3rd phase of villagization (i.e. the forced mass movement of farmers to new villages). This view on the supply crisis is underlined by BRIGGS (1979: 701p.), who emphasizes that it was the rapid compulsory movement of the peasantry during the last phase of villagization from 1973 onwards which virtually put a hold to agricultural development – and not the communalization of agriculture that had been promoted nationwide since 1967. The drought from 1974-76 and the issues in motivating people to work cooperatively intensified the shift in attention of policy from communalization to production rates.

This trend continued throughout the 1980s. Production on the communal plots remained at only 8% of production in an average village, while 20% of village labor was attributed to these plots. Failure to redistribute the fruits of communal labor among the farmers was one of the issues that led to the demise of communal agriculture. If the revenue of communal production was not directly redistributed, but used as a sort of tax income to enable the village to make investments in infrastructure or similar things, collective work effort was even lower (PUTTERMAN 1986: 234).

The way communalization was performed in Tanzania in the 1970s and 80s, however, was not only low in productivity and participation, it was also organized in a top-down manner: Paid party officials, who were the village managers at this time, were responsible for setting production targets and work plans, often without much participation by the village assembly. Minimum acreage laws were imposed by the central state without any peasants' participation. The whole era gives an image of a central and local bureaucracy increasingly distant from the farmer on the ground. According to HEDLUND and LUNDAHL, this is derived from the paternalist view of the Tanzanian officialdom enshrined in Nyerere's ideology, as well as the class interest of a bureaucratic ruling class who, after 1967, had neither an interest in liberal market economy nor in extended farmer participation. This sort of centralized communalization, however, was bound to fail in both production targets and peasant involvement in development (HEDLUND & LUNDAHL 1989: 44–50).

In fact, the way in which production targets were centrally enforced on Ujamaa villages and the peasants were told to work harder, without considering environmental, social or technical circumstances could be seen as a direct continuation of the colonial administration's attitude. And it certainly did not enhance compliance on the village scale (FREYHOLD 1979: 48).

Yet, this was not the only factor coming into play that nurtured the peasants' reluctance to see communal farming as an alternative to their economic stagnation: Over several decades, they had been exposed to all sorts of government projects and development policies, usually with meager results, more work, and no participation on their side. For them to embrace a new style of cooperative enterprises which was again controlled by the central government (e.g. in the form of minimum acreage

laws) would have taken a lot of persuasion or inducement – and most of all a successful example of communal agriculture which they could see for themselves. As it
was, the "normal peasant" felt better represented by a rich and esteemed farmer of
his own village, who dealt with outside government officials and provided help or
wage labor as a benevolent patron. Given the personal experience of the majority of
peasants up until the mid-1980s, this behavior seems the most rational choice – and
it certainly did not help the establishment of any kind of village cooperative agriculture (Putterman 1986: 244–246).

Furthermore, even after the Arusha Declaration, the central state gave priority to
parastatal agricultural companies, not the Ujamaa villages when it came to agricultural investment. More attention was given to cash crops than to food crops, despite
the stated policy emphasizing the increase of production for internal consumption
(Freyhold 1979: 93).

It is the observation of Putterman's study, that the nationalization of the crop
market and the establishment of a monopoly for big parastatals like the National
Milling Company has actually had counterproductive effects concerning collective
agriculture. The prices paid by the parastatals tended to be significantly lower than
prices that farmers could achieve on the black market, which were in fact in the area
of 180-350% higher in the mid-1980s. Additionally, the parastatals tended to pay
farmers late or even below the agreed prices. Since the produce of the communal
farms had to be sold through these channels, productivity on these farms would
have to be in the area of three to four times more productive than on the private plots
to be economically beneficial to the individual peasant. While the author admits that
limiting factors like oil prices and the war with Uganda may have limited the state's
ability to pay market prices to the farmers, he also sees this situation as a proof of the
neglect in the active promotion of collective agriculture. Low consumer prices and
surplus creation for a small industrialization strategy seemed to outweigh the interest of viable prices for agricultural producer cooperatives. This might be attributed
to both the attitude of anti-incentivism and the interest of the bureaucratic class in
extracting surplus created in the agricultural sector for investments and revenue
creation (Putterman 1986: 253–255).

Despite several different attempts at restructuring after independence, such parastatals, as well as the marketing cooperatives for agricultural produce, remained
under the direct control of the central state. Many peasants felt that the cooperatives
were arms of the government. They were not understood as something of their own
belonging. Peasants were not involved in the democratic control of these cooperatives and their use was not fully understood. Rather, farmers joined for social and
economic benefits offered. Therefore, they could not act as a vehicle for inducing
ideological commitment towards collective agriculture (Lyimo 2012: 52).

The practical implication of the state's unwillingness or inability to pay higher
prices to the peasants was that it discouraged the intensification of collective agriculture as a development strategy. Instead of freeing the farmers from the profit
interest of middlemen by nationalizing the crop market and creating a communal
agriculture throughout the country, the opposite was achieved: Individual peasants
were even more reliant on black market middlemen and had to take worktime out

of agricultural activities in order to find buyers and circumvent the restrictions of a controlled market to earn a living income (PUTTERMAN 1986: 255p.).

This tendency is underlined by findings of a study within the Southern Highland Region – including some of the former RDA villages – conducted in 1981/82. In the case study area, maize was the main food crop and at the same time the main source of cash income for the village households. However, selling maize to the National Milling Corporation (the only official market in 1982) was rather seen as a last resort, due to its low purchasing prices. Around 50% of the sample households reported selling crops through unofficial channels (SCHULTHEIS & SESHAMANI 1982: 4.14).

Additionally, PUTTERMAN sees the bureaucratic style of policy and development implementation prevalent in Tanzania as impeding the emergence of collectivism on the village level in several ways: In an approach like Ujamaa which, at least in theory, depends on large-scale political mobilization and voluntary participation, overcoming the peasants' experiences of authoritarian colonial administration was an uphill battle to begin with. However, the widespread paternalistic attitude of the Tanzanian officialdom certainly did not encourage the acceptance of outside input by the peasantry. Development strategies were still implemented in a style of directives rather than suggestions among equals. In practice, the lack of experience in participatory decision-making on the side of the villagers could not be overcome by more changes dictated from outside (PUTTERMAN 1986: 247p.).

So, in spite of having a higher social legitimacy than the colonial administration, the central government of independent Tanzania was not able to create the necessary degree of ideological commitment within the peasantry. During colonialism, the central authorities were mainly seen as responsible for the economic functions of the territory, and in the postcolonial situation "the popular emotional commitment to the new government was both short-lived and at least partially dependent upon the fulfillment of economic promises and desires." (NELLIS 1972: 188). Although several steps – including the abandonment of the chiefdoms as administrative units – were taken after independence in order to establish the social and ideological leadership of the central state, this only added to the reluctance of the peasantry to comply with new strategies that were seen as much as external to their livelihoods as the colonial ideas of development had been (NELLIS 1972: 187–189).

The reliance on TANU – and later CCM – as a vehicle for democratic mobilization did not help either, as most of the local party officials showed the same paternalistic attitude towards the peasants. While the introduction of democratic institutions showed some remarkable results, participation in village assemblies remained low and reproduced a bureaucratic manner of communal organization, for instance in the case of organization of labor on the communal farms. One result of this was the start-up problem, which emerged when bureaucratic village officials planned communal shambas which were too big for the peasants' ability or willingness to work. Another example was the use of communal produce as tax income. Overall, the bureaucratic mentality of the Tanzanian officialdom was reflected in the behavior of village officials and could not induce participation of the peasants in collective agriculture. A patron-client relationship was the usual setting between officials and peasants (PUTTERMAN 1986: 248–250).

The economic advantages of collective agriculture, which were mostly seen as self-evident by the Ujamaa policy, were thought to be enough material motivation for the independent peasants to join the collectives. However, as BUNTZEL criticizes, those possible economies of scale were hard to achieve in a high labor – low capital agriculture like the peasant economy prevalent in Tanzania at that time. Organizational benefits through association in cooperative forms, on the other hand, would only be possible after a (socialist) modernization of agriculture. This means that the economic benefits, which were supposed to drive the peasants into Ujamaa collectives, could only be realized after the establishment of these collectives, and therefore could not be used as a reason to join them in the first place. Even the small and poor peasant had a lot to lose after all, namely his independence as a subsistence producer with his own land. Overall, the Ujamaa implementation would lack almost any coherent plan on how to achieve the envisaged transformation of the rural economy, let alone concrete plans adapted to the environmental, economic, and social conditions in different regions. It did not take power and class relations into consideration and relied too heavily on an idealized image of a peasantry motivated by an equally idealized communitarian past (BUNTZEL 1976: 333–337).

BALDUS underlines the fact that the creation of cooperative villages in Tanzania did not emerge spontaneously but was the result of a conscious ideological decision to establish cooperative agricultural production as a means for national development. However, he concludes that the practical experiences indicate that ideological mobilization in itself is not sufficient to induce the social and economic change aspired for in the Ujamaa policy. Material incentives and tangible benefits of engaging in collective production have to be perceived by the peasantry in order to mobilize them for cooperative development (BALDUS 1976: 29–32). In the period following villagization, productivity on communal plots was significantly higher in villages where an incentive system based on individual work contribution and distribution of the produce was in place. The other village circumstances (e.g. geographical properties) had no significant influence (COLLIER et al. 1986: 131).

PUTTERMAN does see one major reason for the failure of the Ujamaa policy to implement a meaningful collective agriculture in its prevalent anti-incentivism. While this attitude that would put moral and political exhortation and the use of force ahead of material incentives for the individual peasant would not be constitutive of the Ujamaa ideology, the author sees this phenomenon as being noticeable all over the Tanzanian approach to development. In practice, this means that material benefits were usually not taken into consideration when issues in the organization of labor or the unsatisfactory participation in communal agriculture arose at the village level. However, in his view, if the individual peasant cannot see any tangible results from collective work effort, it is not surprising that work on the communal shambas is in decline and that the agriculture of the country continues on its classical development of a few rich farmers and a majority of subsistence farmers. In this view, openly denouncing the material demands of peasants is in no way socialist and cannot lead to the envisioned development goal of a socialist economy. On the contrary, PUTTERMAN sees the use of anti-incentivism as indicative of the strong implicit opposition of the Tanzanian ruling class to socialist transformation: The successful rich peasants were praised for their work effort, while the normal peasant was frowned upon for not working for the community without any material incentives (PUTTERMAN 1986: 250–253).

Aid dependency instead of self-reliance

Apart from these issues concerning the implementation of collective agriculture, the Ujamaa strategy also failed to end the aid dependency that had been problematized in the Arusha Declaration (NYERERE 1967b). Almost ten years after the Declaration, foreign aid was still seen as perpetuating the colonial system of unequal exchange, in which Tanzania had to trade in cash crops for industrial goods (COULSON 1976: 26).

As RUGUMAMU (1997: 188–200) illustrates through several examples, the increasing donor influence on Tanzania's politics assured that the foreign investments mostly helped the donors self-interest or companies from donor countries. Inefficient planning and insufficient foreign exchange resources hindered the ability of large-scale development projects to run at capacity, while the influx of foreign aid replaced domestic resources that would have been needed to sustainably run the state machinery and its social services. At the same time, foreign debt and negative trade balances became an ever-greater burden for Tanzania throughout the 1980s, and exports switched back almost completely to traditional agricultural products. Simultaneously, growing tax burdens on peasants made them return to subsistence production, lowering even more the country's cash crop production. As inflation brought official wages below survival levels, the second market emerged as the only option for people to survive, and the public sector almost naturally had to turn to increasing corruption.

Almost twenty years after the Arusha Declaration, COLLIER et al. conclude that the high reliance on foreign aid and the increasing foreign debt put Tanzania's goal of self-reliance into question. While the Ujamaa villages proved to be successful as providers of social services, they were much less so as agricultural producer cooperatives. Tanzania was still characterized by a non-diversified rural economy with mainly subsistence production. Furthermore, the country showed a pattern of rural isolation, with few transport or market links between its rural populations, even compared to other peasant economies in Africa. Stratification according to educational status was still prevalent, with few secondary education institutions, and even fewer secondary graduates willing to return to the villages (COLLIER et al. 1986: 127p.).

In RUGUMAMU's view, the big influx of aid and the attractiveness of the Tanzanian model helped the ruling class in Tanzania tremendously in establishing themselves, as well as enabling the state to achieve quick progress in social services after Arusha. This sustained international support, disregarding the shortcomings in the practical implementation of the praised policy gave the political leaders the leverage and the resources to push through with policies like villagization in the 1970s. It was only at the end of the 1970s, when the dependence on foreign aid became apparent, that policy backfired for the political class of Tanzania. It also led to widespread patronage and the establishment of a big, but inefficiently managed, state sector and administration, which produced a large number of well-paid managerial position, but little productivity (Rugumamu 1997: 183–186).

3.4 Neoliberal shift and Structural Adjustment Programs from the 1980s onwards

At least from the beginning of rising oil prices in the 1970s, Tanzania was facing increasing difficulties with its trade balance, as the slow speed of industrialization made it impossible for the country to substitute its imports, and its primary export commodities were losing value. The vision of self-reliance appeared increasingly utopian (Shitundu 2002: 143–145). External shocks like the oil crises, as well as internal problems like the unsatisfying effects of the villagization project increased the economic downturn within the country. Stagnation in food crop production put the country's food security in danger, while its agricultural exports increasingly lost competitiveness on the world market. In 1981/82, the national economy reached its lowest point since independence, and the continuing abandonment of village farms illustrated the fading hopes of the rural population in the Ujamaa policy (Bryceson 2010: 77–81). However, driven by the high ideological commitment to its own policy, the Nyerere government were reluctant to search for alternative policies and, in the eyes of some observers, failed to respond adequately to the ongoing crisis (Hydén & Karlstrom 1993: 1397–1400).

In any case, in 1982 the country had to appeal to the International Monetary Fund for assistance, and subsequently had to give in to its demands for the liberalization of its economy. Although the Ujamaa policy was never formally repealed, deregulation and the reduction of state expenses became the new goal of national policy. In 1985, Ali Hassan Mwinyi replaced Nyerere as the President of the United Republic of Tanzania (Mair 1996: 12). Despite the ongoing economic decline, there was almost no opposition movement to the ruling party. As was the case with previous policy changes, most of the discussions on liberalization and economic change were led within the party – and between CCM's socialist and technocratic factions. In 1991, the leadership code of the Arusha Declaration was officially repealed, and in 1992, the one-party state was abolished with the admission of opposition parties (Mair 1996: 23).

The stagnation of agricultural productivity under the Arusha policy was one of the main reasons for the shift in macro-economic policy in Tanzania that started in the 1980s. Increasing international debt and subsequent fiscal limitations forced the state to abandon its controlled agricultural policy. In May 1982, a task force was founded by the Tanzanian government to analyze the current system of agriculture and land tenure in the country and to develop recommendations for changes to the system. According to the task force analysis, there were three different systems of agricultural land use operative in the early 1980s: First the so-called homestead farm, or individual shamba, on which a household produced for their own consumption at their own choice of crops – with the produce belonging to the family. Secondly, the block farm, which was actually a large, communally owned, plot of land subdivided into individual plots for each family. And thirdly, the village farm, on which work was supposed to be collectively carried out by all able-bodied inhabitants of the village – the original Ujamaa farm. All three types of land were under the tenure of the village as provided by the village and Ujamaa village legislations of 1975. The task force found that land tenure and activity-planning under these circumstances was not clearly structured, that collective farms were seen as a burden, rather than as an asset by most villagers, and that the structure of land management was not conductive to private initiative. In particular, the short-term allotment of plots on the block farms was not seen as encouraging long-term investment by the individual farmers (Gondwe 1986: 32–34).

A first statement for the liberalization of agricultural markets was published in 1983. Most important for the future of the national development policy was the devaluation of the Tanzanian Shilling, a cut of subsidies for parastatals, and overall market liberalization, including the lifting of import restrictions. Additionally, price controls were repealed and consumer prices rose as a result. Agriculture was supposed to undergo a process of commercialization to overcome the apparent stagnation in productivity, and tax incentives for private investment were installed to further this concept. Overall, the fiscal restraints implied by the low liquidity of the Tanzanian state meant a continued retreat from agricultural production by the state, whose new role was seen as enabling private investment and production. Productive cooperatives or independent collectives, which were not under state control, like in the early days of independence, were no longer an aim of the rural development policy of Tanzania (URT 2013b: 1).

As a result of its findings, the task force recommended a considerable change to Tanzanian land tenure, with an emphasis on enabling long-term land leases by the individual peasants and long-term allotments of plots on the block farms. It did not yet recommend the change to a private land ownership system in the sense that an individual farmer would be able to buy his or her land from the village and keep it regardless of its use. However, the general tendency of the task force and the emerging new agricultural policy was the preposition that collective agriculture had failed and that measures had to be undertaken to encourage private initiative and investment. From what capital, the small-scale farmers were supposed to make these investments was an issue not touched by the task force in 1982. In 1983, the new agricultural policy (AGRIPOL) was officially adopted by the CCM one-party government and aimed to implement the recommendations of the task force as well as those of privatization and market liberalization by the IMF and the World Bank (Gondwe 1986: 35p.).

This new economic policy did not only affect the agriculture of the country: Had international tourism long been frowned upon under the impetus of national self-relaince and economic independence, the new imperative of private investment and foreign currency needs meant that the natural resources of Tanzania's National Parks and Conservation Areas were now to be tapped. This led to a phase of expansion for the country's tourism sector, which became one of the most important sectors of the national economy by the end of the 20th century. It also unlocked new revenue sources for the Tanzanian state (JOB & METZLER 2003: 13-15; see also JOB & WEIZENEGGER 2003). While the state retained its supremacy on natural resource management, and was able to benefit from the direct and indirect effects of nature based tourism, the concentration of the bulk of tourism activities in few areas, such as the Northern Circuit and the emerging "tourism capital" of Arusha, not only induced new regional economic disparities. It also put increasing pressure on the environment of the most renowned destinations, such as the Serengeti National Park and the Ngorongoro Conservation Area (SCHMID & JOB 2011: 52–54).

In retrospect, the quick and externally induced shift from state control in all sectors of the national economy to the promotion of private initiative and investment was never thoroughly planned or implemented by the Tanzanian state. On the contrary, the central state just retreated itself from agenda setting with the hope that international advisors would present a coherent strategy, and international donors and investors would alleviate the shortage of capital for investment in industry and agriculture that had hampered national development before. However, with the shift of agenda setting to those international actors, privatization dynamics went largely unstructured and increased regional disparities and the economic inequalities in Tanzania as a whole. The new concept of private economy was never able to replace the state as an entity for implementing equally distributed national development across all sectors (HEWITT 1999: 390).

Together with economic liberalization and privatization came a quick retreat of the state from social service provision, and the emerging vacuum led to increasing issues in social services, especially in the rural areas of Tanzania. Furthermore, regional disparities became accentuated, as it was the already more advanced regions with better market access that would profit the most from the new opportunities of the emerging market economy, while more remote areas were left behind (LIMBU & MASHINDANO 2002: 49–51). Figuratively, the reforms imposed by the World Bank and IMF, the quick effort of privatization and liberalization of markets – in short the advent of neoliberalism – actually replaced the empty shelfs that had become the norm in the country's Ujamaa stores with full ones – but only very few would be able to buy what was on them (SCHICHO 2009: 186p.).

In fact, food and consumer prices rose drastically after the macroeconomic changes of the 1980s, which significantly affected the large majority of the Tanzanian population in a negative way. All households, except for the richest urban households, experienced significant losses in welfare throughout the 1990s and the 2000s, with the losses of the latter decade being even higher than before. These welfare losses, which were the highest among the poorest strata of households, can mainly be attributed to rising food prices with only very small increases in real income throughout the same period. Prices for non-food products were also increasing, but did not have the same impact like the rise of food prices in real terms. Combined with the lack of a redistributive tax system, the privatization policy of the 1980s therefore actually led to a real terms welfare loss for the majority of Tanzanians (LEYARO et al. 2010: 35).

These increasing inequalities did also have a strong spatial component: While at least some poverty reduction could be achieved in the urban areas of the country (with regards to a basic-needs approach) in the 1990s, the effects in the rural areas were almost negligible. In this sense, the new development strategy of Tanzania showed a strong urban bias (FAN et al. 2005: 16).

On the producer side, the new agricultural policy fell short of inducing the positive effects promised by the advocates of economic liberalization. By the end of the 1990s, neither labor productivity nor yields for the main food crops had increased, compared to the years of economic crisis from 1979-84. The same was true for production per capita. All of these indicators had either stagnated or even declined, compared to the pre-liberalization era. In fact, the price fluctuations under the new open market environment and the increasing issues in the procurement of farm inputs (caused by the retreat of the state from the distribution of said inputs), led many small-scale farmers to retreat to subsistence farming or to pursue additional economic activities to sustain their family's livelihood. Overall, the new policy failed to create any form of economic progress for the majority of the rural population of Tanzania (SKARSTEIN 2010: 124p.).

Instead of having to rely on poorly paying state cooperatives or the black market, like before, most small-scale farmers did not have any market left for their produce afterwards. When agricultural growth occurred, it was courtesy of the few better-off farmers who were able to access credits through private financial institutions and hence could invest in their business. So, while many new buildings and roads in the urban areas implied the return of economic growth and individual opportunities through foreign investment, the peasants of Tanzania were left stranded in the periphery (PUTTERMAN 1995: 320–322).

Another contributing factor to this increased differentiation in the era of liberalization was seen in the new trends emerging in crop choice and organization of farm labor. New market opportunities induced the cultivation of faster growing, but more labor-intensive crops, which necessitated the employment of more additionally hired farm hands in shorter periods. As the system to organize such excess labor became increasingly contractualized by the bigger producers, it became more difficult for the smaller farmers to find people willing to help them out on the basis of customary social obligations. This further impeded their ability to compete on the new private markets and amplified economic inequalities (PONTE 2000: 1025).

Regarding social service provision, similar tendencies could be observed throughout Tanzania: While until the end of Nyerere's presidency, health facilities would exclusively be seen as a task of the state, the Mwinyi administration encouraged the introduction of private hospitals and health service providers as part of the structural reforms demanded by the IMF. While this actually increased the total number of health facilities in the following years, these private operators did not choose to develop their operations in the areas which had the highest need for better health care, but tendentially opted for the slightly better developed regions which would promise a higher number of paying customers. During the Nyerere administration, on the other hand, the scarce resources of the Tanzanian state were concentrated on creating health facilities in the neediest areas of the country. As a result, health care coverage dropped significantly after the economic shifts of the 1980s, if seen from a spatial perspective (BENSON 2001: 1914).

3.5 Recent development strategies and policies in Tanzania

Despite the large extent of the structural reforms in economy and political system throughout the 1980s, there has never been a complete brake away from the rhetoric of Ujamaa or the glorification of Nyerere as the Father of the Nation in Tanzania. Actually, even after the end of the one-party state in 1992, CCM has dominated all elections in Tanzania and was able to establish something which MORSE (2013) has called a competitive hegemony: Even if there are relatively free and fair elections between multiple parties in Tanzania nowadays, the extent of party structure and involvement, especially in rural areas, which CCM has inherited from the times of Ujamaa, is unmatched by any competitor. And as Nyerere's leadership was neither excessively autocratic, nor in any ways tied to his family for succession, it was the party itself which inherited his political legacy. Furthermore, it was able to achieve a remarkable ability for self-correction and adaptability even through the economic changes of the 1980s (MORSE 2013: 658–661).

The continuing strength of CCM is also seen as the result of the weakness of opposition parties, who suffered from internal conflicts and poor leadership, especially in the formative period of Tanzania's multiparty system in the second half of the 1990s (MPANGALA 2004: 13–15). Furthermore, the dominance of CCM in practically all areas of civil society (due to the fact that it had controlled all organizations in this area before the abandonment of the one-party state), enabled the party to create a true fear of opposition parties among the population. On the other hand, the ruling party continued to receive widespread support for its policies by the electorate, who credited CCM with having managed the economic transition in the best interest of the country (MUSHI 2004: 52–54).

Indeed, the focus of the party on rural development and paternal care for the peasantry were not empty words after all, and material redistributions to the countryside enabled the party to establish a stronghold among rural voters as yet untouched by the opposition. Therefore, even three decades after the end of Nyerere's presidency, the political scene in Tanzania is dominated by the discourse within CCM, and elements of Ujamaa can be found in virtually all of the recent development strategies of the country (MORSE 2013: 670–672).

With that being said, policy papers issued by the respective CCM governments continued to emphasize private initiative over the collective approach of Ujamaa. The Tanzania Vision 2025, which still acts as the overall policy of national development, states a "developmental mindset" as well as "economic and political pluralism" as the driving forces of achieving high standard livelihoods throughout Tanzania. While adjusting to the international development mainstream of good governance, private investment, and the rule of law, the paper is characterized by a sort of opportunistic approach when it comes to attracting international capital to the country. At the same time, the social service component is upheld, but intended to be a shared responsibility of private organizations and the state, which is supposed to provide them in a "cost-effective" manner (URT 1999: 15p.).

Lal's study on postcolonial development in the Mtwara region had a special interest in the echoes of Ujamaa discourse on development. She found them in local resistance to central state infrastructure projects like a gas pipeline, constructed with Chinese support, linking Mtwara with Dar es Salaam. On different occasions, the Tanzanian government took to a discourse of national development interest to defend itself against accusations of land grabbing and resource extraction made by local inhabitants, who were enraged by the negligible benefit the project would have for the region the resources were based in. In the broader picture, the author attests a revival of Third World rhetoric and supposed South-South cooperation and solidarity in justifying the big foreign investments from both China and South Africa into Tanzania in the first two decades of the 21st century. Similarly, President Kikwete's 2010 *Kilimo Kwanza* (agriculture first) program for rural development tries to make rhetorical connections to Ujamaa's focus on agriculture as the base of national development. However, many observers have deemed this green revolution style program to be only focused on short-term commercial development of already advanced farmers. In their view, a program with a focus on the majority of still small-scale farmers dubbed "Wakulima Kwanza" (farmers first) would have been much more meaningful for people centered rural development (Lal 2015: 227–231).

Indeed, the policy initiative of *Kilimo Kwanza* stresses the new focus on private public partnership instead of state interventions. It tries to involve all types of farmers (small, medium, large scale), while at the same time proclaiming a shift in agricultural investments from classical cash crops to food crop production, which are intended to be increasingly marketed. The overall approach is a large-scale push for agricultural modernization through the provision of better seeds, better access to fertilizers, and investments in farm tools and machinery. However, how exactly the policy tries to access the different scales of agricultural production all at the same time, remains unclear – and the only official document provided by the Tanzanian government on the policy itself is a presentation held in 2012 (Ngaiza 2012).

It is probably more useful to see Kilimo Kwanza as a public campaign of raising political support for agricultural development with a strategy based on the 2005 Agricultural Sector Development Program (ASDP). The cornerstones of this program are agricultural investment, capacity building and market creation on the local and national level. In a continuity with earlier privatization programs in Tanzania, local and national components of the program are no longer seen as a direct task of the state, but are supposed to be implemented by state accredited private service providers. There are also major infrastructural investments set out in the program, like a national irrigation scheme, which was also supposed to be implemented as a public private partnership (URT 2005a: 15–21).

The current Agricultural Marketing Policy of 2008 defines the responsibility of the state for the creation of legislation and an institutional framework conducive to economic growth in this sector, while the private sector and international development partners are designated to operate the market for agricultural products as such. Although support in the provision of farm inputs and credits is still considered to be a task of the government, the direct control of the crop market is no longer seen as a mission of the Tanzanian state – in contrast to the Ujamaa era (URT 2008: 24p.). This general division of roles, into a coordinating and overseeing one for the public sector on all levels of government and the role of investing and producing on the side of the private sector on all scales (from the small individual farmer to the big agribusiness company), is also reiterated in the most recent national agricultural policy of 2013 (URT 2013b: 35–42).

Furthermore, the operation of cooperatives and SACCOs is envisioned to be more business oriented. A reform program launched in 2005 is supposed to help this sector to adjust itself to the new liberalized market environment by supporting capacity building and managerial skills within the cooperatives. Additionally, the central government pledged to enhance the financial situation of these institutions by providing credits and fostering the reduction of existing debts (URT 2005b: 22–37).

More than 50 years after independence, agriculture is still the most important sector when it comes to employment in Tanzania, with around 75% of the country's total workforce. It produces 24.1% of the nation's GDP and roughly 30% of its export earnings. An average agricultural growth rate of 4.4% per year means that production increases quicker than the population (2.6% p.a.). However, there is still not enough surplus production for significant increase in wealth or poverty reduction. Food crop production creates about 65% of the agricultural GDP (with maize the most important one at 20% of the total agrarian GDP) and cash crops 10%, the rest is produced by livestock keeping and forestry activities. Food and cash crop production is responsible for around 70% of rural incomes (URT 2013b: 2).

The National Agricultural Policy of 2013 identifies 44 million ha of land as suitable for agricultural activities, of which only 24% (10.8 million ha) were cultivated in 2012, generally by subsistence farmers, who would cultivate between 0.2 and 2.0 ha on average, with relatively low productivity. The policy envisions the expansion of the cultivated area, as well as the intensification of production in more densely populated areas. Within the recent agricultural policy, there is no clear focus on smallholder production (as was the case with the Arusha Declaration, for instance), but rather an approach open to all scales of agricultural producers, including large-scale farming (URT 2013b: 2p.).

The main constraints for agricultural development are seen in the low productivity of land and labor, as well as production inputs. For instance, maize productivity is only around 3.9 t per ha on average, while there would be a potential of 6 up to 7.5 t per ha. Similarly, average paddy production in Tanzania is at 2.0-3.8 t per ha, with a potential of 6-8 t per ha. This low productivity is manifested by the underdeveloped use of irrigation potentials, shortage of farm inputs like fertilizers and improved seeds, and limited access to financial services and capital for agricultural investment. In 2012, only around 450,000 out of the 10.8 million ha under cultivation were under irrigation. This high reliance on rain-fed agriculture makes the Tanzanian agriculture vulnerable to the highly variable rainfalls, inducing high uncertainty in production and possibly in national food security targets. Necessary investments, however, are hard to come by, especially for small-scale farmers, as the rural credit business is seen as a high-risk-low-return venture by commercial banks, which supply over 90% of all rural credit in Tanzania. The poor state of rural infrastructure – especially the road network – amplifies the difficulties of small-scale producers in increasing their production. Furthermore, the shortage of technical support, plant and animal health services and environmental degradation are seen as constraining factors. Last but not least, the policy identifies weak producer associations as well as the insufficient involvement of women and youth as hampering development in this sector. While it acknowledges the detrimental effects of insecurity in land tenure and the depressed prices for primary commodities on the world market, it also criticizes the limited involvement of the private sector into agricultural development in Tanzania – possibly implying a policy more open for private (foreign) investment (URT 2013b: 3–5).

The National Agricultural Policy as well as Tanzania's latest five-year development plan also underline the value of focused investment strategies in predefined agricultural growth corridors, which are identified in climatically favorable regions of the country. In these corridors, market production and larger-scale investment by national and international private companies are encouraged and accompanied by infrastructure investments by the central government, either directly or by public private partnership (URT 2011b: 65p.).

One of these "show-case" corridors is the Southern Highland Agricultural Growth Corridor (SAGCOT) which follows the main road between Dar es Salaam, Mbeya and Zambia and is meant to attract large-scale international funding by combining the favorable climate conditions of the Southern Highlands and the relatively good connection to international markets via the TanZam highway and (theoretically) the TAZARA railroad. The Project was launched together with *Kilimo Kwanza* in 2010 and is still receiving ample support from various international donors (SAGCOT 2015; The World Bank 2016).

Indeed, this project can be seen as an example for the ambivalence of Tanzania's recent agricultural policy: While other projects, like the Tanzania Bread Basket Transformation Project (URT 2011a), directly aimed at peasant production have repeatedly stressed the importance of smallholder food production for the Tanzanian economy as a whole (e.g. through investments in structures like better storage facilities, voucher schemes for farm inputs and support in market access on the village level), the big publicity and the big investment by state and international community literally bypasses the Southern Highlands of Ruvuma. SAGCOT only focuses on investment in places where there already is market access, and leaves it to other programs or donors to care to create one for other places. So, despite the recurring praise for the peasant as the backbone of national agriculture and economy, the national agricultural programs seem to sidestep the vast periphery and concentrate its efforts on the few corridors which are considered to be a worthwhile investment for international capital.

Overall, agricultural production in Tanzania has shown a steady increase in the first decade of the 21st century, as has the national GDP in general. However, this growth has continued to be unevenly distributed across both space and income groups, as the economic differentiation of the population continues to grow. While some achievements have been made in reducing food poverty, the overall effect of Tanzania's economic growth on poverty reduction has remained limited. This is especially true for the poorest strata of the population living in peripheral rural areas. As such, the economic development of Tanzania throughout the 2000s cannot be considered to be pro-poor (HAVNEVIK 2010: 267–269).

4   The Research Process

Research for this project commenced in December 2013 upon securing scholarship funds courtesy of Friedrich-Ebert-Stiftung (FES). It started with a thorough analysis of the available literature with the aim of revisiting the most important elements, steps and changes of the Ujamaa development strategy and implementation in Tanzania. In the next step, a first preliminary field visit was undertaken in May and June 2014, in order to establish the institutional linkages to the St. Augustine University of Tanzania (SAUT) at Mwanza and to arrange research clearance on the side of the Tanzanian Commission of Science and Technology (COSTECH).

The second field visit took place in September and October of the same year, this time with a focus on literature research at the main library of the University of Dar es Salaam, with its rich (and otherwise mostly inaccessible) reservoir on contemporary Ujamaa literature. In the following months, the decision was taken to concentrate the empirical research on the Ruvuma Region in Southern Tanzania, as its plentiful history of basic democratic Ujamaa implementation (see above) appeared to hold the most valuable information for the core aims of this study (for a detailed description of the case study selection process, see chapter 5).

With the decision on the case region taken, the two remaining field visits in February/March and August/September 2015 were designed to focus on the generation of (mostly qualitative, see below) data on the local and regional experiences of various stakeholders with the period of Ujamaa, as well as the subsequent changes in development strategies in Tanzania. Going out from Songea, the administrative capital of Ruvuma Region, the empirical process was started with a series of guideline-based expert interviews with government representatives and various NGOs. Afterwards, preliminary visits to the villages identified as potential case study sites were taken. For three of those villages – namely Litowa, Matetereka and Mbingamharule, longer field visits could be arranged, which were conducted during the last phase of empirical research in August and September 2015. All of the field work within Ruvuma Region was performed with the support of the Archbishop James University College (AJUCO) at Songea, the local branch of SAUT in this area.

4.1   Methodological considerations: How participatory and how extractive?

Given the somewhat problematic history of Tanzania's development strategies regarding the conflict between local initiative and central control which has been discussed throughout chapter 3, this research faced the issue of how to achieve a comprehensive picture of the local perspective on these changing strategies, without confining it to the purely extractive accumulation of data. More specifically, the challenge would be seen in minimizing the researcher's effect on the data itself by eschewing the structural bias that comes with pre-arranged methods like big questionnaires prepared without participation of the research subjects, in this case the inhabitants of the case study villages. A more detailed critique on the limitations of such "classical" forms of rural investigation has been presented by CHAMBERS (2008: 1–24).

In the search for more participatory and less extractive ways of empirical research, two basic concepts were considered for this thesis. Firstly, the *Rapid Rural Appraisal* (RRA) (CHAMBERS 1981) technique, and secondly, the *Participatory Rural Appraisal* (PRA) methodology, as described by CHAMBERS (2008: 85–104), which has become increasingly popular in the field of development research within the last two decades. In fact, PRA has been developed by practitioners and researchers on the basis of the RRA technique since the early 1990s. First clarified by CHAMBERS (1992) and CHAMBERS and CONWAY (1992), PRA and RRA continue to be influenced by CHAMBERS (2007a, 2007b), as well as CORNWALL et al. (2001) and other authors, many of them based at the Institute for Development Studies (IDS) at the University of Sussex, UK.

While stating the importance of the participation of the local population, both in the collection and the dissemination of data, PRA does not stick to a fixed set of inquiry instruments. On the contrary, it "embraces" methodological plurality and "eclectic" opportunism, i.e. it demands the researcher to look for the most appropriate and most participatory method of gathering data, but also to strive for a true understanding of the research object. "Classic" methods like big questionnaires are discouraged, while new methods – both qualitative and quantitative – are commonly created while performing field research. Also, PRA tries to analyse fewer cases over longer periods of time, instead of accumulating masses of data in a short timeframe. Being traditionally associated with more qualitative forms of research, many contributions have proven the ability of PRA methods to also retrieve quantitative information, with the same or even better accuracy than "traditional" research methods (CHAMBERS 2008: 167–191).

In fact, both RRA and PRA share a common set of principles, which are based on the main goal of achieving the reversal of the learning experience. This means, that the researcher takes the position of the student, who wants to learn from the experiences and knowledge of the local community and not the role of a teacher or expert in his or her field of competence. Therefore, flexibility in the pursuit of information and reliance on local informants is encouraged. In order to ensure the scientific value of the emerging results, triangulation of data from different methods is also paramount. From the perspective of the limited resources available for this research, a balance of possible trade-offs suggested by those techniques provides an additional incentive (CHAMBERS 1992: 13p.).

The main difference in the application of either RRA or PRA has been seen in the difference of those applying them and the overall goal of the appraisal as such. While RRA has been used mainly in the scientific context for the use of understanding local realities, PRA is more inclined to use by NGOs and practitioners, who also aim to empower the participants of the study by sharing and discussing the results in the process (CHAMBERS 1992: 11p.).

While continuing to be popular in this context, the application of PRA has also been seen as critical in practice, as there have been tendencies to narrow the definition of participation on the exact adherence to a predefined "participation catalogue" – implying that participation has to be conducted according to external use. This also implies the necessity to address the issue of who exactly is "doing participation" and for whom these results are used (CORNWALL et al. 2001: 7–13).

Coming from this tendency observed in the implementation of the PRA paradigm, CHAMBERS (2007a: 25–28) has argued for a new "eclectic pluralism", which would focus on the core theme of participation and involvement of local stakeholders, rather than to certain brand of research pattern of an exact catalogue of methods. Discussing the same issue, BERGOLD and THOMAS (2012) emphasized that the most basic question in order to consider a research project as participatory or not would be the question on who controls the enquiry at each stage of its design and implementation.

Therefore, the following chapters will try to illustrate the research process with regards to the interaction between the researcher and the local research partners and informants, in order to provide an impression on how participatory and how extractive the empirical stage of this thesis has been.

4.2 Whose research is it anyway?
Between intrinsic interest and local perspectives

With these propositions, the question emerges whose interest and whose reality determinates the design of the research as such. Considering the basic principles of participatory appraisal of any kind, it is supposed that it is the local perspective which should be the basis of enquiry (CHAMBERS 2007a: 19–21).

Nevertheless, one has to consider the fact that the idea for this thesis itself, as well as the focus on the issue of Ujamaa did not come from a local request of any sort, but emerged from the interest of the researcher himself in the respective topics. Therefore, both the overall theme as well as the selection of the case study area (see below) were determined by factors external to the research subjects themselves. In fact, the specific topic of Ujamaa history could be considered as an intrinsic interest of the researcher (TELLIS 1997: 1p.). Consequently, the issue of control over the research progress becomes even more eminent.

The conflict between external and internal perspectives, however, is not unique to human geographic research. In the area of cultural studies, these different perspectives have been defined as the emic approach on the one hand, which represents the description and meaning making of events by insiders or "native members of the culture" (LETT 1990: 130) which is the focus group of a respective research. In contrast, the etic perspective would be the interpretation of an event by somebody external to said culture – in the scientific context, this would usually be the researcher foreign to a certain social group (DARLING 2016).

In order to reconcile this apparent discrepancy between participatory pretense and intrinsic (yet external) motivation with regards to methodological practices – i.e. to use the right methods and ask the right questions – this research has employed an iterative model of empirical research, which has been used in a similar fashion by Darling (2016). Within this framework, the research starts with theoretical and methodological considerations by the researcher. Yet, as the scientific work enters its empirical phase, these research tools may be amended following insiders feedback. In a zig-zag pattern, initiative by the external researcher will be informed by local knowledge, which will determine the next step to be taken.

In the case of this study, the intrinsic interest in Ujamaa was followed up by literature research, which led to the emergence of Ruvuma as the main region of interest and the RDA as one of the main themes for further inquiry. Once arrived in the case study area, local institutions like the partner Universities, NGOs and regional authorities were approached in order to specify the research topic and identify villages suitable for more in depth case studies. In the next step, local village authorities and village based key informants were approached with the help of local research partners. This not only led to the concretization of research questions, but also to the identification of further key stakeholders, like contemporary witnesses and the farmers' groups of the respective villages.

In conclusion, it could be said that the intrinsic interest dominated the first phase of empirical research, while for the actual field work in the villages, local informants took the lead. It was they who described their understanding of Ujamaa, their ideas which informed the coding of the information and their impetus on emphasizing some things, and not others, which shaped the further structure of this thesis.

4.3   Detailed description of methods

After these rather philosophical considerations concerning the design of the research project as such, the subsequent chapters will present a more detailed description of the concrete methods which were used in the field.

4.3.1   Guideline-based Expert Interviews

Qualitative interviews are among the most common methods in the initial stages of any research. Usually, they are conducted with the aim of getting a first impression of the research subject, identifying areas for further investigation and gathering additional contacts within the research area. As the dialogue is one of the most basic elements of everyday communication, it is usually also the easiest way for the initial approach to predefined stakeholders (Meier Kruker & Rauh 2005: 62p.).

For this task of initial exploration of the research topic as well as the research area, the expert interview is seen as one of the most useful tools. "Experts" in this sense can be any group of persons, who are seen to have specific knowledge about the topic and/or the area. As is the case with most expert interviews in human geographic research, the interviews for this study were prepared in the form of guideline-based interviews (MEIER KRUKER & RAUH 2005: 64–71).

Those guidelines were designed based on the theoretical knowledge of Ujamaa and development history in the region presented in the previous chapters. Preidentified groups of stakeholders included NGOs performing development activities in Ruvuma as well as government authorities on regional, district and village level. Further experts were included in the interviews as research progressed, based on information gathered during the field visits. These included the Abby at Peramiho, the National Food Reserve Agency (NFRA) in Songea and YARA, a private company engaged in the provision of fertilizers and other farm inputs in the region. Furthermore, other informants like school principals were addressed in the form of guideline-based expert interviews.

In general, the guidelines were developed during the field visits directly before the interviews (usually on the day the appointment could be confirmed), but informed by the overall knowledge at the respective time of research. Guidelines were kept the same for groups of actors like NGOs, to ensure comparability for later analysis. Individual expert interviews had their own guideline, specific to the respective organization or position. In all cases, some issues of overriding importance were always included in the guidelines, such as the activities of the respective organization, the time the interviewed person has been working at the position of interest, their personal or institutional understanding of development, challenges and Ujamaa history, as well as the perceived changes since the end of Ujamaa. The detailed guidelines for each sort of expert interview can be found in Appendix 1.

Furthermore, the first stage of interviews with the NGOs and government institutions during the field visit in February and March 2015 was used to gather personal contacts and additional information on the eventual case study villages. During this visit, six expert interviews were conducted with NGOs in Songea, two with regional and district government authorities, one with NFRA and one with a former Member of Parliament, also in Songea. One interview was conducted at Peramiho Abby, one with a former villager from Matetereka at Peramiho, and one each with the village government of Litowa and Mbingamharule. Apart from the last two, all of these first-round interviews were conducted in English or German (one of Songea's NGOs, SNC). The interview with the chairman of Litowa was held in Kiswahili with the help of a local translator, while the one in Mbingamharule was conducted entirely in Kiswahili by the author. Another expert interview was conducted at YARA's Tanzanian headquarters in Dar es Salaam, also in English.

The field visit of August and September of 2015 included expert interviews with the village chairman of Matetereka (Kiswahili with partial translation), the head teacher at Matetereka's primary school and an additional NGO interview in Songea, both in English. All interviews were recorded with a digital audio recording device and took between around 15 and 45 minutes, depending on the unfolding of the respective interview. A complete overview on the guideline-based interviews can be found in Appendix 1. For the sake of citation in this thesis, each of these interviews has been assigned the code GBE (Guideline-Based Expert Interview), followed by consecutive numbering and the date of the interview.

4.3.2 Narrative interviews with contemporary witnesses

The concept of (local) narratives has enjoyed increasing interest in human sciences in the last decades. This attention is driven by the acknowledgement that a local, biographical perspective on various social and political events can provide valuable insights into the overall understanding of such phenomena. Specifically, individual political biographies are seen as one field of interest in this context, in an effort to give a voice to the local perspective and the perceptions of people at the periphery of political systems. However, there are still differing understandings of what exactly a "narrative" is: Usually the interpretations vary between the extremes of a purely personal story and the abstract concept of an integrated overall narrative in a given geographical area or group of persons (ROBERTS 2004). Within this methodical discussion, questions also remain concerning how to appreciate narrative data (usually biographical interviews) with regards to an overall understanding of historic reality or causality (PONTI 2012).

An overview on the different streams of thought regarding narratives and their use in social sciences has been provided by ROBERT and SHENHAV (2014). Derived from their understanding of the different uses of narratives, the term will be used in two distinct ways throughout the presentation and the discussion of the empirical results of this study: Firstly, a narrative is understood as a "major topic or grand story" (ROBERT & SHENHAV 2014: 9) of a specific theme in a certain area, such as the narrative of Ujamaa development in Ruvuma that will be presented in chapter 6. It includes the findings of all the different empirical inquiries performed for this thesis.

Secondly, narratives are understood as a specific object or element of this research, i.e. the personal stories which a specific group of stakeholders (the contemporary witnesses) tells about the history of their villages and organizations (ROBERT & SHENHAV 2014: 9p.). It is the latter use of the term which acted as a base for the design of the narrative interviews:

As the main focus of these interviews has been the interest in collecting the personal stories of contemporary witnesses, those interviews were not led by a guideline, but were conducted in an open manner. Resulting from this interest of narrative interviews as such, the participants were usually asked to tell the story of their village from their own point of view. Additional questions by the interviewer were asked if necessary, as the interview unfolded (MEIER KRUKER & RAUH 2005: 67).

For this group of interviews, the chief interest when choosing the participants lay in locating contemporary witnesses of the Ujamaa period, who have been living in the respective communities for an extended time and ideally would have been part of the villages' foundation in the case of Litowa and Matetereka. Furthermore, a flexible approach was taken with regards to the number of interviewees in each narrative interview. Preferably, a one-on-one situation was chosen, although the visits always included the presence of a local guide.

Two such individual interviews with contemporary witnesses of the RDA era were led in Matetereka and three in Litowa, one interview (with two interviewees) in Liweta, and two additional interviews were conducted in the non-RDA village of Namatuhi. In two cases, narrative interviews were led as group interviews involving more than two participants. This was the result of local informants inviting contemporary witnesses for the sake of the interview in Mbingamharule and Matetereka. In spite of the group situation, the participants were still telling their own personal stories in these cases.

All narrative interviews were led in Kiswahili by the author. In six out of the nine narrative interviews, (partial) translation into English was provided by local interpreters. The interviews took between 15 minutes and over two hours, depending greatly on the knowledge of the participants and their willingness to share their stories. All interviews were recorded digitally and a complete overview on the narrative interviews can be found in Appendix 1. Within the following chapters, those interviews will be cited as NCW (Narrative Contemporary Witness Interview), followed by consecutive numbering and the date of the interview.

4.3.3 Group interviews

During the last field visit, the main goal was to locate present day local farmers and understand their knowledge and perspective on (village) development and the Ujamaa history of their area. In order to get detailed information, as well as an overview of the bigger picture of the opinions of the peasantry, the first method applied for this endeavor were group interviews. This form of qualitative research is seen as enabling discussions among the members of the group around a predefined issue, and possibly the creation of new ideas on dealing with it (MEIER KRUKER & RAUH 2005: 71).

While this second possible outcome was not the key interest of this research, the approach was still seen as the most adequate form of involving not only the perceptions of leaders and other individuals, but also those of "common" farmers into the study. Out of the interest in modern day farmers' self-organization, as well as for reasons of practical accessibility, the main target of these group interviews was the *vikundi* (singular: *kikundi*) operating at the case study villages. Vikundi might be described as the Tanzanian equivalent to farmers' cooperatives. However, the different vikundi can be characterized by vastly different degrees of organization and cooperation (see below). Twelve Group discussions were conducted with vikundi in Litowa (6), Matetereka (4) and Mbingamharule (2). The group discussions in Mbingamharule and two of the discussions in Matetereka included several vikundi each. Additionally, two group interviews were held with youth groups.

The design of these interviews was elaborated taking into account the results of the earlier expert interviews and aimed to give the participants the opportunity to explain the nature and activities of their respective group. Guidelines according to the group type were used for kicking off the group discussion as well as for moderating the proceedings and guiding the group trough the different areas of interest (Cooperation, Development, Ujamaa history, etc.). Other than that, the author tried to take a back seat in the emerging discussion and let the group members discuss the issues as freely as possible. All of the group discussions were held and moderated in Kiswahili by the author. As with the other types of interviews, the length of the discussions varied considerably, between around 20 minutes and one hour. All discussions were recorded with a digital audio recording devise. The guideline used for the group interviews is presented in Appendix 1, as is the detailed overview on all of these interviews. The citation within the text will be GI (Group Interview), followed by consecutive numbering and the date of the interview.

Yet, it has to be mentioned, that access to the groups was usually facilitated through actors that could be described as authorities within the villages (village chairmen, wazee, etc.), as direct access to these often loosely associated groups appeared unfeasible without the help of such authorities. In most cases, these persons were present during the group discussions and interacted with the group members at different levels of intensity. Therefore, even if the discussions usually appeared to be led quite openly, and critical opinions on village policy were a norm rather than an exception, the presence of these aforementioned authorities has to be taken into account when evaluating the results of the group discussions.

4.3.4 Village questionnaires

In addition to the use of group discussions, a questionnaire was developed for the villages of Litowa, Matetereka and Mbingamharule, which served the purpose of (qualitatively) understanding the opinion of current residents on the present and past development of their home villages. The questionnaires were chiefly aimed at the farmers of the village and included personal questions on demographic data and opinions as well as questions about agriculture and other income. The agriculture related questions (field size, crop types, etc.) were asked for the household of the recipient, as this is the common unit of production in all of the three villages. Three open questions concerning the challenges of living in the particular village, the state of village development and the knowledge and opinion on Ujamaa history were therefore placed at the end of the questionnaire. In order to better understand the economic and social background of the recipients, questions on the provenience, family size and farm activities were also part of the questionnaire. These questionnaires were the basis for random personal interviews, which were conducted by local research aides in Kiswahili. 100 questionnaires were collected in Litowa, 109 in Matetereka and 95 in Mbingamharule, all of which were later analyzed by the author. The questionnaire itself can be found in Appendix 2, as can the distribution of age and gender among the recipients of each village.

4.3.5 Analysis of qualitative and quantitative data

Qualitative content analysis

The analysis of the qualitative data gathered through the different types of interviews described above, as well as the qualitative questions of the questionnaires, was performed according to the principles of qualitative content analysis. Presented by MAYRING (2000) as an integration of different qualitative approaches to deal with data (communicative studies, psychology, hermeneutics, etc.), it is based on several principles: First of all, the qualitative analysis of content requires the subsumption of the primary data under a model of communication, i.e. the presentation of the circumstances of data creation (in our case, the situation of the interview), the social and cultural background of the interviewee and the aim of the analysis itself. Secondly, it requires the setting and description of the rules, according to which the material has been analyzed. Thirdly, these rules of analysis are used for the categorization of data. This categorization is based on the theoretical foundation of the study itself as well as the results of the interviews. And finally, the description of all the aforementioned steps has to ensure the interreliabilty of the results (see MAYRING (2010: 26–47) for a more detailed description of the basic elements of qualitative content analysis).

Transcription of interviews

After the audio recording during the field visits, the first step necessary for the further analysis of the interviews was the transcription of the audio recordings, in order to get a textual base for analysis. As in any empirical research, the depth of detail for the transcriptions of the interviews was guided by the overall research interest (MEIER KRUKER & RAUH 2005: 75p.). Therefore, neither a commenting nor a full word-by-word transcription was deemed necessary, as the research had no interest in the in-depth linguistic or communicational science aspects of the material in question. As a result, repetitions and similar elements of the conversation were not necessarily transcribed.

The main challenge in the transcription of the interviews, however, was the different languages used in the interviews as such, as well as the fact that some of the interviews had been translated in situ by a local interpreter and others were held entirely in Kiswahili. To account for this fact, in the case of interviews with interpreter, his interpretations were the ones transcribed in detail, while the original passages were only transcribed by the author in case there was a lack of interpretation. In such cases, the transcription was done directly from the Kiswahili audio material into an English interpretation of the text, based on the auditory understanding of the original account. This was seen as the best possibility for achieving comparability between the different types of translations (by local interpreter and by auditory understanding of the author). In the case of Kiswahili-only interview situations, the same technique of direct auditory transcription into English was chosen. In all cases, it was attempted to keep the original structure of the original account's syntax and wording in the English version.

In the case of the interviews held in English, word-by-word transcription was performed, with the level of detail mentioned above.

Coding and selection of relevant information from interviews

After the transcription of the interview material, the next logical step in qualitative content analysis is the identification of data relevant to the research and their organization along the patterns guided by the research questions itself, and thereafter the combination of these data into meaningful categories (Aronson 1995: 1p.). Indeed, in the case of this research, all parts of the interviews were selected for this process of categorization, with the exception of the process of introduction and the questions of the participants directed at the interviewer at the end of each interview. All other parts of the interviews were coded using the Atlas.ti software.

Coding and category-building was done using a combination of deductive and inductive coding (Mayring 2000): Some major codes were already deducted from the interview questions as such (for instance "NGO activities" or "definition of development"). With these codes already clear, the first step in the analysis of the transcripts was now to identify and mark the relevant passages of each interview.

The second step of coding, on the other hand, can be considered to be inductive: The interview transcripts of a specific group of stakeholders (NGOs, Farmers' Groups, etc.) were now screened manually with a technique dubbed "Noticing and Collecting Things (NCT)", which basically means that one goes through one interview after another, marking passages that are noticed to transport a certain content. If in following passages or another interview similar content is found, it is coded in the same way, hence collected (see Friese (2011) for a detailed description of this technique using the Atlas.ti software).

In this manner, new codes were created as subcategories to the deductive categories derived from the questions themselves. In reiterative steps, the new codes collected are screened for consistency and merged together, if necessary (Winters et al. 2010: 1420–1422). Through this process, it was possible to categorize the different opinions on the times of Ujamaa, for instance, based on the local understanding of this time by the participants of the interviews. The final result of this coding process is the base for the presentation of the empirical findings in chapter 6. A detailed description of the respective coding rules applied will be provided in that chapter as well.

Coding and analysis of questionnaire data

Concerning the qualitative data collected with the help of the village questionnaires, the same process of deductive and inductive coding was used. However, since the individual contributions were considerably shorter than those of the interviews, coding was done directly in the excel representation of the questionnaires. Furthermore, in contrast to the expert, narrative and group interviews, the emerging categories of answers could be presented in a nominal quantitative manner. The coding scheme used for the recipients' perceptions of the Ujamaa era can be found in detail in chapter 6.2.4.

For most of the quantitative data derived from the questionnaires, a simple, descriptive representation was deemed to be sufficient for the sake of this research. For instance, in the case of field sizes, number of different crops, and animals owned by the respective respondents. In this case the frequency of each property was simply counted with the help of the excel-mask of the respective village questionnaires, and, if applicable, arithmetic averages could be calculated. In the case of the field size stated by the respondent, categories were built in order to enable a graphic representation of this property (Meier Kruker & Rauh 2005: 114–119).

With regards to the opinions on Ujamaa, which have been coded out of the open, qualitative answers of the respondents, those categories were treated as a nominally scaled parameter. Therefore, a contingency test for nominal parameters according to Pearson was performed, in order to analyze the contingency of these opinions with other parameters such as the age and gender of respondents, their respective village of living or the size of their field (MEIER KRUKER & RAUH 2005: 141p.).

Yet, not all of the data gathered in the village questionnaires have been used for this thesis out of different reasons. For instance, answers to the question regarding the size of the respondents' families did not appear to be reliable, as in many – but not all – cases, the number of children stated in question 2 was the sum of the number of men and women specified above. This indicated that different respondents interpreted the question in a different manner, making the use of these demographic data inadvisable. Regarding the amount of harvest for each respondent, only the number of different crops has been used for further analysis, as the yield itself was not stated in a coherent manner.

4.3.6 Mapping of the former RDA villages and historical transects

The villages of Litowa and Matetereka have been mapped for the use of this study, using classical onsite mapping techniques and locally collected GPS data. The maps were later designed at the Würzburg Institute for Geography, using the data from the field visits and additional satellite imagery provided by google earth.

Apart from giving an overview of the current layout and building structure of the former RDA villages, one key interest of the mapping operation was to locate places of historical interest. In line with the attempt to represent the local perspective on Ujamaa history, the method of historical transect walks was chosen to accomplish this task. Historical transects have been described as a participatory method to gather information on a predefined area of interest, while at the same time enabling local participants to literally lead the way and show the researcher the places they find relevant for their own history. Such walks are therefore not a quiet hike through the area, but an ongoing conversation between the participants and the researcher, who is taking notes on the information which are presented by the locals (KUMAR 2002: 143–147).

Quite often, such walks act as a tool to understand the history of natural resource use or local history in general. In the ex-RDA villages of Matetereka and Litowa, historical transect walks were performed in order to locate and understand the remaining physical sites of the organization's history. In Litowa, the historical transect took place on 22nd of August 2015 and was made with the support of members from the current village government, in Matetereka the transect walk was led by Mzee Mayemba and some fellow villagers on 31st of August 2015. In both cases, the sites identified by the villagers were marked with a GPS device, in order to be included in the village maps later on.

5   The case study –
Ujamaa development in Ruvuma

With this background of research methods and methodological considerations, the thesis will proceed with the presentation of the case study itself: The development of Ujamaa in Ruvuma. First of all, a short overview on the selection process of the case study area and the definition of the different stakeholders will be given. Afterwards, the basic characteristics of the research region of Ruvuma will be presented in chapter 5.3, while the case study villages of Litowa, Matetereka and Mbingamharule will be described in chapter 5.4.

5.1   Selection process of the case study area

The overall goal of this thesis has been to shed new light on the changing development paradigms in Tanzania in general and the development of the Ujamaa ideology and strategy in particular. Thorough research of the available contemporary and post-Ujamaa literature from both Tanzanian and international scholars underlined the crucial role of the early communitarian movements in the Ruvuma Region, and the history of the RDA in particular, in the unfolding of the Tanzanian development approach. Therefore – and in consideration of the limited resources in time and manpower – the decision was taken to concentrate the empirical research on this region, rather than selecting case study sites from several different areas within the country. While this decision certainly limits the possibility of arriving at a general picture of the local effects of changing development paradigms all over Tanzania, it enabled the research to deliver a more in-depth perspective of the development history of this particular region.

Once the regional scale of the study was decided, it became clear that data had to be collected from both RDA and non-RDA villages, in order to create a broader picture of development narratives on the ground. Concerning the RDA villages, the three villages of Litowa, Matetereka and Liweta became the center of attention from early on: First of all, all of these villages had received relatively high interest in the contemporary literature, and several descriptions and scientific papers were available as a starting point for research (see INTERVIEW WITH E. NDONDE 1975; WENNER 1970; TOROKA 1973; IBBOTT 1969, 1970; BRAIN 1977; COULSON 1982; LEWIN 1973; MUSTI DE GENNARO 1981). Therefore, all of these three were visited during the third field visit to explore the possibilities for further research.

Secondly, the village of Litowa played a crucial part in understanding the organizational development of the RDA and Ujamaa in general, and proved to be a very valuable study area, being the first RDA village (COULSON 1982: 263; IBBOTT 2014) and the central place in the association's history. On the other hand, Matetereka had been described as "the last Ujamaa village" in Tanzania by EDWARDS (1998), who had produced a valuable account of the proceedings of the original Ujamaa cooperative of that village after the disbandment of the RDA. Several interviewees in EDWARDS' account could again be found during research in 2015 (*NCW 4; 3/6/2015; NCW 10; 8/31/2015; GI 11; 9/3/2015*). As logistic and administrative support was hard to come by in Liweta, it was eventually eliminated as a case study site, although one narrative interview could still be conducted there.

For the non-RDA villages, the concrete historical entanglement with Ujamaa appeared to be of secondary importance. Practicability and accessibility therefore were the chief interest in the selection of those villages. With the help of Xaver Komba, a valuable local contact in Songea, his hometown of Mbingamharule provided an excellent opportunity for the non-RDA case study. Additional interviews were led in Namatuhi, to the South of Songea.

5.2   Definition of focal groups and stakeholders

The most important focal group for this research on understanding the effects of Ujamaa development on the rural population of Tanzania were the members of the peasantry themselves. Therefore, the perception of those small-scale farmers was the main interest of both group interviews and the village questionnaires in the case study villages.

During the research, farmers' groups – or vikundi (singular kikundi) in Kiswahili – emerged as one of the most interesting group of actors for the understanding of both the perception of Ujamaa history by the local peasantry, and the persistence of cooperative ideas on the village scale. Kikundi in Kiswahili is the general term for any kind of "group". However, within the village environment, it is understood as an association of farmers. Yet, vikundi should not be equated with the European concept of farmers' cooperatives. While they certainly share some of the same basic ideas, the range of activities as well as the scope of collective actions varies greatly between the different vikundi that have been analyzed for this research. Some of the groups are merely common organizations to express their members' interests to other stakeholders, others try to achieve a low-key form of social insurance by pooling their members' cash reserves and giving payouts for certain immediate needs like hospital bills or school fees. Many have a system of pooling the agricultural produce of the individual farmers, in order to achieve higher prices at the markets and improve their bargaining power when dealing with middlemen. Some of the vikundi, however, are operating a certain extent of collective agriculture, mostly for cash crops like soya. The cash income generated by such activities is then split among the group's members, or used for investment in agricultural inputs for the next season. The inner organization of the vikundi is usually of a basic democratic character, with all the members meeting regularly to agree on the group's activity and electing a chairperson, bookkeeper and similar positions for the day-to-day management of its assets. The varying activities of the groups involved in this research will be described in chapter 6.2.3.

Secondly, the need for contemporary witnesses made the group of village elders, or *wazee*, another focal group of interest. It was assumed that they could act as contemporary witnesses for practically the whole Ujamaa era, as well as the subsequent changes occurring in their villages. Narrative interviews were the main method of choice for understanding the members of the wazee group. As most of the wazee are small-scale farmers themselves – and in some cases vikundi members –, those individuals are part of both focal groups. Furthermore, some other contemporary witnesses, like former students of the RDA school, took part in narrative interviews. In general, all representatives of this focal group were identified by local informants. In the case of Matetereka, the names of many wazee, who were involved in the establishment of the village, were already known thanks to EDWARDS' (1998) information on the subject.

Thirdly, in order to include the view of younger village members on development and Ujamaa, group discussions with village-based youth groups were conducted in Litowa and Matetereka. This last group of stakeholders may actually act as an example of the general approach of this research towards the planning of interview situations. Indeed, the general groups of interest were defined before the setting off to the case study area. However, during the actual visit, a very open attitude towards the involvement of additional interview partners was taken. With the youth, only the village of Matetereka had a more or less organized youth group, while the interview with the young farmers of Litowa consisted of an ad-hoc group of interested participants. While this approach might negatively affect the representativeness of their statements, it was seen as a practical implementation of participative research, which actually demands the flexible incorporation of the local situation (CHAMBERS 1992: 13–15).

Apart from this inside view on development on the village scale, public administration (on regional, district and village level) was identified as another group of stakeholders. In addition to their knowledge on the research subject, the involvement of these actors not only served as a source of information, but also as a necessary requirement for getting access to the local level. Last but not least, the NGOs involved in different development projects within the region could be seen as an obvious stakeholder in the development scene of the research area. Their information acted as a valuable starting point for the deeper understanding of local development interactions.

5.3 The Ruvuma Region in Southern Tanzania

In the following chapters, an overview of the basic topographical, ecological and socio-economic settings of the Ruvuma Region will be given.

5.3.1 Basic Physical and Agro-ecological Features

The Ruvuma Region is situated in the extreme Southwest of Tanzania, bordering Malawi to the West (at Lake Malawi/ Lake Nyasa in Tanzanian terms) and Mozambique to the South, between a Latitude of 9°35' to 11°45' South and a Longitude of

34°35′ to 38°10′ East. It covers an area of 64,493 km², of which 54,839 km² are considered to be arable land, 6,425 km² forests and 29,79 km² water surface by the Tanzanian administration. To the North, it boarders Iringa Region and to the East Mtwara Region. Ruvuma is part of the Southern Highlands of Tanzania, which can reach as high as 2000 m a.s.l. in the Lukumburu Mountains in the North of the region. The West of the region is characterized by the equally high Matengo Mountains, before descending rapidly to the shore of Lake Nyasa, which fills the bottom of the East African Rift valley. The Southern and central parts of Ruvuma are made up of lower plains and undulated terrain, dissected through the namesake Ruvuma River and its tributaries – which form the main drainage system of the area – flowing between the lower areas of Eastern Ruvuma and Mozambique before leading into the Indian Ocean. Its main tributaries are the perennial Njuga, Likonde, Ngembambili and Lukimwa Rivers. The Western slopes of the Matengo and Lukumburu mountains are drained through the Ruhulu river system into Lake Nyasa, and from there on into the Zambesi River system (URT 1997a: 1, 1997a: 24).

Map 1: The research region of Ruvuma

An overview of the Region can be found in Map 1, which also illustrates the administrative borders within Ruvuma. The places of research are highlighted as well.

Ruvuma's climate is considered to be moderate given its tropical location, with average peak temperatures of 30°C in October and November and lower temperatures in June, July and August, which can reach as low as 13°C in the Matengo Highlands. The average temperature for Ruvuma is 23°C. Apart from extraordinary dry years, there is enough rainfall available in the region, averaging between 800 and 1800 mm per year, with the amount of rainfall decreasing gradually from West to East. Due to its location in the South of Tanzania, Ruvuma experiences only one long rainy season, which lasts from December until mid-April (URT 1997a: 3p.).

The far Western and the Eastern parts of the Region have a relatively high risk of dry spells in mid-season (February), while the central parts, especially around Songea town have a high reliability of rains throughout the season. In fact, the Southern Highlands growing season, which usually spans 130 to 140 days per year, is considered to be the most favorable in all of Tanzania, due to the combination of reliable rainfalls and relatively low temperatures. This gives good conditions for water-demanding crops like banana and finger millet, but also an excellent environment for the cultivation of maize. The latter also benefits from the ideal soil moisture conditions in much of the region, which enables the plants to access enough water even after the end of the rainy season (SCHMIED 1989: 17p.).

Considering the natural vegetation of the area, most of it was covered by Miombo woodlands in the past, with the species of *branchistegia*, *julbernia* and *isoberlinia* being the most common trees. The Miombo woodlands are under increasing threat from human activities, especially the demand for firewood and charcoal production. Therefore, the woodlands have mostly been replaced by bushland thicket and grassland on the lower slopes, and the area covered by Miombo woodland has declined. (URT 1997a: 5p.).

Songea Rural District, the district in which all case study villages are situated, covers an area of approximately 13,455 km², after Namtumbo District has been created out of the Eastern part of the original Songea District in 2002. The climate here resembles the average for Ruvuma region, with mean annual rainfalls between 800 and 1200 mm and one long rainy season (November to May). Generally, rainfall increases with altitude in this district, resulting in relatively drier lowlands and humid highlands (especially in the far North of the district). The natural vegetation is also similar to the region's average. To the North, a small section of Selous Game Reserve lies within the borders of the district (SDC 2013: 3–5; EDWARDS 2003: 227).

5.3.2 Political and Administrative Organization

Ruvuma Region is one of the 30 administrative regions of Tanzania, of which 25 are located in mainland Tanzania, as of 2012 (URT 2013a: 1). Under the current system of Tanzanian government and administration, the Regions are the second level of government directly below the national government in mainland Tanzania, while in Zanzibar, the islands' own government acts as an additional tier dealing with political issues only concerning the archipelago. The creation of regions dates back to German colonial times, when administrative sublevels were created in the first place. The system was significantly altered by the British and then again with the advent of independence, and also saw major transformations afterwards (SEMBOJA & THERKILDSEN 1994: 807p.).

The number or regions has increased since independence in an attempt to further decentralization in development planning, and several new regions have been formed across Tanzania. Nevertheless, the Regions in their latest form, established by the Regional Administration Act of 1997, remain the central government's arm on the ground: They are headed by a Regional Commissioner, who is appointed by the Tanzanian President himself and acts as his direct representative for the whole region. There is no own legislative organ on the regional level itself, but the Commissioner is advised by a Regional Consultative Committee over which he presides. This consultative organ does include elected officials from the region, including the Members of (National) Parliament from the respective region, but also other appointed officials like the District Commissioners. The whole setup of the Region in Tanzania is thought to be first of all an administrative unit, but secondly also a body overseeing the implementation of national development policies on the regional level (URT 1997b).

Below the regional level are the Districts, which have also seen various changes since independence. The introduction of some elements of local government on this level was originally the result of the colonial government's reaction to demands for more direct control, that led to a local government reform between 1950 and 1955. In the Ruvuma area, it was mainly the demands of the Ndenduele chiefdoms that led to this development (EDWARDS 2003: 202–204). This had also been the first time that local government on village level was introduced.

After independence, however, changes by the new central government actually reduced the power of elected district structures in favor of party appointed officials on the same level. With the decentralization act of 1972, local governments were actually denied further financial autonomy, and the year of 1975 saw the end of Districts as political units in favor of the Regions above and the villages below, which had been upgraded as a central planning organ by the Ujamaa Village Act. While the legislation of 1975 actually included the introduction of district level elections, these were never held. All in all the reforms of the 1960s and 70s were dominated by the bureaucratization of all local levels of government, and especially the district level (SEMBOJA & THERKILDSEN 1994: 807–810).

Only in the early 1980s were district structures seen as political again, rather than purely administrative bodies, and the District Council as an elected parliament was introduced in 1984. The council is headed by the District Executive Officer, while a District Commissioner is the highest appointed representative of the central government on district level. Districts can have their own sources of revenue and also receive funding (usually the majority of their funds) from the national government, from which the councils pay technical staff and officials for various tasks – like development, education, security, etc. They are thought of as an entity of connection between the villages and the village councils, but also as a further level of implementation of central government's policies. The Districts could therefore be seen as the highest level of local government as well as the lowest of national government – a sort of intermediary structure (WILY 2003: 6).

From the reintroduction of the District Councils in 1984 until 2002, Ruvuma Region was divided into four districts: The rural districts of Tunduru, Mbinga and

Songea (rural) and the municipality of Songea town. In 2002, Namtumbo District was created out of the eastern parts of Songea Rural, in a move that caught many local authorities by surprise (EDWARDS 2003: 227; URT 1997a: 1).

Later, Mbinga District was also split into two, and the new Nyasa District was established at the shores of Lake Malawi (Nyasa in Tanzania), so that today there are five rural Districts and one township in Ruvuma Region (URT 2013a: 95p.). The further subdivision of districts might not be over yet, as there have been talks about the creation of a new Madaba District in the far North of the Region, which would include the village of Matetereka (*GBE 16*; 9/1/2015). For the time being, however, all three case study villages are situated within the boundaries of Songea Rural District, which warrants a few more details on this district itself:

The Songea Rural District Council was established as an administrative unit on 1st of January 1984, following the Local Government Act No. 7 of 1982, which provided for the establishment of Districts as the third level of government in Tanzania (below the national and regional levels). It lies in the center of Ruvuma Region, between Mbinga District to the West and Namtumbo District to East. In the South, it reaches the boarder to Mozambique, while to the North, the District boarders Morogoro and Njombe Regions. In the central South, the district encloses Songea Municipality – sometimes referred to as Songea Urban (District) – the capital of Ruvuma. The District Council is the legislative organ of the District, comprising of 17 elected members (1 for each ward), 6 special seats (for certain groups) and one Member of (national) Parliament. The district is further divided into 3 Divisions, 17 Wards and 64 Villages (SDC 2013: 3).

These 64 villages form the basic unit of Tanzanian politics and administration. Since the times of the Arusha Declaration, the village was seen as the core unit for rural and national development (NYERERE 1967b), and the assembly of all its adult inhabitants became the highest authority of decision-making for the village – at least in theory. Under the one-party system in Tanzania, the party chairman and the party secretary, who were elected by the party branch members, automatically filled the positions of village chairman and village secretary as well, illustrating the strong central and party dominated element of the theoretically local decision-making process (SCHULTHEIS & SESHAMANI 1982: 4.1-4.4).

With the Local Government Act of 1982, the importance of the village assembly was reaffirmed and the authorities of the villages themselves were amended: From now on, villages were able to release by-laws for their villages and were given financial sovereignty – although just like the District Councils, they relied on national funding. The duality of elected and appointed officials, which is a typical feature of Tanzanian administration, is also present at the village level. Here the village chairman (mwenyekiti) is elected by the whole village and is the chair of the 23 other elected members of the village council, the local parliament. On the appointed site, the village manager or secretary (mtendaji) is a part of the village government, and is also part of the village council, bringing the total to 25 members. Apart from the fact that chairman and secretary are no longer identical with the respective party offices, the structure itself has not changed since the introduction of a multiparty system in Tanzania. At all times during the five-year election cycle, the village assembly of all inhabitants remains the highest legislative organ of the village, and all elected representatives only act on its behalf. One of the most important functions of the village government is the administration of village land, which is also an area of common conflict between different actors. As the village is not necessarily seen as a settlement structure but first of all as an administrative unit, villages in Tanzania regularly include various nucleated settlements or sub-villages and can have quite expansive territorial extent in areas with low population density. In general, a village in Tanzania is supposed to have between 275 and 400 households (2,000 to 4,000 inhabitants) – and if a village gets significantly bigger, it is usually split up into two new villages by the way of promoting a former sub-village to a village in its own right (WILY 2003: 4–6).

Just like the district council, village governments are seen as a key institution for the promotion of social and economic development in rural areas by the current National Agricultural Policy (URT 2013b: 38). Furthermore, they are supposed to take part in the creation and implementation of sectoral plans (e.g. agriculture) and mobilize the financial and human resources for local development interventions, as well as to supervise the implementation of extension services provided by higher levels of government. Last but not least, local government authorities are in charge of land administration as well as the general administration of the respective village and the implementation of relevant laws on the local level.

5.3.3 Socio-economic profile

Ruvuma is still one of least densely populated and most rural regions of Tanzania. Nevertheless, it has seen a rapid increase in inhabitants since independence, as has Tanzania in general. In 1967, 395,447 people were living in Ruvuma, a number that has since increased to 783,327 in 1988, 1,113,715 in 2002 and 1,376,891 at the last national census in 2012. Between 1978 and 1988, the annual growth rate of the population was 3.4%, which was above the national average of 2.8% in the same time span. The annual growth rate has subsequently dropped to 2.5% between 1988 and 2002 and 2.1% between 2002 and 2012, respectively (URT 1997a: 7p., 2016: 15).

During the period of villagization, the resettlement of the whole rural population into 307 Ujamaa villages was considered to be achieved in Ruvuma in 1977. Back then, most of the resettled villagers were still living in provisory dwellings, without appropriate conditions for health services, water supply, education and other social services (GAMA 1989: 140p.). In 1997, the percentage of rural population living in the then 547 villages of the region was estimated at over 90%, in a settlement pattern still very much influenced by the villagization of the 1970s, and only 5-8% in the district headquarters, usually referred to as "towns" or "trading centres" (URT 1997a: 7).

Between 2002 and 2012, population growth has mainly occurred in these urban areas of the region, were the number of inhabitants has been growing at 6.9% annually, while in the rural areas, the average growth was only 0.9% per year. Nevertheless, there are still around 75% of the inhabitants living in rural areas (URT 2016: 13). As in most areas of Sub-Saharan Africa, Ruvuma has a high percentage of younger population, which is reflective of the relatively high fertility rates (URT 2016: 21p.).

A more detailed look at the distribution of the Region's population according to age groups is presented in Fig. 5. One of the peculiarities within this distribution is the relative shortage of male population from the age of 15-19 onwards, which is indicative of the comparably higher tendency of the male population to leave the region in the search for paid work opportunities in other areas of the country.

Figure 5: Population Distribution for Ruvuma Region 2012

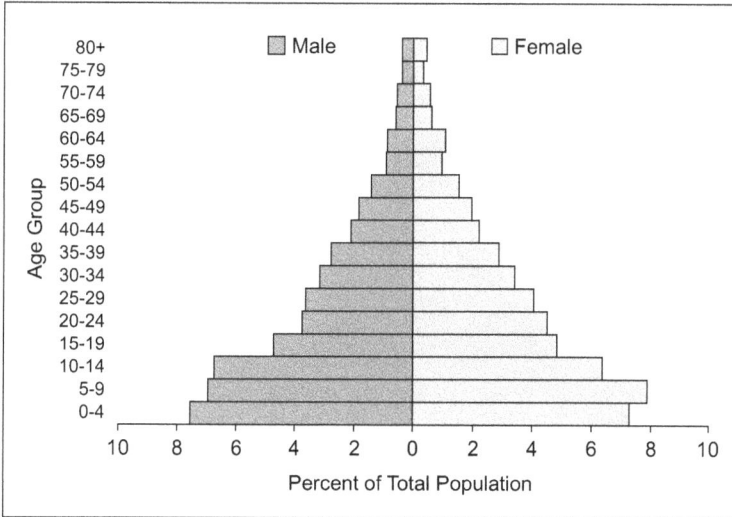

Source: URT (2016: 21)

Figure 6: Population Distribution for Ruvuma Region 2012, rural

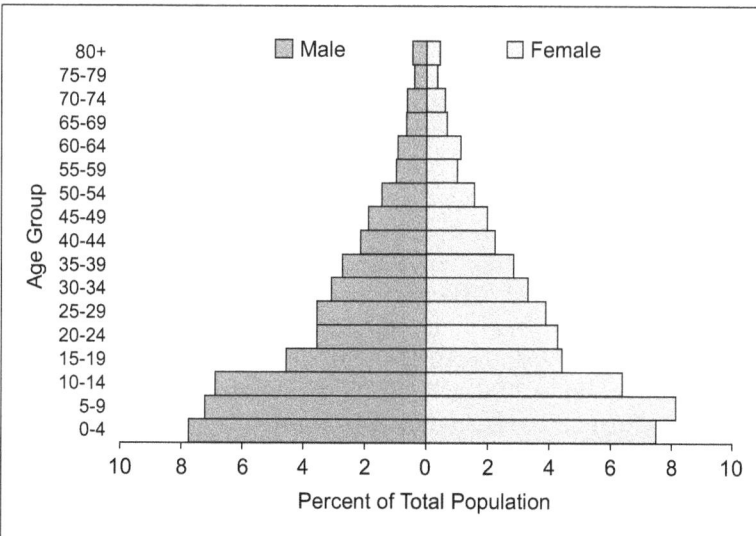

Source: URT (2016: 22)

This tendency becomes even more pronounced when taking a look at the distribution of the rural population in Ruvuma (Fig. 6), which illustrates the lack of perceived economic opportunities, especially in the village environment. In a social situation in which the male is still seen as the main breadwinner of the family, it is the young men who will first leave their home in the search of better opportunities elsewhere (see also chapter 6.2.6).

On the other hand, the discrepancy between the male and female parts of the population is less pronounced in the urban part of Ruvuma Region (see Fig. 7), which basically comprises of Songea Town.

Figure 7: Population Distribution for Ruvuma Region 2012, urban

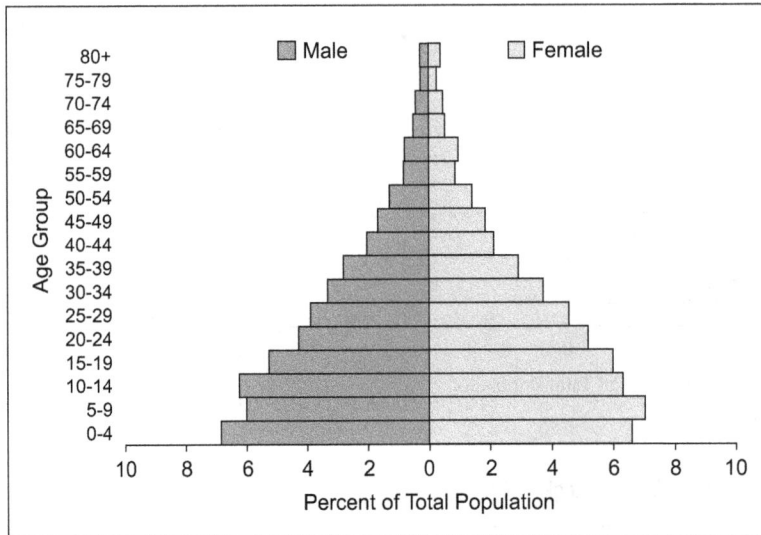

Source: URT (2016: 22)

The average household size across the region has been counted at 4.5 persons (4.6 for rural households) in 2012, compared with 4.7 persons in 2002 (URT 2016: 31), which is still higher than in 1967 (4.0 persons) but a decrease when compared to 1988 (5.3 persons per household) (URT 1997a: 7p.).

Farming was by far the most important economic activity of Ruvuma's inhabitants in 2012, as it was the main occupation of 79.2% of the working population of the region and 79% of all households in Ruvuma were active in agriculture. Maize is by far the most important staple food and therefore the most important crop throughout the region. Around 220,000 out of the 238,000 agricultural households were engaging in maize cultivation in 2012, while 50% of all households in Ruvuma were also engaging in some form of livestock keeping, mostly as an add-on to their farming activities (URT 2016: 94, 125-127).

According to the regional agricultural sample survey of 2007/08, annual crop farming provided the most important cash income for 93% of all rural households (91.1% in Songea rural), while 5% came from employment in other sectors, and only

148

0.4% from livestock keeping (URT 2012: 13p.). Around 35% (Songea rural 46.4%) of households were engaging in cash-income generating off-farm activities (such as permanent or occasional employment), 22% of these households had two, 9% more than two such activities (URT 2012: 20p.). For the overwhelming majority of agricultural households within the region, most of their cash income was generated by the sale of food crops (69% of households), cash crops amounted to the main cash income in 13% of the households, other casual earnings for 4% and livestock keeping for less than 3% of the households (URT 2012: 89).

In Ruvuma Region, there is a total land area 773,000 ha available for smallholder cultivation, of which 64% were used in the year of the last survey in 2007/08, giving an area of about 2 ha used for agriculture per household – a figure that resembles the Tanzanian average. Within the region, land utilization ranged between 82% in Tunduru and 50% in Songea Rural District (URT 2012: 21p.).

Generally, Ruvuma has one of the lowest rates of land utilization in Tanzania, resulting in the lowest number of households who suffer from a shortage of land (URT 2012: 91). During the 2007/08 agricultural season, 30.5% of the land available to smallholders was used for temporary monocrops (239,000 ha) and 87,000 ha (18,7%) for permanent monocrops. Temporary mixed crops were cultivated on 65,000 ha (8.3%) and permanent annual/mixed crops on 59,000 ha (7.5%). Fallow made up 147,000 ha (18.7%), natural bush 84,000 ha (10.7%) and uncultivated land 49,000 ha (6.2%) of the total land available (URT 2012: 22).

In terms of crop area, maize is the most important annual crop in Ruvuma, being cultivated on 50% of the utilized land area, followed by cassava (19%), paddy (16%) and beans (13%). Other crops each represented less than five percent of the cultivated area in Ruvuma (URT 2012: 25). With nearly 210,000 ha, cereals are cultivated on 60% of the total area planted with annual crops, roots and tubers make up 17% (62,000 ha), pulses 12% (44,000 ha) and oil seeds and nuts 9% (34,000 ha) of the total area. The cultivation of cash crops takes up only around 1% of the total area of annual crops (URT 2012: 25).

Almost 150,000 ha were cultivated with maize in 2007/08, bringing in 237,000 t of harvest. This represented an increase in maize production of 32% up from the 179,000 t produced in 2003. Before that, there had been a constant decline of maize production from 1994 until 1998 (from 203,000 to 158,000 t), followed by an increase of 48% in 1999 and relatively constant production levels until a drop in 2003 (URT 2012: 28). Paddy is the second most important cereal in Ruvuma, nearly 56,000 t were produced in 2007/08 on 48,000 ha – a yield of 1.1 t/ha on average. Compared to 2003, there has been an increase of paddy production by 8% p.a., which can be attributed to the extended area of cultivation (38,000 ha in 2003), while the yield per ha remained almost constant (URT 2012: 28p.). Other cereals cultivated within the region include finger and bulrush millets, sorghum and wheat. 12,000 t of other cereals were produced in the 2007/08 agricultural year (URT 2012: 29–31). Concerning roots and tubers, Cassava represented the most important crop, being cultivated on 57,000 ha with a total production of 100,000 t, representing around 92% of area and production of roots and tubers in the region (URT 2012: 31p.).

Almost all of Ruvuma's agricultural land is cultivated by hand, with very limited use of technical equipment like ox-ploughs and tractors. Nevertheless, the use of inorganic fertilizers in Ruvuma is among the highest in Tanzania and it had a higher percentage of fertilizer use than any other region of the country. This relatively high usage of fertilizers can partly be attributed to Ruvuma's status as one of the "Big Four" Regions for maize production in Tanzania (together with Iringa, Mbeya and Rukwa – all part of the Southern Highlands) and the Region's important role as the nation's bread basket. This status was actively promoted by the regional authorities from the 1970s onwards and encouraged the use of inorganic fertilizers by smallholders. However, inappropriate use of them has led to several problems concerning soil depletion and environmental degradation in some areas of Ruvuma (URT 1997a: 35–37, 2012: 91).

Given the relatively low population density and high food crop production, Ruvuma experiences comparatively high food security levels, with 51.4% of the agricultural households responding that they never experienced issues in food sufficiency and another 27.8% claiming they "seldom" experienced such problems. On the other hand, 13% experienced issues in meeting household's food requirements sometimes, 4.8% often and 3.0% always had problems with achieving food sufficiency. In Songea Rural District, 62% of households experienced some frequency of insufficient food supply (URT 2012: 89).

This characterization of Ruvuma as a region with surplus production of food crops, especially maize, was underlined by the representative of the National Food Reserve Agency (NFRA), which is operating a food reserve center in Songea town. According to his statements, the maize stored there, which is collected from all over the region, is very rarely used for food shortages within the region itself. Rather, it is sent to regions with higher population densities like Dar es Salaam or areas which are more prone to drought in northern Tanzania (*GBE 13*; 3/13/2015). Throughout the region, 71% of the households normally enjoy three meals per day, 28% have two meals and 0.6% of the households only can afford one meal per day on a regular basis (URT 2012: 88).

Adult literacy has been increasing throughout Ruvuma in the last censual decade, from 76.8% in 2002 to 84.4% in 2012. However, there are regional differences in literacy, with the range being between 94.3% in Songea Town and 71.1% in the very remote Tunduru District to the East of the Region. Nevertheless, the latter was able to achieve the biggest advance in adult literacy in the decade in question. The adult male population had a generally higher literacy rate than the female one (88.3% to 80.8%), as did the urban population in comparison to those residing in rural areas (93% urban, 81.4% rural), while higher literacy rates are generally found in younger age groups (URT 2016: 62–68). Among the members of agricultural households aged 5 years and above, 50% had completed some form of education in 2008 (the same percentage as in 2003) and 35% were still in school at the time of the survey. Around 15% of rural household members had never attended any form of school. The percentage of household members who had completed any form of education was the lowest in Tunduru district at 41% (URT 2012: 19p.).

Songea Rural District

In 2012, there were 174,000 people living within Songea Rural District (URT 2013a: 98). Of the total working age population of the District, 71% engage in agriculture, while livestock keeping is of very little economic importance. Most of the agriculture is characterized by traditional techniques and low subsistence yields per area. There are some development activities on district level, which aim at increasing agricultural productivity through the introduction of farm machinery like tractors and government subsidies for fertilizer by the use of voucher schemes. According to the district council, this has led to an increase in maize production from 5-8 bags per acre in 2007/08 to 40 bags in 2011/2012, although the reliability of these data appears questionable[4]. Main food crops are maize, paddy and cassava, as in the rest of the region, while cash crop production includes sunflower, simsim, soya beans, cashew, tobacco and coffee. The district council has sponsored 680 t of improved maize seeds to its smallholders via the voucher system in 2012/13 (SDC 2013: 5–7).

In Songea rural district the utilized land area is 0.79 ha per household, of which 0.33 ha are planted with annual crops. Maize production uses a total of 29,300 ha and paddy production 5,100 ha; 5,400 ha are planted with permanent crops, of which banana cultivations are the most important form with 1,300 ha of planted area. Only around 1,400 ha out of the 54,300 ha of planted land in the district used irrigation systems, while the remaining area relied exclusively on rain fed agriculture – the smallest percentage in the whole region. 91% of agricultural households were reported to have been able to sell some of their produce in the 2007/08 season and all households were using some form of crop storage during the process, mostly relying on traditional storage facilities or storage in bags. Only 4.7% of the agricultural households in Songea Rural District were accessing credit for agricultural investment, of which 48% was provided by NGOs and Development projects, 26% through cooperatives and 16% through SACCOS. 68% of households were accessing agricultural extension services (URT 2012: 93-94, 127, 138, 140, 168).

Within the district there are 95 primary schools with 702 teachers, who teach around 32,000 primary and 5,000 pre-primary pupils. The deficit in teaching personnel is estimated at 180 teachers, while there is also a shortage of 223 class rooms (with 743 existing) (SDC 2013: 10p.). There are 23 public and three private secondary schools in Songea Rural, with a total of 4,179 pupils (SDC 2013: 11p.).

The district's health services include one hospital run by a voluntary agency, two government health centers, as well as 23 dispensaries run by the government and 13 by voluntary agencies. The most severe health issues are Malaria and HIV/Aids, followed by respiratory diseases and diarrhea. Malnutrition is not a severe issue within the district, with only 0.2% of the population affected. HIV prevalence was at 3.4% (all numbers for 2011/12 (SDC 2013: 12–14)).

Around 80% of the households get their water supply from within 500 m distance from their place of living (URT 2012: 94) and water supply infrastructure by the district council has reached 52 out of the 64 villages, albeit with a service level of only 65%, and mostly by basic hand pumps (SDC 2013: 15).

Concerning road infrastructure, there are no tarmaced district roads, only the main Songea-Njombe, Songea-Mbinga and some stretches of the Songea-Tunduru

---

4 One bag of maize equals 100kg, by the Tanzanian Weight and Measures Act of 1982. However, use of measurements is notoriously inconsistent in Tanzanian agriculture and practitioners have found deviations of up to 48% between standardized and actual weight of bags sold at Tanzanian crop markets (TANZANIAN MARKETS-PAN 2013: 3).

roads have tarmac. 23% of district roads have a gravel surface, the rest are simple earth roads that become very slippery and are prone to mud traps during the rainy season. Only 75% of all district roads are considered to be passable without problem throughout the year (SDC 2013: 18p.).

Land and boarder mapping for its villages is another task for the District Council. So far 16 out of 64 villages underwent this mapping process whereby they now have the right of occupancy for their village lands. 10 villages have conducted Participatory Land Use Management (PLUM) assessments, although the data presented by the district council are for the 2003-06 period. However, no new mapping or planning activities seem to have been conducted before the publication in 2013. According to this source, Matetereka was one of the 10 "PLUM" villages (SDC 2013: 19p.). Yet, own field visits in 2015 led to the impression that no representative of the village government was actually aware of these plans, nor did they appear to be used in any sort of village development activity (*GBE 15; 8/30/2015*).

5.4 The villages

After this short introduction into the research region of Ruvuma, the case study villages of Litowa, Matetereka and Mbingamharule will be presented in the following chapters. This section is meant to give a first impression of the respective history of these three villages, as well as some basic data on the economic activities of the inhabitants. For the RDA villages of Litowa and Matetereka, the results of the historic transect walks and the mapping will also be presented. All of this will act as a background for the narrative of development emerging from the other empirical findings of this study which will be presented in chapter 6. Some basic impressions of the two additional research sites of Liweta and Namatuhi can be found in Appendix 3.

5.4.1 Litowa – The first Ujamaa village

The village of Litowa, built on a small ridge in the lush hills of Southern Songea District became the cradle for RDA's revolutionary approach to putting the idea of Ujamaa into practice. Detailed descriptions of the daily lives of this village can be found in Kate Wenner's (WENNER 1970) account of her stay as a volunteer in 1966/67, as well as in Ralph Ibbott's republication of his earlier accounts of the RDA's history and his role as a sort of embedded adviser to the wajamaa throughout the association's history (IBBOTT 2014).

During that time, Litowa became an example and role model for many small-scale farmers from the Songea area, who went on to found their own villages based on communal work, basic democratic decision-making and the vision of a socialist future. At the time of WENNER's visit, there were 13 villages inside RDA, and Litowa – being the most mature and advanced settlement – became a kind of service village for the whole organization. Inhabitants of all member villages came to learn and new approaches and techniques in farming were tested in Litowa, for application in all of the villages – if successful. It was also the site of RDA's own primary school, as mentioned earlier. All of the houses in Litowa were built on the ridge, while the communal fields (mostly maize) lay in the surrounding valleys. The houses were constructed in a rectangular shape, out of mud and wattle, and covered with grass roofs. Often two houses were erected adjacently to each other, connected by grass fences to form a home for two families. The biggest building of the village was the Ujamaa hall, where the villagers would gather for dining together, before holding the twice weekly Ujamaa Assembly, the highest institution for common decision-making. After the assembly was closed by the chairman, the members would join in singing political songs, praising their way of development and their contribution to the building of the nation. The meetings were announced by ringing the metal wheel in the center of the village, after the men and women came back from their daily work on the fields and proceeded to wash themselves before the bell was rung three times to announce the commencement of the joint dinner. The children of Litowa did likewise and joined the proceedings of the meeting. After the meal, the assembly was opened by the chairman, and topic after topic was discussed in lively fashion, until consensus could be reached on how to carry on with whatever was on the schedule (WENNER 1970: 17–33).

These meetings were seen as emblematic of the spirit of Ujamaa within the community and took place every Tuesday and Thursday night. Church was held by a priest from Peramiho every Sunday at the Ujamaa hall and was another important part of the community life. Usually, the only African member of the Peramiho Seminary, Father Mbunga, would hold mass. He also led a movement of replacing the old German hymns with new African church songs, and became very popular with the inhabitants of Litowa (WENNER 1970: 85p.).

The shamba had 150 acres and belonged to everybody. Maize was cultivated as the main food crop on the fields on the bottom of the valley, while tobacco was the main cash crop and grown on top of the ridge across the valley (WENNER 1970: 124). The farmers of Litowa were always keen on learning of new farming techniques, like improved spacing for maize cultivation. However, if new ideas were brought in, for instance by an extension worker or agricultural expert from the outside, the whole village would discuss whether or not to use the new technique, and if applied, to evaluate its success. In this way, the shamba of Litowa was known to produce higher yields and better qualities than any of the surrounding villages (WENNER 1970: 126–129).

Apart from the RDA school (see chapter 3.3.1), a nursery was set up in Litowa with the support of Wenner in 1966. One of the main reasons for the establishment of the nursery in Litowa was the need to attend to the nourishment of the pre-school children. Traditionally, this task would have been taken care of by their grandmothers, but in Litowa, there were mostly young couples, who made up the village – and they had to take care of the communal field work. Apart from this pragmatic reasoning, the decision was made to provide the young children with the best food available in the village, rather than the worst, as was the traditional way. Therefore, the nursery was given the number one priority in allocation of the limited food resources of the community. Through this approach, the child death rate was almost zero in Litowa, as compared with up to 50% in surrounding villages, in WENNER's anecdotal account (WENNER 1970: 60p.). The dispensary at Litowa was operated by Ngomaty, the village chairman, and would often attend to patients from other villages, which had no medical services. It appears as if the dispensary was fairly well stocked for its remote location, although more severe cases had to be transferred to the missionary hospital at Peramiho (WENNER 1970: 71).

Despite such remarkable results and the dedication to bring development to the village, traditional customs and ideas were still very important to the people of Litowa. The chapter describing the death of a young girl gives a good impression of the villagers and their community between tradition and future. In the Ujamaa meetings, everyone was allowed to speak and votes were seldom taken, usually a topic was debated until consensus could be reached. While members of the community saw themselves as equals, traditions, like letting wazee speak first, were still very important in the proceedings. Some of the wazee, however, still had issues with a perceived loss of status, for instance if they had to sit on the ground, while the younger board members used chairs. Furthermore, the belief in spirits, curses and other elements of animism was still very much alive in the community, even if they were committed to new technologies like tractors or modern medicine. Those beliefs manifested themselves in extreme situations, like the aforementioned death of the young girl (WENNER 1970: 90–99).

Maternal health was another area in which modern development and tradition were sometimes at conflict in Litowa. While one of the younger women was trained to be a midwife, the older women had reservations about trusting her judgement, when complications arose during giving birth. In most cases, however, complicated cases were transferred to Peramiho hospital, where another issue could be found: As the missionary hospital was adhering to catholic rules, some operations would not be performed, such as tying the fallopian tubes to impede another pregnancy, even if it was diagnosed that this woman would die if going through another birth (after having already suffered from three complicated pregnancies). In such cases, women had to rely on the government hospital in Songea, and be very discrete about it, even within the Litowa community (WENNER 1970: 154–165). Later on, the trained midwife would set up a rudimentary delivery room within the village, and less complicated cases could be dealt with there. With the extended dispensary, Litowa was becoming a health center for the RDA (WENNER 1970: 166p.).

Litowa's reputation for being a sort of socialist model village was so well known that even the Israeli ambassador at Dar es Salaam got word of it. For him, the organization of daily life and the organization of labor had a great deal of resemblance to the kibbutzim in Israel, and he wanted to get more information on the village. A visit was arranged, and while the ambassador was impressed with the villagers' success, the villagers were puzzled to learn that there were other farmers so far away that had a similar approach to development. Millinga, who was by then the leader of

SERA was invited on a journey to Israel, to experience a kibbutz first hand in 1966. When he came back, he immediately began to share the knowledge of his hosts, as well as his admiration for their success as he deemed the environment to be much harsher there in comparison to Litowa (WENNER 1970: 195–204). When reflecting on the core values of the villagers that led them pursue their model of cooperative development and collective farming, WENNER (1970: 235–237) argues that it was first and foremost their desire to take control over their own lives, to create a more prosperous future for themselves and their children. It was their own interpretation of Ujamaa, their own work and their own decision to choose hard work and freedom, which made them join a village like Litowa.

Litowa after the RDA

Litowa was probably hit the hardest by the disbandment of the RDA, as the self-organized form of development that was started there was thoroughly destroyed. From being one of the model villages for national development, Litowa turned into being a stagnating little place, like so many in this remote part of Tanzania. A survey on Ujamaa development conducted in 29 sample villages of the Southern Highlands at the beginning of the 1980s ranked Litowa number 23 in overall development and 27th in village prosperity. Agricultural production was low on both private and communal fields and even the once revolutionary approach to participatory village government had apparently given way to a very low ranking in quality of communal decision-making (SCHULTHEIS & SESHAMANI 1982: 9.8-9.12).

EDWARDS (1998: 18) remembers seeing the remains of the once prosperous past everywhere around the village, abandoned buildings and machinery illuminating the demise. During own field visit in 2015, the ruins of RDA structures could still be seen adjacent to the village headquarters – all of them fallen beyond disrepair. The cattle-dip was out of use and hardly recognizable as it had become engulfed by the reemerging bush, the water-tank and the piping system erected during the village's heydays were out of use and the women of Litowa had to get their water from the river – as if the development during the 1960s had never happened.

Village Layout and historically relevant places as remembered by the villagers

As described in chapter 4, the village of Litowa has been mapped in 2015. According to any information available in literature, as well as the statements by local authorities, this was the first time such a map was created. The mapping itself was conducted in the central part of the village, which is Litowa itself. As has been mentioned before, the village as an administrative unit includes some further nucleated settlements which could not be visited during the field study (the general setting of Madamba, the bordering sub-village to the West, is included in the map). Litowa itself has a linear layout, with most of the residential building lined up along the main dirt road which follows the topography of the area and runs along the top of a small ridge in a Northwest-Southeast direction (see Map 2).

Map 2: Litowa

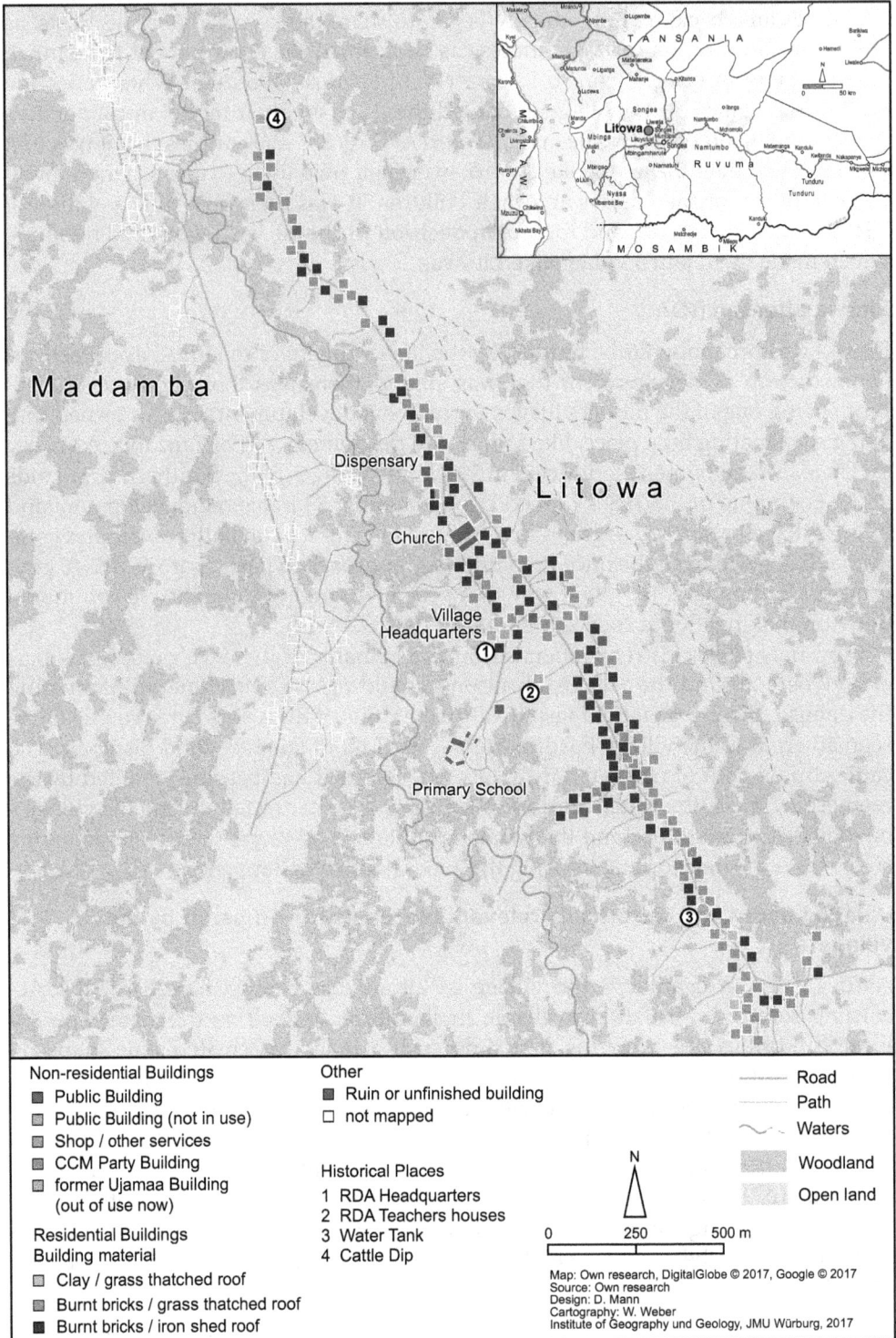

Madamba

Litowa

Dispensary

Church

Village
Headquarters
①

②

Primary School

③

④

Non-residential Buildings
- ▪ Public Building
- ▪ Public Building (not in use)
- ▪ Shop / other services
- ▪ CCM Party Building
- ▪ former Ujamaa Building
  (out of use now)

Residential Buildings
Building material
- ▫ Clay / grass thatched roof
- ▪ Burnt bricks / grass thatched roof
- ▪ Burnt bricks / iron shed roof

Other
- ▪ Ruin or unfinished building
- ▫ not mapped

Historical Places
1 RDA Headquarters
2 RDA Teachers houses
3 Water Tank
4 Cattle Dip

Road
Path
Waters
Woodland
Open land

N

0   250   500 m

Map: Own research, DigitalGlobe © 2017, Google © 2017
Source: Own research
Design: D. Mann
Cartography: W. Weber
Institute of Geography und Geology, JMU Würburg, 2017

The central place of the village is situated between the village headquarters and the dispensary. Today, the village headquarters consist of several rooms in a burnt brick, iron shed building, which is directly connected to the party office of CCM. Further notable public buildings include the church and the primary school, where four teachers were taking care of around 370 students, as of 2015. As can be seen on the map, there are very few shops or other services within the village and all of the shops consist of only one-window stores or simple wooden street stalls.

Most of the residential buildings consist of walls made from burnt bricks, which are produced on site by stacking clay bricks on a pile with holes for adding wood and burning the bricks. Very few residential buildings still have clay walls. Roughly one half of the houses have an iron shed roof, which has to be bought at the market, while the other half sport a grass thatched roof made from local material. The houses vary little in size (mostly two to three rooms), but some consist of several residential buildings arranged around a courtyard. Most of the houses within the village have a small garden around them, while the actual fields are located at varying distances around the village.

During the historical transect, some places were pointed out by the participants as being relevant to their understanding of Litowa's past. Those places are indicated by the numbers on the map. The most important site in this context can be found at number 1, were the ruins of the formers RDA headquarters can still be seen. Unfortunately, none of the participants was able to give an exact account of the specific functions of each of the buildings. In 2015, only the decaying brick walls were still standing and the areal was plastered with bush. According to local information, it was at this site where the RDA had its head office, where the Ujamaa assemblies took place and where the collective dinners were held afterwards. Nowadays, village meetings are held adjacent to the old RDA buildings on the open space in front of the new village headquarters.

The next place visited during the transect was the Litowa primary school. However, the current buildings which are arranged around a central courtyard are a more recent structure, not identical with the original RDA school. As of 2015, only students from the village of Litowa itself are visiting the school, and there is no boarding anymore. This means that students coming from other settlements within the administrative boarders of Litowa have to walk several kilometers to and from school each day. The only remains of the old RDA school were identified by the participants in the form of two deteriorated residential houses for teachers (number 2 on the map).

The next important historical place which was shown during the transect was the water tank (number 3) in the Southern part of the village. In the days of the RDA, water from the river was pumped up into this round stone tank and then distributed within the village through a gravity fed pipe system. According to local information, the system was in operation for several years after the disbandment of RDA, but the pump itself has since fallen beyond disrepair and the village would have no financial capacity to invest in a replacement. Regrettably, nobody at the village was able to provide clear information on the exact years of operation.

The basic layout of Litowa appears not to have changed since the time of the RDA, although the residential houses have been modernized and enlarged in many cases. The only further place that seemed noteworthy to the participants of the transect is the former cattle dip, indicated by number 4 on the map. This structure is now engulfed by bush and fallen beyond disrepair. Its construction had been one of the last development projects implemented under the tutelage of the RDA, and was meant to support the collective cattle keeping of the village by enabling better animal health care. At the high point of this operation, the villagers had around 300 heads of cattle, according to local information. In 2015, there was no collective cattle keeping in Litowa, and only very few villagers were keeping small numbers of cattle on individual basis.

Since census data are only available for the entire administrative area of the village, it is not possible to give a reliable number of inhabitants for the settlement of Litowa proper, which is shown in the map. In 2012, there were 1,703 people living in all of Litowa village, according to the most recent available census data (NBS 2012: 191).

Economic Activities of the villagers in 2015

According to personal information from the village chairman, maize production per acre is around 300 kg per year and every household would have a private shamba between 3 and 6 acres under cultivation, with the fields being shifted every three years. Other crops commonly grown include rice (in the valleys), cassava and sesame. Soya production in the village had started in 2014, by his accounts (*GBE 7; 2/26/2015*).

Figure 8: Distribution of field sizes per household in Litowa

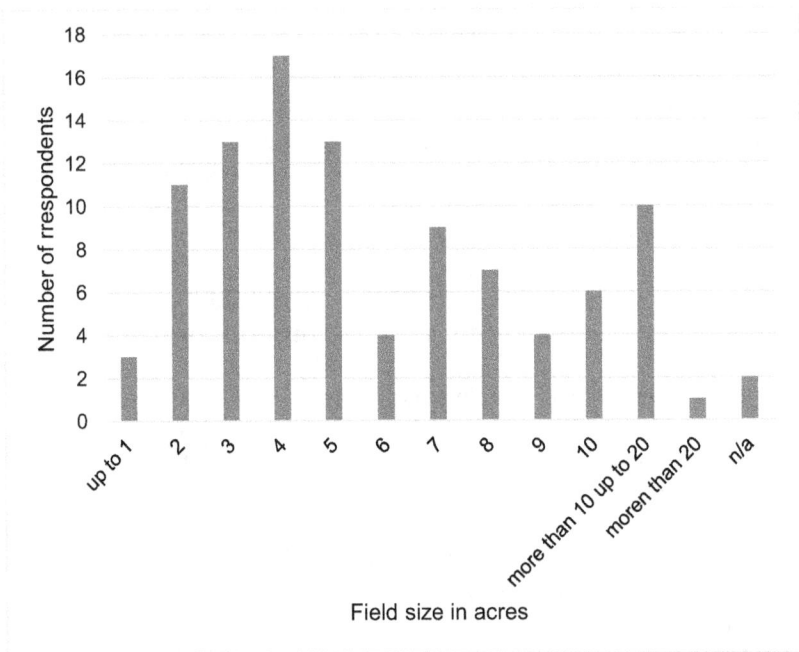

Field size in acres

Source: own survey

Exactly 100 villagers from Litowa responded to the village questionnaires in 2015. All of the respondents in this village were performing agriculture and can therefore be considered as farmers. As the family can be considered the basic unit of production in the rural areas of Tanzania (see above) all questions relating to the economic activities of the respondents were directed at those of their family or household as such. Out of the three case study villages, Litowa took the middle spot concerning average field sizes per household, with 6.75 acres. Most farmers were cultivating fields between one and five acres, while ten farmers had more than 10 acres under cultivation. Only one shamba was bigger than 20 acres. The distribution of field sizes per household can be seen in Fig. 8.

Most of the households in Litowa (38%) were cultivating two crops on their fields on a regular basis, 13% were only cultivating one crop, 27% three crops and 19% four different crops. Only three households were cultivating more than four crops on their land. By far the most common crop under cultivation in all three villages was maize (mahindi), and in Litowa, it was cultivated by 99 out of the 100 responding households. The most common secondary crops in this village were maharage (common bean) with 39% of households and ufuta (sesame) with 36%. Soya had been cultivated by 26% of the respondents in 2015. 47% of the households were stating that they would consume all of their produce themselves in 2015, while 53% were also selling some of their produce at the market, as a cash source for their family. Only 12% of the respondents were employing additional workers from outside their families for their farm work, the lowest percentage of the case study villages. On the other hand, membership in vikundi was the highest in the Litowa sample, with 53% of respondents stating that they were active in one of the farmers' groups in the village.

With regards to animal husbandry, the large majority of households in every village were keeping some animals, with chicken, goats and pigs being the most common ones. Overall, animal husbandry was performed by 94% of the respondents' households in Litowa. In this village, 90.4% of those households held chicken (12.5 on average), 56.4% had goats (7.4 on average) and 41.5% had pigs (3.8 on average). 12 of the responding households were keeping a total of 43 cattle at the village. Only 25% of respondents had other forms of income apart from their agricultural activities, and only 55% were regularly having three meals a day – the lowest percentage of all three villages in both categories. 43 out of the 100 respondents had two meals a day and two had only one meal per day on average.

5.4.2 Matetereka – Tanzania's last Ujamaa village?

The village of Matetereka is situated to the very North of Songea Rural District, close to the border to Njombe, 150 km north of Songea and approximately 12 km off the Songea-Njombe main road. It belongs to Wino ward and lies on two Y-shaped ridges between 960 and 1300 m a.s.l. The original Ujamaa village (Matetereka A) is situated at the very end of this ridge, while the sub-villages Matetereka B and C are subsequent additions settled during villagization. In 1994, the population of all three sub villages was 2,242 people in around 320 households (EDWARDS 1998: 10), mostly of the Wabena ethnic group (and some of the Wapangwa) with only a small increase of population occurring up to 2012, when there were 2,652 inhabitants in Matetereka (NBS 2012: 191). The village is characterized by a very favorable climate for agriculture, with good soils, rainfalls of around 1200 per year (in one long rainy season) and moderate temperature due to its highland location (LEWIN 1973: 189).

During Edwards' visit in 1998, coffee was grown as the main cash crop in the village, with maize being the main food crop. Apart from coffee cultivation, additional cash income was derived from the sale of beans, groundnuts, bananas, finger millet and cassava. Most households can achieve two maize harvests per year, as in the dry season, maize is cultivated at the valley floors, while it is cultivated on the ridge tops during rainy season. All fields are usually located within 5 miles of a farmer's compound, with up to 1 ha per household being cultivated directly around the compound. The latter is used for permanent types of agriculture, with coffee, banana and other crops grown on the same field, making use of the different heights of the respective crops. Another one to three ha are located in the surrounding areas. Around 1 to 2 ha per household were cultivated each season, and the land is allotted by the local government. In contrast to the times of the RDA, all farming is carried out by hand, as no tractors or ox ploughs are available. Even in 1998, a small number of farmers were employing laborers on their land, and there was a small amount of non-farm enterprises (bars, small shops, masons, carpenters, etc.) located at the center of Matetereka A. In 1998, all houses were already made of burnt bricks, with ca. 50% topped by an iron roof (see Map 4 of 2015 for comparison), three shops and three milling machines were operating and the cattle dip was still in use. According to EDWARDS, the gravity fed water supply system was installed in 1993, providing a tap within 100 m of most compounds (during the field visit in 2015, most of the taps were not working anymore). Wood collected from the surrounding Miombo woodlands has been the most important source of energy, as there was (and still is) no electricity supply in Matetereka (EDWARDS 1998: 10–12).

As was the case for Litowa, Matetereka took off in the early days of independence due to enthusiastic young farmers, who wanted to help in building the nation according to Nyerere's vision. In contrast to many such initiatives that failed (including at least four in the Wino area), Matetereka profited from its founders' pragmatic step-by-step approach, as well as the support of the RDA – especially in the early days of the village (LEWIN 1973: 189).

It all started in January 1962, when six men from the village of Wino (the center of Wino ward) wanted to start communal cash-crop production on this fertile ridge. Their move found support with the local authorities, including a man named Lukas Mayemba, who was the Ward Party Chairman of TANU at that time. Gervas Mkomba became the first village Chairman, and Abel Njalika the first village secretary (both were interviewed in 2015, see below). Until 1964, the communal farm was known under the name of Mahiwa, and the early wajamaa were only staying in temporary structures from Monday to Friday, while returning to their home villages on the weekends. The name of the village was changed to Matetereka, to avoid confusion with another settlement known as Mahiwa in the same area. The new name is supposedly the kibena term for a riffle cartridge and was coined by Njalika, as he had found some of these while helping with his father's beekeeping activities in the area during his youth. In August 1964, Mkomba and Njalika were invited by Ntimbanjayo Millinga to attend a three-day seminar on the RDA's activities in Litowa. Being attracted to the RDA's approach of communal farming and living, the villagers decided to move to Matetereka fulltime, and from 1965 onwards they started to prepare permanent houses for their families. By January 1966, all families had relocated at Matetereka. The process was accelerated through the lending of a tractor by the RDA. They started to implement similar structures of communal farming and decision-making like in Litowa and were able to cultivate 15 acres of coffee, 10 acres of maize and two acres of groundnuts communally in the 1966 season. Later on, a brand-new tractor was donated to the village by the RDA, which seems to have been in use until at least 1992. It was used to carry Matetereka's children to the Litowa school, as well as for the transport of maize. To outsiders, the village was known for its strict organization and work plans, and sometimes was criticized for appearing like a colonial sisal farm, due to its apparent discipline (EDWARDS 1998: 13–15).

Nevertheless, all work plans and other issues were agreed upon by the Ujamaa assembly, which were held after a long working day on the fields, just like in Litowa. This, however, did not discourage long an lively discussions at the assembly of Matetereka's "radical democracy" (LEWIN 1973: 190). Apart from the implementation of village democracy, equally high importance was given on the education of the youth, as children in this village would "start living as socialists before they are two" (LEWIN 1973: 191).

Survival of the Ujamaa group at Matetereka

After the RDA's disbandment in 1969, Matetereka was the only of the original 50 Ujamaa villages under the tutelage of the Department for Ujamaa Village Development, in which the institutions of its original Ujamaa group survived more or less intact and even survived the impact of villagization during the 1970s (EDWARDS 1998: 18, 41).

When the CC's decision to bring the Association's assets under state control was carried out by the delegation in 1969, the villagers were able to circumvent the expropriation of their possession through clever political tactics and the remote location of their village, compared to the other member villages of the RDA. Nevertheless, there were conflicts with the new Regional Commissioner, who tried to enforce central control on rural development and Ujamaa cooperatives (EDWARDS 1998: 18–22).

The impact of villagization led to additional tensions between the original Ujamaa group and the new settlers who came from all parts of Tanzania and were settled at the new sub-villages B and C. The main source of conflict throughout the 1970s and 80s was the perceived wealth of the original group and their unwillingness to share the fruits of their cooperative with the new arrivals. The original wajamaa on the other hand, were reluctant to share material benefits, as they thought the new village members were supposed to create their own base of living and were only willing to give them their knowledge, but not the readymade product of their attempt on collective development. New members were accepted into the group after 1969, if they were willing to adapt to the way of doing things, and the group reached its peak membership in 1980 at around 140. After that, block farming started at Matetereka, and the numbers declined continuously to about 25 members in 1998, many of them still from the first generation of settlers. Nevertheless, the village received many rewards as best developed village in the region throughout the 1980s (EDWARDS 1998: 29–35).

The tensions reached their braking point in 1987, when Lukas Mayemba was replaced as chairman of the village while he was on an educational visit to Bulgaria (which was granted as a present to the village by Nyerere himself). From thereon, different factions from the three sub-villages continued to argue about the importance of village (i.e. government) land vs. land owned by the Ujamaa groups of the village. The original group's activities declined throughout the 1980s, and a large amount of their land was no longer cultivated communally. In the 1990s, an ongoing legal battle between the Ujamaa group and the village government over the group's coffee plantation commenced, as the new chairman of the village insisted on turning all arable land into village land (EDWARDS 1998: 35–38).

While still existing in 1998, the last continuously existing Ujamaa group of Tanzania sold all their assets and ceased to exist in 2000 (*NCW 4; 3/6/2015*), although many of the last members are still engaged in cooperative agriculture (mainly the Kujitegemea Group, which can be seen as the direct successor (*GI 11; 9/3/2015*), and some in the Tangawizi Group (*GI 7; 9/2/2015*)).

Nevertheless, Matetereka remained one of the most prosperous and developed villages in the Southern Highlands area (SCHULTHEIS & SESHAMANI 1982: 9.8-9.12) even in the decade following the disbandment of the RDA. EDWARDS (1998: 44–49) sees the good organization, high motivation and experience of the original wajamaa group as the main factors for this success. Instead of abandoning their model of self-controlled development and falling into the role of passive recipients of central government interventions, the group at Matetereka introduced the RDA model as the leading development strategy even under the new political structure. By a combination of adaption and resistance to the new development environment, they were able to carry on with being one of the leading villages of Tanzania in almost all aspects of development.

Village Layout and historically relevant places as remembered by the villagers

Thanks to the research conducted by EDWARDS (1998), there was more detailed information on the geographical situation of Matetereka available than in the case of Litowa. The basic pattern of land-use for the entire administrative area of Matetereka village has not changed since and can be seen in Map 3. For the further understanding of the research findings, the three sub-villages of Matetereka A, B and C play an important role. As in the case of Litowa, the general Layout of the village is indicated by the topographical situation, with all residential areas concentrated in a linear fashion at the top of the ridges along dirt roads, and all other forms of land use dispersed in the remaining village area. Indeed, Matetereka does have a land-use plan dating from around 2005 which is kept in the village headquarters, but has no relevance to the actual activities of the village government. The normative categories of land use are the same as in this map based on Edwards (*GBE 15; 8/30/2015*).

Map 3: Land use and basic settlement pattern of Matetereka

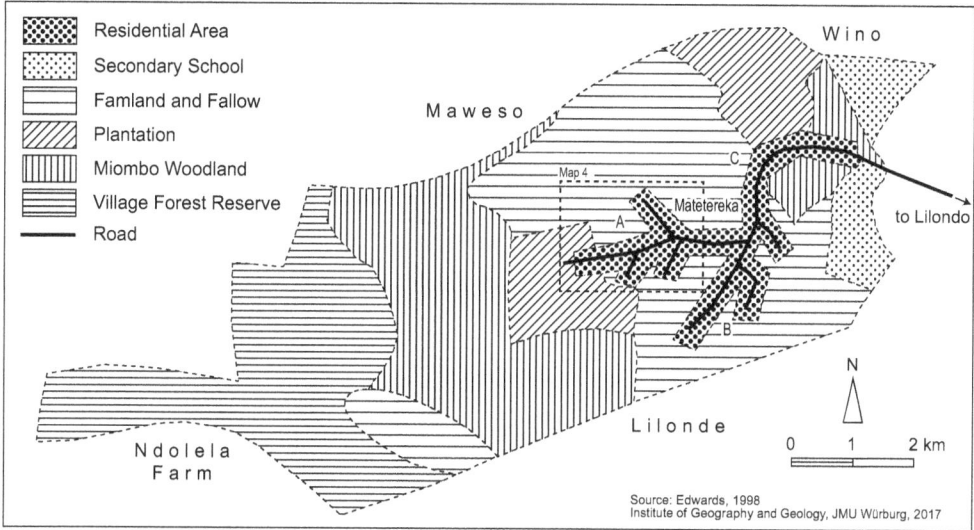

The oldest part of the village, founded by the original Ujamaa group in the 1960s is Matetereka A at the very end of the ridge. The other parts, B and C, were only settled during the era of villagization in the 1970s, when a large group of people was resettled to the area. During the field visit, a more detailed settlement map of Matetereka A was created, which can be seen in Map 4.

The most important buildings, like the village headquarters, the CCM office, the primary school and the church are located in the eastern part of Matetereka A and act for the whole village. The layout and structure of these buildings is very similar to those found in Litowa. However, the actual center of Matetereka A is characterized by several stores and simple pubs, indicating a much higher level of commerce when compared to Litowa.

The residential buildings of Matetereka A are almost entirely made from locally produced burnt bricks, and iron shed roofs are much more common than in Litowa. Most of the houses are comprised of several buildings arranged around a courtyard and surrounded by a small garden. As in Litowa, most of the actual fields are dispersed around the remaining village area. In contrast to Litowa, the residential areas are spread out along several ridges, courtesy to the local topography.

During the historical transect walk, several places of historic relevance were identified by the participants. Thanks to the extensive knowledge of Lukas Mayemba, the description of these places has been more detailed than in the case of Litowa. First of all, a group of buildings in the very center of Matetereka A was named as the location of the former Ujamaa group activities. Among them was the former Ujamaa store, built in 1968 (number 1 on the map), where commodities for personal consumption were acquired at large by the group and then distributed to its members, in order to achieve better prices for the individuals. Adjacent was a guest house

Map 4: Matetereka (A)

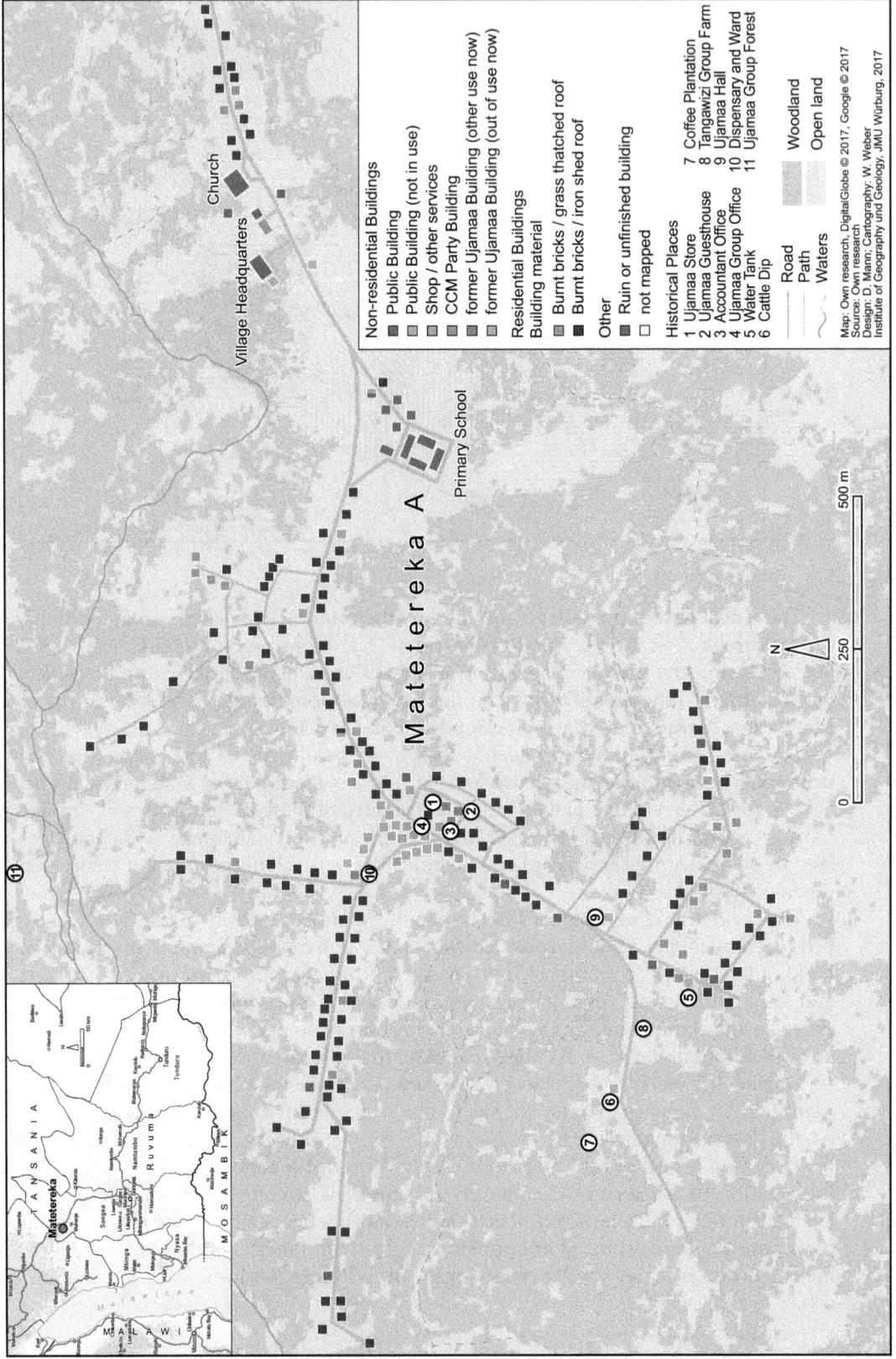

Non-residential Buildings
- Public Building
- Public Building (not in use)
- Shop / other services
- CCM Party Building
- former Ujamaa Building (other use now)
- former Ujamaa Building (out of use now)

Residential Buildings
Building material
- Burnt bricks / grass thatched roof
- Burnt bricks / iron shed roof

Other
- Ruin or unfinished building
- not mapped

Historical Places
1 Ujamaa Store
2 Ujamaa Guesthouse
3 Accountant Office
4 Ujamaa Group Office
5 Water Tank
6 Cattle Dip
7 Coffee Plantation
8 Tangawizi Group Farm
9 Ujamaa Hall
10 Dispensary and Ward
11 Ujamaa Group Forest

— Road
— Path
— Waters

Woodland
Open land

Matetereka A

Church

Village Headquarters

Primary School

Map: Own research, DigitalGlobe © 2017, Google © 2017
Source: Own research
Design: D. Mann; Cartography: W. Weber
Institute of Geography und Geology, JMU Würburg, 2017

0   250   500 m

owned by the group, which was used to accommodate guests of the village (number 2), as well as the office of the group accountant and the store for farm machinery (number 3). All of these three buildings were owned by the group until 2000 and then sold to a private owner for other uses. The actual head office of the Ujamaa group is on the other side of the road (number 4) and currently out of use.

At the top of the village, there is a water tank (number 5), very similar to the one found in Litowa. It was supposedly fully functioning up to around 1990, and the wind-powered pump which brought the water up from the river has since fallen beyond repair. Further along the same path, the participants pointed out the remains of the decaying cattle dip (number 6), which is out of use and overwhelmed by bush, just as in Litowa. As of 2015, there is no communal cattle keeping in Matetereka.

In the same area, the former coffee plantation of the Ujamaa group was visited (number 7). After the end of the group in 2000, it was bought by the Kujitegemea group, but is now out of use due to the legal battle between this group and the village government (see below). Several of the coffee trees have been uprooted and destroyed, and the rest were in very bad shape at the time of the visit. The foundations of the planned office of Kujitegemea group was pointed out at the same site, but construction is on hold until the final verdict has been spoken. On the way back to the residential part of the village, the participants indicated the location of the collective ginger field owned by Tangawizi group (number 8), which was one of the ongoing collective agricultural activities of the original members of the Ujamaa group as of 2015.

Further down the main road, the transect walk took a longer stop at the former Ujamaa hall (number 9). This rather large building is currently owned by Wino Saccos, a local savings and loans cooperative, only used occasionally for formal events or festivities (for instance, a wedding reception took place there during the time of the researcher's stay in Matetereka). Originally, however, it was constructed shortly after the abandonment of the RDA, as one of the first projects of the village's Ujamaa group conducted without the support of the association, and owned by the Wino Development Association, an institution that was supposed to replicate RDA's functions on ward level. It acted as the main gathering place for the Ujamaa assembly and other common events. The village's nursery was also operating in several smaller rooms within the building until 1987. After that, the classrooms were used by the village's secondary school, before it was moved to its current location on the road to Lilondo (see Map 3).

Back in the center of Matetereka A, the dispensary of the village was identified as another one of the important buildings of the Ujamaa era (number 10). At the time of the field study, one doctor and three nurses were working at the dispensary, which is now under the government's tutelage. It has only one bed for potential patients, while the adjacent sick ward – which was also constructed as an Ujamaa project – is currently out of use. The final place of interest during the transect was the former forest owned by the Ujamaa group (number 11), which was also bought by the Kujitegemea group in 2000 and has since been the subject of legal battles concerning the ownership of former Ujamaa group property (see below).

Economic Activities of the villagers in 2015

Regarding the agricultural activities of the villagers in Matetereka in 2015, there was the biggest range of households' farm sizes among the case study villages. Out of the 109 respondents to the village questionnaires, 102 were engaging in farming activities. Most farmers (41 in total) had fields up to 5 acres in size, while 15 farmers had more than 20 acres under cultivation. It was also the only village were respondents were stating that they did not own their shamba, but were only renting it from a landlord – these cases are shown independently in the figure, without acreage (8 respondents, between 2 and 4 acres) – and the highest number of respondents without any shamba. Also, some respondents were mentioning that they would own more land than they would cultivate. In this case, the area under cultivation is represented in the figure. The average area under cultivation was 10.6 acres – the highest out of the three villages surveyed during the research. The distribution of field sizes can be seen in Fig. 9.

Figure 9: Distribution of field sizes per household in Matetereka

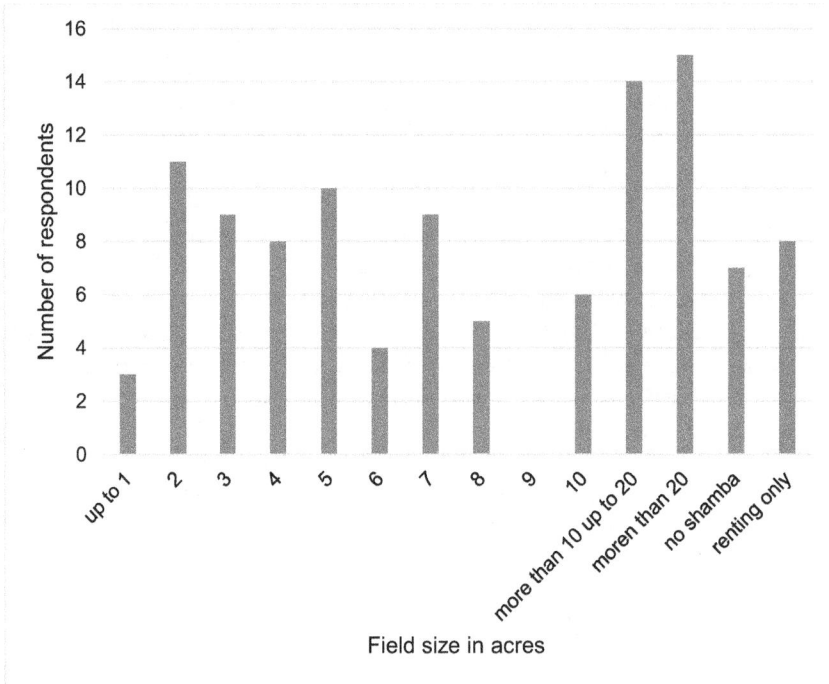

Source: own survey

As in Litowa, most farmers in Matetereka were cultivating two crops on regular basis, with this peak even more pronounced at 51% of farming households. 5.9% were cultivating only one crop, 25.5% three crops and 11.8% regularly cultivated four different crops on their fields. Another 5.9% were cultivating more than four different types of crops. Regarding crop choices, 92.1% of the farming households of the sample were cultivating maize, and 76.5% were cultivating common beans. Karanga (groundnut) was the third-most important crop with 30.4% cultivating it. Only one household had started soya production in Matetereka, and none were growing sesame. 19.6% were growing different types of banana (Ndizi and Migomba). None of the respondents were growing coffee in 2015, which had been one of the most important cash crops in the times of Ujamaa (EDWARDS 1998: 11p.), another indicator for the effect of the legal battle between the village and the Ujamaa group's successors. Only eight out of the 102 farming households in Matetereka claimed that they would only produce for their own consumption, while the remaining 94 were also able to sell some of their crops on the market, and 45.1% of the farming households were employing additional labor at some point of the growing season. The membership in farmers' groups was the lowest in Matetereka, by comparison, with only 24.5% of the whole sample stating their group membership.

Out of all respondents from the village, 73.4% stated that their household kept animals. Out of these animal-keeping households, 73.8 percent were keeping chicken (13.5 on average), 42.5% had pigs (2.7 on average) and 28.8% were holding goats (4.3 on average). In Matetereka, more respondents stated that their households would regularly enjoy three meals per day than in Litowa, at 56.9%, while 37.6% claimed their households had only two meals per day. No respondent stated that his or her household had to rely on only one meal per day in this village. Matetereka also had the highest percentage of respondents having additional occupations, besides their agricultural activities, with 40.4%.

5.4.3 Mbingamharule – Changes in a non-RDA village during and after the Ujamaa era

In contrast to the two aforementioned villages, Mbingamharule[5] never shared the unique development history of RDA. Situated in the South of Songea District, around 3 km off the Songea-Mbinga Main Road, it sits in relatively low, undulated terrain. It receives between 1000 and 1200 mm of rain each year, with the vast majority of precipitation occurring in one long rainy season between December and May. The months of June through August are considered to be the colder months, while the period leading up to the rainy season is considered to be the hot season (September to November). Average temperature is around 20°C, with monthly averages ranging between 18.9°C and 25°C (SDC 2012: 10).

The center of the village is marked by the primary school, a relatively large catholic church and a small local hospital. In 2012, the primary school had 585 students, who were educated by eight teachers in 11 class rooms. The village development plan states that there would be demand for at least two additional class rooms and three teacher accommodations (SDC 2012: 14). A few dukas (small shops) and eating

---

5 Note that there is no spelling of Mbingamharule commonly agreed on. In many sources, it is actually spelled "Mbingamhalule", and both versions are used by the local authorities. For this study, the spelling "Mbingamharule" was used because it appears to be closer to the spoken form of the village's name by its inhabitants.

places are also found in the village center (own observation). As there has been no evidence of a grassroots period of cooperative development comparable to Litowa or Matetereka, the decision was taken not perform a similar historical transect walk in Mbingamharule. Accordingly, no map of the village has been produced. Today, Mbingamharule is one of the bigger villages in this part of Songea District, having had 2,708 inhabitants at the last census in 2012 (NBS 2012: 193).

Local history has it that Mbingamharule was the birthplace of Chief Mharule of the Wangoni, who fought against the German invaders during the Maji Maji uprising. Later on, a school was built at this place, but until villagization, there were not a lot of people living in Mbingamharule itself. Peasants in this area were still living in small, scattered hamlets, and students would come to the school walking ten kilometers or more. Only in 1974, when operation vijiji reached the area, the school and the church were identified as a suitable place for a nucleated village. A large amount of people were moved to the place, but at least according to local sources, there was no force involved at Mbingamharule (*GBE 11*; 3/11/2015).

The establishment of the settlement as an Ujamaa village, under the villagization policy in 1974, had far reaching consequences for local development: Before, it had been a quaint place that had seen few changes since colonial times. Local wazee felt that life was very hard in those days, that they were missing a lot of basic things and would describe the living conditions before the arrival of Ujamaa as "duni" (inferior; *NCW 6*; 3/11/2015).

Afterwards, the centrally organized development policy focused on the provision of social services, beginning with the expansion of the school, the building of the hospital and other primary services, which was seen as progress in living standards. As in other areas of the country, the idea was that once the people had been brought together, they would also start developing in a cooperative way. Indeed, local sources verify the existence of a village shamba and collective agricultural activities throughout the 1970s, but overall results remained disappointing, and people started to abandon the communal agriculture and returned to their private fields (*GBE 11*; 3/11/2015).

In recent years, new development initiatives by the Tanzanian government have improved the infrastructure in the village, although the local road to the Songea-Mbinga main road remains unpaved and prone to mud in the rainy season. Water supply in the village does reach every neighborhood, but the pressure is still too low to guarantee secure access by every household. Furthermore, works had begun to connect Mbingamharule to the national electricity grid at the time of research (*GBE 11*; 3/11/2015; SDC 2012: 11).

Economic Activities of the villagers in 2015

In Mbingamharule, a total of 95 inhabitants responded to the questionnaires, with 91 stating that they had their own shamba, while four did not have their own field. According to the numbers of the village development plan, 81% of the farmers had their own fields, while 19% were renting their shamba in 2012 (SDC 2012: 16). As in the other villages, the bulk of respondents had between one and five acres under cultivation, but their percentage was even higher than in Litowa or Matetereka, with

168

75 respondents in total stating field sizes up to five acres. Only one respondent had more than 10 acres, and the average farm size was 4.1 acres – the lowest average acreage of all villages. Yet, 30 respondents stated that they would employ additional work for their agricultural activities – more than in Litowa but less than in Matetereka. The distribution of field sizes can be seen in Fig. 10.

Possibly reflecting the relatively small areas under cultivation for each household in Mbingamharule, the majority (52.7%) of farming households were only cultivating one crop, 29.0% had two crops, 8.6% three and 7.5% four different crops under cultivation. Only two households in total were cultivating more than four crops in Mbingamharule. Maize was the dominant crop in this village as well, with 86% of farming households cultivating it. The secondary crops were less pronounced than in the other villages, with 20.4% growing soya, 16.1% paddy, 12.7% sesame and 10.8% common beans. Out of the 93 respondents giving accounts of their households' agricultural activities, 58 (62.4%) stated that they would only produce for their own consumption, while the rest were selling some produce at the market. This was the highest percentage of food-only production across the three samples in this study. 42.1% of all respondents were members in one of the villages' farmers' groups.

Figure 10: Distribution of field sizes per household in Mbingamharule

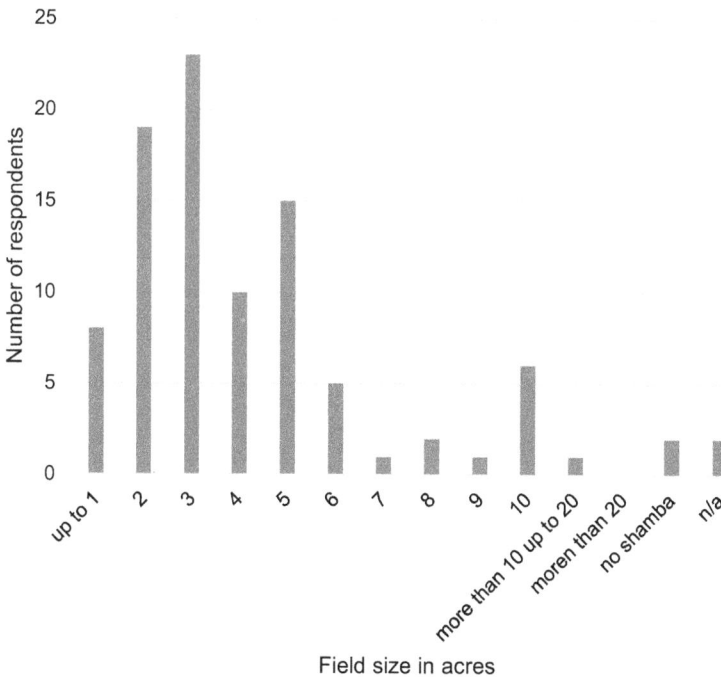

Field size in acres

In 2012, 75% of the adult inhabitants of the village had agriculture as their main occupation, while 19% had both agriculture and animal husbandry (SDC 2012: 12). Among all respondents of the questionnaires in 2015, 73.7% stated that their households would keep animals. Yet, in comparison to the other villages, in Mbingamharule there was a much lower tendency among the animal keeping households to keep more than one sort of animals. 47.1 percent had an average of 20 chicken, while 40% of animal keeping households held goats (5.4 on average). 20 percent kept pigs (3.5 on average) and 17.1% had cattle, with an average of 6.6 heads per cattle keeping household. 28.4% of respondents had additional occupations other than farming, and the village had the highest percentage of households enjoying three meals a day as stated by 71.6% of all respondents from that village, 26.3% had two and only 2.1% had one meal per day.

6 Findings: The narrative of development in Ruvuma

Within this section, the findings of the field studies will be analyzed by dividing the emerging narratives gained from interviews and village questionnaires into two different perspectives: "The view from outside" will address the perceptions of actors that are not a direct part of village live, i.e. the regional and district development authorities, as well as the various NGOs involved in development activities based in Songea. Thereafter, the "inside view" of the villagers on Ujamaa will be presented. After that, chapter 6.3 will show the emerging image of the local perceptions and definitions of development before presenting the challenges which the different stakeholders are seeing for their own development, as well as that of their villages and the region as a whole. Finally, chapter 6.4 will summarize and discuss the different findings from the field study in relation to the original research question: What is left from Ujamaa?

6.1 Ujamaa: The view from outside

The following chapters will give an impression of the perception of Ujamaa by "outside" stakeholders, i.e. those who are not directly based inside the village communities. Special emphasis will be given on the views of the different NGOs and their activities in Ruvuma.

6.1.1 Regional and District government

According to the Tanzanian structure of government, regional and district authorities have a distinct role in the planning and implementation of regional development strategies (see chapter 5.3.2). Although they are directly involved in local development as well, they are considered to be part of the outside view on Ujamaa development within the framework of this study, as "inside" in this sense is only the direct evidence on the village level. Both the regional headquarters of Ruvuma Region and the District Office of Songea Rural District were approached during the field visit, in order to gain an understanding of the perception of local Ujamaa development by these authorities. Unfortunately, neither office was particularly forthcoming in the provision of data and first-hand documentations on the Ujamaa era. Therefore, two interviews with the Regional Development Officer and the District Planning Officer (respectively in charge of development planning in their level of government) will have to suffice for this insight. Neither of the two interviewees was originally from Ruvuma, and their general interest in the particular history of Ujamaa within the region appeared to be quite low, as was their understanding of its specificities. At least the Regional Development Officer, however, appeared to have some knowledge of the early attempts of cooperative villages in the region, albeit with a lack of detail:

> "Uhm, Ujamaa…. It started before we have. Since we turned to independence in, in the early 50s (sic!), eh…There was some initiative from the government to try to speed up development at the grassroot level. So, one of the inputs which was done, was the – to establish Ujamaa villages …. In 1957 [67?], they made some ujamaa villages, people were working together, planning together, implementing projects together."
> Anthony Nginga, Regional Development Officer, Songea (*GBE 12*; 3/12/2015)

Without further elaboration on what appears to be his knowledge of the RDA and possibly other early villages, he went on to describe the further actions of the Tanzanian state in implementing Ujamaa: Villagization, which had shaped the structure of the Region much more thoroughly than those early villages anyway:

> "From that, in 1972, there was ehm another project, which was adopted by the government, which is villagization. And planning coordinated from the Region, according to the environment, and the resources they have. And then it was followed, in 1975, where the government announced, that all the village, all the- all the established eh villages, that all the people should be live together in the village there. In order to facilitate the government to provide services, social services, such as water, dispensaries and so on. So, when we started in 1974, people were establishing collective, communal projects, like farms, eh, … Especially in Ruvuma, where we are very prominent in producing maize."
> Anthony Nginga, Regional Development Officer, Songea (*GBE 12*; 3/12/2015)

Yet, while he came to the conclusion that the socialist period within the region was truly over now, he still remembered that some of the Region's villages rose to quite a prominent status during the Ujamaa era – specifically because of their high degree of cooperation and their success in collective farming:

> "Ok, but, that of course, as currently we have changed now. I can say we are not that type of socialistic. It's just, eh, capitalist way today. Because people are not working together, they are – just everybody is doing on his own. No, not that thing which were done collective, eh, during that time. Now, they are not doing something like that. So, in Ruvuma, from my memory, we have some villages, which were – which became very popular on Ujamaa. Especially Matetereka. Some, some villages managed even to have, even to run the projects, but eventually, they are, nowadays, that project died. But, ok, collective work, markets, … It was Matetereka, and something Litowa, and eh, ehm, in Mbinga. In Mbinga, there were, during that early eighties, there was some villages which managed to have…, some collective, communal projects. Like, to have, eh, I think during that time about ten villages were formed in [Ruvuma] (…) But as the time goes, I told, but the projects are not existing."
> Anthony Nginga, Regional Development Officer, Songea (*GBE 12*; 3/12/2015)

Unfortunately, the District Planning Officer, Charles Mihayo, was not able to give more detailed information on his perception of the Ujamaa history, mainly because he felt that he had been working at this position for too short a time to give a valuable evaluation. Nevertheless he concluded that Ujamaa as such was definitely over in Songea Rural District (*GBE 8; 3/2/2015*).

6.1.2 The "NGO Nexus" of Songea

Being the administrative capital of Ruvuma Region and the biggest settlement (just over 200,000 inhabitants in 2012; NBS 2012: 197) in the Southern Highland region south of Mbeya, Songea serves as a hub for various NGOs which are operating within the region. At least 50 different NGOs currently have offices in town (*GBE 4; 2/24/2015*) and various organizations have common projects or are coordinating otherwise regarding their development activities throughout Ruvuma Region. There has also been a network of all NGOs in Songea (called Songo), but according to local NGO representatives, there are currently very few activities of this network, which was described as a "sleeping man" in this context (*GBE 5; 2/24/2015*).

The different NGOs

During the research, representatives from six different organizations were interviewed in seven interviews at their respective offices in a semi-structured way, focusing on information on their activities, their perception of challenges and their definition of development. In the second part of each interview, their knowledge and opinion on the Ujamaa history of the region was at the core of interest, as well as their evaluation of the changes since this era. Most of the respondents did not have an extended knowledge of Ujamaa history – usually the fact that they were not yet in Ruvuma in those times, personally, was cited as a reason. In this case, the changes they had observed during their stay in the Region were asked for. Six of the interviews were conducted during the first field visit in Ruvuma, between February and March 2015, and served as an opener for understanding the general development environment of Ruvuma. Out of these six NGOs, four were dealing directly with development initiatives for local farmers, namely Caritas Songea, RUCODIA (Ruvuma Commercialization and Diversification of Agriculture), Songea Network Center (SNC), and MVIWATA (*Mitandao wa Vikundi vya Wakulima Tanzania*; Tanzanian Network of Farmers' Groups).

Caritas Songea is running various assistance and market creation programs for small-scale farmers, as well as supporting them in the setting up of groups for saving and internal lending schemes (SILK). Caritas, as a Catholic Church organization, runs under the archdiocese of Songea, but offers support to people of all denominations. They have been active in Songea since before independence, and were originally more focused on charity and relief operations. Their current focus, however, is more on income-generating projects for the local peasantry. Their most important activity from the perspective of this research turned out to be the "Soya ni Pesa" ("Soya is Money") program, which is sponsored by the United States Department for Agriculture (USDA) and implemented by Caritas. In this project, farmers can learn how to cultivate soya for income generation. The produce is then sold to the market, with Caritas organizing the buyers for the farmers. Usually, these soya projects are operated by farmers' groups (*GBE 1; 2/23/2015*; see also chapter 6.2.4). The impact of this program on the creation of such groups proved to be considerable in the case study villages. Therefore, one additional interview was conducted with the program coordinator of Soya ni Pesa at the conclusion of the second field visit (*GBE 17; 9/9/2015*).

The second NGO, RUCODIA, also deals with creating markets for small-farmers, as well as the diversification of agriculture in Ruvuma. One of their programs includes the cultivation of sunflowers as income generation opportunity. In contrast to Caritas, RUCODIA is only active within the region, they have been operating since 15 years (*GBE 2; 2/23/2015*).

SNC, on the other hand, is a fairly new addition to Songea's NGO scene, founded by a local priest from Mbingamharule, who had gone to Munich, Germany for his doctorate in theology. Upon return, he started this NGO, which also organizes farmers' group in various villages throughout the Region. They are also planning to create a technical training center in Songea, where young primary graduates from the villages could get training in carpentry, mechanics and other professions (*GBE 10; 3/10/2015*).

Last but not least, MVIWATA operates as an NGO itself, offering training and technical advice to farmers' groups, but is also acting as the national network of those groups. It is also a member organization of the international network Via Campesina. They are active in the whole of Tanzania. Their main focus of work is the creation and support of farmers' groups (vikundi), through which the organization facilitates its capacity building activities, as well as their advocacy for the political recognition of small-scale farmers from the Tanzanian periphery. At the time of research, MVIWATA was active in 24 villages across Ruvuma. Apart from their general advisory role, this NGO also implements concrete projects, if funds are available. One of these projects is the support of small farmers to get traditional land right titles. For this undertaking, villages in which enough farmers' groups are willing to participate have been surveyed and demarcated, followed by mapping and demarcating the individual plots. Five villages in Namtumbo and three in Songea Rural District had been mapped at the time of the interview and another six villages in Tunduru District were scheduled for the remainder of 2015. Indeed, although MVIWATA relies on a group approach for all of its activities, it underlined the importance of individual – and legally recognized – ownership of land by the peasants, which is why they saw the land rights project as their most important activity (*GBE 3; 2/24/2015*).

MVIWATA is also closely connected to some other NGOs in Songea, who care for different sectors, and their success in enabling more than 800 farmers to get traditional title deeds for their land was also recognized by them (*GBE 5; 2/24/2015*). All of those four NGOs were seen as representing a cross section of organizations active in development interventions with a focus on small farmers in Ruvuma.

Two other Songea based NGOs were also visited in the early stages of the research: TMMTF, the Tanzania Mineral Mining Trust Fund, which mostly deals with small-scale mining operations in Eastern Ruvuma (*GBE 5; 2/24/2015*), and PADI (Tanzania Mission to the Poor and Disabled), an organization caring for marginalized groups in rural areas, with a special focus on the needs of older people, disabled persons and the poor in general (*GBE 4; 2/24/2015*). Although most of their activities were less closely connected to the research interest, their representatives were able to contribute some valuable insights into the development scene of Ruvuma, as well as on the situation of the rural population itself.

PADI was concentrating its activities on marginalized groups in remote rural areas and has been active in Ruvuma since 2000. Actually, the organization itself was founded locally and started operation with a microcredit scheme involving ten beneficiaries in one village. In 2015, they were lending microcredits to 1,500 people, according to their own accounts, and serving 20 wards in Songea rural district, plus seven in Njombe district. The second field of activity was a chicken based income generating scheme for their focus groups, which started in 2001 and involved more than 4,500 beneficiaries at the time of the interview. Additionally, the organization was involved in improving water supply in 73 villages by supplying funds for improved wells, and nine boreholes, which were provided for secondary schools across Songea district. The organization was especially proud of their own development and boasted winning three national awards for the most effective NGO in Tanzania from 2011 through 2013. As was the case for all of the NGOs involved in the research, its representatives would first approach interested villagers and the village authorities by the means of a public meeting in which they would lay down their ideas and the conditions for getting support from the organization. People who then wanted to get involved in these activities would form groups which would act as a vehicle for the NGO to address its beneficiaries and provide training for the group members if necessary (*GBE 4; 2/24/2015*).

TMMTF was different from the other participating NGOs, as its main focus was advocacy and capacity building for small individual miners involved in the mining of precious stones and minerals in Ruvuma, but also small-scale coal mining. However, it also focused on environmental sustainability and was cooperating with other NGOs involved in agricultural development when it came to provide alternatives to mining once the resources were depleted in a certain area. Founded in 2000, the organization was also catering for HIV/Aids prevention programs in areas of high population mobility (i.e. mining and road building areas) and land rights issues, which affected its focus group just as much as the small farmers of Ruvuma, as "mine grabbing" by richer actors was a common concern throughout its area of activity (*GBE 5; 2/24/2015*).

NGO's perception of Ujamaa and its relevance for their work

Some of the NGOs working in direct contact with the local peasants gave very detailed accounts of their perception of the changes in Tanzania since the end of Ujamaa and their impact on the local scale. They assessed that the focus of the national development policy has since switched away from the rural poor. As a result of the new market economy, every person would just care for their own well-being and the mutual social security, which was offered by the Ujamaa approach, has since vanished. Yet, a communal idea of working together would still be paramount to achieving development on local scale:

> "But nowadays. People they are serving for their own benefit, first. If they are suffice excess, you can be given other person. So, this is a very very big challenge. And farmers, they are still – I think, they still have the mind, people, they are still think of our, our poverty. The government are thinking of our poverty. But within the government, they have moved from Ujamaa now in the capitalism, now. So, people they are seeing they are on their own – then, farmers. This is very challenging, even to our leaders: They are not focusing, let us say, the poor people, how they are living. They are thinking how we should be dealing. Then, to the people. So, the Ujamaa, Ujamaa, the government is saying we cannot work in Ujamaa, now we are following the other way of economy. You cannot depend on Ujamaa. But for me in some cases we should teach people a, a communal live."
> Brio Mgoyo, Caritas Songea (*GBE 1*; 2/23/2015)

Other NGO representatives underlined these changes in the economic policy of Tanzania. However, in their opinion, the new form of organizing economic activities has not yet sunken in at the peripheral rural areas of Ruvuma. Indeed, many of those peasants would still believe they were living under Ujamaa, at least to the eyes of an outsider:

> "What I can say that most of the people they think that they are still in the Ujamaa. They think so, because, you know, things are changing to those, eh, big cities. Those who know, who are, who are nearby maybe to their industrial area. But here, people still think, that maybe you are still using the system of Ujamaa and not capitalist. I tell you that we don't know, in all Tanzania, maybe you can assist me. You do know if we are in the Ujamaa, really? or partial, or we are in the capitalist? But according to the free market, we think that maybe we are in the capitalist, but the people in the rural area, they don't know, ya. They don't understand about the – eh – the competition of the market. Hm, I don't know are we in the Ujamaa? (...) The, the villagers say, themselves, they are ujamaa village. But, what they are doing in the village now is quite different from the era. There is nothing that you can.... We are not using to, eh, the economic activities, is by individual ownership. Now. It is an individual ownership project. Before – during the Ujamaa – eh, the economical activities were owned by the, all the community. That maybe the big change is, they see now. And, by the time being, the government was using to buy all the product of the farmer. But nowadays, is a market competition. Ya, that's the changes."
> Ladislaus Bigambo, RUCODIA Songea (*GBE 2*; 2/23/2015)

The second observation of this statement – of Tanzanian being a "mixed system" that still retained elements of the past Ujamaa policy – was also accounted for by other respondents, like Iskata Msigwa from PADI, who felt that Tanzania currently was somehow "in between" (*GBE 5; 2/24/2015*) the old ways of Ujamaa and the new system. In any case, the difficulties of small scale farmers in adapting to the new market environment were seen as a big challenge to RUCODIA's work on the ground.

On the other hand, this persistence of former elements of collective organization and cultivation was seen as an asset by some NGO representatives, as it helped them in their work of organizing farmers' groups for income generating activities. The tradition of Ujamaa in the villages could therefore be understood as implying the preference for a group approach when implementing such projects:

> "Ya, there were Farmers, they, let's say, (…) do it as a community. And this approach is very nice. Us, we are using group, group approach. Supporting farmers not individually, but through their groups. This approach is like, working with Ujamaa, to solve their, their own challenges in the villages. If say, we support, you are dealing with the everybody but without any group, you are dealing with no one. But through this living together, and joining together, supporting each other, they solve their problems together. So, during Ujamaa, my problem is his problem."
> Brio Mgoyo, Caritas Songea (*GBE 1; 2/23/2015*)

In a similar fashion, Xaver Komba from SNC underlined his experience that the inception of such groups as vehicle for further development interventions was made very easy through the general understanding of the group approach by the peasantry. Because of their personal experiences of organizing collectively in the Ujamaa era, there was little reluctance in joining such groups in the present, or in seeing them as one possible way of achieving personal development through cooperation with other farmers of the same village. The challenge, however, lay in the phase after the creation of such groups: Many of them would actually do very few activities and show a lack of organization when it came to group finances, which would in turn lead to many of them actually folding within their first year. Indeed, the biggest issue in recent group organization would be for the groups to actually do something, rather than just wait for further interventions by NGOs and other donors after their inception (*GBE 10; 3/10/2015*). In a similar fashion, the representative of MVIWATA stated that there was not that much remaining from Ujamaa to build on when forming farmers' groups and that a lot of education on cooperative operation was needed in most cases (*GBE 3; 2/24/2015*).

Although all of the six Songea NGOs worked with groups as their main vehicle for involving their different focus groups in their respective development activities, some of the organizations pointed out the significant differences between the present practice of group involvement and the old idea of Ujamaa:

> "They are in groups, but each one is doing his own activities. Because, doing activity together, it has been experienced that it is – that there is a failure, because one be a hard worker, or not. Some can be lazy, and therefore they are organized into groups, but each works at his own piece, ok. But the group is just there to help them to be together, to share ideas, to solve the problems together, or to share the experience, and be easily

monitored. But not working together, having one chick, or chicken together. Working together, having a cattle pen like that one, two goats or chicken, or cattle, and then they say it is ours? No, it is not working. It is not working."
Iskata C. Msigwa, PADI Songea (*GBE 4*; 2/24/2015)

On the other hand, there was commonly an understanding of the benefits which the Ujamaa policy had had for the inhabitants of Ruvuma's remote villages – which are the area of work for the NGOs now. And while some remaining ideas like the spirit of communality were seen as generally beneficial for the work of their organizations, there was also a clear understanding of things which had not necessarily changed for the positive:

"Ujamaa is no longer. Ujamaa is no longer in Tanzania. This dream we had this before, but now, I think we are implementing different [things] now. Because we have already inviting a lot of investors here. We have very big gap between the rich men and the poor men, yes. So, if there is a gap between the rich people and poor people, then there is no Ujamaa – as introduced by Mwalimu Nyerere. But, we still have a unit, we still have no… – we don't have tribalism in Tanzania. Still our country is a very peaceful country."
Wilbert Matumbi, TMMTF Songea (*GBE 5*; 2/24/2015)

Changes in Ruvuma

As stated above, many of the NGO representatives felt that they were too young or that they had not been in the region long enough to give a decisive depiction of all the changes that have happened since the period of Ujamaa. Nevertheless, all of them were aware of the many changes that had occurred in their field of expertise since they became active in the development scene. Some of them were virtually excited regarding the success which their organization's involvement had brought about, and concentrated their narration of the changes on this perspective:

"[Our beneficiaries were coming] from smaller project to bigger project, and have managed to have cattle keeping. Now, they are able, they have managed to construct biogas. We have got pictures, and, eh, the actual space, if you want to see. From using charcoal, or firewood, they are using biogas now. So, that is some changes. Those who were not able to send their children to school, they have managed to send. Up to the university level. From our support."
Iskata C. Msigwa, PADI Songea (*GBE 4*; 2/24/2015)

Representatives from MVIWATA also saw change in the form of more farmers being able to address their issues and express their needs to government officials and other stakeholders as one result of the organization's capacity building (*GBE 3*; 2/24/2015).

Wilbert Matumbi of TMMTF credited some of the development initiatives of the government and the various NGOs for bringing some sort of progress to the region in the last 15 years. Specifically, the central government's program to build more hospitals and health centers, as well as the investment in secondary schools for each ward, were seen as very positive and bringing development on the ground. The influx of investors in coal mining operations and the general population growth of Songea and the whole region would also create new market opportunities for the bulk of small-scale cultivators in Ruvuma. On the other hand, the government's attempts to support small-scale farmers through various measures had failed to reach the remoter villages of Ruvuma in his view, and those people would completely rely on the initiative of organizations like MVIWATA to get a shot at progress (*GBE* 5; 2/24/2015).

Others, like Xaver Komba of SNC and Ladislaus Bigambo of RUCODIA, perceived the changes in Ruvuma as rather limited to a minority of farmers, who would be able to appreciate the new economic system and take their personal benefit out of it – either because they possess a higher level of entrepreneurship than their peers or because they have easier access to capital for investment. In any case, progress in the last 15 or 20 years had failed to reach the majority of the rural population of the region. However, those two NGOs representatives did not want to conclude if this came from a general reluctance to change and progress by the peasantry, or a lack of material opportunities to capitalize on the new conditions of market economy – or a combination of both (*GBE* 2; 2/23/2015; *GBE* 10; 3/10/2015).

So, with this general picture of the perception of Ujamaa and the following changes in Ruvuma by the NGOs in question, it is worthwhile to look closer at one particular program which proved to be very important for the research on the village level: Caritas' Soya ni Pesa project.

The "Soya ni Pesa" program

This income-generating project deserves further presentation, as its results were connected with all of the farmers' groups which have been analyzed in Litowa and Mbingamharule. Soya ni Pesa aims at creating a forthcoming base of cash income for small farmers in the villages of Ruvuma. It started in 2012 and is scheduled to continue through 2017, with a funding of 10.6 million USD provided by the United States Department of Agriculture (USDA). The program tries to achieve this goal by four program stages: First of all, it gives advice to farmers if they want to perform mutual savings and credits in an approach called SILK (Saving and internal Lending methodology), in which farmers, attached to the program, can buy shares and can give small credits to their neighbors every four weeks. These loans are specifically meant for investment in soya farming by the recipients. The second stage of the program provides the farmers with improved seeds for soya, where Caritas see themselves in the role of a connector between the researchers working on improved seeds and cultivation techniques on the one side, and the farmers on the other side. The third stage is the provision of training plots, where the farmers involved can get training on how to use these seeds and cultivate soya. The actual production of soya is most commonly done by the group members on their own individual plots. The last stage is the marketing of their produce, in which Caritas facilitates a connection between the productive farmers' groups and different private buyers (*GBE* 17; 9/9/2015; SₙP 2017).

Soya production was first introduced in Ruvuma by the Peramiho Mission in 1960. The Region itself is considered to be among the areas with the highest natural potential for increased soya cultivation in Tanzania and, like in most parts of the country, the soya bean does not need additional fertilizers or chemicals for crop storage under normal circumstances. With this beneficial environment, the reliability of markets for the produce has been considered as the key limiting factor to the further expansion of soya production in the Region (MALEMA 2006: 29p.). The potentials of soya cultivation, as a cash crop for small-scale farmers, have already drawn the attention of several international NGOs (see, for instance, RONNER et al. 2013 and RONNER & GILLER 2013). Furthermore, the Tanzanian government is attempting to support the peasant production of soya through the provision of extension services and guidelines on cultivation techniques (URT 2006).

In the case of Soya ni Pesa, Caritas itself does not buy the produce, but cooperates with different bulking traders, while ensuring good prices for the farmers. In line with Caritas' preference for group activities stated above, the project is only accessible for organized farmers' groups. At the time of research, the project involved 252 groups with over 4,000 farmers in 44 villages within the Songea Rural and Namtumbo Districts of Ruvuma Region, although not all of them were doing SILK and soya production, but may only participate in one half of the total program. According to the project coordinator, Neema Lutatenekwa, Caritas would usually look for existing farmers' groups in the villages and see if they are open to join the program. However, if there are no existing groups in a certain village of interest, the NGO would start with a community sensitization meeting and encourage the creation of new groups. They would also offer assistance in writing the groups' constitution, registration, opening of bank accounts and other institutional requirements. She did not state how Caritas is choosing the villages for this group creation process (*GBE 17*; 9/9/2015).

Lutatenekwa stated that the farmers, in general, have been very open to this concept of collaboration, although she stressed the necessity of material benefits and the importance of year-round activities, to keep the individual farmers engaged in the project:

"They are interested with the groups, but farmers are interested more in the groups which they saw the results after one, two to three. Within one, two to three months. For example, as I said, we are working with save-internal-lending, and we are working with production, so sometimes we have different types of group. We can have the group, which are doing production only, now that, we can have that group, but it is a zero-zonal group, the production only. But in case of SILK and production, because SILK is a continuous process within the year, so they save, take loan, within the year, then they share, then they start again. So, for the kind of groups which are doing both, saving-internal-lending and production, these are existing and the farmers are interested in those groups. But, this production, they can be there during production season, but when you go there during off-season… [they don't do anything together]"
Neema Lutatenekwa, Soya ni Pesa Project Coordinator,
Caritas Songea (*GBE 17*; 9/9/2015)

Therefore, the main focus of the program in 2015 was to encourage those groups only doing SILK to start production, and vice versa. Concerning the economic results of the program, Lutatenekwa evaluated the results as fairly good. Yet, there is a considerable issue with price fluctuation: According to her information, prices for soya sold through the program were around 200 TSh per kg at the initiation of the program, but then a company bought the soya for 800 TSh per kg in the 2012/2013 season, which induced a sharp rise in the number of farmers producing soya in 2013/2014. This inevitably led to problems in finding enough buyers in that season. In the last 2014/2015 season, there were fewer farmers as a result of this, which – in cooccurrence with a lot of produce lost by insects and crop diseases – led to prices climbing as high as 1,000 TSh per kg and middlemen buying the soya directly from the farmers at the villages (*GBE 17*; 9/9/2015).

For Tanzania in general, soya is overwhelmingly produced by small-scale farmers, who are responsible for 99% of the total production of this legume. The market for this crop is almost entirely national, and there are no official data on the export of Tanzanian soya available. Apart from some few companies in Dar es Salaam, the processing of soya is most commonly done by small-scale local enterprises in regional trading centers. Still, the national market for soya products for both human consumption and animal feed is very limited. The preferences of the majority of small-income consumers have been cited as the main reason for this limitation.[6] On the other hand, while the global market for soya beans and soya products is growing continuously, Tanzania has not been able to compete with the big producers of soya on the international level so far (Wilson 2015: 5–7).

In spite of these challenges, Caritas was optimistic about adding even more farmers to the project and giving them enough know how to deal with production and market issues after the conclusion of the program (*GBE 17*; 9/9/2015). Apart from Ruvuma, the Soya ni Pesa program is also operating in the neighboring Regions of Njombe and Morogoro. Furthermore, the *Tanzania Soybean Development Platform* for the promotion of soya as a cash crop suitable for the economic improvement of small-scale farmers has been launched in cooperation with other NGOs, government institutions and research facilities. This initiative is also seen as an attempt to create a bigger and more reliable market for soybeans in the country (SNP 2015).

Summary

All of the NGO representatives who took part in this research were giving an account on their understanding of the Ujamaa period, although some of them preferred to concentrate their statements on the changes they had observed in their own time of activity, rather than going too much into detail about the times of Ujamaa as such. Furthermore, all of the NGOs were basing their activities in Ruvuma on a group approach, rather than approaching their clients individually. Most of the respondents concluded that there was not much remaining from the times of Ujamaa, concerning the concrete practice of collective agriculture, for instance, but also agreed that the mindset of the times of Ujamaa was still very much present with the rural popula-

---

6   See also Mishili et al. (2009) for an overview on the Tanzanian bean market and the effects of consumer preferences.

tion. Indeed, several interviewees considered this persistence of cooperative think-ing on the village scale to be a big asset for their own work as NGOs, as it made it much easier to find people who are willing to join group activities in the first place. On the other hand, there was also the observation that the practical implementation of such group-based activities was facing considerable challenges, and some NGO representatives attributed this to a loss of cooperative knowledge since the times of Ujamaa. All respondents concluded that the changes since the end of Ujamaa did not benefit the majority of the rural population, and observed the negative effects of the withdrawal of the Tanzanian state from the most peripheral areas. Nevertheless, some interviewees also saw some progress in the post-Ujamaa development strate-gy, at least for some individuals in the rural areas.

Overall, the importance of the Ujamaa era for the current development of Ruvu-ma was seen as rather high, but more as a general concept of collective development and as a mindset and less with regards to any material achievements which would still remain from that era.

6.1.3 Other actors

Two further views from the "outside" could be collected during the first field visit in Ruvuma: One interview was led at the Benedictine Mission at Peramiho, and an-other one was conducted with Mr. Damas Mbogoro, a former Member of Parliament who is now working as a lecturer at AJUCO in Songea.

The role of Peramiho

One of the oldest actors in rural development in Southern Tanzania is the Bene-dictine Abby at Peramiho, founded by brothers from St. Otilien, Germany in 1898. Established as a missionary enterprise during the German colonial period, the Abby now has around 2,000 ha of land under cultivation with different crops, as well as pastures for cattle keeping. The complex is employing 200 people in agriculture and other services, as well as around 300 employees at the missionary hospital, which is renowned as being the best in this part of the country. Furthermore, there is a tech-nical training college on site, with around 150 students learning to be mechanics, electricians and similar professions, as well as the college of the hospital with about 60 students. All of these operations are described as "human development" by the Abby (GBE 6; 2/25/2015). The farm of Peramiho also has been regularly involved in the development and testing of new, locally suitable farming techniques or crop variants, in an effort to increase the agricultural productivity of the region (URT 1997a: 36).

Peramiho and the Ujamaa legacy

Despite its history of being one of the most active institutions in the development of rural Ruvuma, Peramiho has always had an ambivalent connection to the Ujamaa policy, especially in the time of RDA's inception in the early 1960s. Some of the internal conflicts between the new African generation of priests, who wanted to be a part of the building of the nation, and the older German fathers, who were more concerned with cultural issues like church sermons have been accounted for in WENNER's first-hand description from Litowa (WENNER 1970: 85p.).

In general, the ideology of self-reliance that was intended by the emerging Ujamaa concept did not fit well into Peramiho's paternalist approach to the development of their farmers. In the early days, Litowa's activist settlers had their own disheartening experiences with some of the Benedictine fathers, who treated them like children and wanted to give them "development" as a gift from above. As a result, mutual antipathies grew between the self-organized farmers and the representatives of Peramiho, who did not understand why these stubborn idealists refused their help (IBBOTT 2014: 229–232).

RDA's activities and development strategy, in particular, were demonized by the Peramiho mission as communist project – even long after the disbandment of the association (MEYNS 1977: 165). Even in 2015, these anti-communist sentiments may be part of the negative evaluation of Ujamaa in general that was given by the Prior of the Abby, Father Fidelis:

"To me Ujamaa was one of the bad policies, which had destroyed the economy of this country. That's my position. I can't change it – it's true, I believe on it. To me, Ujamaa killed the economy of Tanzania. Destroyed it, ruined and so on – the economy of Tanzania. People were made to be poor by, eh, because, eh opportunities, for development were limited. Ya. That's what I know about Ujamaa. Now, how far has been successful to me was – what was at least a positive element of Ujamaa, is just, eh, solidarity, the field of solidarity, unity and so on. That's the only way I can say. Solidarity, unity, among the citizens of this country. Ya, and of course there has been peace, ya, also, was also a result of Ujamaa. Ya. But, economically, Ujamaa, eh, to me it was irrelevant."
Father Fidelis, Prior of Peramiho Abby (*GBE 6*; 2/25/2015)

Apart from this negative perception of the economic results of Ujamaa, which is certainly not exclusive to Father Fidelis, his account of the history of Litowa gives a vivid example on how little the development initiative of these farmers has been appreciated by the missionaries, just a few kilometers away. Even in the present, the depiction of RDA, and Litowa in particular, is dominated by the suspicion of foreign intervention and alien ideas as the motivation behind this peasant movement:

"Yes, what I know, especially Litowa, I don't know if the same applies to Liweta and Matetereka – Litowa was a model of Ujamaa na Kujitegemea policy, eh, there were some people from – Russia I think – that came to work there on how to developed this form of Ujamaa na Kujitegemea. Eh, it worked at first because everything was imposed from outside: Machinery, eh, equipment and machineries and so on and so on. So many equipment came from, I mean economic support, financing it so on was done from donors, or I mean from those or some part of it from the government. But, people did not understand that thing, because it was like, it was imposed, like putting something there, without eh, that people being informed of it. That's why it didn't really, eh, when those expatriates from Russia, I don't know where – left, then the whole thing collapsed,

because it was not made to be theirs! Ya...from the very beginning. I mean they were, the locals were not so much involved on running that institution. In founding and running that institution, that's why when those expatriates left, the whole collapsed..."
Father Fidelis, Prior of Peramiho Abby (*GBE 6*; 2/25/2015)

Even more striking is the immediate connection to alleged Russian expats as the source of their revenue and also the reason for their failure after those people were thrown out. According to this research, there has never been even one expat from the former Soviet Union living in Litowa or other RDA villages, and most of the international support came from UK, Switzerland, and other "Western" countries. When inquiring about the fact that Litowa was actually started by a former student of Peramiho's own seminary (Millinga, see above), the argument against their movement turned political:

"Yes, but it was political figures of a particular movement. The aim was politically motivated. People of course in this period where not so much educated. They were told just go there and found a village and so on. But, eh for what purpose? Why? So, this are questions I don't, I doubt if they were asked and they were addressed. Eh, the reason to my stand is that when those expatriates left, nothing works. If you go there now, you can see only buildings, nothing is standing there, ya."
Father Fidelis, Prior of Peramiho Abby (*GBE 6*; 2/25/2015)

The opposition of high ranks of Peramiho to this "particular movement" could not have been clearer throughout the interview. On an interesting side note, it should be mentioned that the first visit to Litowa on the following day was accompanied by Brother Augustine of Peramiho Abby, who also acted as an interpreter on that day. During the interview with Mzee Soko (*NCW 1*; 2/26/2015), he misunderstood Soko's account of the early days of Litowa, as was later reconstructed by the help of the audio record: When Soko spoke about Ibbott, as one of the leading figures of the movement, Augustine understood "Abbott" and concluded that the first move had actually been led by the Peramiho Abby itself! Without overinterpreting this kind of misunderstanding, it might add another impression of how little actual knowledge there is within Peramiho, about the Ujamaa history of its immediate vicinity, and how many misconceptions and negative attitudes towards grassroots initiative are still prevailing among one of the biggest development actors of the region.

In concordance with his earlier remarks on Ujamaa, Father Fidelis did see a lot of changes happening in Ruvuma since then, mainly concerning the effects of market economy and privatization. These changes, however, are seen as overall progress and an increase of opportunities for the local population, as compared to his perception of the "state economy" under Ujamaa:

"Now that thing of, the first thing is – which brought some changes – opening the markets, buying and selling, commerce. The second thing, which also improved life standards to the people, is privatization, and therefore liberalization of economy. Because from there, people started doing business, ehm, they, eh, their products, their agricultural

products had markets, ya, ya. Also, people were employed, 'cause of investment, and so and so on. Therefore, investment came, people doing business, also international institutions, multinational companies coming in and doing business, automatically people – many people were employed not by... In the past, almost all were employed by the state, now many people were, are employed by the private sector. To me that's the key development which I see. Also, the, the policy of privatization and, eh, free markets has brought so many motor vehicles, as you see them. Ya, now that has employed a lot of people, and people are easily, get services so easily, like movement: People can move from one place to another, use a lot of motorbikes, ya, motorbikes. ya, and cars and so on and so on. Therefore, now there are so many changes."
Father Fidelis, Prior of Peramiho Abby (*GBE 6*; 2/25/2015)

The narrative of Damas Mbogoro, former Member of Parliament

Some further interesting views on the history of Ujamaa in Ruvuma came from Damas Mbogoro, who is currently working as a lecturer for economics at AJUCO in Songea. He is himself a Ruvuma native, born in Mtema village in Wino ward, close to Matetereka. He was studying at the University of Dar es Salaam, where he was also a contributor to some of the Economic Research Bureau's papers on Ujamaa village development in the 1970s. He then went on to study in Canada, and returned to Tanzania in 1981. Mbogoro became a Member of National Parliament for the Peramiho constituency in 1985 and held his seat until 1995. In this time of transformation for the country, he was working for the department of economics under Ali Hasan Mwinyi's term as president of Tanzania (*GBE 9*; 3/10/2015).

His general idea about the history of Ujamaa was that it was "really a great concept. And in many aspects, we have changed" (*GBE 9*; 3/10/2015). From his perspective, the idea of Ujamaa was all about developing people, while under the post-Ujamaa strategy, the focus was on economic development and individual entrepreneurship. And in his varying functions, he observed the many changes that came to Ruvuma and the country as a whole during these years:

"It is very big, the change. And, eh, maybe for the greater or for the worse. Ehm, you know, getting individual initiative – it is now very very important. (…) So, through the big firm in Tanzania, and most of them are private. So, eh, the in the, eh, the changes: changes, from national [level] to individual this applies for the big cooperatives or anything. You say: this is my area, this is my area, this is a big change. Nationally, people technically, the ruling party – even the opposition parties – pretend to be socialist. But if you go to the rural areas, they don't understand, if you talk of socialist, they won't understand. So, they are also pretending to be socialist, but virtually they are waiting for changes to go on so on. But you get contradiction now, you know, fights over land, and, eh seeing there getting everything. And they are getting foreigners, taking what is theirs. And they think by themselves: what's happening? They don't understand why somebody came to take a piece of land. And says, give me that land. For them it's not about the ownership. And, eh, they are going to be there and eh, they have problems. So, transition is low. But, ehm, in terms of how the economy is managed, there is no, eh, sort element of socialism left."
Damas Mbogoro, Former Member of Parliament, Songea (*GBE 9*; 3/10/2015)

In his view, there were hardly any tangible structures left from the times of Uja-maa within the Region, apart from what he remembered from Matetereka and their continuing Ujamaa activities. Furthermore, he was very aware of the importance of the first settlers of Litowa for the development of Ujamaa as a national concept, but implied that there would be virtually nothing remaining from those times. That would be except for the structure of the leadership, and the understanding of how to develop a project on the village level, which in his view survived the end of Ujamaa policy and would act as an asset to further development in those villages, especially in Matetereka (*GBE 9*; 3/10/2015).

The most interesting part of this interview, however, might be Mr. Mbogoro's account of the end of Ujamaa as a national policy, since in his function as a member of the department of economy, he was directly involved in some of the macroeconomic policy changes that would settle the fate of Tanzania's socialist period:

"Ya, eh, so in terms now at the policy level: if you go to the changes in Ujamaa policy [that] started in 1985. At that time, I was Member of Parliament for Peramiho constit-uency. I came from the University of Dar es Salaam, I was researcher there and then I became Member of Parliament. And then during the government, and eh, eh, you know the change in president place [from Nyerere to Mwinyi]. (...) But the changes we were making, because, I think the economy was small. So, the changes we were making, [to get an] an economy which eh yields money. Eh, so for quite a long time we discussed and, they are continuing, and ehm, they are slowly getting set to this changes, and, ehm, what else? [We] Changed the constitution. These days, there is no complaint if the Shilling is devaluated. By then it was a problem: 1985, they – we had big discussions; 'why, why they devaluate our shilling. why, why'."
Damas Mbogoro, Former Member of Parliament, Songea (*GBE 9*; 3/10/2015)

The devaluation of the national currency was one of several measures which were implemented by the Mwinyi administration from 1985 onwards, with the aim of transforming the country's closed and state controlled economy into an open market economy, as it had been demanded by both The World Bank and the IMF as a pre-condition for financial support to Tanzania's struggling national budget (see chapter 3.4). Indeed, it had been these macroeconomic difficulties, which in Mbogoro's view made the reform of the national economic system inevitable:

"Hm, ah, there were internal and external, and, eh reasons. The internal [reason] was most people saw it was not working, from 19..., eh, we were in the war with Uganda, 78 to 79, and then the economy, virtually from that time began to deteriorate. And, eh, then we had a lot of financial problems. (...) Ehm, basically, – you know I'm an economist – by then I came from Canada, and when they started these sort of economic reforms, and eh, 82, now 81 I came back, I landed and I looked around, and eh, look, generally like we had an economy which is not really, I mean, you see people, not having their basic needs, it was hard times. Then when I came down here from Dar [es Salaam], I brought a tooth brush, and they were surprised, there was nothing like that here.

So, the effect of the war, somehow, and eh, I think, I don't know if we had friends or not, who [were left for the country], but nobody was ready to help. The IMF and World Bank they were not giving any more loans, because, eh, the bad economic policies. And then I also took a look and they were not wrong, this World Bank people. The economy just looked bad. So, actually 1985, when there was a change of president; by then the first President Nyerere was removing in 1985, and eh, he refused to devaluate the shilling, he didn't like that. But I think, as an economist, I was by then in the department of economics, so we were thinking on what's wrong, and, eh, why is everything so bad. Eh, so when new president came, Mwinyi, and, eh, then he started, I think it was right to change the economy of this country. An, eh, this started with the devaluation, because the IMF said: Ok, we give you a loan, but the shilling [has to be devaluated]. Ya, and of course I came from academics. There was a national congress, and eh, when I became a Member of Parliament they said come, come and join the cabinet. And then of course there was also some the leaders of departments and we worked together and eh, they say, if we want to have progress in development, then the economy we have to change. And that's when we agreed that Ujamaa was done, because we had to do the currency devaluation right now we have to take matters in control and eh, you know, including live style and no market unfortunately, there were a lot of markets but you following the market also. So, finally, somehow, but there was lot of, eh, misunderstandings at the end. I told the others that I was very much pro devaluation, very very much. But we needed to change, people saw the benefits of it."

Damas Mbogoro, Former Member of Parliament, Songea (*GBE 9*; 3/10/2015)

So, with these definite decisions taken on the national level, the next question was how the people on the ground, in his constituency, would react to these changes. According to his memory, the first effects of the new economic policy were not necessarily welcomed by the people of Ruvuma, but – at least in his observation – the majority of the rural population did not suffer from the implications of the currency devaluation, as they did not have a lot of connections with the international markets:

"It was interesting, you see, when we started, people asked: 'What is devaluation?' When they agreed to the external devaluation, we were monitoring, what was happening on the ground. Ehm, up to the time I finished ten years [of my term in parliament], they were still checking. You know devaluation was, eh, people were afraid, because most of the people going to the bank, eh, [but] most of the part of devaluation does not affect most of the people, because they were not going to buy things from outside. (…) Then of course the government, concerning the value of the export [there was a bigger impact]. There was a campaign to farmers, for getting more money, and eh, even now they don't complain about. Their live has been shielded from the cruelling part of devaluation. When it came to build their own house from local market, they managed to buy iron sheets, then they make contact with devaluation, but they make bricks themselves, so you know. So, the shilling now is about 1800 a dollar, nobody complains. ... And that's what we, but we shielded, the [normal people] ... Particularly on key sectors. (…). I negotiated whit the IMF, and, eh of course they wanted but then I said, look, I'm not in charge of this structure, I'm in charge of something else.

So, trust me, so we went a long way. So then, unfortunately, Ujamaa is gone now. So, if you wanted knowledge of Tanzania somehow, we were moving very quick and I was in the kitchen, somehow. But now I'm retired, I'm lecturing here, that's here is where it started."
Damas Mbogoro, Former Member of Parliament, Songea (*GBE 9*; 3/10/2015)

Up to this day, Damas Mbogoro is convinced of the necessity of the economic transformation of the 1980s, and while he still sees a lot of challenges for development, especially to the small-scale farmers of Ruvuma, he thinks that without the shift away from Ujamaa, the situation in the country would be much worse than it is today (*GBE 9*; 3/10/2015).

6.2   Ujamaa: The view from inside

So, with these statements from more or less closely related outsiders in mind, the following chapter will try to go one step further into the rural narrative of Ujamaa and have a closer look at the ideas, perceptions and opinions of the villagers themselves. First of all, the stage will be given to those who were there the whole time – the contemporary witnesses of Ujamaa in Ruvuma.

6.2.1   First hand experiences: Contemporary witnesses of Ujamaa of Ruvuma

When setting off to visit the remote villages of Ruvuma, I had already read many stories, personal accounts and scientific literature, which dealt with the experiences of the first Ujamaa villages in this area and gave an impression on the personal motivations and ideas that inspired the peasants to create these villages. However, in order to truly understand the history of Ujamaa – in Ruvuma and in the rest of this country, it seemed of utmost importance to find first-hand evidence of the personal stories behind the movement which would change Tanzania in so many ways. Given the fact that 2015, the year in which the field studies were conducted, marked the 54th anniversary of Tanganyika's independence, it was assumed that at least some inhabitants of the case study visits would have been living there long enough to act as contemporary witnesses for the whole period of Ujamaa development. Their first-hand experience of the historic events and its effects on village life would therefore be an invaluable asset for the research project as a whole. Indeed, the villages of the RDA were mostly founded by young idealist activists, who were then in their 20s. In both the RDA and the non-RDA villages that were visited during the field study, several wazee were willing to share their personal story of development. These narratives of ujamaa will be the foundation of the following chapter.

188

Stories of a new beginning – The idealist youth going to the countryside

So, how did it all begin? As described in chapter 3, a radio speech by President Nyerere, addressing the youth of the country, urging them to go to the countryside and help to build the nation after Uhuru, is widely seen as the starting point for the grassroots Ujamaa movement that unfolded in Ruvuma and reached its peak with the development of the RDA.

In Litowa, it was Mzee Joakim M. Soko, a former teacher of the RDA school, who would give a vivid account of those first days of the village. To his memory, it was indeed a group of young activists from TANU Youth League, led by Millinga, who came to the place that would become Litowa. Singing political songs about building the nation, they arrived at the small ridge to begin their project. Soko himself was not a part of this group, he was then living in a nearby village, at Maposeni. He remembers the people of his and the other surrounding villages being skeptical about these young people, who were coming to the bush – ill prepared in their view – with nothing but their motivation. Many of the villagers were anxious about the newcomers, and thought they would bring chaos to the area (*NCW 1; 2/26/2015*).

Mzee Soko highlighted the role of John Millinga and Ralph Ibbott throughout the whole interview, although at times he was unsure about the exact timeline and especially the role of Ibbott (see also below). In any case, it was Millinga, who approached the *bwana shamba* (the man in charge of agriculture) of one of the surrounding villages, whose name was Winfred Songa. Songa helped them to get a better understanding of agriculture, to get their communal farm going. Millinga also went to the leader of Maposeni, to explain his project, and that he wanted to mobilize the youth, just as Nyerere had told to the nation. Eventually, the village leader agreed and went to tell his villagers to let the youth do their thing. Furthermore, the leader was now convinced that these young activists might actually bring development to the area. Indeed, many young peasants from the surrounding area would soon join the settlers at Litowa – and Soko was one of them. He, too, was eager to learn more about this new thing called Ujamaa and the ideas those people had for developing themselves and their country (*NCW 1; 2/26/2015*).

Mzee Shawa, who was also living near Litowa when Millinga and his group arrived, gave a similar account of his first impression. For him as well, fascination and surprise at the unusual ways these people behaved soon turned into motivation to join and to become a mjamaa (a socialist) himself. He founded his own family in Litowa and raised four children there. Two of them are still living in Litowa as farmers themselves (*NCW 9; 8/24/2015*).

The news of the new developments at Litowa soon spread in the immediate vicinity, where another group of young farmers was working to set up a communal farm at Liweta, some 10 km to the East. Firsthand accounts of the early days of this village could be gathered in an interview with wazee Bele Kumasi Nyoni and Lucia Eluka (*NCW 3; 3/3/2015*). According to their memory, the original settlers of Liweta were TANU Youth League members as well, who were motivated by Nyerere's speech and decided that it would be better to work collectively, rather than to carry by themselves. They found a place for their project and founded their farm at Liweta. In their account, the two wazee of Liweta asserted that Ralph Ibbott had a very high importance for the development of the early Ujamaa villages – as was the case with many interviewees, who were asked about the local Ujamaa history. One could even get the impression that it was him, rather than the Youth League members, who initiated the movement:

> "And there was this white man, known as Ibbott. Ibbott had an idea of ujamaa. He said you can come together and work together."
> Bele Kumasi Nyoni and Lucia Eluka, Liweta. Interpreted by Dennis Mpazagade (*NCW 3; 3/3/2015*)

In any case, the settlers of Liweta were in dire need of advice, and as far as Nyoni and Eluka remember, it was Ibbott himself, who then came to Liweta and advised the settlers on how to work together. At this time – it appears to have been within the first two years of Liweta – they were only working on the field during the day and would return to their original villages at night. After the advice from Litowa, however, they decided to stay there on a permanent basis and to look for more people to join in the surrounding villages:

> "Then they came, they said, why work alone, let's find other people. So, they started convincing people nearby. Then one after another, they were coming to work over there [pointing in the direction of the old Liweta settlement]. Then Ibbott asked them, how do you see? Working from home, or working while sleeping here? They said, sleeping here would be much better than walking back home. And from there they started establishing small houses, here in Liweta. Now, when the nearby communities saw this kind of Ujamaa initiatives, then they were actually impressed. They saw, ah this is a good idea, let's join. So, enthusiastically, they joined the move. So up that day they formed a kind of Liweta Ujamaa village."
> Bele Kumasi Nyoni and Lucia Eluka, Liweta. Interpreted by Dennis Mpazagade (*NCW 3; 3/3/2015*)

Nyoni and Eluka were among those who joined. They both were seeking a better life and a new perspective for their future. According to Mzee Nyoni, people from four to six villages came together to form Litowa (*NCW 3; 3/3/2015*).

At the same time, seven young men in the far north of Songea District, at Wino village, were also thinking about what Nyerere had said. They wanted to do farming, but they wanted to do it differently from how they had learned from their ancestors, who farmed in family units. So, they went out into the highlands, and found their place for a cooperative farm in 1961. At first, there were around thirty people who joined the effort, but only six of them pushed through with it. At the beginning, everybody was cultivating one acre individually, or together with their wives. In 1962, they cultivated the first shamba together, where they planted groundnut as a cash crop. Mzee Abel Njalika was among them; he recalls the early history of Matetereka (*NCW 10; 8/31/2015*):

"So, in '63, we continued to cultivate together, but with a bigger extend. We were now also growing maize, beans, we also introduced coffee, as a cash crop. We started to cultivate on around 15 acres."

Mzee Abel Njalika, Matetereka (*NCW 10*; 8/31/2015)

As their small cooperative went on fairly well – better than most of similar group farms in the area at that time – they were able to extent their operations each year. By this time, Mzee Lukas Mayemba was the chairman of the TANU party branch in Wino, and got news of the settlers of Matetereka, who had secured a loan of 1,000 Shillings for buying cattle and an ox-plough. He would soon join their movement himself (*NCW 4*; 3/6/2015).

In 1964, Ralph Ibbott and Ntimbanjayo Millinga had already heard about the farmers at Matetereka, and paid a visit to them. The first contact with the RDA proved to be decisive for the future of their efforts. Abel Njalika and Gervas Mkomba, the chairman, were invited to visit Litowa, to get an insight into their organization:

"We went on a seminar in Litowa, for four days. Really, we could see what they had changed there. They stayed together, the work was hard, they had a plan for work, for everything. They had a very certain way of doing things. But there was also joy. A lot of things. So, we also changed the way of how we would do things here. (…) So, on this seminar, we really learned a lot of things. (…) It all started with this seminar. (…) Back then we were just a cooperative, in '64, when Ibbott and Ntimbanjayo Millinga came, and then when I went to the seminar, there.

I came back, we discussed, if we wanted to go on with Ujamaa, true Ujamaa. So, we decided we were ready for it. So, all of us should stay here, and work together, rather than having to come so far. You would leave for work at 8 a.m. and arrive at 9, 10, maybe 11 o'clock... So, we decided it would be better for all of us to stay together. Just as we had seen in Litowa. Therefore, the wanachama [group members] decided to make a plan to move together by 1965. The first thing was to build houses, for everyone with his wife. In those times, the RDA lent us a tractor, to help us with cutting the trees and to build the houses. And also, to prepare more fields. So, after this, the wajamaa, in '65, they were building houses and farming for food – maize, mainly. We also had the coffee plantation, but we now also needed a shamba for food. So, once we were able to cultivate enough food, we started living here from 1966. We cultivated and started living together. 1966, January, we brought our families here."

Mzee Abel Njalika, Matetereka (*NCW 10*; 8/31/2015)

It becomes clear from this evidence that the RDA had a profound impact in the early days of villages like Matetereka and Liweta: Advice from Ibbott and Millinga not only assured the first farmers at these places to go on with their cooperative farms, but it turned their attention from just farming together as an add-on to their original private shambas in their home villages, to creating entirely new settlements in which they would not only cooperate in agriculture, but organize the whole community based on cooperative principles. Furthermore, in both cases, the main motivation appears to have been the idealist notion of creating something new, as well as to contribute to the "building of the nation" as Nyerere had coined it. Neither land shortage in their home villages, nor other limiting factors in their "old lives", were described during the interviews. This is true not only for the original group of settlers, some of which could be interviewed at Matetereka, but also for people like Soko and Shawa of Litowa and Nyoni and Eluka of Liweta, who all stated that they moved to these respective villages because they were interested in what they had heard and seen from the first group of settlers.

Nevertheless, in all the interviews, the material benefits that were created by the Litowa approach to development, took an important part in the accounts, indicating that idealism may have been the motivation for founding these new cooperative farms in the first place, but that material success was the factor which kept them going and which attracted additional settlers from adjacent areas. Specifically, it was the initial success of Litowa, as well as the willingness of Ibbott and Millinga to search for and reach out to other grassroots cooperatives across Ruvuma, that sparked the creation of cooperative villages in the Region.

On the other hand, some contemporary witnesses from other villages had a completely different account of this period immediately after independence. This was certainly true for Stanislaus and Merkiol Senda from Namatuhi: In their area, the news of the new settlements like Litowa and Matetereka was met with great skepticism. Even today, both of them were convinced that those young people were sent there by the state, or that those other farmers were only joining them because they wanted to evade taxes, or get other benefits. Apart from that, they generally did not have a high opinion about the idealists at those villages, who were working for free – in their view – and who could not possibly achieve any results in their way of doing agriculture. Unsurprisingly, none of them joined the movements in the area, and little would change in their hamlet until the arrival of villagization (see below) (*NCW 8*; 3/11/2015).

Mbingamharule, as well, was not affected by any of the early cooperative movements of the Ujamaa era and would remain unchanged until villagization. However, in contrast to the accounts of Merkiol and Stanislaus Senda, there were no suspicions about the young activists in Litowa expressed by the wazee of Mbingamharule (*NCW 6*; 3/11/2015).

Life in an Ujamaa village – personal accounts of the RDA period

For those who had joined one of the new RDA villages, however, a new period of their lives began: The life in an Ujamaa village. All of those wazee from Litowa, Liweta and Matetereka, who took part in the interviews, had a vivid memory on how life was in the early days of Ujamaa. All of them underlined the importance of dining together, working together, and sharing the fruits of their labor together.

> "They did everything together. Cultivating together, harvesting together. Then if in your family, you don't have enough food, you have to say, then you are given. So, they used everything together. They were also keeping cattle together. So, they had everything."
> Bele Kumasi Nyoni, Liweta. Interpreted by Dennis Mpazagade (*NCW 3*; 3/3/2015)

192

Mzee Shawa shared the same depiction of life in Litowa in those days (*NCW 9; 8/24/2015*), as did the wazee of Matetereka, when speaking about the time after 1966, when they had started living together in their new village (*NCW 10; 8/31/2015*). The effects, which their connection through the RDA brought to the villages, were appreciated by the common villagers and the leadership alike. The school in Litowa was one of the examples of this cooperation which most interviewees referred to. And the children who attended this school, themselves, also enjoyed the benefits of having a school which taught them practical Ujamaa:

"My father was one of those who started with Ujamaa, I was still a child. When I was a child, Ujamaa started, and we came here [Matetereka], and I started to study Ujamaa. The school, the school we studied in was in Litowa. We learned Ujamaa. We went with the car, and came back with the car, that was a big advantage. (…) when we were children, we were with a mzungu [a European person], who cared for the small children. We went to the shamba, and we understood. She was teaching a lot of things, usually, this and that. We ate there, it was very good. Later on, indeed, the mzungu had to go."
Former student of RDA School (f), Matetereka (*NCW 10; 8/31/2015*)

Yet, the RDA was not only an education project and it proved to be very helpful in assessing and caring for the specific needs of its member villages, as the following account illustrates:

"Therefore, the RDA helped us a lot, to progress in Ujamaa, and also to reach self-reliance. The RDA brought some sheep here, to get wool for the cold climate. One of the youth was trained for this. Therefore, we could set up the sheep keeping and the production of wool."
Mzee Abel Njalika, Matetereka (*NCW 10; 8/31/2015*)

Again, statements like these underline RDA's general approach to development: If there were certain needs, like warm clothing because of Matetereka's highland environment, the Association would not just try to get hold of clothing with the help of their international donors. On the contrary, in the sense of their understanding of self-reliance, they tried to give the people involved the means to care for their needs themselves.

In many of the personal accounts of the wazee of former RDA villages, one can still feel the pride the villagers took in their project. Mzee Soko was particularly detailed in pointing out the visits of Mwalimu Nyerere, and how the president was impressed by the development those peasants were able to achieve. Apart from Ibbott, Soko remembered many different foreigners coming to see the village or even staying to help with its development. They came from all over Europe, some from Germany, some Israelis, some Americans – they all came to Litowa (*NCW 1; 2/26/2015*).

The end of RDA – first hand

The abandonment of the RDA in 1969 marked the sudden end of the story of a new beginning, as the wazee had experienced it. It certainly came as a shock to everybody, especially to those who were not among the village leadership and therefore did not have a direct exposure to the several conflicts between the RDA and various levels of government (see chapter 3). The event itself was perceived most harshly in Litowa itself, where Mzee Soko still has a vivid memory of this fateful day:

> "As I said it was 1969, it was during noon time, when the village got the news. They didn't know anything, they were very surprised. But, soon what they saw, the cars were coming, many of them. From one up to twenty-eight. And after reaching here, they started to collect people. Leaders, whoever, important persons. All of them. All people were grabbed, Ibbott was here, everyone was there. And after reaching, they saw that there was a minister, called Peter Kisumu. He was sent by the president. And they put all people in the Ujamaa hall, and told them to sit down."
> Mzee Soko, Litowa. Interpreted by Brother Augustine (NCW 1; 2/26/2015)

After everyone was sitting down in an atmosphere of anxiousness and surprise, it was Peter Kisumu, Nyerere's delegate, who broke the news to the villagers:

> "[And they told them] from today, this is the end of RDA. And after reaching a point, he said, – and after seating – he said that if people they having questions. And people almost were silent, except one: He said; 'we are here, and we came here under Nyerere. If Peter Kisumu has been told by Nyerere that you have to stop, its ok, no more, finish.' And people they were silent because, they were shocked."
> Mzee Soko, Litowa. Interpreted by Brother Augustine (NCW 1; 2/26/2015)

None of them truly understood the reasons behind this move, since they all perceived themselves as faithful followers of Nyerere's Ujamaa policy and builders of the nation. They would follow the orders, and nobody was putting up a fight against it. Only later, did the people of Litowa try to make a sense of what had actually happened. For Mzee Soko, he admitted that he was not sure until today about the real reasons behind it. For him, the most important factor appeared to be the presence of foreigners within the village – and also a sort of envy by local and regional bureaucracy, who felt that they could not achieve the same level of development as the RDA villages. They were enraged by the fact that they did not have direct control on the activities of these peasants:

> "What he says is that what was happened was amazing, it was really high. And of course, it could create the doubts, that before the government feared, even if it was under the regional and town council. But the village was higher than the town council itself. The capacity they had. And, they reached a time that the leaders wasn't have a say here. And that one could be among the things which made the leaders to say, no, that we stop there, because we have no access."
> Mzee Soko, Litowa. Interpreted by Brother Augustine (NCW 1; 2/26/2015)

In his narration, Mzee Shawa recalls that life became very hard after the end of RDA in Litowa (NCW 9; 8/24/2015). The most immediate effect was the departure of the foreigners, especially of Ibbott and his family, as well as the leaving of the non-Litowa students from the RDA school. The car was also gone, as Mzee Soko remembers:

> "The village was stopped. People, for example Ibbott, he left here 1971, and they didn't. He left here unwillingly, and the foreigners, they left early. (…) They had RDA before, it was closed in 1969. But they started another, they said 'Ruvuma Development Fund', later on. Which means, they changed the name, instead of association, they said 'fund'. But it wasn't the same ways as at the beginning. And all the property was taken, almost. The cars and so forth. There were so many things."
> Mzee Soko, Litowa. Interpreted by Brother Augustine (*NCW 1; 2/26/2015*)

The people of Liweta felt the same sort of destruction upon the disbandment of the RDA, and strong sentiment underlay their accounts of this part of village history. There, as well, reference to the end of RDA's school was made:

> "He is saying, everything was destructed, there was no Ujamaa again. Every person was doing on his own. He is saying even the education system was destructed."
> Bele Kumasi Nyoni, Liweta. Interpreted by Dennis Mpazagade (*NCW 3; 3/3/2015*)

The students themselves were not happy about returning to their home villages, where long walks to other schools awaited them, instead of the cooperative home of Litowa's school. Even worse than this inconvenience, however, was the fact that those schools did not teach Ujamaa, as they had come to appreciate in their time at Litowa:

> "I began to learn there, I studied there for four years. So, four years I studied there, after that, I was told that I had to go back. First, I went to the school in Irani, near Maweso, others went to Wino. And that was because the RDA had collapsed, it had died the RDA. Therefore, when we came back, we had to go all the way to Maweso, on our feet, to go to study. We would start early in the morning, to go to the school. Later on, we got hosts there, so we could stay there and study. We studied there – I started in 67 in Litowa, and I finished in Maweso. I finished there. (…) But Ujamaa, I could not learn there."
> Former student of RDA School (f), Matetereka (*NCW 10; 8/31/2015*)

In order to continue with Ujamaa, they had to go different ways than before, and the following account by another former student gives a glimpse of how the students of that time dealt with the changes coming upon them from the Association's disbandment:

> "I also want to share my story. In 65, I started with the school in Litowa. So, we went from here, with the car, at the beginning of the term, and at the end, we would return. When the RDA collapsed, I was in standard six, so for standard seven, I had to go to Wino. Because I could not take standard seven there [in Litowa] I had to go to Wino, on my feet. But there was no other class to which I could go, it was very tiring. So, I finished school in 71. After that, I went in to training at Mzee Mayemba, to learn ufundi

(craftsmanship). It was good. Later on, I became a teacher of craftsmanship. So, that is how we continued with Ujamaa, through cooperation among ourselves."
Former student of RDA School (m), Matetereka (*NCW 10; 8/31/2015*)

People who were more involved in the politics of those days, like Lukas Mayemba, also shed light on the reasons that could have led to the party's move to abolish the RDA. In many ways, he was giving the same propositions as Mzee Soko of Litowa, but, being a party insider back then, he had a more detailed understanding of what exactly caused the government to fear the peasants' own organization of Ruvuma so much:

"As the Ujamaa developed, people from the system were skeptical. They knew this would be a threat. Because, there are some graduates from university, who graduated, and went directly to leave, to Litowa. So, this actually developed some kind of fears to this people. So, there was a kind of conflicts. But Nyerere was still supporting it. But these other – the delegates of Mwalimu, questioned him: 'How come a person who graduates from the university, then goes to stay in the village?' He said: 'ah, you leave them, they are going to learn there. When they feel, they come back to the government, and we give them a kind of employment.' So, the fear developed from the government itself. They thought that they establishing this, this will probably change into communism. Communism, not socialism. So, this was their kind of fear."
Mzee Lukas Mayemba, Matetereka. Interpreted by Dennis Mpazagade (*NCW 4; 3/6/2015*)

It also becomes clear from this statement, that the RDA was not merely one way of trying cooperative development for Mayemba. To him, it was Ujamaa itself. The attack on the RDA, in his eyes, therefore was an attack by the party elite on Ujamaa itself. Their fears led to the end of RDA, and nothing else, in his view. The presence of "white man" being the most important single factor on which this fear was founded:

"The major cause was the government. So, the government feared, that there might be some hidden agenda, because there are white men coming. But when it was registered, it didn't show, who will come to run it, but now there are so many white men. Actually, this was kind of fear that the government had. They feared probably this will grow bigger and bigger and bigger. So, to cut it short now, is to close it. Now, there are some people like this man [Mayemba], who tried to question: 'why do you close it? Can you tell us what's wrong with RDA?' Then there was no clear response. Rather than harsh response: 'sit down!!!', this was what he was told, 'sit down'. And they were told by the minister by then. So, this was when RDA collapsed."
Mzee Lukas Mayemba, Matetereka. Interpreted by Dennis Mpazagade (*NCW 4; 3/6/2015*)

The decision of the TANU Central Committee was final, and the villagers and their leaders had no other option than to comply with it. It was the decisive end of RDA's network and the end of locally organized development for all but one of its member villages. This village, as has already been told, was Matetereka.

196

The second beginning. Matetereka after the RDA

Some of the factors that have contributed to the survival of Matetereka's Ujamaa group have been described in chapter 5.4.2, based on EDWARDS' (1998) findings. Many of the accounts of that study were independently confirmed by the interviewees of the field visits in 2015. For the sake of creating an understanding of the internal perception of their continued cooperative development, and as a basis for the analysis of the final end of their Ujamaa group in 2000, shortly after Edward's visit, some of their accounts will be presented in this section.

Lukas Mayemba, one of the key informants in Matetereka, had himself been part of Kisumu's delegation to Litowa and therefore was the first among the village's leadership to get news of the incumbent end of RDA. When he returned to Matetereka, however, the atmosphere was different from those described in the other villages. Instead of succumbing to the shock, the villagers of Matetereka discussed their options and decided that the virtues which kept them going in the first place – hard work and the goal of self-reliance – were still there to be used, regardless of the supporting structure which was now gone:

> "So, we decided to carry on, and we said we will be stronger, on our own. The first thing we need is Kujitegemea (self-reliance), we don't need the mzungu (white person), we don't need a lot of people, we don't need additional help. For us, we can go on."
> Mzee Lukas Mayemba, Matetereka (NCW 10; 8/31/2015)

Indeed, the post-abandonment political environment was not completely hostile to their efforts, because on national level, the implementation of Ujamaa had just begun – and with the Europeans out of the village, the government had not so much to complain about:

> "He says, the intention of the government was to see the white men out. So, when these people went away, the government started to preach again the Ujamaa. So, they started a lot of seminars, seminars across the country. And he was among the facilitators. So, they were teaching the people the good of Ujamaa. So, people started to practice Ujamaa."
> Mzee Lukas Mayemba. Interpreted by Dennis Mpazagade (NCW 4; 3/6/2015)

On the contrary, the new nationwide scope of *Ujamaa vijijini* required for people with experience in the creation and the operation of cooperative groups on village scale, and therefore Mayemba and other leaders of Matetereka were highly sought advisors for the Ujamaa "school" at Tabora, where people from all over Tanzania were supposed to be prepared for the development of the new villages. However, Mayemba's hopes of contributing to his vision of Ujamaa in this way became dire very quickly. The difference between the government's words and its actions was too apparent, after all:

> "After the collapse of RDA, the government actually started again to preach the good of Ujamaa. But their questions, him and the other colleagues, with Ujamaa, they had was: 'how can you preach Ujamaa. Why don't you practice Ujamaa? You are preaching

Ujamaa, why are you living in Dar es Salaam? In very good houses.' At the same time, at that time, he was in Dodoma also preaching ujamaa, as a facilitator – no in Tabora. In Tabora. So, he questioned himself: 'how should I preach what I don't practice? So, I better go home to practice socialism.' Now, the question is: 'how will I get permission from Tabora to even Iringa, Ruvuma or Mbeya' – nearer by his home. Then he said: 'let me tell them that my mother sick, so when I go back I will be able to attend her.' Then bosses rejected: 'no, we can't allow you.' So, what he decided, he resigned. He said, 'I can't keep on preaching what I don't practice. Let me go back to my people and practice socialism.' So, he came back here."

Mzee Lukas Mayemba, Matetereka. Interpreted by Dennis Mpazagade (NCW 4; 3/6/2015)

When trying to understand people like Mayemba, it becomes clear that they had a deeply felt conviction in their idea of local development. And as they saw themselves as true, down to earth socialists, the only way of living up to their own standards was to go back to the village they had started, and to continue to develop from there. It was also the only way, in which they thought they would be able to contribute to the building of the nation, and to act as an example for their compatriots: By showing them how to run an Ujamaa village, first hand.

This combination of idealism and a pragmatic developmental approach was also noticeable with other returnees to Matetereka. Moses Njalika, the brother of Abel Njalika, the first secretary, was part of SERA when the RDA got abolished. As part of his tasks, he had been sent to Liweta for two years in order to care for the milling machine and the tractor. After the RDA disbandment, he came back:

"In 1969, when the RDA was abolished, I was at Liweta. So, I came back and saw what had changed. They were self-reliant, they were growing coffee as a cash crop and sold it, and they were farming their food, like maize, beans. Everybody was growing, they were not doing it alone, they were doing it like Ujamaa. They harvested together and brought the produce to the market together. (…)

So, we had this village shop, together with the other wajamaa (socialists) and we were having different services. For example, our children, they didn't know a lot about. We were only like five wajamaa, people who called themselves wajamaa. And the development of government was a problem, because now the government wanted to make Ujamaa. Really, in this system, the youth had to go to different places, if they wanted to go to school up to standard seven. That was a problem. Another issue was water, there was no sufficient supply of water. So, we got the money to buy a machine, a pump, to get better water supply from down there. Once the machine worked, we had our water. And our children, they needed milk. Enough milk, for the health of the children.

So, … A lot of things we changed. We had a system to ensure that everybody had three meals. We cared for the water supply… And also, the milling machine, and we had to ensure a sufficient water supply. To care that the people had good services and the children had three meals, and water."

Mzee Moses Njalika, Matetereka (NCW 10; 8/31/2015)

This first-hand account may serve as an example of how those returnees assessed the new situation: The organization was still there, but a lot of things were missing. And these issues had to be tackled one by one. Moses Njalika, for instance, continued his work as the village mechanic, caring for the tractor and the machinery in Matetereka. He went on to educate other young people to be able to deal with these machines. In 1972, he became village secretary himself, and he also was the secretary of the Ujamaa group until 1991 (*NCW 10; 8/31/2015*).

That was the way of operation at Matetereka; if things were missing, they had to be built. And, as it becomes clear from the previous statement, the creation of "wajamaa" – of socialists who knew what they were doing, was one of the top priorities. Yet, as the RDA school which was built for this purpose in Litowa was no more, a new school was the order of the day:

> "Therefore, the Ujamaa continued, and we built our own school, and we taught the Ujamaa. We finished our school of Ujamaa. Then we went on to work, just like usual… And again, in those times in school, we would go back and do work of Ujamaa. We are doing work of Ujamaa. Therefore, we went on to teach Ujamaa later on, until the Ujamaa collapsed for good."
> Former student of RDA School (f), Matetereka (*NCW 10; 8/31/2015*)

Still, not all the things could be acquired locally, and the loss of the RDA support system brought considerable challenges to the village. This did not mean, however, that there was no solution to these shortcomings, even if they sometimes had to bring them to the national level:

> "He just described the challenges that he faced when he came to run ujamaa in this village. So, he phoned here the Regional Commissioner, who was also surprised: 'how comes a person resigns and comes to the village? To do what?' So, when he came here, he found so many problems. Social problems, no dispensary, children are dying because of malaria and the other diseases. Cattle also are dying. So, what he did, he informed the Regional Commissioner, to resolve the problems. And the Regional Commissioner he said: 'how can I resolve? We waste time as a government to take care for only fifteen people.' So, what they did, they prepared a kind of memorandum. They highlighted all the problems they faced, and went to Dar es Salaam to see Mwalimu Nyerere."
> Mzee Lukas Mayemba, Matetereka. Interpreted by Dennis Mpazagade (*NCW 4; 3/6/2015*)

Whether this move had been as successful for other villages in Tanzania, which did not attract Nyerere's personal interest, cannot be answered by this study. In Matetereka's case, its name still had value, much to the discomfort of regional development staff:

> "After Dar es Salaam, a team from the government, of government officials, came here to Songea, to see the problem. Political party members. Actually, for the purpose of resolving this issue. So, they organized some meetings, and so forth. And it was realized that the problems were very big. Bigger than what they had explained. Now, what was

the conclusion: the Regional Commissioner was fired. Ya, Mwalimu fired him. That was the end of the story. So, the man, who were fired blamed Mayemba, as the one who actually caused him to be fired. So, they became some kind of enemies. (…) The results of his fight, they got a dispensary, water, and this, eh, cattle dip. They got it. And the water. All these services were brought here through his efforts. And he's saying that they now have a very good dispensary, which was actually build in 1969. (…) So, despite all these problems, they kept on working and producing. After the collapse of RDA, they continued with their socialism."

Mzee Lukas Mayemba, Matetereka. Interpreted by Dennis Mpazagade (*NCW 4; 3/6/2015*)

Through these efforts on various scales, Matetereka was not only able to keep its original cooperative structure intact, but also became a sort of show-case village for what the whole idea of *Ujamaa vijijini* was about. So, ironically, after the destruction of the original RDA structure, Matetereka became a legitimized role model for rural development in Tanzania for doing exactly the same as before, but on its own. Many people were coming to the village, accordingly, and the villagers saw this as a confirmation for their undertaking:

"Now really, in those times, we also had contacts to a lot of places, and many people came to find work, because our economy here was good. and because the economy was good, the life was also good. There were a lot of good houses, the work went well. So really, a lot of other villages were impressed by us, because the life was so good. Before, people were not knowing how to even survive, then they even had a nice bedding. All because of our Ujamaa activities that we did together."

Former student of RDA School (m), Matetereka (*NCW 10; 8/31/2015*)

And even after the end of RDA, the village was attracting new villagers, who wanted to join the effort:

"So, I came here in 70. When I came here in 1970, I had heard about Ujamaa, and I was interested in Ujamaa. So, after I came here, in 1973, I thought I had to decide what I wanted to choose for my life. So, for me this was the education of children. So, I went to Mahiwa, to learn this profession. When I came back, they had already constructed the nursery school over there, for the education of the small children. So, that's why I stayed here, to teach small children. So, I became a nursery teacher. So, those were the reasons to stay, and to teach the children. (…) We played a lot of games, and also taught them. But, for me it was just like the school for the big children. Studying and all. There were times were two mamas would also help. We would teach the children until noon, and then they would get milk. Because, we had enough cows in the village, so the children could get very fresh milk."

Former nursery teacher (f), Matetereka (*NCW 10; 8/31/2015*)

From the perception of the participants at least, things were going on pretty well in Matetereka after the end of RDA, at least until the impact of villagization. At that time, the system of collective work and communal organization at Matetereka had already been well established, and the development of the village was making good progress under the leadership of Mayemba and the other members of the original Ujamaa group – as Telesphor Mwenda, a Matetereka native, remembered in an interview conducted in Peramiho in February 2015:

"Now, where Ujamaa started exactly, is where is Matetereka A. There – and I was living there, from 67 – now they had a system, first of government, they did that collectively, they had a chairman of the village, the Ujamaa village, this was Mister Lukas Mayemba, who was actually a charismatic leader, and he is still alive. I'm not in contact, but he is still there. And, eh, there was a general secretary, known as Moses Njalika, general secretary. They had a certain type of an executive secretary, somebody who was dealing with practical questions. [He] Was the elder brother of Moses, was Abel Njalika. This was organizing some activities of all the days. And now, under this leadership, the people were working together, all.

Therefore, all the mornings, the bell was ringing, and then people was going there and see what is the work for today. So, there was a program prepared there every day, he was writing, all, all women of this zone are to work in the garden, do this work; and men are to go to this work. Apart from those specific duties, some were taking care of, like cattle, some were taking care of the garden; those were more or less experts, so they were always there. But, all others to see every day what is the program, the daily program of work. And they are going to work there. And, eh, people were working, for example cultivating, the cultivating using hand hoes, but also, they had – I remember – in some moments they also had a tractor, which was helping those cultivating that great farm. So, they would cultivate a lot of maize, they had great plantation. Eh, coffee, and great plantation of sugar cane, great plantation of, eh, mangos, of oranges, eh, many types of fruit they had there. They could sell them there and outside there, and they could have some [income]. I think that moment they could buy even cars. They bought a certain lorry, certain moment. And, eh, their plan was to be together, make all together.

I remember when I was a student, even the school opened, we all could wear uniform of the same color and everything. It was prepared for all children. So, we went to the school all of them, clean, but eh, due to that organization of the village, etc. And, eh, that was the life, generally. And, eh, a system even of familiarity. For example, a question of, morals questions, therefore, the leaders were responsible and the parents were responsible to the young people, children – in moral questions. Even though these are not their children, because they are part of the, this part of this Ujamaa village, they were responsible also. So, it was something like a family, eh, in that moment. And, eh, ok. It was very interesting, people could visit, etc. Eh, but slowly, it went down, due to some political changes."

Telesphor Mwenda, former resident of Matetereka, Peramiho (NCW 2; 2/28/2015)

Villagization

Interestingly enough, the impact of villagization did not take a big part in the accounts of the wazee from Litowa. Mzee Soko, who had given an emotional report about the abandonment of RDA did not tell anything about the influence of any new settlers during villagization, and Mzee Shawa seems to have a positive opinion on Ujamaa, even after the end of the Association – although in general he never really discriminated between the phases before and after the abandonment (*NCW 9;* 8/24/2015). In any case, there appears to have been no significant impact of villagization on the life of the two wazee in their own perception.

In Matetereka, on the other hand, the arrival of many new settlers during the villagization campaign was the starting point of many of the conflicts that are still going on between the different parts of the village. Indeed, in the perception of people like Mayemba, it even contributed to many of the quarrels with higher authorities at that time, and he himself came under scrutiny for his alleged non-cooperation with the new settlement policy of the country:

> "Now, 1974, the campaign for Ujamaa came in, so all Tanzanians were supposed to engage in Ujamaa. Now what happened, some people from other villages shifted to this village, came to live here. So, this raised another concern: they said we have everything, our economy is strong. Now if this people come in and we share, this can be very dangerous for our economy. Now what we do, we have to give them their portions, so start from grassroots, they will learn, we will become their teachers. So, this actually was perceived negatively by top officials at the government. They said: you are very bad people, this guy is initiating, he is critical, he is criticizing Ujamaa, he doesn't want to involve others. So, this actually brought some problems to the village."
> Mzee Lukas Mayemba, Matetereka. Interpreted by Dennis Mpazagade (*NCW 4; 3/6/2015*)

In places like Namatuhi, villagization changed the nature of the area even more dramatically. All the people living in the scattered settlements of the surrounding area were ordered to move to Namatuhi, by a direct instruction from the central government. Some people followed this directive quietly, others had to be brought in by force, as the Sendas remember it. However, in their memory, collective agriculture was never really established in their village. The people just could not see the benefits of working together, and work on the communal shamba was seen as a necessity by external order. In 1977, the idea of forced collectivization of agriculture was dropped in Namatuhi, and replaced with a sort of Ujamaa by projects (*NCW 7;* 3/11/2015; *NCW 8;* 3/11/2015).

In the view of Merkiol Senda, such projects like building or repairing classrooms of the village school or other public buildings had been common in the area even before villagization. For him, the whole Ujamaa idea was brought in from the central government and had absolutely no benefit to the local peasantry. He couldn't understand what the use of this policy was supposed to be, and he felt very happy that it ended: "The failure of ujamaa really wasn't a problem of the ordinary people. It was truly one from above. A problem from above" (Mzee Merkiol Senda, Namatuhi; *NCW 8; 3/11/2015*).

Although the changes affecting Mbingamharule during the time of villagization appear to have been as severe as in Namatuhi (there had not been a village as such before as well, see chapter 5.4.3), the wazee interviewed there did not have the same negative perception of the effects of villagization as those of Namatuhi – even if there was sometimes the perception that the government was directing everything

(NCW 6; 3/11/2015). Nevertheless, the practical advantages of the new nucleated settlement outweighed these reservations:

> "Well in the past, to get good services was big problem. But after we became a village, it changed a little bit and it became good. The individuals, they had better services and healthcare."
> Mzee Majini Johni Deo, Mbingamharule (NCW 6; 3/11/2015)

The development after villagization was therefore seen as progress, in the eyes of these wazee. Still there was a lot to be improved, especially concerning the economic development of their village:

> "Before, when we went on individually, we missed a lot of things. But, well the live was not very good, it was inferior. But after 1974, when we became an Ujamaa village, we were together, and it changed a little bit. We got different services, easier. And since we were many, things changed a little bit. But even then, the economy was still a problem. The economy was a problem, in this village, there was only one business, and this was cultivating food crops. And the profit of this was little."
> Mzee Johni B. Komba, Mbingamharule (NCW 6; 3/11/2015)

Yet, the times of cooperation sounded just like in the other villages, which had a background in RDA:

> "Well we did everything together, we built the school, got education. Everything together. All of us were together in this, the youth, the wazee."
> Mzee Petro Komba, Mbingamharule (NCW 6; 3/11/2015)

The end of Ujamaa

The end of Ujamaa in Tanzania is most commonly seen in the end of Nyerere's presidency in 1985 and the subsequent economic and political changes implemented by his successor Ali Hasan Mwinyi (see chapter 3.4). In Matetereka, however, the original Ujamaa group continued with its activities even after that. Throughout Matetereka, therefore, the end of Ujamaa is seen much later, in the year 2000, to be exact:

> "We reached a phase where now Ujamaa is no longer existing in this village. He says there were actually some people, who withdrew themselves from Ujamaa. Because they had some kind of mentality. Few people were still practicing Ujamaa. So, some of the people withdrew from Ujamaa. He himself with the other colleges kept on with it, Ujamaa. So as time goes, there raised again conflicts. Those who withdrew from Ujamaa wanted some property from Ujamaa. They said, we owned together this property, so we have to divide, so they decided to go to court. So there the court, the judgement at the court was, you sell everything, then you divide. So, they did this. By 2000 they sold everything and divided equally. So, nothing belongs to Ujamaa. So Ujamaa was collapsed at that day."
> Mzee Lukas Mayemba, Matetereka. Interpreted by Dennis Mpazagade (NCW 4; 3/6/2015)

As a reaction to this, a kikundi called Kujitegemea was founded by the original wajamaa and other villagers with similar political conviction in 2000. Mayemba and many others wanted to continue with cooperative activities, so he and his wife flew to Scotland to meet with Ibbott and Edwards. They were able to raise around five million TSh from donors, and used it to buy two of the assets of the original group: The trees and the coffee farm. They continued their cooperative activities based on these operations, and the old members were also seeing their new kikundi as a vehicle for younger people to try out different cooperative development projects (NCW 4; 3/6/2015).

> "In 2000, we ended the Ujamaa group. So, we had been continuing with Ujamaa, even after the end of Litowa. We wanted to develop with the system of Ujamaa. From Litowa, we had learned the Ujamaa. Four of us, including Mayemba and myself, we wanted to continue with Ujamaa in any way. But we also knew, if it was only the four of us, we would fail. But now, we needed more than just us. So, that's why we decided to teach the youth, on how to do Ujamaa, to get more wajamaa. So, in 2000, we started a new group, we made a work plan for each year, and see how to continue."
> Mzee Moses Njalika, Matetereka (NCW 10; 8/31/2015)

However, in 2014, the coffee farm was impounded by the village government. The new village chairman had obviously promised to do so in his election campaign, in order to give the former Ujamaa land to all people of the village, as he put it (NCW 4; 3/6/2015). This kikundi was also part of the analysis of farmers' groups, presented in chapter 6.2.3. The ongoing conflict over the last pieces of Ujamaa property in Matetereka also reached the ear of some of the village's former residents, who described the general issue in the following manner:

> "Ujamaa now, in Matetereka has brought a very serious problem. People are in a very serious conflict. Due to the fact that those who belong to that group of wajamaa, had already possessed, for example, great pieces of land, as a group, eh, even buildings – they built a lot of buildings, important buildings. They made there even, even, nursery schools, etc., and, eh, they had built, eh, even centers for women, something like that, eh. Now, with that they possessed a great, a piece of land. Now, nowadays in Tanzania, the problem of piece of land has started, now there are, eh – the one who is the chairman of the village, is one who is totally against Ujamaa. Therefore, that was the problem. So, he started to say: No, this pieces of land, we don't recognize you as a group, because Ujamaa doesn't exist now, etc. So, that time there is a very serious conflict."
> Telesphor Mwenda, former resident of Matetereka, Peramiho (NCW 2; 2/28/2015)

Life after Ujamaa

Unsurprisingly, many of the wazee from Litowa, Liweta and Matetereka regretted the end of Ujamaa and felt that the new individual system was a step backwards in development. They liked working together and were satisfied with their achievements as wajamaa (NCW 3; 3/3/2015). Some felt that there was "not much development afterwards, because the agriculture declined, the tractor was gone." (Mzee Shawa, Litowa; NCW 9; 8/24/2015).

Even if they had continued the organization as a group in Matetereka, the eventual end of "original Ujamaa" brought discontent among the founders of the village, as expressed by Mzee Gervas Mkomba:

"So, he says currently every person works on his own. And they are no longer cultivating or working as a group, as union (...). He is not happy, and he was comfortable with the Ujamaa. Ujamaa is no longer, every person works alone. He liked working with the group, so he is not happy with the current situation."
Mzee Gervas Mkomba, Matetereka. Interpreted by Dennis Mpazagade (NCW 5; 3/6/2015)

This feeling of the loss of the cooperative thought and the practice of working together, was expressed by many of the former wajamaa of Matetereka A. The change of system was also perceived as a loss of knowledge on how to cooperate in the first place, and how to achieve development together:

"Now, I really think, the times of Ujamaa and today are very different. Because, in the times of Ujamaa, we really had a lot of affection, and we were doing things together! ... Then, nobody was going without help. But now, the affection is gone. The wind changed, and the leaves got blown away very quickly. A lot of bad things happened. Really, now there is no affection anymore, and the wisdom got lost"
Former nursery teacher (f), Matetereka (NCW 10; 8/31/2015)

In line with this, the general evaluation of the times of Ujamaa within this group of contemporary witnesses was overwhelmingly positive, while the rise of an attitude of caring only for oneself was lamented:

"Generally, the activities of Ujamaa were good. Now, there are activities of individual persons. The activities of Ujamaa, for me as I recall, we did our activities together, including working our shamba together and cultivating. Even if you had to go to the hospital for two or three months, if you would return, your tasks would already be done, because there was mutual help. But, nowadays, if a person cannot do his/her tasks for any reason, no one would do it for him/her or help."
Former student of RDA school (m), Matetereka (NCW 10; 8/31/2015)

Former Ujamaa leaders like Moses Njalika were assessing the changes on a broader scope. In his view those changes did not only alter people's attitudes, but also destroyed the whole idea of having common social services, owned by everybody within the community. The results of this are, in his view, detrimental for the society as a whole:

"I would like to add, maybe, that in the times of Ujamaa, we did all the things, the private ones and those of society, together. But now, the communal functions, like school, the service of water, health, they are collapsed. Like it was told, in those times we had water, now there is no water. Then we were caring for the water supply, we were building it together. Now, communal services like this, there are none. So, things like this are only available for people who have money. But, most among us they don't have money. In those days, all the children, regardless if their families had income or not, were going to school. Now, these things are gone. If you can afford it, you go to school. The same is true for health. Before, we were considering this a communal task, and everybody helped each other. If you were successful, you helped the society. Now, things like that are gone. (…)

So, I think, those are some of the differences. Now, there is no education, on how to cooperate, how to do things together. Everybody just wants to get education for themselves. Therefore, in this system, I have to care just for myself, and my relatives. In the system, before, it was me for us. That's the difference. We were working together, we were constructing the houses together, the children were going to school together, in case of illness, we cared together. But now, this is gone. The sense of cooperation, of mutual affection is gone, and everybody is just caring for him or herself and his/her things."
Mzee Moses Njalika, Matetereka (NCW 10; 8/31/2015)

The wazee of Mbingamharule were less pessimistic about the changes, but still some of them lamented the loss of solidarity and social services that came with the transformatory period after Ujamaa, and they do not perceive much development happening afterwards:

"The main change is now, everybody is on his own. You are on your own. And I say your, because, the people have destroyed it. (…) In the times of Ujamaa for instance, the medicine was free, but then the government changed that policy. And the small development, until now the development is small."
Mzee Johni B. Komba, Mbingamharule (NCW 6; 3/11/2015)

In the case of Stanislaus and Merkiol Senda, on the other hand, they had only experienced Ujamaa as a forced project, brought upon them by the power of the state – a project, in which they never felt they had any control over their own development in Namatuhi. The communal farming appeared useless to them, and as they could not see any tangible results of these efforts, they were delighted when the whole policy came to an end in the 1980s. For them, everybody caring for his own land was the best way of doing agriculture. In the communal projects, like the building of a school, they could see some benefits for themselves and for their offsprings. This idea of the necessity of tangible results appeared very important in their account of the village history. In the present, they do see the issue of young people not caring as much for the community like before. However, this idea of caring for each other, for them, did not have to do so much with Ujamaa, but more with the traditional idea of working together for communal projects. Collective farming from above did not fit into this idea of solidarity. On the contrary, it was seen as a waste of time and as counterproductive for development. And it was this experience of the new settlers coming to Namatuhi against their will, and the forced implementation of collective farming, which to Merkiol and Stanislaus Senda became emblematic for the whole Ujamaa policy. Against this background, it is not difficult to understand why those wazee are still skeptical of any development initiatives brought from the outside and why they are convinced that everybody is better off after the end of Ujamaa – even given the lack of communal interest by the youth which they observe. They, at least, have no interest whatsoever in elements of Ujamaa coming back to Tanzania (*NCW 8; 3/11/2015*).

Summary

It has become clear from these accounts of the contemporary witnesses interviewed for this research, that the period of Ujamaa affected the lives of the interviewees in many ways. Those participants, who had themselves been part of the early time of RDA villages, all gave vivid and very positive accounts of their stories of a new beginning. They were proud to be a part of a new movement that would help to build the nation. Those elders who had been coming to these villages a little later, like the interviewees from Litowa and Liweta, emphasized the fact that it was a combination of the fascination with the Ujamaa ideal and the tangible results they could observe in these villages that made them join the collective settlements in the early hours of independence. All of them shared the depiction of working together, living together and helping each other as their most important memories of this era. And all of them were shocked by the abandonment of the RDA, as it contradicted their own identification with the state's goal of reaching socialism and self-reliance.

After the end of RDA, however, the experiences of the wazee of Litowa and Liweta were thoroughly different from those of Matetereka. Only in the latter village, did the original wajamaa find the will and the resources to continue with their model of cooperative development within the new centralized environment of Ujamaa. In the other villages, few accounts were made on the history after RDA.

From those contemporary witnesses of the non-RDA villages of Namatuhi and Mbingamharule, differing statements were given: While in Namatuhi, the early cooperative villages were frowned upon skeptically, such negative attitudes towards the RDA were not present in Mbingamharule. In both cases, the impact of villagization and "ujamaaization" from above were seen as severe. Yet, while in the case of Mbingamharule, many positive aspects of villagization – like social services – were described, the respondents from Namatuhi only saw the negative effects of this policy. Nevertheless, in both villages, the effects of the forced introduction of collective agriculture were seen as negative and production was considered to be insufficient. Therefore, contemporary witnesses from both villages welcomed the end of communal farming in their communities. In Matetereka, villagization and the impact of new settlers was identified as a major cause for conflicts within the village.

In all of the former RDA villages, the contemporary witnesses regretted the end of Ujamaa in the country, as well as the abandonment of the RDA. They hardly saw any positive effects of the post-Ujamaa period in their villages, or even in the country as a whole. In Mbingamharule, the attitude towards the post-Ujamaa era were more ambiguous, and some of the new economic opportunities were explicitly welcomed. In Namatuhi, the end of Ujamaa was very much welcomed by the interviewees.

6.2.2 Political actors: Village authorities and their view on Ujamaa

In order to conduct any kind of research on the village level, engagement with the local authorities, especially the village chairman and the village secretary are a sine-qua-non-condition. Apart from their valuable knowledge on village development in general, their view on the village's history during the Ujamaa era and the subsequent changes on the local level were of key interest. In all three case study villages, the village headquarter (ofisi ya kijiji) was approached, to arrange the possibility of research and to gather information on the village itself regarding economic activities and other development issues. While this general information on the villages has been included in the case study description in chapter 5, the following passages are focusing on the perception of Ujamaa among the village authorities. In all villages, the village chairman (mwenyekiti) took part in the interviews; in Mbingamharule, the village secretary or manager (mtendaji) was also present during the interview.

All three village chairmen saw the general development of their villages as the main task of their office, as well as them taking a connective role between the government as such (at all levels), the village council and assembly, and the citizens in general. The mtendaji has the additional task of taking care of bookkeeping and organizing village assembly and council meetings. All of the interviewed village office holders were elected the year before, although in the case of Mbingamharule, the chairman had been in the same office before and had now again taken the position after a hiatus of five years (*GBE 7*; 2/26/2015; *GBE 11*; 3/11/2015; *GBE 15*; 8/30/2015).

General depiction of the Ujamaa era by village leaders

In the village of Litowa, there is a relatively young village chairman in office, Michael Komba, who showed a very high interest in the idea of the research and would also facilitate the meeting with the different vikundi within the village. In a way, he was the first interviewee to make the connection between the modern-day farmers' groups and historical Ujamaa in the village. Despite his young age, he was able to give a quite detailed account of the local history, even though in his opinion, the wazee would surely know more about it. In particular, he attributed a high importance to the presence of Ralph Ibbott in the early days of Litowa and the time gap between the first settlers led by Millinga and the arrival of the British advisor was non-existent in his accounts (*GBE 7*; 2/26/2015). Equally important to Komba was the idea of cooperation and mobilization, which he himself described as having a kikundi, and the material developments that this group made in the times of Ujamaa:

> "They had a primary school, they had a tractor, they had a shamba, where they were growing crops together, also they had cows, a lot of them (…) they had a machine, which was pumping the water into the tank up in the village (…). Ibbott was here, they had a kikundi, a group of Ujamaa, they were working together and introducing different services."
> Michael Komba, Chairman of Litowa (*GBE 7*; 2/26/2015)

The chairman of Matetereka, who is also allegedly involved in the legal battle with the Kujitegemea group about some of the original Ujamaa assets of the village, still has the usual depiction of Ujamaa as a system of collaboration between people. However, from his statement, it also becomes clear that during Ujamaa, the government was having most of the project under its control, and not the people themselves – a fact which he sees critically:

"Ah, ok, what I know about Ujamaa. The people were working together, and they grew together [the crops]. So, everybody worked for Ujamaa. It was a complete unity. So, all the people they worked together, and helped each other. In this system, they had an organization of work for everybody, so that everybody would be fine. So now, in this system, the government, not the people on themselves, the government made big projects, like building the school and other things, and a car for the village, etc."
Remigius W. Njafula, Chairman of Matetereka (*GBE 15*; 8/30/2015)

He recalls some of the benefits of having the RDA as a network, however:

"And then they worked together in whole Ruvuma, to get capital. There was help in that."
Remigius W. Njafula, Chairman of Matetereka (*GBE 15*; 8/30/2015)

In Mbingamharule, the memory of cooperative work was also the most important topic concerning the depiction of Ujamaa by the village authorities. In their view, the people of their village tried to follow the central government's idea of cooperative development, but did not achieve the results they had hoped for:

"Now, during Ujamaa, it was like everywhere. We were cultivating together, on a common shamba, we tried to reach self-reliance and development. (…) But the development was disappointing, because everybody went back to work on their own, they didn't like to be together."
Ernest S. Madau, Chairman of Mbingamharule (*GBE 11*; 3/11/2015)

So, despite the differences in their villages' history, present-day village leaders shared the same general depiction of Ujamaa. The next question was, how they would evaluate the period of Ujamaa, as well as the changes for their villages.

Evaluation of the changes through and after Ujamaa

The village government of Mbingamharule was indeed very reflective on the impact of villagization, which made their place an Ujamaa village. They also acknowledged the positive effects that this central policy had on the provision of social services for their community, very similar to the accounts made by the contemporary witnesses:

"I think generally, our village, from when it started, a long time ago was a quaint village, until 1974, when the government decided that from now on this would be an Ujamaa village, that people would move here and that this would be better. The biggest benefit was supposed to be that once the people would live together, they would be in contact together, do all the activities together, for the benefit of the village and our country as a whole. Another benefit would be, if our citizens are in one place, all of the primary services could be provided more easily."
Omare Kamare, Village Manager of Mbingamharule (*GBE 11*; 3/11/2015)

In Litowa, the village chairman also shared the overall assessment that had already been given by the wazee of his village, as he remembered the many material benefits that the Ujamaa period had created. Some of them were still in use in his village, and this added to his positive perception of the past. On the other hand, he described the changes that were brought upon Litowa, when people, who could afford it, bought the once communal assets and others, who could not, were left behind in development:

> "What remained here up the time being, the school, for example, the dispensary, were constructed in that time. Eh, buildings, but they are not in a good condition. And he said, the farms, they are still there, but people they are not making them in common, they are not sharing the work. Everyone is possessing on his own. And people they started to do so after the village as a whole rejected and was doing nothing. And the people they said: now, we get something from that shamba and then they started to use that on their own. Therefore, people, according to their way, they had cows and cows – they reached a point where they were not able to manage as a village, and the chairman said – the former one – said, if people, the village people are able to buy it, for the individuals, for the families, it is fine. And then I think they had a meeting, like which they had before, and they discussed it and reached a point where they were able to do so. People, who were able to buy it, they bought it for their own family. And now some people they are having cows. Which in former times they were under common [ownership]."
> Michael Komba, Chairman of Litowa. Interpreted by Brother Augustine
> (*GBE 7*; 2/26/2015)

By contrast, the representatives of Mbingamharule were more optimistic with regards to the post-Ujamaa situation of their community, and also praised the vikundi as a new engine for development on the local scale:

> "But now, thanks to the vikundi, we are on a good road. A good stage, we have good food, etc. Even now most is cultivated for food, but there is also business. The people have vegetables. So, this is good. They have their personal supply of vegetables and the like. So, it changed a lot."
> Omare Kamare, Village Manager of Mbingamharule (*GBE 11*; 3/11/2015)

The chairman of Matetereka, too, acknowledged the difficulties with the new capitalist system, especially the challenge of getting capital for development in the first place. On the other hand, he appeared to be convinced that the new way of doing things was superior to the old one of Ujamaa, as it relieved the people from working for the government, as he perceived it – and that this had in fact improved the standard of living in his village:

> "I think the main challenge here in the capitalist system is capital. You know, in the capitalist system, each people they have to own their own property, so if you don't have a big capital, you can't produce in large area. But during Ujamaa period, the people

210

produced more for the benefit of government only. But the people themselves, they were getting a low amount of money, just for feed only, and not for other uses. And he explained that, when you look the Ujamaa period and the capitalist period, nowadays in the capitalist period the people have changed, from a lower standard to a higher standard, somehow, many people they build their house in high quality, compared to Ujamaa period."

Remigius W. Njafula, Chairman of Matetereka. Interpreted by Josephat Mwasulama (*GBE 15*; 8/30/2015)

Summary

Overall, each of the village representatives was aware of the local history of their village and gave quite detailed accounts of the particularities of the Ujamaa era in their respective communities. Regarding the evaluation of the era, only Michael Komba of Litowa showed an overwhelmingly positive assessment of the past, while the authorities from the other two villages saw both positive and negative changes since the end of Ujamaa. In particular, the new individual freedom in economic opportunities was praised by Remigius Njafula of Matetereka. Nevertheless, all village leaders saw the idea of cooperation in the new form of farmers' groups (vikundi) as one of the most promising approaches for progress in their communities.

6.2.3 Farmers' groups: Practical Ujamaa or pragmatic adaption?

As described in chapter 5.2, the farmers' groups within the case study villages emerged as one of the most valuable sources of information regarding the Ujamaa legacy within those communities. For the sake of this thesis, the main question regarding these vikundi was whether those present-day farmer organizations could be seen as a reminiscence of Ujamaa's tradition of grassroots economic development, or if those groups are just a pragmatic adaption of the farmers to incentives like NGO support.

The vikundi interviewed for this research

In total, 23 farmers' groups took part in 12 group interviews during the field visits in the three case study villages. Although it was preferred by the research design to have one interview for one kikundi each, this proved only to be feasible in Litowa (six groups and six interviews) and Matetereka A (two groups in two interviews). In Matetereka B, two vikundi took part in one group interview, while in Matetereka C, three groups from this sub-village took part in one interview. In Mbingamharule, getting a good setup for the discussions turned out to be the most difficult, and let to a very dense situation especially during the first group discussion there (*GI 13*; 9/8/2015), when a total of seven vikundi participated in a meeting at the village headquarters. The second group discussion in this village took place with the participation of group members and non-members at the side of a funeral celebration (a big social event for the whole village) and involved around 100 participants.

Representatives from four groups took part in the actual discussion there, with one of the groups (TMK) having already been part of the first group discussion in Mbingamharule.

These differences in the scale of discussions was caused by the fact that the research had to rely on local guides – mostly representatives of the village headquarters, another limitation – who took charge of arranging the meetings with the various groups. In spite of these limitations, the results are considered to be valuable for the understanding of local development within the research area and will be presented in this chapter. Whenever possible, direct quotations will be citing the name of the respective vikundi and the place of the interview. In some cases, in which more than one group took part in the discussion (namely, Matetereka C and Mbingamharule), it could not always be determined to which group the person making the statement was belonging. In these cases, only the citation "Group member, village" will be used. In the case of the two groups from Matetereka A, both of them included some of the original settlers and Ujamaa group members, whose names were already known during the discussion. In these cases, direct citations will include the name of the respondent.

Regarding the age of the different groups, considerable differences could be observed between the different locations. While the groups of Matetereka B were founded in 2002 and 2003, respectively, and the Kujitegemea group of Matetereka A was founded in 2000, as the direct successor of the original Ujamaa group, most vikundi were substantially younger: Tangawizi group (Matetereka A) was founded in 2012 and involved partly the same group of people like the Kujitegemea group. The groups in Matetereka C were all founded between 2009 and 2010, while those in Mbingamharule gave no clear statements regarding their inception, but stated they had been operative for in between two and three years only. One group (Siliki) was founded a little bit earlier in 2011. The youngest groups on average could be found in Litowa, with Kanyanga Twende dating from 2012 and Juhudi Group from 2013 being the only groups operating there for at least one year. The other four groups visited in this village had only started their activities in 2015, the year of research.

The number of groups involved in each village depended first of all on the willingness and the availability of the group members themselves. Generally, this availability was high, courtesy of the fact that these interviews were held during the dry season, in which there was relatively low necessity for immediate farm work for the members.

In Litowa, there were a total of eight groups operative in 2015, as by the account of the village chairman (*GBE 7*; 2/26/2015), six of whom were willing to take part in the group interviews. In Matetereka, eight groups were active in the whole village in 2015 (*GBE 15*; 8/30/2015), of which seven took part in the interviews. In Mbingamharule, a total number of 14 groups was named by the villagers (*GI 13*; 9/8/2015), of which 10 were represented in the group interviews. Therefore, the following statements are considered to give a comprehensive insight into the operations of these farmers' groups and the opinions of vikundi members in the three case study villages.

Types of activities

As already mentioned, the groups in Litowa are fairly new organizations. All of them have started a sort of mutual saving and loan system, whereby their members contribute a certain amount of cash in regular intervals to the group. On the one hand, this money is used to act as a private savings account, in order to enable the individual farmers to buy seeds and, if possible, fertilizer in time for the next planting season. Shortage of money for these kind of farm inputs was regularly named as one of the biggest challenges by the farmers, and this system is seen as a possibility to cope with this issue (all groups in Litowa, particularly Mtakuja Tangine (*GI 2*; 8/24/2015)). The second function of this saving scheme is to act as the basis for small loans for the members, in case of personal hardships like illness, but possibly also for investment in agriculture – although the capital is usually not sufficient for this task, especially in the case of the younger groups (*GI 4*; 8/24/2015).

Some of the groups were also engaged in income-generating activities. The Kanyanga Twende group, for instance, was using some 100 acres of forest for timber production. However, the timber was not sold, but rather used for the production of 22 boxes for beekeeping, which were distributed throughout the group's forest. Yet, there seems to be no accessible market for honey and it was only sold locally. At the year of research, the beekeeping activities of the group were on hold altogether, with lack of funds for protective equipment cited as the reason by group members. This may give some insight on the volatility of vikundi activities. Nevertheless, the group found a more worthwhile income generating activity in Caritas' Soya ni Pesa project, for which each member is producing individually. The soya is then collected by the group and sold to buyers which are organized by Caritas (*GI 1*; 8/22/2015).

The other established group of Litowa, Mtakuja Tangine, is also taking part in Caritas' soya project. Each member was cultivating half an acre of soya in the last season. Sesame and beans are also grown on half an acre by each member individually and then marketed through the group. They are also trying to buy fertilizer and other inputs together, in order to achieve better prices (*GI 2*; 8/24/2015).

Of the other four newer groups, only Umoja group had already been able to get a harvest in in their first year. They, too, were growing soya on one acre per member. The whole group appeared to be very enthusiastic during the interview concerning the returns of this activity, and were planning to increase the production for the next season. As with the other aforementioned groups, the returns of soya production are also used to increase the capital of the kikundi, apart from paying dividend to its members (*GI 6*; 8/24/2015).

The other three groups stated that they were still in the process of collecting the funds from their members, but all were planning to start soya production for the next season (*GI 3*; 8/24/2015; *GI 4*; 8/24/2015; *GI 5*; 8/24/2015). An overview on the vikundi of Litowa and their respective activities is provided in Table 1.

Just like in Litowa, the vikundi of Mbingamharule were all taking part in the cultivation of soya through the Caritas sponsored Soya ni Pesa program and were also

Table 1: Overview on Farmers' Groups in Litowa

Name of the kikundi	Year of foundation	No. of members	Group activities				Plans for the future
			Saving and Lending	Agricultural	Animal husbandry	Others	
Kanyanga Twende	2012	34	Yes	Growing soya for Soya ni Pesa on individual plots.	No	Beekeeping (on hold because of lack of equipment). Tree farming (no market outside the village)	Trying to get enough capital to get machinery (at least an ox plough and a milling machine).
Mtakuja Tangine	2015	30	Yes	Growing soya for Soya ni Pesa on individual plots. Buying farm inputs together.	No	None	To get a common shamba and to increase soya production to at least one acre for each member.
Juhudi	2013	17	Yes	Every member is growing half an acre of soya, sesame and beans each, which is marketed together through the group. Soya is sold through Soya ni Pesa.	No	None	To get enough capital for investment, get a common shamba for the kikundi and to get fertilizers for this shamba together. To get enough money to get a mode of transport for the group, like a motorcycle.
Mshikamano	2015	25	Yes	Planned, when enough capital is collected.	No	None	To start soya production for Soya ni Pesa. To get enough capital for investment, get a common shamba for the kikundi and to get fertilizers for this shamba together. Thinking about various crops to be used for collective farming. To create profit for their members.
Juhudi (2)	2015	14	Yes	Mutual advice. There are plans for a common shamba.	No	None	To start soya production for Soya ni Pesa. To start collective cultivation of soya and other crops. To start mutual help in non-agricultural activities like building houses.
Umoja	2015	30	Yes	Growing soya for Soya ni Pesa on individual plots.	No	None	To use profit from first year of soya production for investment in a milling machine, in order to market maize together. To increase soya production, and to start a common shamba for this. To get cows and start producing milk. Envisioning a cooperation among all the vikundi to get a tractor for the village.

Source: own survey

214

providing a mutual saving and lending scheme for their members (*GI 13; 9/8/2015; GI 14; 9/10/2015*).

In most cases, the soya farming was conducted in a similar way like in Litowa, with each member growing a certain acreage of soya beans, which would then be marketed by the kikundi through the help of Caritas. There is also a limited amount of collective work at the soya demonstration plot. Most of the groups also stated that they would engage in other group activities, like helping each other when building or improving houses and similar things (*GI 13; 9/8/2015*).

Two groups, however, stated a higher degree of cooperative operations: TMK Group, for instance, has a rotational scheme of cultivation, in which the whole group would work on one plot of a member for one day, then go on to the next member, and so on. They are also planning to keep animals as a group and share the income generated from this activity (*GI 14; 9/10/2015*). The oldest group in Mbingamharule which took part in the discussions – Siliki, founded in 2011 – is already active in sharing advise on animal husbandry among its members, although the animals are kept privately. However, they stated that they do have a common shamba for the kikundi, on which they grow soya and also maize (*GI 14; 9/10/2015*). Table 2 illustrates the activities of Mbingamharule's farmers' groups.

Table 2: Overview on Farmers' Groups in Mbingamharule

Name of the kikundi	Year of foundation	No. of members	Group activities				Plans for the future
			Saving and Lending	Agricultural	Animal husbandry	Others	
Twende na wakati Ukombozi Mshikamano Kambarage Upendo Muungano	2012/2013	Around 20-30 each	Yes	Sharing advise and mutual help on members' individual shambas. All groups participating in Soya ni Pesa, growing soya on individual plots.	No	Some vikundi have small businesses and shops together.	Few concrete plans for the vikundi. Individual members want to increase cash income through group activities.
TMK	2012	22	Yes	Rotational help in cultivation among the members. Also, growing soya for Soya ni Pesa on individual plots.	Planned	Mutual help in non-agricultural activities like housing improvement among its members.	Step by step development - improve agriculture, housing and financial situation of its members. Start with animal husbandry.
Siliki	2011	25	Yes	Cultivating maize and soya on common fields, selling soya through Soya ni Pesa.	Sharing advise for individual husbandry	None	Increase cultivated area, introduce collective cattle keeping.
Thinka	2012	Unclear	Yes	Growing soya for Soya ni Pesa on individual plots.	"a little bit"	None	
Caritas	2012		Unclear	Growing soya for Soya ni Pesa on individual plots.	No	None	

Source: own survey

For all the groups from Litowa and Mbingamharule, which were taking part in the Soya ni Pesa program, soya cultivation was solely seen as a welcome opportunity to get access to a relatively secure market for this cash crop. None of the vikundi engaged in this project were performing any additional steps in the processing of the soya beans, nor stated that they would be interested in doing so in the immediate future.

In contrast to this relative uniformity of vikundi in Litowa and Mbingamharule, the situation in Matetereka appears to be more diverse and is different for each of the sub-villages. In Matetereka A, the Kujitegemea group is the same Kujitegemea group that was founded as a successor of the original Ujamaa group in 2000 (see chapter 6.2.1 for details). Since 2014, the conflict caused by the impounding of the group's assets by the village government took up most of the group's attention. A court case was filed against the village government by the group, and the decision was still pending at the time of research. The group was therefore not doing any of its genuine activities, as the government's actions were cited as hindering all of them. Before that, they were looking into different new ideas, one of them being

Table 3: Overview on Farmers' Groups in Matetereka

Name of the kikundi	Year of foundation	No. of members	Group activities				Plans for the future
			Saving and Lending	Agricultural	Animal husbandry	Others	
Matetereka A							
Tangawizi	2012	14	No	Cultivating ginger and beans on common fields, selling together at the market.	No	None	Increase production. Looking for other groups to cooperate and make their field a learning farm. Thinking of adding additional crops.
Kujitegemea	2000	12	No	Common coffee plantation (former Ujamaa farm), but on hold due to legal conflict.	No	Tree plantation (former Ujamaa property), but also on hold.	Hoping to overcome the legal issues with the village government and restart their activities.
Matetereka B							
Tupo tayari	2003	11	Using the profit from common agriculture and tree plantation.	Growing maize and beans together, mostly for food, but selling surplus produce together.	Keeping three cows together	Owning a tree plantation, selling for the market.	Hoping for more support from the government.
Sisi kwa sisi	2002	20	No	Sharing advise	Keeping cows	None	Increase cattle keeping, goal is to have one cow for each member. Hoping to get enough capital for machinery.
Matetereka C							
Tuinuke kiuchumi	2009	27	Yes, with group account.	Sharing advice and pooling resources to buy farm inputs.	No	None	Determined to contribute to village development by increasing their production.
Tuvitange	2009	12					Planning to introduce sesame cultivation. Hoping to get enough capital for machinery.
Tuvumiliani	2010	10					

Source: own survey

the establishment of a fishing pond (*GI 11*; 9/3/2015). Many former wajamaa were also engaged in the Tangawizi group, founded in 2012. As its name suggests, these farmers were mainly engaged in the production of ginger (Tangawizi in Kiswahili), but also beans as a cash crop, both of which are cultivated collectively. The lack of fertilizer was cited as a limiting factor on their ginger production (*GI 7*; 9/2/2015).

Both groups in Matetereka B were well established and were providing saving and lending for their members. Both of them are also keeping cattle together, although Sisi kwa Sisi only started doing so in 2014, while Tupo tayari has been keeping three cows for milk production for a few years and was also assigned a designated grazing area by the village government. The latter group is also selling trees and has an area of five acres under common cultivation for food crops like maize and beans, in addition to their individual fields. They are also cooperating on these private plots. This group also stated that they have a high frequency of group meetings, up to three times a week, to coordinate their different activities and to decide how to use profits (*GI 10*; 9/3/2015).

By contrast, none of the groups in Matetereka C was having common agricultural activities, although some of the members were contemplating the inception of collective animal husbandry for income generation, as well as for use in farming. The three vikundi there were only involved in saving and lending for their members, and were also using their accounts in order to buy farm inputs collectively for their members (*GI 9*; 9/3/2015). The features of Matetereka's farmers' groups can be found in Table 3.

The issue with collective farming

Persisting or newly established forms of collective farming within the case study villages were seen as a key interest for this research, as it was proposed that this could be an indication for the persistence of Ujamaa elements within the area. Therefore, the question of whether group members would engage in some form of collective agriculture, for instance by virtue of a common shamba for their group, was regularly asked at the beginning of the group interviews – usually as a follow up question to the first description of group activities by the members.

However, the insistence in looking for such proposed remainders of Ujamaa legacy may have led to an initial misunderstanding of the concept of communal agriculture of these groups by the researcher: Many Litowa vikundi reported farming soya together on an area of about one acre (for instance Mtakuja Tangine Group: "(…) this year, they are cultivating the soya together, they have one acre which they cultivate together "(*GI 2*; 8/24/2015), and also Juhudi Group (*GI 3*; 8/24/2015) and Umoja Group (*GI 6*; 8/24/2015)). First, this was understood as some form of newly incepted communal farming. Later analysis of the interviews, as well as triangulation with the interviews with Caritas Songea (*GBE 1*; 2/23/2015; *GBE 17*; 9/9/2015) and with the village chairman of Litowa (*GBE 7*; 2/26/2015) indicated, however, that most probably the vikundi members were referring to the Caritas demonstration plot in Litowa, where they cultivated together as a learning experience.

This would explain the apparent contradictions, which are found in those group discussions, whereby groups already engaged in soya cultivation regularly stated both that they were farming together AND that each individual member was farming soya on a specific area on their individual shamba (0.5 to 1 acre usually). Nevertheless, it also appears to be within the plans of some of the mentioned vikundi to increase collective production, at least for soya:

> "We have a common shamba for soya, with one acre. But, now we are planning to increase this."
> Member of Umoja Group (m), Litowa (*GI 6; 8/24/2015*)

> "We are growing individually. Soya, it is our project to grow together. Now, this year, everybody in this group has cultivated one acre, individually. In the future, we want to cultivate this together. But this year we have grown individually. Then, we want to start to cultivate two acres together, and then go on from there."
> Member of Umoja Group (m), Litowa (*GI 6; 8/24/2015*)

This seems to be the standard approach of Caritas, as the program coordinator in Songea did not understand the question if communal farming was a requirement for joining the program, and rather explained the training elements (mono cropping or intercropping, spacing, etc.) repeatedly (*GBE 17; 9/9/2015*). VAN DER BOM (2013: 25–30), who provided an overview on the early stages of the Soya ni Pesa program in other villages of Ruvuma, also described the emphasis of the NGO on these demonstration plots for training purposes on the village level. Collective production, on the other hand, was not within the overall goals of the project. This makes it reasonable to presume that there is indeed no collective farming activity for any of the Litowa groups regarding soya, apart from the common training plot. This leaves some of the Matetereka and Mbingamharule groups as the only vikundi which were performing some extent of collective farming (see above), at least at the time of research.

"They worked together, they ate together" – Group members' depiction of Ujamaa

It may be useful at this stage to recall the openness with which the question regarding Ujamaa was presented to the groups. The basic impetus was to get to know their opinion on the times of Ujamaa. Nevertheless, most of the responding groups started with a depiction of these times, how they had experienced it themselves – or what they knew about the times, if they were too young to have been there themselves. By far the most common first description of Ujamaa was the expression – in one way or another – that they worked together, ate together, and cultivated their fields together:

> "In the times of Ujamaa, generally, they did everything together, the ate together, all things were done together, all things were Ujamaa. The agriculture, the gardens, etc. all things. A kikundi ujamaa."
> Member of Mshikamano Group (m), Litowa (*GI 4; 8/24/2015*)

> "I think in times of Ujamaa, we had everything, mashine (machine ya kusaga – a milling machine, usually just referred to as "mashine"), a tractor, a car. They could buy everything. they worked together, ate together. The grew the maize together, then they cooked it together and ate it together. That is what I know about Ujamaa."
> Member of Mtakuja Tangine Group (f), Litowa (*GI 2; 8/24/2015*)

Similar stories were shared by the other groups of Litowa (*GI 5; 8/24/2015; GI 1; 8/22/2015; GI 6; 8/24/2015*). In all groups of the village, the stories about the communal activities (working, harvesting, eating) were as vividly told as the material benefits that the village had during those times. The tractor, the car and the milling machine, which were all owned communally, were regularly mentioned, as was the school that was built in those days. Last but not least, the water supply was another major theme when recalling Ujamaa history. At least according to the members' memory, a working pump and the water tank are deeply connected to the period of Ujamaa – and the lack of a functioning water supply in the present is seen as a huge step backwards:

> "Well, in the times of Ujamaa, we had water supply. With the tank, just over there. We had a pump, to bring the water from the river. With a pipe, all the way from down there up here. Well, afterwards, the life changed and it went astray. They were developing for what they needed. They needed water, they build a pump. A lot of things. Yet, we got – well as the chairman said, where did it go? In the past, the wazee here, they were really with Ujamaa. When I was born, there was Ujamaa. There was a building, milling machine, cattle keeping together... the whole day. And in the end, you were eating, together. It was really here."
> Member of Juhudi Group (m), Litowa (*GI 3; 8/24/2015*)

In Matetereka A, most of the personal experiences of the older group members have already been described in chapter 6.2.1, but the accounts of the younger members didn't differ much from their stories, or the depiction of Litowa's groups – special reference was made to the organization of work in those times:

> "I think it was their times [referring to the wazee within the group]. They were going together. They were working together. Everybody was working, because they were doing their work in specified times. So, everybody had a task given, and a time to do the work. That and of course there were also activities which they did together."
> Member of Tangawizi Group (m), Matetereka A (*GI 7; 9/2/2015*)

Work and education where indeed recurring aspects in the depictions of Ujamaa in those groups, especially by members who had been there since the beginning:

> "Really, I myself, it started 1965, when we were young. First, we got knowledge, on what to do. Secondly, we made structure of work. Third, we didn't have fear. The times made me, until today, in Matetereka. We taught the youth a profession, for free. How to be a builder, a carpenter, we taught for free, Ujamaa. So, for the youth to come to Ujamaa. Sometimes, I think for the people it is difficult to understand Ujamaa, in this village."
> Member of Kujitegemea Group (m), Matetereka A (*GI 11; 9/3/2015*)

Notwithstanding, even members who came to the village in a time when Ujamaa was on the demise in the rest of the country, would be impressed by the nature of Ujamaa in Matetereka:

"Well I came here 1987. But when I came here, I could see what Ujamaa was all about, because I could learn so much."
Member of Kujitegemea Group (m), Matetereka A (*GI 11; 9/3/2015*)

In the other sub-villages, the depictions were less enthusiastic. Some members in Matetereka B remember Ujamaa as being like one big kikundi, which had some benefits, but also brought issues concerning the fair organization of labor and the sharing of benefits, as well as the conflict between the original wajamaa and other groups in the village:

"When we had Ujamaa, we had one kikundi together. The structure was good, as long as everybody contributed. But when there came more people, it became very difficult. It became difficult to get help. For example, there was only this one group with a milling machine, so when the normal citizens (wananchi) needed to mill, it became difficult."
Farmers' Group Member (m), Matetereka B (*GI 10; 9/3/2015*)

Concerning the vikundi of Matetereka C, the depiction of the village's past was mostly negative. Reflecting many conflicts that had already been narrated by the wazee of the original village, most of the participants in this sub-village felt that they had the short end of the stick during Matetereka's extended Ujamaa operations. As in B, the monopolization of the milling machine by the Ujamaa group was cited as one of the negative issues during that time (*GI 9; 9/3/2015*). Overall, the attitude of the original inhabitants was seen as commanding and presumptuous against the new arrivals of the villagization period. Those and their descendants make up most of C's population today. In their view, they experienced a sort of Ujamaa from above, as they were feeling like going back to primary and "were told [what to do], not doing by ourselves" (Farmers' Group Member (m), Matetereka C, *GI 9; 9/3/2015*). Generally, Ujamaa was experienced as a system of the leadership only, and this was not appreciated:

"Maybe, Ujamaa brought development in those times for Tanzania. But for the village – and this was an Ujamaa village – the wananchi just worked. After that it became an Ujamaa village, and the whole country, together with Matetereka. And the name of Matetereka was known everywhere, that this was Ujamaa. But it was a system of the leadership, not for the wananchi, the kikundi cha ujamaa (Ujamaa group). And this Ujamaa, in those times, it was a system, for them, not for us (...) For me Ujamaa ended because it was a system of the leadership, and it was bad. Maybe for them it was good, but for us self, it was bad."
Farmers' Group Member (m), Matetereka C (*GI 9; 9/3/2015*)

Up until today, this divide between the original settlers and the later arrivals is lamented by the participants at C. They feel that the attitude of the old wajamaa has not changed since their group ended in 2000. Furthermore, the economic success of those former leaders is contributing to their negative perception by the group members at Matetereka C.

"Until now in this village. These people of Ujamaa they have nice houses, and some business, only among themselves, everything is a thing of Ujamaa. Even if it's now finished. It is many things. So up until now, this is a problem for many, because they think they own all of it."
Farmers' Group Member (m), Matetereka C (*GI 9; 9/3/2015*)

The group members of Mbingamharule were more general in their depiction of Ujamaa in their village. Still, they emphasized the change from collective agriculture, right after villagization, towards a more project based approach to communal work later on:

"We were doing things together, in this village. Having our crops together, on the village shamba, later we had something called ujami, where we did some works together."
Farmers' Group member (m), Mbingamharule, (*GI 13; 9/8/2015*)

Within this statement, the last part describing "ujami" is referring to collaboration in non-agricultural activities. As it has already been described by the wazee of Namatuhi (*NCW 8; 3/11/2015*), Ujamaa activities on the village shamba were later on replaced by specific working events, such as repairing or extending public buildings. Nevertheless, vikundi members from Mbingamharule described "togetherness" as the central structure of Ujamaa, in work as well as in social life:

"I think what is important about the structure of Ujamaa. The people were together, they ate together, they enjoyed together. Together, that was everything in Ujamaa."
Farmers' Group member (m), Mbingamharule, (Mann 10.09.2015)

Better or worse? Groups' evaluation of the Ujamaa period

As by general impression, the farmers of Litowa took a lot of pride in the history of their village. At the same time, the sentiment of being a kind of "forgotten place" that had lost a lot of its former achievements was deeply felt. Statements like the following were the norm during the group discussions throughout the village:

"(…) in this village, when there was Ujamaa we were the first village. The first Ujamaa village in whole Tanzania (kijiji cha kwanza kabisa ujamaa!). Now Litowa, there is not much left, all is very little. We don't have water (…) water to drink, clean water. From a water pump, we don't have. No water. Now, when there was Ujamaa, when this was an Ujamaa village, even president Nyerere knew about this village. He came here and saw: This is Ujamaa! Now, we don't have water (…) it is everything so low now."
Member of Mtakuja Tangine Group (m), Litowa (*GI 2; 8/24/2015*)

"I think it was good, because, they had cattle, they could slaughter and had meat, for a very cheap price. It was very good development. They helped each other with their crops. They had a car. A lot of things. They had a village shop, they had social services."
Member of Juhudi (2) Group (m), Litowa (*GI 5; 8/24/2015*)

221

The Umoja Group was especially enthusiastic in their assessment of the Ujamaa period, and this was just one of the many positive statements by group members:

"So, just as our bookkeeper said, the times of Ujamaa were very good in development. They had good development because the people joined in, because they worked together."
Member of Umoja Group (m), Litowa (*GI 6*; 8/24/2015)

Within the groups of Matetereka A, there was also positive assessment of the Ujamaa era in general, as "it contributed, it contributed a lot. It contributed things like, the idea of how we to work. This is helping us until today. We know a lot about how to do each type of work."(Member of Tangawizi Group (m); *GI 7*; 9/2/2015). And even the younger members were agreeing with this positive impression:

"For me Ujamaa of the times back then, they were working together, different from today. Today the young people think Ujamaa is not good for them, that it was only a thing of the wazee... In general, Ujamaa was good for young people and the wazee. In my opinion."
Member of Kujitegemea Group (f), Matetereka A (*GI 11*; 9/3/2015)

In stark contrast, the impression of an "Ujamaa from above" was very strong in the groups of Matetereka C. And while generally agreeing that Ujamaa itself was not a bad idea, the participants made it very clear that they had not enjoyed the local brand of Ujamaa at Matetereka:

"Ujamaa is good, Ujamaa is solidarity. Ujamaa is bad when the leaders want to decide what to do for each person. That was what the Ujamaa of Matetereka was, but it contributed only for the leaders, not for the normal people."
Farmers' Group Member (f), Matetereka C, (*GI 9*; 9/3/2015)

And they most certainly did not want it to return to their village, because "that would be like going back in development." (Farmers' Group Member (f), Matetereka C; *GI 9*; 9/3/2015). Yet, the overall effect of Ujamaa for the economy was perceived as very negative by some group members there, as well: "I think it was bad for the economy of the country, the economy was very low. In Ujamaa times it was really not good." (Farmers' Group Member (m), Matetereka C; *GI 9*; 9/3/2015).

The general impression of the two vikundi in Matetereka B could be seen as a sort of middle-ground between the other two other sub-villages. They thought that it was a good thing, a good step in development. They actually reflected that it started just like a kikundi and was good, as long as everybody contributed. But as the whole village became one big kikundi, it was difficult to organize, and there was not a lot of profit left for each person. So, right now, they think it is better to work in a small kikundi, where they can organize easily and have the freedom to decide what to do with their profits, rather than having to share it with everybody. They also recall that in the times of Ujamaa, there was only one machine belonging to the original group and it was difficult to access it for the ordinary people (*GI 10*; 9/3/2015).

In Mbingamharule, the overall assessment of the group members was positive (*GI 13; 9/8/2015*), although some participants were skeptical about the practicability of Ujamaa's development approach in the modern environment and thought "that maybe, Ujamaa would not be a good solution for the present." (Farmers' Group member (m), Mbingamharule; *GI 14; 9/10/2015*). Older participants, on the other hand, took a more philosophical perspective on the issue and assured the audience that "the thoughts of Mwalimu were good, and they are good for development until this day. Ujamaa was a very good thing." (Farmers' Group member (m), Mbingamharule; *GI 14; 9/10/2015*).

"The smell of Ujamaa"

One of the areas of interest, when approaching the vikundi of the case study villages, was the question of whether the members would make a reference between their current activities as a group and the period of Ujamaa. Indeed, one has to admit that as the research was conducted in a manner in which the aim of understanding Ujamaa was very clear to the participants of the group discussions, this might have encouraged them to seek this connection, in order to please the researcher as a person. Nevertheless, the question regarding the participants' opinion on Ujamaa was asked in an open manner, without direct reference to the group activities. All statements going in this direction can therefore be regarded as coming from the participants themselves. The most direct connection between the local history of Ujamaa and their own experiences as a group came from a member of the Umoja group at Litowa:

> "We here in Litowa in our group, we want to make things together and develop together. So, this group here is a little bit like Ujamaa. We have started like Ujamaa. Surely, the system has changed, and everybody is now eating their ugali at home, in the system of today. So, it is different. But, there are still people who have stayed together. A lot of people. Because, in a village like Litowa, where there has been Ujamaa here. Historically, people they are saying Litowa was the first Ujamaa village of Tanzania. Therefore, it is very easy, because the smell of Ujamaa is still there. Therefore, it is very easy."
> Member of Umoja Farmers' Group (m), Litowa (*GI 6; 8/24/2015*)

This member received ample support for his description of the group's spirit, which in their understanding was based on the history of their village itself. Although they had only started their group at the beginning of 2015, they were already seeing progress of their work, which might explain the general enthusiasm for going forward. However, the other main reason for themselves was this "smell of Ujamaa", the remembrance of the once great past ("the first Ujamaa village in Tanzania"), which made it "very easy" for them to create an idea of cooperative work among their members. Just as in the past, they would sit together regularly and discuss what to do as a group (*GI 6; 8/24/2015*).

Identification with this idea was generally strong in Litowa, even if some of the younger group members did admit that they did not quite understand all of their forefathers' ideas:

"I think about the times of Ujamaa, that our wazee know more about it. For us as group members, we don't know much, but we understand the environment of Ujamaa, the idea of Ujamaa, we as group we bring Ujamaa and we go on as Ujamaa."
Member of Juhudi Farmers' Group (m), Litowa (*GI 3*; 8/24/2015)

In this sense, the history of Ujamaa nurtured the founding of new vikundi in Litowa in the perception of its members (*GI 3*; 8/24/2015; *GI 6*; 8/24/2015). Similar opinions were also shared by a member of the TMK Group in Mbingamharule, who stated that "if there had been no Ujamaa, there would be no vikundi. The vikundi are the heirs of Ujamaa." (Member of TMK Group (m), Mbingamharule; *GI 14*; 9/10/2015).

In Matetereka, the opinions on how much the local history may have helped the groups to start their work, are clearly divided along the lines of conflict between the original Ujamaa group at Matetereka A and the residents of Matetereka B and C (see also chapter 5.4.2). The two groups which have been interviewed in Matetereka A – Tangawizi and Kujitegemea – still have a lot of members that had already been members of the original group, and therefore see their current group activities as directly inspired by the local history of Ujamaa (*GI 7*; 9/2/2015; *GI 11*; 9/3/2015). This is especially the case for the Kujitegemea Group, which was started as a direct successor of the original Ujamaa group in 2000 (*NCW 4*; 3/6/2015). On the other side, the members of the vikundi at Matetereka C, who in general had a negative opinion on the original settlers, and had expressed their discontent with the ways those people were organizing the village in the past, wanted their groups to be seen as a genuinely different way of Ujamaa:

"Now we have an individual system, and together we have vikundi. Therefore, the whole country still has Ujamaa, but not the Ujamaa of those times. The Ujamaa of those times was bad, and was from the leadership, not the Ujamaa of ourselves – and that was not good."
Farmers' Group Member (m), Matetereka C (*GI 9*; 9/3/2015)

In this sense, the next step of analysis was to take a closer look at the perception of the differences – or similarities – between the recent vikundi and the Ujamaa of the past.

"In unity, there is strength" – similarities and differences as identified by the group members

In this passage, the main interest lay in understanding how the members of the various farmers' groups saw the structure, the general aim and the activities of their respective kikundi in comparison to their perception of the Ujamaa era. Farmers who had already been actively involved in the formation and the continuation of Matetereka's original Ujamaa group, approached the topic in an idealistic way, and drew a direct connection between the idea of a kikundi and other forms of cooperative development:

"You can call it communism, you can call it Ujamaa, you can call it ushirika (cooperative), you can call it kikundi. All of this, it is, it is all the same idea. There are small differences, true. But each of them says: in unity, there is strength!"
Moses Njalika, Member of Tangawizi Group, Matetereka A (*GI 7*; 9/2/2015)

The main difference for them was the scale in which a present-day kikundi is operating. A difference also brought forward by younger members of these groups:

"So, they were doing their work everywhere [in the village]. For the group, now we are doing the work in a certain place. And then everybody is also doing their work at home. Therefore, that has changed, how we do work together."
Member of Tangawizi Group (m), Matetereka A (*GI 7*; 9/2/2015)

Indeed, there was acknowledgement of the difficulties of operating in this new environment of individual agriculture and market economy, as "for us elders, the biggest challenge is capitalism. If we grow things, we need a market here. That is the first challenge." (Moses Njalika, Member of Tangawizi Group, Matetereka A; *GI 7*; 9/2/2015). So, while trying to continue with a form of collective agriculture of which they are convinced, many of their members have reservations on the current economic system of the country. Furthermore, the concrete issue of the ongoing conflict with the village government concerning their coffee plantation is impeding the work of the Kujitegemea Group, the second vikundi made up mostly of old wajamaa in Matetereka (*GI 11*; 9/3/2015).

Apart from those groups with this sort of direct personal continuity to Ujamaa, there is the Umoja Group in Litowa, whose members are drawing a direct line from the way the founders of their village organized in the past to their own collective activities:

"They had good development because the people joined in, because they worked together. And truly, this is the same in this group. We are together, we are doing our activities together. We are one [Umoja, also the name of the group]. Just like they did in the times of Ujamaa, we are doing it together. We are doing our activities, we are doing our plans together, not one by one. Just like the RDA."
Member of Umoja Farmers' Group (m), Litowa (*GI 6*; 8/24/2015)

This group in general was showing a high identification with the values and practice of Ujamaa, as they perceived it. Furthermore, the other vikundi of Litowa were acknowledging Ujamaa as a sort of role model for their group, albeit with a different scope. In contrast to the members of Tangawizi Group, however, they did not see the limitation on just one group as opposed to the whole village as a restriction, but rather as a positive aspect in organizing communal activities:

"They are now repeating the same, the same system but with a different kind of taste. They are saying, currently, they are doing the same, they are learning the same, they are teaching each other on how to improve themselves. But, every person is let on his

or her own. He has to work individually. And thereafter, they make evaluation. That if they agreed all to do some activities independently they have to go and check, whether anyone has fulfilled. So, whoever fails to fulfill, he gets punishment. This is within their constitution. If you reject punishment, you will be fired from the group."
Members of Kanyanga Twende Group, Litowa. Interpreted by Dennis Mpazagade (*GI 1*; 8/22/2015)

Other groups from Litowa were arguing in a similar fashion, sometimes stressing the fact that the Ujamaa of the past, as done by the wazee, could not be replicated by the youth of today:

"Now we are doing this group and start to work together, but everybody keeps his/her independence. We start to work together a little and help everyone. But the Ujamaa of juzi (the day before yesterday) that was the life of the wazee. The youth of today cannot do it [in the same way as they did]."
Member Mtakuja Tangine Group (m), Litowa (*GI 2*; 8/24/2015)

In the village of Mbingamharule, most group members were sharing a similarly high commitment to the values of Ujamaa, while underlining the novelty of their own form of Ujamaa in comparison to the past:

"And he says, the Ujamaa is coming now again, in this village. People are working together. But with a system known a chama, a kind of group. Whereby, the group of people, arrange: so today we cultivate, or to help this man, tomorrow we go to help this farm, and the day after we go to this farm. A kind of rotation. This is the kind of Ujamaa they have here. [...] they are saying, we practice it, through helping each other. We save some money, when a person gets a problem, he comes a lend from the group. This is the kind of Ujamaa they are saying. So, this is Ujamaa of their kind."
Member of TMK Group (m), Mbingamharule. Interpreted by Dennis Mpazagade (*GI 13*; 9/8/2015)

Nevertheless, the ideological commitment towards Ujamaa appeared to be very high:

"The thing of Ujamaa. Ujamaa, really it is a Kiswahili term. It means we are together. Ujamaa is a life of self-reliance, in questions, in well-being, in economy. Now they are saying, in each kikundi, we are doing Ujamaa. We are working together, we protect each other, that is their Ujamaa. We are in this game together, this Ujamaa. We are not on our own. If we would market alone, we would go nowhere. This is a sort of Ujamaa, to reach self-reliance, in protection, in well-being, in economy."
Farmers' group member (m), Mbingamharule (*GI 14*; 9/10/2015)

This kind of conviction was indeed a little too much for some of the other kikundi members present at the same interview, who thought that this sort of proclaimed pledge towards Ujamaa would lack a practical basis – as the times of a village shamba are long gone in Mbingamharule, after all:

"After that, we say we are still together, we are doing this and that, and like in Ujamaa, we help each other. That's what they say, but they all have their own shamba and what not. Still they think it's Ujamaa, but just as they are sitting here."
Farmers' group member (m), Mbingamharule (GI 14; 9/10/2015)

In contrast to those groups, the vikundi of Matetereka B and C saw much bigger differences between the organization and activities of their groups and the period of Ujamaa as perceived by them. Independence in decision making and the sharing of possible economic gains appear to be the most important aspects in their understanding of a new form of Ujamaa.

"I think another thing, it is different now. We have democracy now. And the first thing is economy, democracy and development. I think everything has a beginning and an end. And now we have vikundi, and we have a lot of them. I think therefore we say, Ujamaa was bad. We had some development. But now it is different, and we want to go ahead. Not as one, but as many."
Farmers' group member (f), Matetereka C (GI 9; 9/3/2015)

The last sentence "not as one, but as many" is particularly interesting, as it gives a positive interpretation of the downscaling of communal activities. As already mentioned, the particular form of Ujamaa that was prevalent in Matetereka, even after the end of RDA, was not seen as a grassroots form of collective agriculture, but rather as an Ujamaa from above – and it was just as negatively perceived if it came from the old settlers of the village as it was when the people were moved there during villagization by the central state.

The vikundi members of Matetereka B did not share the same resentment towards their village's past, but still insisted that independence in economy and general decision-making was beneficial to the activities of their groups, and that they would prefer the current order of things in comparison to the Ujamaa of the past.

"I think, the Ujamaa of the past – it was the whole village. So, when there was money, there was little money for the whole village. But now, this vikundi of today, when we produce a lot, then we have the freedom to go to the bank, and we can choose what to do with it. But for the whole village, the work was very difficult. Very well, these times we had a car and so on, a tractor – in these times, the times of Ujamaa. But for the project of vikundi, it is better that there is no Ujamaa. Because we only have to discuss among our ten members, what we want to do. That is easier."
Farmers' group member (m), Matetereka B (GI 10; 9/3/2015)

Inspired by Ujamaa or "soya boom"?

Despite the evidence for the different identifications with Ujamaa history as an inspiration for the vikundi analyzed, the question remains whether this sort of intrinsic motivation has led to the creation of the respective groups, or if external factors are the reason behind their formation. This is especially true for the vikundi of Litowa, and to lesser degree to those of Mbingamharule. All of these groups have a relatively short history, at most dating back three years. All of the groups of Mbingamharule were involved in the production of soya for Caritas' Soya ni Pesa program (*GI 13; 9/8/2015; GI 14; 9/10/2015*), as were many of those in Litowa. The groups who were not yet cultivating soya for this income-generating program were planning to start to do so for the next season. From the data collected during field work, this question cannot be answered with certainty. It seems reasonable to assume that the relative success of the first groups involved in soya cultivation sparked the interest of other farmers to form similar groups.

In Matetereka, the situation appears very different for each sub village: The two groups form Matetereka A were either directly founded by former wajamaa (Kujitegemea (*GI 11; 9/3/2015*)) or are to a large extent constituted by members of those times (Tangawizi (*GI 7; 9/2/2015*)). The main motivation for their inception lay in the continued commitment of its members to their practical implementation of Ujamaa – just as it had been the case after the abandonment of the RDA.

In Matetereka B, both groups showed relatively high commitment to the idea of Ujamaa, while at the same time stressing their conviction towards a more independent approach, less influenced by the wazee of the original village. The two groups also have a comparatively long history, dating back to 2002 and 2003, respectively (*GI 10; 9/3/2015*).

For Matetereka C, a lot of the motivation to form these groups remains unclear, especially since members stated that their groups would not help them very much in coping with the challenges of daily life. Nevertheless, the cooperative thought is well established among their members and they referred to their activities as a new (and better) form of Ujamaa (*GI 9; 9/3/2015*).

In any case, the Soya ni Pesa project has not yet reached any of the sub-villages or groups in question. Therefore, it seems reasonable to assume that the inception of vikundi came as an endogenous adaption to personal development needs. In the case of Matetereka A, it was the most suitable form to continue cooperative work after the irrevocable end of the Ujamaa group in 2000. In the case of Matetereka B and C, it appears as a strategy to cope with the challenges of lack of inputs, capital and market as a group, rather than as individual farmers, but with full control on individual contribution – a feature that was perceived as missing in the "last Ujamaa village of Tanzania" before the turn of the millennium.

Summary

What has emerged from the group interviews with the vikundi of Litowa, Matetereka and Mbingamharule is the fact that all of these groups were not only giving a description of the Ujamaa period as they perceived it, but were also making connections between their own group activities and the collective organization of their villages during the days of Ujamaa. The group members of Litowa, Mbingamharule and Matetereka A, in particular, were seeing their groups as a sort of heir to the idea of Ujamaa. Many of them underlined the idea that their collective experience of the Ujamaa era both inspired their current activities and made collective organization easier, as the "smell of Ujamaa" was still there.

Even though the groups of Matetereka B and C took a more critical stance in their evaluation of the Ujamaa period in their village – especially with regards to the perceived dominance by the original settlers of Matetereka A – they still saw the concept of Ujamaa as an inspiration to their own efforts as a group.

So, in conclusion, while the respective interpretations of Ujamaa differed between groups and villages, the importance of the ideas of Ujamaa was regarded to be very high by all responding groups. With regards to the material benefits of the Ujamaa period to their villages, only the groups from Litowa and Matetereka A were sharing a positive perception of those achievements, while the others did see some benefits but also the negative sides of village-wide organization of collective work. In this sense, most groups did state that they would prefer their own approach of group-wise organization compared to the times when communal activities were done together by the whole village population.

6.2.4 Views of the villagers in general

While the vikundi analysis proved to be a valuable way forward in the understanding of local perceptions of Ujamaa development in the case study villages, it could only access the impression of the organized peasantry. In order to gather further perceptions, as well as to broaden the empirical basis, individual farmers were interviewed by local research assistants in the form of one-on-one questionnaire-based interviews. Participants were randomly selected by the assistants themselves. The question on their opinion on the times of Ujamaa was presented in the same open way as in the guidelines used for the vikundi group interviews, in order to increase comparability. Coding for the analysis of their statements was derived from the codes developed for the group interviews.

Depiction and evaluation of Ujamaa and differences between the villages

In many cases, the ways in which the Ujamaa period was depicted by the respondents of the individual questionnaires in the case study villages reflected the depictions given by the vikundi members of the respective villages: In Litowa, the main theme in the respondents' statements was working together and collaborating for development. Most of the statements were relatively short, only consisting of one or two sentences of depiction and, in some cases, comparing Ujamaa to the present (see below). Most notably, the theme of concrete material benefits (like the tractor or the water supply), which had been very prominent in the group interviews, was missing in the statements of the village questionnaires, although the provision of social services and mutual help was mentioned by some respondents. In comparison, the statements were the most sophisticated in Matetereka, often both describing the past and evaluating it using different examples. The core depiction of Ujamaa as a time of cooperation and all people working together was also very much present. References to the impact of Ujamaa on the development of the village itself were more common than in Litowa. While also emphasizing the theme of working together, depictions were mostly held very general in Mbingamharule, and mostly without making an evaluation of this depiction in comparison with the present.

Table 4: Coding guidelines for the opinion on Ujamaa. Village questionnaires

Category	Indicators for coding	Example for statement given (Kiswahili)	Translation of statement
Positive	• Clearly positive evaluation of Ujamaa • Positive evaluation of description of Ujamaa	"wakati wa ujamaa maisha yalikuwa mazuri" Litowa "wakati wa ujamaa watu walikuwa wanaishi hata bila usumbafu" Mbingamharule	In the times of Ujamaa, the life was good/better. In the times of Ujamaa, the people were living without hardships.
Negative	• Clearly negative evaluation • Negative in comparison to present • Negative evaluation of description given	"maisha sasa ni mazuri kuliko yaa ujamaa" Litowa "Ujamaa ulileta maendeleo kwa watu wachache tuna sio wote" Matetereka	Life now is better than during Ujamaa Ujamaa brought development for a few people, but not for us (it is not ours)
Ambiguous	• Positive and negative elements in Ujamaa description	"Malengo ya ujamaa yalikuwa mazuri, lakini watu waliokuwa wanaongoza ujamaa walitumia ujamaa kwa maslahi yao binafsi" Matetereka	The goals of Ujamaa were good, but the people who were the leaders of Ujamaa were only using Ujamaa for their own interests."
Description only	• Only description of Ujamaa perception • No evaluation of this description	"Ujamaa uliwafanya watu waishi pamoja" Matetereka "wakati wa ujamaa watu walifanya kazi kwa pamoja" Mbingamharule	Ujamaa caused/made people to life together." In the times of Ujamaa, the people were doing their work together."
Unclear	• Position of respondent remains unclear • No personal description of Ujamaa given	"tunahitaji kupata pembejeo" Litowa	We need to get farm inputs
Distanced	• Personal non-involvement as reason for lack of knowledge	"sikuwepo"	I was not there
Don't know	• Lack of knowledge stated	"sijui"	I don't know

Source: own survey

In order to create a broader understanding of the different opinions of the farmers concerning the Ujamaa era in relation to their age, gender, vikundi membership and other properties, their statements in question 14 of the questionnaire (see Appendix 2) were categorized according to their main proposition (see Table 4). Statements which were openly declaring Ujamaa as "good" or as better in comparison with the present were categorized as "positive", in the opposite case they were named "negative". In case the statement had both positive and negative aspects, it was coded "ambiguous". Furthermore, statements which only included a description of Ujamaa, without clearly stating an opinion on this perception were deemed to be "description only". If respondents directly stated that they wouldn't know anything about it, the category is "don't know", if they stated that they were not there, or not born yet, and therefore did not like to make a statement, this was coded as "distanced". If the statement had no clear connection to the topic or remained otherwise unclear, it was coded "unclear". Lack of statement was marked as "n/a". Since the decision of not giving any kind of statement on one's opinion was seen as an active decision by the respondent, these cases were still used in the further analysis of the evaluation of the Ujamaa period.

The differences observed in the case study villages were considerable, and can be seen in Table 5. The first big difference can be seen between the former RDA villages of Litowa and Matetereka and Mbingamharule. In the latter case, there were considerably more respondents who were just giving a description without evaluation (33.7% as opposed to 5% for Litowa and 6.4% in Matetereka), also there was by far the highest number of non-respondents to the question (n/a), at 29.4%, compared to just around two percent at the other villages. If respondents were giving an evaluation, it was mostly positive, however, at 18.9% of all respondents, with only 4.2% giving negative statements on Ujamaa – the lowest percentage of all villages.

Table 5: Evaluation of the Ujamaa period by inhabitants of the case study villages (N=304)

| Village | Number of respondents (percentage) | | |
	Litowa	Matetereka	Mbingamharule
Positive	48 (48%)	32 (29.4%)	18 (18.9%)
Negative	21 (21%)	25 (22.9%)	4 (4.2%)
Ambiguous	2 (2%)	8 (7.3%)	2 (2.2%)
Description only	5 (5%)	7 (6.4%)	32 (33.7%)
Unclear	7 (7%)	2 (1.8%)	3 (3.2%)
Don't know	13 (13%)	15 (13.8%)	7 (7.4%)
Distanced	2 (2%)	18 (16.5%)	1 (1.1%)
n/a	2 (2%)	2 (1.8%)	28 (29.5%)
Total	100 (100%)	109 (100%)	95 (100%)

Source: own survey

This apparent difference between Mbingamharule and the former RDA villages is thought to be indicative of the significantly lower interest in the history of Ujamaa in a village without a prominent history in cooperative development of its own. As the other items of these questionnaires, without any opinion on Ujamaa stated, were regularly completed in a coherent manner, the high percentage of "n/a" answers to question 14 is seen as a valid expression of this lack of interest and not as a sign of incomplete interviews. Therefore, the results of the questionaires from Mbingamharule were used for the further analysis of the opinion on Ujamaa.

The highest "approval rate" for times of Ujamaa could be found in Litowa, with 48% of all answers giving positive statements, as opposed to 22% negative ones, very few people were only describing Ujamaa without giving an opinion in this village, and very few were ambiguous or unclear about it. In Matetereka, the share of negative statements was a little higher than in Litowa (22.9%), but considerably less positive statements were given (29.3%). The village was also notable for the observation that significantly more respondents (16.5%) were giving "distanced" answers, stating that they "were not there" to see it or not born yet, and could therefore not comment on the Ujamaa period nor give at least their personal perception of it. Such "distanced" answers were far less common in the other two villages (around 2% each). There was also the highest share of "don't know" answers, at 13.8%. Both facts, combined with the prevalence of relatively long and detailed answers in the other categories, might indicate that in Matetereka, you only take part in the discussion of Ujamaa if you think you have a good knowledge about it.

Overall, a Pearson χ^2 test for contingency determined a relation between the village of the respondents and their evaluation of the Ujamaa period with a 99% level of significance, as the observed χ^2 as cross-table difference between observed answers and expected answers in the case of independent variables was 283.75, while the critical value χ^2_{crit} for this table would be 32.0 at this level of significance.[7] The corrected Pearson coefficient of contingency (C_{corr}) for this table is 0.86, indicating a high level of contingency between the village of the respondent and his or her way to evaluate the times of Ujamaa.

Furthermore, the answers from the positive and negative categories in Matetereka differed from the two other villages qualitatively: Instead of relatively short and general statements, opinions from Matetereka would reflect the general conflict within the village, with many positive statements being particularly idealist in nature, stating that "During times of Ujamaa we the young ones of the past (who are elders now) thought very high of socialism and we wanted Ujamaa to go on forever" or even: "Socialism was a great savior for the people of Tanzania" (Questionnaires, Matetereka). On the other hand, many negative comments directly criticized the leadership for forming Ujamaa according to their interests and perceiving that Ujamaa in this village had only benefited a few, i.e. the leadership.

Age of respondents and its relation to the view on Ujamaa

Regarding the distribution of categories within the villages, considerable differences could be observed depending on the age group of the respondents. Generally,

---

7 Throughout the thesis, critical values for the χ^2-distribution were taken from the table provided by MEIER KRUKER and RAUH (2005: 178).

positive opinions were more prevalent in the 51-65 and above 65 age groups, than in the 35-50 age group. However, the distribution varied heavily among the villages. Most notably, the youth of Litowa showed a very positive attitude towards the times of Ujamaa, in comparison to their contemporaries in the other villages. As it would have been expected, the percentage of respondents answering "don't know" or giving distancing statements was the highest in the younger age groups across all three villages, yet in the case of Mbingamharule, non-response was most prevalent among the 51-65 age group. With the data of all three villages combined, the highest rates of positive evaluations of Ujamaa could be found among the two oldest (51-65 and above 65) age groups, as well as with the youngest respondents of the questionnaires (14-18). The latter group however, was not very large within the total sample, so that this observation must not be over evaluated. The respective percentages of answers by age group are shown in Table 6:

Table 6: Evaluation of the Ujamaa period by age group, all villages (N=304, 8 with no age stated; n=296)

Evaluation of Ujamaa	Percentage of respondents					
Age group	14-18	19-25	26-35	35-50	51-65	above 65
Positive	58.3	26.7	25.8	27.5	48.8	47.4
Negative	0.0	15.6	20.6	17.5	9.3	15.8
Ambiguous	0.0	2.2	6.2	2.5	7.0	0.0
Description only	8.3	11.1	12.4	22.5	9.3	15.8
Unclear	0.0	0.0	4.1	6.3	0.0	10.5
Don't know	25.0	26.7	13.4	5.0	7.0	0.0
Distanced	8.3	13.3	7.2	6.3	4.7	0.0
n/a	0.0	4.4	10.3	12.5	14.0	10.5
Total	100.0	100.0	100.0	100.0	100.0	100.0

Source: own survey

As it has been the case with the data sorted by village, a Pearson test for contingency was undertaken. Respondents, who did not state their age in the questionnaire were taken out of the consideration, leaving the sample size at 296 respondents. The difference between observed answers and expected answers for independent variables was x^2=111.50 – well above x^2_{crit} for 35 degrees of freedom, which would have been 57.34 at a 99% level of significance. This indicates that there is a significant relation between the age of the respondents and their evaluation of Ujamaa in our sample. The corrected Pearson coefficient of contingency C_{corr} is 0.52 for this table, meaning that there is a modest contingency between the age of the respondent and their evaluation of Ujamaa. However, contingency is lower than between the village of residence and the evaluation of ujamaa.

Field size of the respondents

Another interesting relation which was made possible by the questionnaire data, was the one between the size of a respondent's shamba and his or her opinion on Ujamaa. To evaluate a possible relation between those two factors, the field size data of all three villages were combined, while those respondents who gave no information on their shamba or who stated that they did not own a field themselves (i.e. that they had no field at all, or that they were only renting it) were left out of the consideration. This resulted in a remaining sample size of 283 for this evaluation. As Table 7 shows, the relation between the size of one's field and his or her opinion appears to be different from what one might think intuitively: The percentage of positive attitudes towards the period rises as the field size of the respondents increases. While only 12.7% of those owning up to two acres gave positive evaluations of the Ujamaa era, this percentage rose to 48.5% for those owning between six and eight acres, and then up to 51.2% for those cultivating more than 10 acres. In a similar fashion, the rates for "don't know" and "description only" answers were the highest with respondents who had the smallest fields within the sample:

Table 7: Evaluation of the Ujamaa period by field size, all villages (N=304, 21 with no own fields or no field size stated, n=283)

Evaluation of Ujamaa Field size of respondent (in acres	Percentage of respondents					
	up to 2	>2 to 4	>4 to 6	>6 to 8	>8 to 10	>10
Positive	12.7	27.5	37.3	48.5	47.8	51.2
Negative	16.4	20.0	5.9	21.2	8.7	22.0
Ambiguous	3.6	3.8	2.0	6.1	0.0	2.4
Description only	20.0	15.0	15.7	12.1	17.4	7.3
Unclear	3.6	3.8	3.9	3.0	0.0	7.3
Don't know	21.8	7.5	13.7	6.1	8.7	2.4
Distanced	5.5	8.8	9.8	0.0	4.3	4.9
n/a	16.4	13.8	11.8	3.0	13.0	2.4
Total	100	100	100	100	100	100

Source: own survey

In this case as well, contingency analysis resulted in a significant relation between the field sizes and the evaluation of Ujamaa stated at a 99% level of significance (χ^2=101.18, while χ^2_{crit}=57.43). Corrected contingency was at C_{corr}=0.56, indicating a modest level of relation between one's field size and his or her opinion on Ujamaa – higher than the contingency of age and Ujamaa, but lower than that of village of residence and Ujamaa. Indeed, the differences of field sizes from the samples of the different villages (as presented in chapter 5), might explain some of the observed differences in evaluation by the respondents: Most respondents with small fields up to two acres could be found in Mbingamharule, where there was also the highest occurrence of descriptive or "don't know" answers to this question. On the other hand, Matetereka had the highest occurrence of relatively big field sizes, and indeed those relatively affluent respondents showed a high rate of positive answers. Nevertheless, this contingency between field size and Ujamaa evaluation in general, and the high occurrence of positive answers with growing field sizes in particular, might also indicate that those farmers who have big shambas now, feel that they have benefited from the system in the past on a personal material level, while those with small fields don't feel that they have got any benefits of the Ujamaa system. In other words, within the sample, there is no tendency of the relatively "wealthier" peasants to oppose Ujamaa. On the contrary, it is this group of peasants who ex-perienced the material benefits of this system and therefore carry positive opinions about it. On the other hand, those without material benefits are hardly convinced by the past and show considerably lower interest in it.

Farmers' group membership and opinion on Ujamaa

Given the high prevalence of positive evaluations of Ujamaa during the inter-views with the farmers' groups, it appeared to make sense to also investigate the relation between the membership in such a group and a person's opinion on Ujamaa. Out of the 304 respondents to the questionnaires in all villages, nine did not state their status of membership or non-membership and were therefore taken out of consideration, resulting in a sample size of 295 in this case. As Table 8 illustrates, most of the categories of answers occurred in similar rates with both groups. However, among those respondents who gave an evaluation and not just a descriptive answer, positive attitudes towards the Ujamaa period indeed were higher among members of vikundi than they were among respondents who were not part of any group.

Once again, the contingency test showed a significant level of relation between vikundi membership and opinion on Ujamaa at a 99% level of significance. χ^2 was 22.27 for this table, while χ^2_{crit} would have been 20.09 at this level of significance. Corrected contingency was calculated at $C_{corr}=0.37$. This indicates that there is a still modest, but comparatively low level of contingency between group membership and the opinion on Ujamaa, when held against the relations between this opinion and the other categories of respondents (village, age, field size).

This does not mean that the evaluations presented by the vikundi members during the group interviews presented above are representative for their villages as a whole, but it indicates that those opinions are not necessarily completely different from those of villagers who are not participating in any group activities. In fact, the statements on Ujamaa made by the respondents of the questionnaires indicate that the village as such has the biggest influence on the view of Ujamaa, followed by the field size and the age of the participant. In comparison to those contingencies, the one between farmers' group membership and evaluation of Ujamaa appears weak – although both categories are by no means independent from each other.

Table 8: Evaluation of the Ujamaa period by membership in farmers' groups, all villages (N=304, 9 with no membership status stated, n=295)

Evaluation of Ujamaa	Percentage of respondents		
	All respondents	Members	Non-members
Positive	32.2	40.3	26.7
Negative	16.9	15.1	18.2
Ambiguous	4.1	4.2	4,0
Description only	13.6	14.3	13.1
Unclear	4.1	3.4	4.5
Don't know	11.5	10.1	12.5
Distanced	7.1	2.5	10.2
n/a	10.5	10.1	10.8
Total	100.0	100.0	100.0

Source: own survey

Summary

It has been the attempt of the analysis of the questionnaires to deliver a more general image on the opinions of Ujamaa prevalent in the three case study villages. For this purpose, the qualitative answers or the questionnaires were categorized in order to enable a basic quantitative analysis. While this study can by no means be considered representative for the respective communities, the results from these random samples underline some of the basic differences in the perception of Ujamaa between the villages, which could already be observed during the qualitative interviews. Furthermore, it determined that the contingency between the village of residence and an individual's statement on Ujamaa is far bigger than that between other personal properties and the opinon in question. In particular, the membership in a farmers' group appears to have the smallest contingency with the opinion on Ujamaa, which in turn indicates that evaluations taken by group members during the qualitative interviews are not necessarily completely different from those of other villagers, just by virtue of their membership. Last but not least, the observation that the relatively affluent farmers (i.e. those with the biggest fields) of our sample actually have the highest rate of positive opinion on Ujamaa might indicate that they perceived their material success as a result of the Ujamaa period. The age of the participant also showed significant contingency with his or her opinion on Ujamaa.

6.2.5 Women and Ujamaa

The historical background

As it has been discussed in chapter 2.3.2, Julius Nyerere saw the role of women as one of the main weaknesses of "traditional" African societies and therefore as one of the main issues which modern Ujamaa would have to address (Nyerere 1968f: 108p.). Consequently, the position of women within the RDA villages and the view of women on the period of Ujamaa, in general, deserves a closer look within this study. Given the limitations of access and the case study design, only a few insights into this wide topic could be produced. Nevertheless, this chapter will try to give a short impression on the role of women in the history of the case study villages.

From a present-day perspective, the policy of Ujamaa actually normalized gender roles in Tanzania according to its concept of the traditional extended family. Women were seen as caring for the domestic sphere, while the male role was constructed in the public sphere. From this point of view, Ujamaa essentially strengthened a binary model of gender roles, while emphasizing the equality of women in all aspects of public life and encouraging women's participation in building the nation (Lal 2015: 127p.).

The foundation of villages like Litowa and Matetereka itself illustrates the general idea of gender roles in the early independence era in rural Tanzania: All of the RDA villages were founded by young men, who later brought their wives and family to live in the new settlement. Only in the case of Litowa, two unmarried women, who were TANU Youth League members themselves, took part in the creation of the village – and both left Litowa when they married men from other villages. Basically, it was always the husband who would decide the place to live in those times (Ibbott 2014: 167).

Inside the new villages, there was the shared notion that women did have their place within the development of the nation. However, if it came to the roles of men and women inside the family, traditional attributions were perpetuated, and if a woman did not want to take part in this or that activity of the village, it was seen as the husband's responsibility to discipline her. Only in small steps were women regarded as full members of the village. The creation of women's groups also helped their voices to be heard at the Ujamaa assembly, when before they would just sit in the back without taking part in the discussions (Ibbott 2014: 168–172).

While gender roles remained traditional in many ways, the RDA villages differed from the old situation in Tanzania in the way that women's additional work in the domestic scene (child care, caring for the house, cooking food, etc.) was actually regarded as valuable work by their communities. This was underlined by the fact that women would receive equal shares of the village's revenue, even if they would spend less hours on the fields if they were caring for a newborn child, for instance (Brain 1977: 243).

Many interesting observations regarding the role of women during the RDA period can be found in Wenner's memories from her stay in Litowa. Even if all villagers saw themselves as a big family of socialists, there was a clear, very traditional understanding of gender roles, and especially the tasks of women. In a way, women got the short straw in village development, because even if they were seen as full-scale members of the cooperative, who would join in all types of labor, they still had to do their daily chores of feeding children, cleaning the houses, etc. At the Ujamaa assembly, it was not very common for women to speak up, as it was the traditional understanding that women were to be seen, not heard. All positions within the village committee were held by men, as were all members of the SERA. Planning village activities and implementing development plans was seen as practically a male concern. Only with the establishment of an own women committee in 1966, the women in Litowa slowly began to organize themselves and to take a more active role in which was still very much a Men's Ujamaa (WENNER 1970: 214–224).

For example, three women of the village were given the permanent task of running the nursery. However, at least in the beginning, the project suffered from the disregard of the community's men for the women's care work. Women in Litowa were seen as equals in the sense that they had to attend to the same sort farm related work as the men, and as Litowa was first and foremost a farming village, there were some reservations about other types of work. This increased the difficulties for the women to take pride in this new form of work, as WENNER recalls. Most prominently, the village manager, who was in charge of organizing the work schedules, was skeptical about taking so many women "off-work". The situation finally improved after child malnourishment was effectively wiped out by the work of the nursery (WENNER 1970: 61).

Similarly, the introduction of sewing classes faced the same sort of reservations, although the men of Litowa did see more direct benefits of this work, as it would reduce the amount of cash needed to buy new clothes that could not be produced in the village. After the lessons were established, however, the sewing became a sort of a closed women's club, where they could discuss village matters without the observing eyes of the men. WENNER's report on the sewing lessons gives a good impression on the role of women and their own perception of their part in Ujamaa development during the times of the RDA (WENNER 1970: 62–68).

Women in this study

No questions specifically designed to evaluate the role of women were included within the field studies. This was mainly done out of the understanding of the own limitations of a male outsider addressing these issues within a rural village community. Nevertheless, the gender of the respondent has been noted on the interview citations throughout this thesis, in order to give the reader the possibility to evaluate the similarities and differences in their statements.

All of the interviews with the farmers' groups included female participants. Yet, the involvement of women in the discussion varied considerably. In Mbingamharule, for instance, no woman would contribute, even if there were almost exclusively women participating in the first group interview (GI 13; 9/8/2015). This was explained by a male participant in a very "traditional" way: "for us here, if there is a man [present], the women are not talking..." (Farmers' Group member (m), Mbingamharule; GI 13; 9/8/2015).

On the other hand, women were very engaged in the group discussion in Matetereka C (GI 9; 9/3/2015), and also took active part in the discussions at the other sub-villages. The Sisi kwa Sisi group in Matetereka B also had a female chairperson (GI 10; 9/3/2015). In Litowa, men did considerably more talking than the women throughout the group interviews, but female contributions were also common.

Only very few comments made throughout the group interviews specifically made reference to the women's perception of Ujamaa, but underlined the idea that those times also brought benefits to the female village members:

> "I think, for us as women, the Ujamaa helped us a lot. If there is a problem in life, with the forest, etc. Our solidarity helped us a lot to get development, even at home. Even if Ujamaa died, still with this group we are building together, and we help each other. There is help, when we want to know about growing a specific crop, for instance. There is help. So, it helps a lot in life. We are together."
> Member of Tangawizi Group (f), Matetereka A (*GI 7; 9/2/2015*)

Some accounts on the work of women and the idea to establish a nursery in order to enable the women of the village to take a bigger part in the agricultural work were also brought forward by the contemporary witnesses in Matetereka A (*NCW 10; 8/31/2015*), resembling the descriptions of WENNER and IBBOTT presented above.

When analyzing the statements of the village questionnaires, some differences between male and female respondents could be observed among all three villages (see Table 9). Generally, positive statements were less prevalent among females than among males, with the biggest gap between those two genders in Matetereka. The same was true, however, for negative statements, which were especially rare among female participants. Furthermore, significantly more females than males would respond with "don't know" or distanced statements than their male counterparts, as well as not answering at all, especially in the case of Mbingamharule. Obviously, the females were less eager than the male villagers to give their personal opinion on the times of Ujamaa.

When looking at the statistical significance of these observations, the χ^2 test again resulted in a significant level of relation between the categories of gender and opin-

Table 9: Evaluation of the Ujamaa period by gender, all villages (N=304, 13 with no stated gender, n=291)

Evaluation of Ujamaa	Number of respondents (percentage)	
Gender	Male	Female
Positive	60 (36.4%)	37 (29.4%)
Negative	38 (23.0%)	10 (7.9%)
Ambiguous	7 (4.2%)	5 (4.0%)
Description only	22 (13.3%)	21 (16.7%)
Unclear	7 (4.2%)	5 (4.0%)
Don't know	12 (7.3%)	21 (16.7%)
Distanced	8 (4.8%)	11 (8.7%)
n/a	11(6.7%)	16 (12.7%)
Total	165 (100%)	126 (100%)

Source: own survey

ion on Ujamaa, with an observed χ^2 of 42.98 against a critical value of χ^2_{crit}=20.09 at a 99% level of significance. Indeed, the corrected contingency between those categories was calculated at a modest level of C_{corr}=0.51, which indicates that the gender of a respondent and his or her opinion on Ujamaa are depending on each other. By comparison, this contingency is higher than that of the vikundi membership, but lower than that of field size and age – and much lower than the one between the village of residence and the respective evaluation of the ujamaa period.

6.2.6 The View of the Youth

In the times of Ujamaa, the education of the children and youth to be prospective wajamaa (socialists) themselves took a great part within the national policy (see NYERERE 1967a), as well as in the activities of the RDA villages in the 1960s. The idea then was that the older people actually did not have to learn about socialism, because they had lived it before, but that the younger ones had to learn about it actively (see above). With much of the research relying on the information of contemporary witnesses and the members of farmers' groups, the question on how the younger generations perceive the times of Ujamaa also had to be addressed. This was especially the case for the former RDA villages, in order to illustrate what kind of picture the youth of Litowa and Matetereka had of their own history.

With regards to primary education, the whole concept of education for self-reliance appears to have survived only in very limited aspects: In the Matetereka Primary School, there are still students' projects like a school shamba and a school forest, which are tended by the students themselves. However, there seems to be no concept for teaching the local history of the village, as the curriculum is centrally arranged by the Tanzanian state, and there is no idea of education outside of teaching along standard books. Therefore, the era of Ujamaa is only dealt with in broad strokes in the history subject, without a local twist. The fact that teachers at Tanzania's primary schools are rotated nationwide and, therefore, no local knowledge is included in the teacher's body might add to this lack of local consciousness on village history (GBE 16; 9/1/2015).

Additional qualitative information on young villagers' opinion on Ujamaa may be added, at this stage, from group interviews in Litowa and Matetereka. In both cases, young villagers were keen to point out the differences between the times of Ujamaa and the present system, and the change from a communal, cooperative to a "private" system. Evaluations of this apparent change were mixed among the youth. In Matetereka, the differences were mainly seen in the organization and the role of the government:

> "I think, firstly, that everything was organized by the government. Now we do it privately, everybody on their own, we develop individually. But only few profit."
> Member (m) of Semani Youth Group, Matetereka A (GI 8; 9/2/2015)

In Litowa, on the other hand, the young farmers were more concentrating on the material benefits that they were seeing in the past:

240

"He says during Ujamaa, the situation was good, they had everything, the development was high. They used to use water from the taps. But currently, they are fetching water from the river, so they are saying it would be better, if Ujamaa comes back, so the life would be good. He prefers Ujamaa to the current situation."
Young farmer (m), Litowa. Interpreted by Dennis Mpazagade (*GI 12*; 9/6/2015)

The depiction of the material benefits of Ujamaa was more ambiguous in Matetereka, and some of the youth group members doubted the fair distribution of those gains:

"The system of Ujamaa, I think it brought development, but only for the government. For the individual person, the situation was inadequate. You had a nice building for politics. The government made good income, but for the for the private persons, they didn't have money. They had a very inferior life."
Member (m) of Semani Youth Group, Matetereka A (*GI 8*; 9/2/2015)

In both group interviews, the participants also discussed the idea if a return of Ujamaa, or elements of it, would "come back" to Tanzania, and if this would actually improve their situation. The majority of both groups had reservations on such ideas, albeit with different perspectives. Youth group members in Matetereka did not only see Ujamaa as an idea of old people from the past, but also thought that the development under the current system actually was preferable:

"Maybe, the system of the past it was the one of the wazee wajamaa (socialist elders), for them the system was good. Now it has changed, and in this system, everything is private. A system of self-reliance, because everybody is doing his/her own work privately. And I think the place changed more through the private system."
Member (m) of Semani Youth Group, Matetereka A (*GI 8*; 9/2/2015)

In Litowa, on the other hand, the young farmers had a more positive view of the past, and while they thought it would not necessarily be a good idea to just repeat the ways of their ancestors, they apparently found some inspiration in their concept:

"Now for me, if Ujamaa came back, our lives would be like that of our wazee of the past. They were doing everything together, it was really hard work. For me now, it is the vikundi of this village, who try something similar. Because in the vikundi, they work together. The have projects, in these vikundi to do together, just like Ujamaa."
Young farmer (m), Litowa (*GI 12*; 9/6/2015)

Indeed, this connotation of a new form of Ujamaa was widely shared in this group discussion – a notion already observable among many of the farmers' group members in Litowa as well (see above). The ideas of Ujamaa were the thing that counted, for the young farmers of this village:

"He also prefers to have Ujamaa in terms of sharing ideas. He says, through Ujamaa, people can come together, and exchange some views and ideas, then they move forward.

And he also concurs with the point of working in small groups."
Young farmer (m), Litowa. Interpreted by Dennis Mpazagade (*GI 12; 9/6/2015*)

So, at least as of 2015, there seems to be an understanding of the younger population regarding the history of the Ujamaa era, and some young farmers do indeed see the cooperative thought of that period as an inspiration for their own activities. Given the apparent lack of recognition of local history inside present-day's education system, however, there appears to be some concern that the villagers' own history might be lost one day, when the last contemporary witnesses of Ujamaa will be gone.

6.3 Perceptions of development and current challenges by the different stakeholders

After this consideration of the different ways outsiders and insiders were looking at the times of Ujamaa, the next area of interest lay in the perceptions and definitions of development and challenges to development which the different stakeholders had expressed during the field study.

6.3.1 Local definitions of development

In order to gather an understanding of the development environment of Ruvuma, it was crucial to analyze the underlying definitions of development, which acted as the base for the development activities of the different actors on regional and village level. In this section, the definitions given by those actors will be presented from two sides: The "outsider" perspective by NGOs, government personnel and other actors, which are not directly based inside the village communities, and on the other hand the "insider" perspective of village governments, vikundi and other groups from the villages themselves.

Outsiders

To categorize the following statements as an outside view might raise some questions, as all of the respondents are involved in various development activities which are conducted on the village level. However, as the people who were giving the following definitions are not living in the villages themselves, and are therefore not a direct part of these communities, they are still considered as outsiders, albeit with a qualified knowledge of the village environment.

Inquiry for these perspectives on development as such started with the NGO expert interviews in Songea. Some of the NGO representatives in Songea appeared to be very reflective on their definition of development, with regards to earlier approaches practiced by their organizations. They were eager to make sure that nowadays, development was all about enabling people to improve their lives by themselves and insisted that this was the base for all of their development interventions:

"You know, I think development is helping the people to help themselves. That's what I find very important, because you can give it, but they don't, you know – you don't assist them, you don't help them, because it's not sustainable. I think, the component of sustainability comes in clearly where he says: You know you can better teach somebody how to fish instead of giving him a fish, isn't it? So, that is very clear in our, in the Caritas approach, you know. Prior than the earlier approach, which was giving, giving, giving, now we don't give anymore, but we train and we teach people. So, there are no handouts anymore, and people also pay their own transport, sometimes their own lunch... So, I think, development for me means, that you, you know, you support them in supporting themselves. I think that is for me very clear. Because otherwise it will not be sustainable."
Welmoed Ryphema, Caritas Songea (*GBE 1; 2/23/2015*)

When further inquiring on which kind of development they had in mind for the people to achieve by themselves, the core theme was that of basic needs, like housing and food, which had to be cared for, and generally to be able to achieve improvements in any of these categories:

"Generally, what is desirable to, for the people. From just that, moving from the lower living standard to the, at least the, they can live as a human being, they have a good shelter, they have food, they have their basic needs of them. They have, well they have focused in the development issues. The eh, the Caritas, you know the office is very broad, but, eh... eh just looking at the livelihood of the people: Are they getting food? Can they pay the school fees for their children? Can they pay for the medical cost? Can they support the farming with the crop? And, eh, the shelter. That's the way we are seeing. We are just measuring, even in the indicators, to see how the project contributes to these, eh, the life of the communities. If we have sent the project at least, eh two to three years, we are just assessing to see from where we started: Is there any development from where they have [been] and where they are now. Go to stages which have taken place, that contributed by the project. So, we are just focusing in that scenarios."
Brito Mgoyo, Caritas Songea (*GBE 1; 2/23/2015*)

Other NGOs shared this idea of how to assess development on the ground: "It means, you can say – purchasing power, for instance. Who can purchase? Who can afford his, eh problems? Can take you smoothly, people to school, eh children to schools." (Ladislaus Bigambo, RUCODIA Songea; *GBE 2; 2/23/2015*). Rachel Teri of MVIWATA and Iskata Msigwa of PADI also argued in the same direction of measurable change on the grassroots level as being the most useful definition of development from their perspective (*GBE 3; 2/24/2015; GBE 4; 2/24/2015*). For Xaver Komba from SNC, development in his understanding also carried a certain extent of novelty: To create something new, in order to go ahead. The notion of improving the basic conditions of living on the village scale was also an important factor for him (*GBE 10; 3/10/2015*). There was also the widely-shared notion that in order for any development intervention to be successful, i.e. sustainable, it had to benefit the people on the ground. Other actors involved in the development scene of Ruvuma, like the Peramiho mission, also underlined their view that this sort of tangible results on the village level were a precondition to development as such – possibly also a reflection of earlier, more caritatively oriented development interventions that had been the norm a few decades ago:

> "…development is good, only when people are mainly the beneficiaries and involved from day one, ya. That will lead to sustainability of those projects for development. If they are not involved from day one, they don't know what's going on, they are just benefitting, without knowing what or, eh, where they get those, eh, … there will be no, you know, sustainability of that project, they end up somewhere."
> Father Fidelis, Prior of Peramiho Abby (*GBE 6; 2/25/2015*)

An additional aspect of defining development in the sense of development opportunities was stated by Wilbert Matumbi of TMMTF in Songea, who underscored the importance of peaceful conditions for any kind of development. This was one of the reasons why, in his view, conflict moderation between different stakeholders was one key activity of his NGO: If there were no conflicts about land or other issues, small farmers would actually be able to produce enough to develop further – if they had a market (*GBE 5; 2/24/2015*).

With regards to the district and regional representatives in charge of development issues, replies to the question on their own definition of development were less detailed, and did not involve reflection on former strategies for rural development applied by their respective offices. Indeed, they shared the most basic of development definitions:

> "On development, I can – simply I can say to change from one stage to another. Ya, change from one stage to another in aspect of, let's say, social, economics. To change maybe from, eh, a certain kind of life standard, to another life quality."
> Charles Mihayo, District Planning Officer Songea Rural (*GBE 8; 3/2/2015*)

Without specifying which areas were to be looked at for analyzing those changes:

> "To me, eh, aha, I can say, it's just, eh, anything... Any changes from the situation which is... I can say, which is to worse, to the better. So, to a situation which is more better. Better as now, actually."
> Anthony Nginga, Regional Development Officer, Ruvuma Region (*GBE 12; 3/12/2015*)

It might be an overinterpretation of these short comments to deduct a shortage of reflection on their own activities on the side of government representatives. Yet, the general impression from both the regional and district development institutions was that any action, which would induce this movement from a lower to a higher standard of living, was good enough to be called development – even if there was no problematization of how these stages would be defined.

Insiders

The statements given by insiders on their definition of development have been categorized into four broad themes which could be deducted from the group discussions on the village level. This should by no means imply that these definitions would be mutually exclusive, or would have been presented as such by the participants. On the contrary, all four elements were regularly included in any of the discussions, with different focuses depending on how the respective discussion unfolded. Nevertheless, this broad categorization is meant to illustrate the connotations which the villagers had on the definition of development as such and how they themselves presented the interconnections between the different aspects.

"From a lower stage to a higher stage"

The idea of development as moving from a lower to a higher stage was quite common with the participants on village level, and was in many cases the starting point of the discussion among group members. After the statement of defining development as a succession of stages, they usually gave some concrete examples on what stages they had in mind:

> "I think, it is going forward, from a low place to a higher one, to build up a house or something. To get more possibilities, to build and take development. To build a small house, to get a machine. To develop the village and make it a better place. It is very little now."
> Member of Juhudi Group (m), Litowa (*GI 3*; 8/24/2015)

This notion was shared not only by farmers' group members of all case study villages, but also by youth group members in Matetereka (*GI 8*; 9/2/2015) and the young farmers in Litowa (*GI 12*; 9/6/2015). Some of the farmers' groups not only defined development as a process going through different stages, they also saw development as a shared responsibility of both the government and their own contributions:

> "I think, development means, to go from a level, a low level of life, to a higher level. And also, the government has to contribute. We are doing a little thing here, but also the government has to do something."
> Member of Tangawizi Group (m), Matetereka A (*GI 7*; 9/2/2015)

Furthermore, there was a high identification with their own groups as the vehicle for achieving this higher stage of development. For instance, by being able to increase their production as farmers' groups:

> "For me development means, we don't have a lot. But it means to go from a low stage to a high one. Maybe from one acre to grow two, such things."
> Farmers' Group Member (m), Matetereka C (*GI 9*; 9/3/2015)

"A car, a tractor…"

In many cases, material possessions with a practical use for agriculture and daily transport were seen as embodying the concept of development. The image of having a tractor as a sign for development was particularly strong among some vikundi members in Litowa (e.g. Kanyanga Twende Group (*GI 1; 8/22/2015*) and Umoja Group (*GI 6; 8/24/2015*)). In the other villages, too, progress in agriculture was seen as emblematic for the concept of development as a whole – again revolving around a perceived linear succession of farm machinery. The following statement is just one of the examples of accounts anchoring on this concept:

> "Maybe for me, development, would be something like from cultivating by hand to get to a stage where you have for instance a tractor, like were you don't have to walk for twenty kilometers on your feet, but you can travel easier, were you can get a bicycle, at least. That would be development. After that a car, maybe, that is development. To go from cultivating by hand to a tractor or power tiller, for agriculture."
> Member of Kujitegemea Group (m), Matetereka A (*GI 11; 9/3/2015*)

Apart from the obvious advantage for their own agriculture, the use of such equipment to enhance the possibility of reaching different places – be it in the village or accessing a market in town – was a common idea of illustrating development from the villagers' point of view. In this sense, the image of being able to switch from the lower to the higher form of transportation was seen as a viable definition of development:

> "Development, I want to explain it using some examples. For example, now, we are moving by our feet. If this kikundi is running good, tomorrow we might travel by pikipiki (a motorcycle). Ok? That means developing. If our project is successful, the day after tomorrow, we might have a car, and reach there. But I think in these times, without the kikundi, there is no development. That would be my example."
> Farmers' Group Member (m), Mbingamharule (*GI 14; 9/10/2015*)

On the other hand, the provision of decent infrastructure like roads, water and electricity by the government was also mentioned as being both a sign for and a precondition to development – and the lack of both infrastructure and transportation was seen as an impediment to local progress:

> "For me it is things like the road, electricity. Now there is no electricity, and the road is a big problem. To get to the shamba on this road is hard. To get anywhere is very difficult on these roads. To sell the produce, e.g.… Also, there is no car. Or tractor. So, for me development is things like that."
> Farmers' Group Member (m), Matetereka C (*GI 9; 9/3/2015*)

The youth, as well, understood improved mobility as one of the key aspects of development in the village environment:

"I think the main issue is the low level of economy. For instance, if you had a bicycle to get to the shamba and home, or then a pikipiki, that would be development."
Member of Semani Youth Group (m), Matetereka (*GI 8; 9/2/2015*)

"A decent life"

In the course of the group discussions, the definition of development as being a succession of stages, and the various material embodiments of these stages, were usually followed by a sort of integrating and powerful definition of development: Development as the possibility to have a decent life (Maisha mazuri), as opposed to the inferior living conditions they were facing right now:

"I think, as I understand it, and what is also the general idea of our group, it is to cooperate and to get from insufficient conditions to conditions where you can have a good life."
Member of Kujitegemea Group (f), Matetereka A (*GI 11; 9/3/2015*)

This decent life, again, is characterized by the most basic material conditions, which are deemed necessary, and their improvement over time:

"To have a good house, to maybe get a better one. A good house. That for me is the first thing in development."
Farmers' Group Member (f), Matetereka C (*GI 9; 9/3/2015*)

Or, in other words, "when you have the ability to sleep inside, in a nice bed, in a good house, that is development." (Farmers' Group Member, Mbingamharule; *GI 14; 9/10/2015*). This basic-needs approach was also shared by some of the village leaders:

"I think, first, that everybody can have three meals a day, (...) to be able to build a good house, clean water, that at least."
Remigius Njafula, Chairman of Matetereka (*GBE 15; 8/30/2015*)

Similarly, the youth was seeing this as the most conclusive definition emerging from their own discussion, and defined the stage of being developed as such in the following manner:

"What they say, most of their answers, because they – most of them they say, this person has developed, if he has a nice house, a nice place to sleep, and sufficient food. Most of them, that's their answers. Then they say, this person has developed..."
Young farmers (m). Interpreted by Dennis Mpazagade, Litowa (*GI 12; 9/6/2015*)

For some of the young villagers, the idea that somebody who had all these things was already "developed", however, was not their understanding of basic needs. Actually, they saw these basic needs as "the first stage" of development, which would imply that there was no development at all so far in their village – at least not for everybody:

247

"I think, the first stage of development is to have your needs in life cared for. Therefore, I think if everybody thinks about what he/she needs, we will hear many things. But that is not development. The challenge here is, to have the capital even to get medicine, many things, you go back. So generally, for me development is the ability to lead a decent life."
Member of Semani Youth Group (m), Matetereka (*GI 8*; 9/2/2015)

All the other material things that were mentioned in this group discussion (cars, tractors, etc.) would therefore represent further stages of development, which should only be sought for after these basic needs had been catered for.

Individually, or as a group?

With these propositions, which all imply material possessions as the definition of development, the question arises, if the inhabitants of the case study villages would only see individual possessions as a form of development, or if they would rather understand development has having access to these goods collectively. Statements like the following would rather imply an individual idea of development:

"So, that person defines development, in terms of what you own, a person with a shop, a person with milling machine, a person with a car, and a person with, with power, electricity."
Members of Kanyanga Twende Group, Litowa. Interpreted by Dennis Mpazagade
(*GI 1*; 8/22/2015)

However, at least with the vikundi members, it was asserted that ownership of things like a tractor or cattle as a group would also meet there definition (*GI 1*; 8/22/2015). Indeed, development was most often conceptualized has entailing profit for the individual person, as well as for the whole group:

"I think to make a little profit, to advance a little, maybe get a credit to expand. To help each other to develop the agriculture, because now it is very low. To make a little profit, also for the private [member]."
Member of Juhudi Group (f), Litowa (*GI 3*; 8/24/2015)

Especially in Litowa, the discussion on the definition of development, as such, would soon turn into a discussion on what the group members would see as development for their groups – illustrating again a very direct understanding of these groups as vehicles for development of both the individual farmers and the village as a whole. In some cases, progress of their group even became the definition of development in general, in which case development would be "to advance as a group, to have a common farm. For the group to help with problems, to create business." (Member of Juhudi (2) Group (f), Litowa; *GI 5*; 8/24/2015).

The strong connection between their definition of development and the activities of their groups was not exclusive to Litowa, however: Some respondents from the other villages would go so far as to imply that the development of the individual farmer would not be possible without cooperation, as the impediments

for a small-scale farmer on his or her own would be insurmountable. Group organization would therefore be the only possible way of development in their
situation:

> "For me development, there is development for the individual, and development in
> general. And the development of the individual is only possible through development of
> the whole together. That is why we have this group, to have at least, some development
> of the individual. The individual development is insufficient, if the whole development
> is. Therefore, development is to go bigger, to go ahead and to overcome challenges.
> Through work and agriculture."
> Farmers' Group Member (m), Matetereka C (*GI 9*; 9/3/2015)

This notion was underlined by other kikundi members: Development is the development of the individual, which in turn is only made possible by the development of the group:

> "I think, development is the development of each. For each person to have their house,
> and also the development together (…). For me it is a lot of things. To come from noth-
> ing to one, that is development. To get from one together to five, that is development."
> Member of Tupo Tayari Group (m), Matetereka B (*GI 10*; 9/3/2015)

While such statements by inhabitants of villages like Litowa and Matetereka,
with their very own history of cooperative development, might indicate that this
is a very local phenomenon, the group members from Mbingamharule did see this
connection as well, and emphasized this understanding of their vikundi's activities
(*GI 13*; 9/8/2015; *GI 14*; 9/10/2015). A finding that implies that there is still a strong
connection between the thought of cooperation and mutual help and the concept of
development as such in Ruvuma – at least among the farmers' group members of
the case study villages. Village authorities, as well, were including this idea in their
definition of development. The importance of this understanding of development
as going from one stage to the next one through the work of grassroots groups, was
neatly summarized even by the village leaders of Mbingamharule – a village without RDA history, after all:

> "Well, generally, development is to get from one stage to another. You could say maybe,
> development begins with the development of you and your family. You are doing it
> every day, year, whatever the timespan. But also, secondly, for development, in general,
> for us it means the development of our citizens. So, if all the wananchi develop, we have
> development. But, development is also brought by the different vikundi, who engage in
> agriculture. This can bring development to this place. Together with the development
> activities they can reach different stages, with a lot of jembe, we can develop the village,
> like having a godown, water, the road, electricity, the school, the church. So, we can
> reach community development."
> Omare Kamare, Village Manager, Mbingamharule (*GBE 11*; 3/11/2015)

Summary

There are several conclusions to be drawn from the analysis of the definition of development by the different stakeholders, both inside and outside the villages. First of all, all groups of respondents agreed that development for them meant a succession of stages – from a lower to a higher stage of development. These stages were most commonly illustrated by material possessions, such as a good house and better tools for agriculture, like a tractor or a milling machine. At the same time, the understanding of the ability to lead a decent life was generally understood as the first stage of development in this context.

Secondly, while usually the personal form was chosen to illustrate the different stages ("a person with a car, a person with electricity, etc."), there was also the common understanding that in order for each person to reach these stages of development, common activities were necessary. In particular, the concept of having a tractor or other farm tools as a sign for development was not necessary seen as an individual goal. On the contrary, most farmers' groups wanted to own such things together, in order for every member to benefit from development. Overall, it becomes clear from the evidence of the field study, that non-material definitions of development (such as a "happy life") are not found within the interviewed stakeholders, and that each of their varying definitions was always illustrated by technological or economic advancement in the basic environment of their daily lives: agriculture.

6.3.2 Perception of the current development status in the case study villages

With these individual definitions of development in Ruvuma as a background, the research interest concerning the inhabitants of the case study villages focused on their perception of the development of their own home villages. Therefore, as part of the village questionnaires circulated in Litowa, Matetereka, and Mbingamharule, respondents were asked about their opinion on the development of their respective villages. The question was posed in an open manner (see Appendix 2), without predefined categories which would imply evaluation of different aspects, in order to give respondents the possibility to add their own understanding of the question.

Category building was instead deferred to the analyzing phase of the research. For this task, the main statements were extracted from each questionnaire and then used to lead a deductive coding process for the creation of categories which would be comparable across all villages. A mind map design of the statements was produced in order to visualize the different connotations brought forward by the recipients. By this process, it was also possible to show the frequency of certain types of statements, in order to illustrate the relative importance of certain answers. Therefore, the individual statements were added as sub-branches to the respective main categories. The results of this process can be seen in the "developmental mind maps" created for each of the villages, which are presented in Figures 11 through 13.

The colors shown for each category in these developmental mind maps were chosen with the intention to enhance the clarity of the figures only, and have no further meaning regarding the results as such.

The main categories of answers emerging in this process were evaluations of the development status (good, low, etc.), statements that included perceived conditions for development (cooperation, hard work, etc.) and ideas for improvement (either concrete plans or general ideas, which would help in village development in the eyes of the respondents). Indeed, the subcategories or individual statements of conditions for development and ideas for improvement were sometimes very similar. However, the main category was chosen first, in order to illustrate the way in which the statement itself was presented. For instance, the statement "hard work of all villagers" without any context would be included in the "conditions for development" category, while a similar statement "Work of villagers together with the government" would be counted as an idea for improving the development of the village.

Further main categories were introduced if the individual statements would not fit within the three aforementioned main categories, for instance the statement that "development here is difficult" or "life is hard", which were not seen as evaluations of development status. The same goes for non-answers (n/a) or statements like "don't know".

When looking at the emerging developmental mind-maps of the villages, considerable differences appeared between the three villages in question. Within Litowa, most respondents answered the question with a relatively short evaluation of the development status of their village, with the majority of those giving a direct assessment without further describing the things that led to their respective evaluation. Of the 48 respondents giving such evaluations, 21 were seeing the development of their village as low or bad, while only eight were describing it as good and six persons seeing it as average. Three respondents thought that there was no development in their village at all. A total of 14 villagers from Litowa were giving their impressions of conditions for village development as a response to the question, with five of them seeing the hard work of villagers as one of these conditions. The other perceived conditions were quite individual and can be seen in detail in Fig. 11.

Concerning the ideas for improvement, which were brought forward by 20 respondents, those were also very diverse, with only "jobs for the youth" named by more than one respondent. Other ideas included better provision of loans, more cooperation in various fields, different ideas on how to improve access to farm inputs and how to create a better market for the local farmers. 18 villagers made statements which would not fit in the three main categories of answers.

In Matetereka, one of the main differences in the answers to the question of village development was the amount of detail given by the respondents. While a similar number of participants gave evaluations of the village's development status (44), these answers usually not only included a simple assessment (good, bad, average, etc.), but also a reason for this view by the person responding. To illustrate this sort of detail, the statements that were included in each evaluation are added as subcategories on the developmental mind map (Fig. 12).

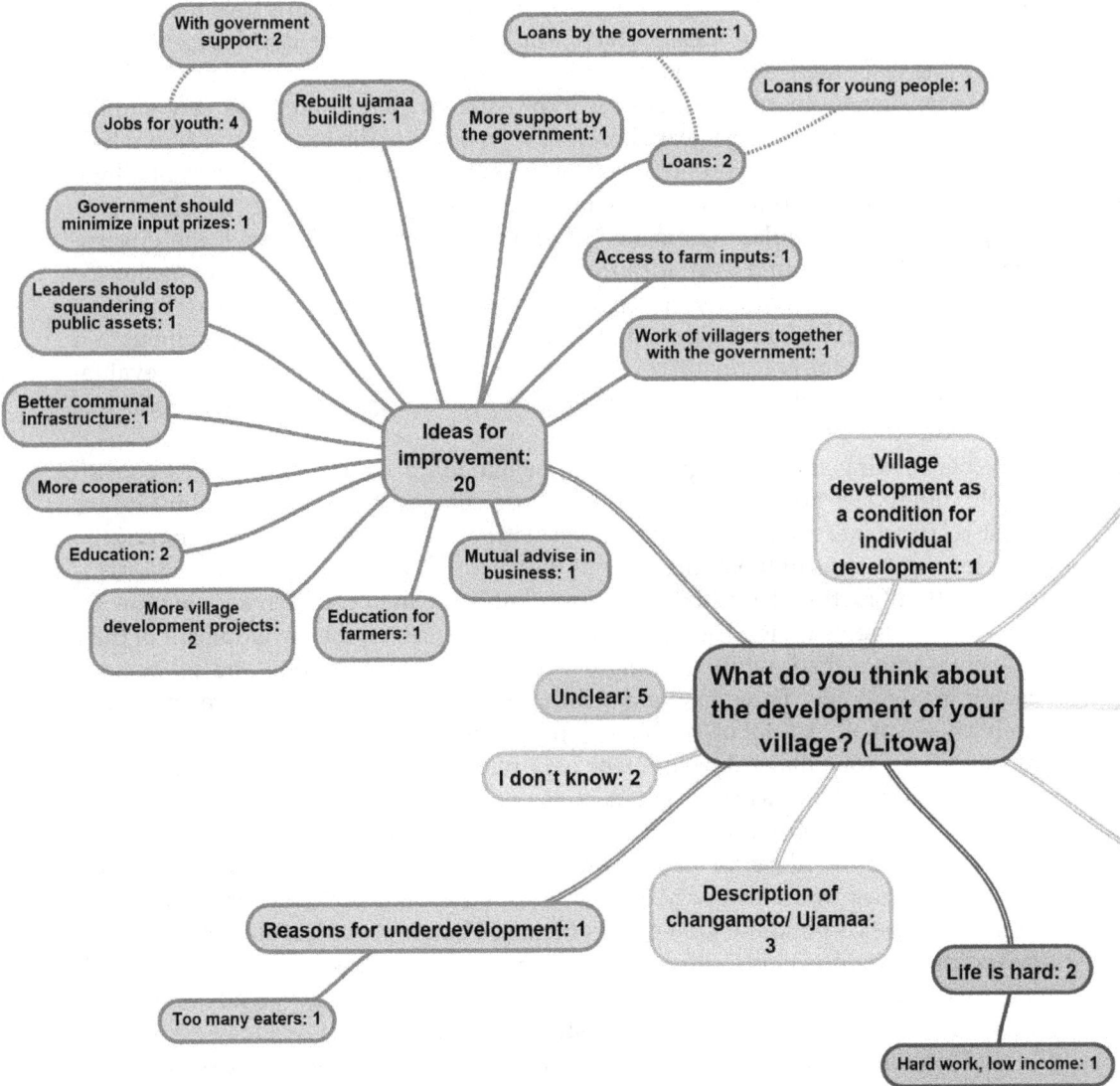

Figure 11: What do you think about the development of your village? (Litowa).

With government support: 2

Loans by the government: 1

Loans for young people: 1

Rebuilt ujamaa buildings: 1

More support by the government: 1

Jobs for youth: 4

Loans: 2

Government should minimize input prizes: 1

Access to farm inputs: 1

Leaders should stop squandering of public assets: 1

Work of villagers together with the government: 1

Better communal infrastructure: 1

Ideas for improvement: 20

Village development as a condition for individual development: 1

More cooperation: 1

Education: 2

Mutual advise in business: 1

More village development projects: 2

Education for farmers: 1

What do you think about the development of your village? (Litowa)

Unclear: 5

I don't know: 2

Description of changamoto/ Ujamaa: 3

Reasons for underdevelopment: 1

Life is hard: 2

Too many eaters: 1

Hard work, low income: 1

Source: 100 questionnaires analyzed from own survey

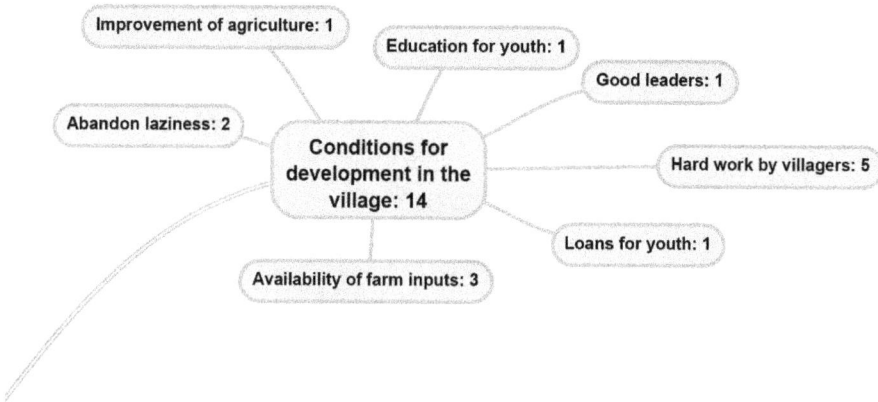

Improvement of agriculture: 1

Education for youth: 1

Good leaders: 1

Abandon laziness: 2

Conditions for development in the village: 14

Hard work by villagers: 5

Loans for youth: 1

Availability of farm inputs: 3

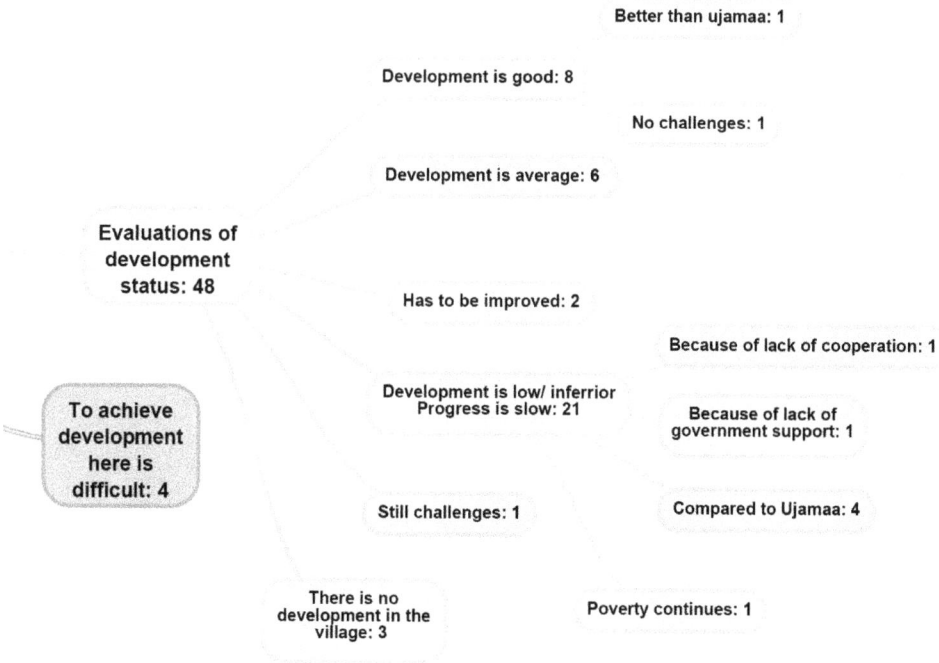

Better than ujamaa: 1

Development is good: 8

No challenges: 1

Development is average: 6

Evaluations of development status: 48

Has to be improved: 2

Because of lack of cooperation: 1

Development is low/ inferrior Progress is slow: 21

Because of lack of government support: 1

To achieve development here is difficult: 4

Still challenges: 1

Compared to Ujamaa: 4

There is no development in the village: 3

Poverty continues: 1

Figure 12: What do you think about the development of your village? (Matetereka)

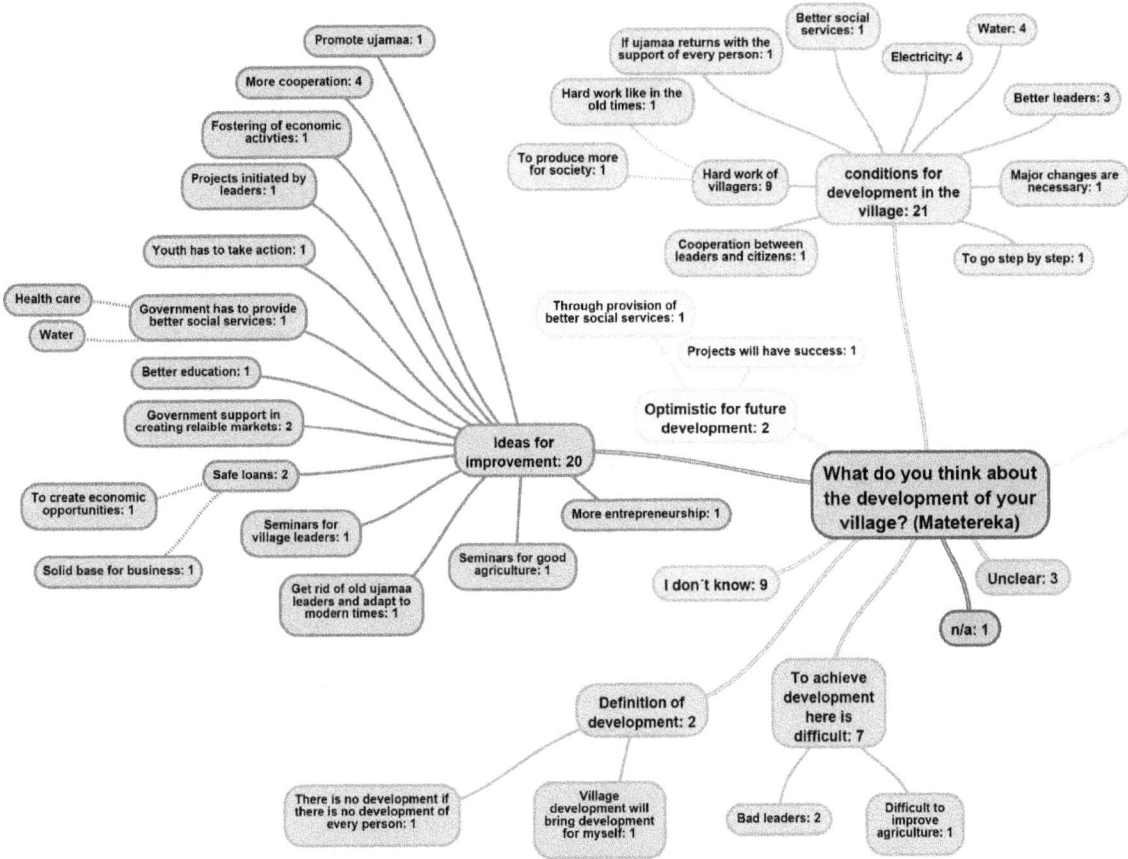

Source: 109 questionnaires analyzed from own survey

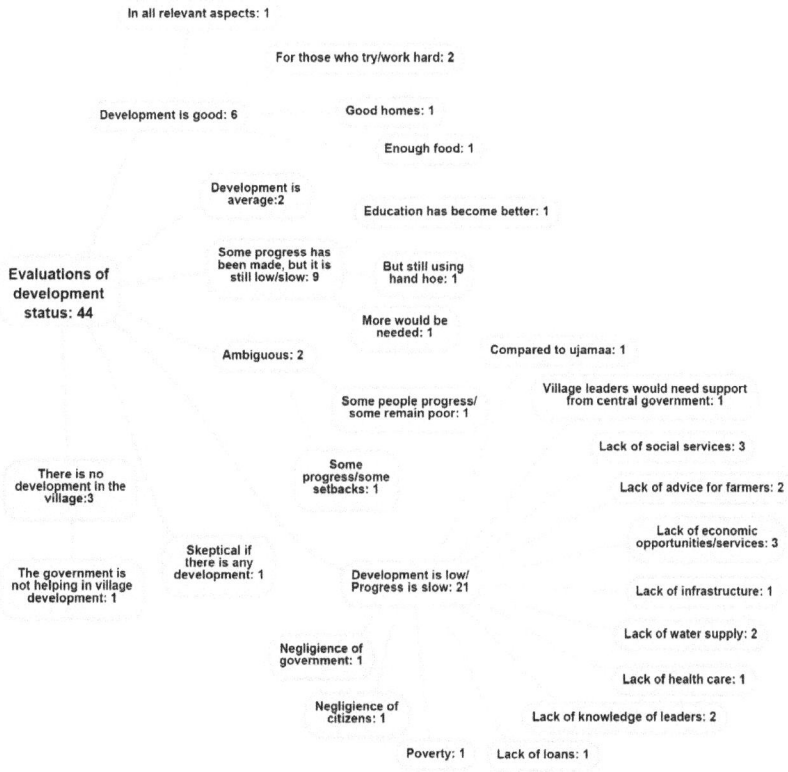

In all relevant aspects: 1

For those who try/work hard: 2

Development is good: 6

Good homes: 1

Enough food: 1

Development is average: 2

Education has become better: 1

Evaluations of development status: 44

Some progress has been made, but it is still low/slow: 9

But still using hand hoe: 1

More would be needed: 1

Compared to ujamaa: 1

Ambiguous: 2

Village leaders would need support from central government: 1

Some people progress/ some remain poor: 1

Lack of social services: 3

There is no development in the village: 3

Some progress/some setbacks: 1

Lack of advice for farmers: 2

Lack of economic opportunities/services: 3

Skeptical if there is any development: 1

The government is not helping in village development: 1

Development is low/ Progress is slow: 21

Lack of infrastructure: 1

Lack of water supply: 2

Negligience of government: 1

Lack of health care: 1

Negligience of citizens: 1

Lack of knowledge of leaders: 2

Poverty: 1

Lack of loans: 1

Figure 13: What do you think about the development of your village? (Mbingamharule)

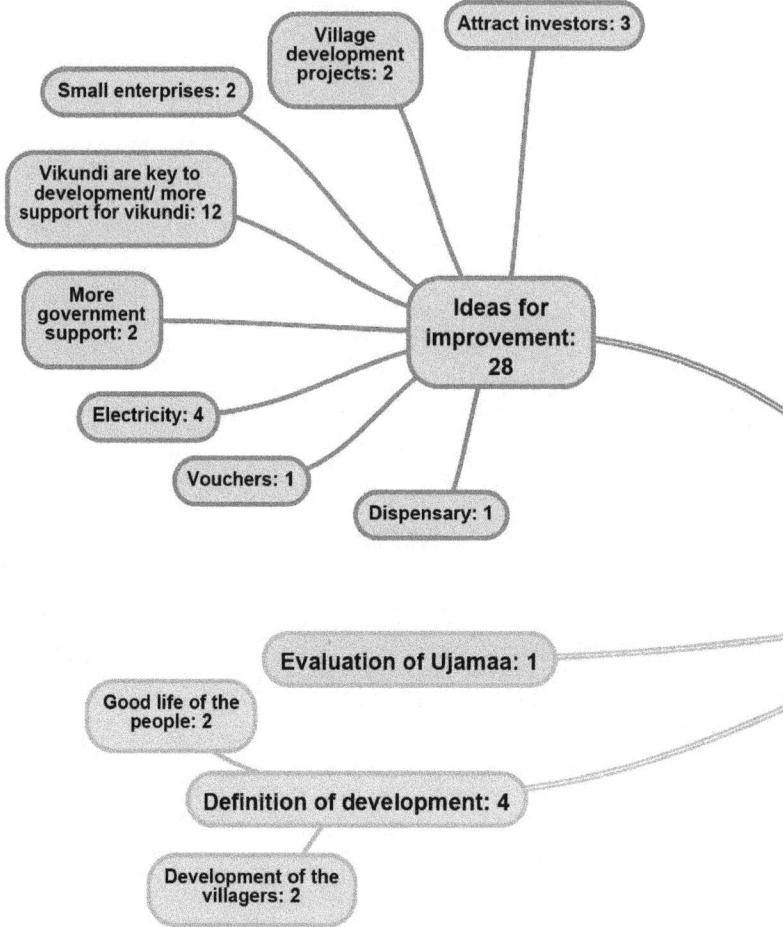

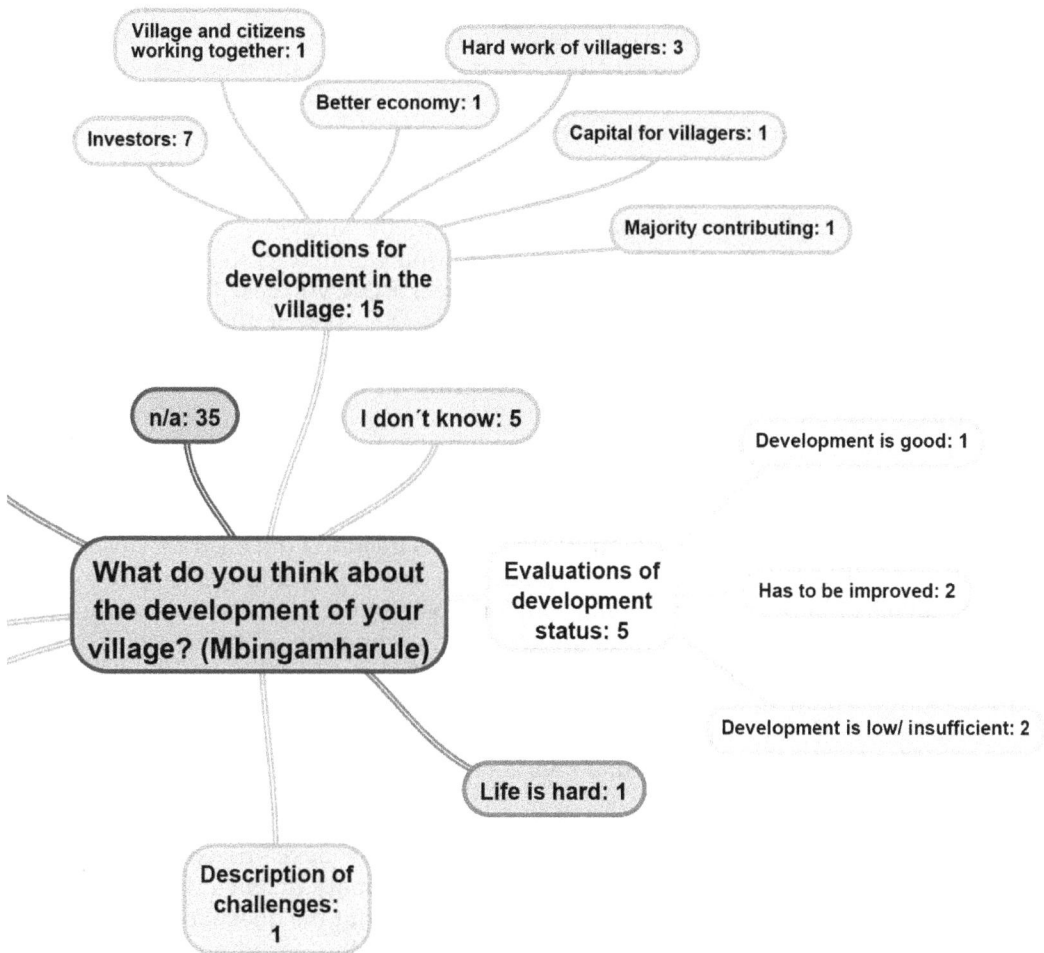

Village and citizens working together: 1

Hard work of villagers: 3

Better economy: 1

Capital for villagers: 1

Investors: 7

Majority contributing: 1

Conditions for development in the village: 15

n/a: 35

I don´t know: 5

Development is good: 1

What do you think about the development of your village? (Mbingamharule)

Evaluations of development status: 5

Has to be improved: 2

Development is low/ insufficient: 2

Life is hard: 1

Description of challenges: 1

Answers stating low development were similar in frequency to Litowa (21), and a number of perceived reasons for this low or slow development of the village were given – for instance the lack of social services (3) or the lack of economic opportunities (also 3). On the other hand, six respondents were seeing the development as good in Matetereka, and nine were seeing some progress, but characterizing it as too slow or too little to be characterized as good development.

When it came to conditions for development (21 statements), hard work by the villagers was also the main subcategory to this, stated by 9 respondents. Apart from further statements including "work related" conditions, like in Litowa, people were also mentioning water or electricity as a major (missing) condition for development in Matetereka. Regarding the ideas for improvement, made by 20 respondents, these were also quite diverse and in many ways resembling the ideas brought forward in Litowa. Some answers, however, like the suggestion to "get rid of the old Ujamaa leaders", or to give seminars to the (current) village leaders, might be another indication for the long history of political conflict within the village.

In many aspects, the questionnaires from Mbingamharule showed a picture completely different from those of the two former RDA villages. The first apparent difference was the reluctance of answering the question at all, as 35 out of 95 respondents choose not to reply. Secondly, only five respondents were giving their evaluation of village development when answering the question (1 good, 2 has to be improved, 2 bad/low).

On the other hand, similar numbers of people were giving conditions for village development (15) and even more recipients suggested ideas for improvement (28) than in the other villages. Within the conditions, the theme of hard work of villagers was still present (3 answers), but most answers included the need for investors or donors in their statements (7) – an issue that was not mentioned at all by the respondents of Litowa or Matetereka. Similarly, within the ideas for improving the situation, a total of 12 respondents underlined the importance of farmers' groups (vikundi) as a vehicle for development, while the issue was hardly a topic in the other village questionnaires. The need for investors on the side of conditions for development was also reflected by ideas on how to attract investors on the improvement side (3). The detailed developmental mind map can be seen in Fig. 13.

Summary

Overall, more comprehensive perceptions of the villages' development status were given in Litowa and Matetereka, with the latter even more detailed. In Mbingamharule, very short assessments were the norm throughout the questionnaires. In all villages, similar numbers of respondents were giving ideas for improvements and stating conditions for village development. An evaluation of the present-day situation was far more common in Litowa and Matetereka, than in Mbingamharule.

In Litowa, conditions for village development were generally more concerned with the work of the villagers or the agriculture as such, while in Matetereka infrastructure-related topics were also common. In Mbingamharule, the need for external investments was particularly prominent.

Concerning the ideas for improvement, they were more diverse in Matetereka and Litowa than in Mbingamharule, where the high number of respondents seeing farmers' groups as the main tool for village development was especially striking.

6.3.3 Challenges to development in Ruvuma

After clarifying the understanding of development by the stakeholders involved in the research, as well as the perception of village development by the individual villagers, the final element in understanding the development environment of the case study area was the inquiry about the challenges which the different focal groups perceived to be the most important ones for the development of the region and their villages, in general, as well as their life as individuals, specifically. These perceptions have been sorted according to the groups of stakeholders of this research, with the farmers' group members and the respondents of the questionnaires being included in the group of the local peasantry as such.

View by NGOs

The NGOs in Songea were very explicit about the challenges in their development efforts, both regarding their own operations and the general environment for development in Ruvuma. Although all of their main activities are nowadays led by the interest to create sustainable development by enabling people to care for themselves, the legacy of former, more charity driven approaches can sometimes be challenging for project implementation:

> "Well a big challenge still is the dependency syndrome, I think. You know, especially for Caritas, because we came – we are from the church – and people are very much used to, eh, everything which comes from the church is for free. So, if we go and we propose a project, people are kind of like, you know, depending that we will give them everything and that they don't have to contribute anything. That is still a challenge for us, although it's getting better and better and better. Because we did research, and we found out that people nowadays are ready to contribute also towards, eh, projects. But I mean, you know, in the heart – in the mindset of people, it's still a very big problem."
> Welmoed Ryphema, Caritas Songea (GBE 1; 2/23/2015)

Apart from this issue of the farmers' perception of their organizations, the political situation in Tanzania, after the transformation from Ujamaa to a liberal economy, creates challenges for the small farmers on the ground. In spite of the official focus of Tanzanian rural development policy, which is still supposed to be on the economic development of the majority of small-scale farmers, the NGOs perceive a gap between policy and practice. Large government projects, such as South Crops, which theoretically aim at the improvement of agricultural productivity on the village scale, would hardly be known by the peasants on the ground. And while there are programs on virtually every level of government to assist small-scale cultivators to improve their production and enhance their market access, hardly any peasant would have access to these programs in Ruvuma. On the contrary, these forms of subsidies would mostly benefit the more advanced farmers and some few big agricultural companies. Land grabbing and late payments by state agencies buying produce from small-scale farmers would add to an increasing gap between the majority of poor farmers, without access to cash income or capital, and a few more advanced farmers, who benefit from government development programs (*GBE 1; 2/23/2015*). Indeed, the information differential between those groups also leads to middlemen undermining government's attempts to guarantee good prices for small-scale farmers:

"But this is from the government really very very challenging. When you see, last season, the government has said they buy maize from farmers, at least they have the better price. So, we see this very very nice for farmers, because there is trouble in selling their maize and the government they said they will buy it. For 500 [TSh] per kg, direct from farmer. But what happened, the rich people went to the small holder farmers, they bought their maize in the 200 per kg, and then they sold to the government for 500 per kg. So, you see, the farmers have spent a whole season, with a lot of costs – [and] somebody who has done nothing, just moving to the village and taking maize, selling to the government, have made a lot of money. So, you cannot make farmers move from this situation. And the government they say they have bought, let's say 300,000 tons from farmers. But farmers they are poor, they didn't receive the money you are sending."
Brito Mgoyo, Caritas Songea (*GBE 1; 2/23/2015*)

The relative remoteness of Ruvuma would also add to this issue of information flow to small-scale farmers, and with the very limited availability of transport options, this inevitably leads to a general problem of market access and economic opportunities, as was underlined by MVIWATA (*GBE 3; 2/24/2015*). While these issues are generally appreciated by representatives of other NGOs, they also added that the farmers, themselves, would be particularly reluctant to adapt to changes in the agricultural economy, compared to other regions in Tanzania:

"Ya, the difference in Ruvuma, as we see we are in the remote area, so far – other actants they don't like to come direct to Ruvuma; say that it is so far away, from maybe the city or.... Ehm, the difference is also that, changing cultures with the people, is – almost, is slowly, in Ruvuma, especially for Songea Rural. Except, except Mbinga District. There are people who are committed. If you talk something, they can implement what you talk. But the other, other areas they – you can say they are lager [there are more of those, than of the others]; taking slowly changes, ya. Relating to other regions, like Mbeya and ya, Ruvuma. In Mbeya, they are so sharp in changing. (…) Challenges, big challenges is the – the infrastructure – but also the commitment of the people. Infrastructure is one, but also the commitment of the people. They are taking changes slowly. Ya."
Ladislaus Bigambo, RUCODIA Songea (*GBE 2; 2/23/2015*)

This statement was partly endorsed by Xaver Komba from SNC, who identified the lack of education as the primary issue within Ruvuma, which would result in a lack of planning capacity by the peasants, especially if they are involved in group development projects: Since there are only few farmers who would have a basic understanding on how to organize group development projects and to evaluate the results of such projects, many farmers' groups would actually not make a lot of progress and are prone to cease operations after one or two seasons. In his view, the remoteness of Ruvuma contributes a lot to this shortage of knowledge, as it would regularly be "the last Region in Tanzania" to implement new development strategies. He cited internal as well as external political factors as contributing to this apparent backwardness of the region (*GBE 10; 3/10/2015*).

Furthermore, some of the NGOs also saw a major challenge in the sustainability of their own organizations, as it was virtually impossible – at least for national NGOs not connected to a big international organization – to get a steady flow of funding for all of its projects (*GBE 4; 2/24/2015*). This was especially true for an organization like MVIWATA, which as the national network of farmers' groups technically relied on its members' contributions for its organizational overhead. Yet, many members would never actually pay their fees, which puts the NGO's Songea office in a permanent struggle to attain project funding from international donors for continuing its work (*GBE 3; 2/24/2015*). TMMTF was facing similar issues (*GBE 5; 2/24/2015*).

View of Political actors

The challenge of the lack of education was also perceived as one of the main issues for development by the district representative, and as one of the causes for the widespread poverty in Songea Rural District. The second main complex of development challenges was, in his view, the overdependency on maize as the main food crop and source of income for the peasantry, worsened by the lack of funds for agricultural improvements:

"The big challenges? For Songea Rural...There are so many challenges. But, eh, ehm, big challenge I can say, ehm. The rate of literacy, literacy. Illiteracy. Other challenges is poverty. Poverty. Because the illiteracy is very high in the rural area. Because they don't like to go to school. The poverty, and other challenges. So, right now, the dependency, sometimes dependence on one type of, eh, food crops, as a cash crops. For instance, cultivating maize: They are very big, but there is also no funding, no money in the rural areas. Those are the challenges: Illiteracy, poverty, and a dependence on maize, as their main [source of income]."
Charles Mihayo, District Planning Officer Songea Rural (*GBE 8; 3/2/2015*)

The Regional Development Officer on the other hand, took a more internal view regarding the challenges for the work of his agency for development:

"Now, actually, most of challenge we are taking – especially for community development department: First of all, we have a shortage of staff. According to the, the structure, at the district level there is ward and the villages. So, we need to have, a, eh community development staff at the ward level. (…) So, there are some wards which have no staff, who can mobilize people to participate. (…) Ya, uhm, ah, another challenge I think is financial obstacles. Financial sources are not enough for the staff to perform their, their responsibilities. (...) Even transport facilities. In the ward, one ward can have three up to six villages, so when, at ward level, at ward headquarters it needs to have a visit to the villages. So, eh, they are lacking transport facilities."
Anthony Nginga, Regional Development Officer, Ruvuma Region (*GBE 12; 3/12/2015*)

Both statements, however, illustrated the general lack of funding for public offices which are supposed to deal with regional development, thereby underlining the perceptions of many NGO representatives of the apparent failure of implementing government sponsored development programs on the ground.

In Litowa, education and lack of capital for the farmers were the main challenges, as seen by the village chairman. As a result, farmers in his village would neither have the capacity to invest in the improvement of their agriculture, nor the knowledge on how to enhance their cultivation, even if they had the funds.

> "One of the factor is capital. They are missing capital, it could be true. And still there is a thing, like a lack of skills. All education, in the agriculture and general could help with. Because they say they are running, but they are not aware how they are running. Are they running – economically, progressively, or not? They are just doing it. They just cultivate, harvest what they have. You harvest and what you expanded before, you don't bother about it."
> Michael Komba, Chairman of Litowa. Interpreted by Brother Augustine
> (*GBE 7*; 2/26/2015)

Approaches like that of Caritas, which was providing a training shamba for the Soya ni Pesa project inside the village, where therefore highly appreciated by him (*GBE 7*; 2/26/2015). Another big complex of challenges, which was named by all three villages' headquarters, was the lack of infrastructure, especially water, and public education facilities:

> "So, they don't have water supply. And he said secondly, they don't have a secondary school here. And it is in a peripheral area. This village is in a peripheral area. Therefore, the government started the day schools. Day schools, not boarding schools. Therefore, the children to go there and come back, even in time is a tough job. Therefore, people they are reluctant. And going and coming, is hard."
> Michael Komba, Chairman of Litowa. Interpreted by Brother Augustine
> (*GBE 7*; 2/26/2015)

The lack of a decent market with reliable prices for small-scale farmers was seen as the main reason for the lack of capital – with the shortage of public infrastructure, like good storage facilities, such as a godown, as contributing to these difficulties. Consequently, investments in such structures, as well as in the improvement of the public water supply were seen as the key objectives for village development. However, there was a lack of funding in both areas:

> "For our development, one challenge is, well first. Our citizens are farming. But there is no reliable market for this. The government has a market, but takes a lot of time to pay. And even if they are trying to expand, up to now our citizens will use most of their harvest for subsistence. So, if you have harvest, there is no service, for buying, so this is a contributing factor. And they are not paying the wananchi, be it the Saccos or the government, for their maize. So, the market is a big problem.

The second challenge, for us to develop, is water. We get the water through neighborhood groups. So, every neighborhood has water, but to develop, we would need water for every house. Therefore, it still is insecure for the water to reach everybody, him, me, you...that would be important. But still, the water supply is not sufficient.

Also, another challenge for us is, maybe related to the market, we would need a new godown for our harvest. As a government, we try to get funding for this. But there is still a lack of money to construct a good godown. The one we have is not very good. Another one, maybe, there is still an issue related to medicine, that is a problem. That would be a task for the government. If we could solve this, it would be better for our citizens."
Omare Kamare, Village Manager, Mbingamharule (*GBE 11;* 3/11/2015)

Market and infrastructure were also seen as the most imminent challenges in Matetereka:

"Maybe, the biggest challenge in Matetereka: First, it is water, the water supply does not work well. Secondly, there is no electricity (…) so secondly (sic!), the market for agriculture, there is no secure market, (…) if you grow a lot, you still get very bad prices. (…) Maybe, the provision of business, and eh, it's very small-scale agriculture. There is no capital. It stays very small."
Remigius Njafula, Chairman of Matetereka (*GBE 15;* 8/30/2015)

The View of the Peasants

The view of the peasants of the case study villages has been derived from the group interviews with the vikundi, as well as from the results of the household questionnaires. Many of the peasants' views reflect those of their local governments, indicating a general understanding of their issues by their political leaders.

Market

As it was the case with these village authorities, most vikundi characterized the lack of market access as one of their main challenges in life:

"The market for the produce for us as wananchi wakulima (common farmers), we still don't have a market. Be it maize, or rice. There is still very little. We do the work with the hand hoe, but we don't have profit. We need better prices!"
Member of Mtakuja Tangine Group (m), Litowa (*GI 2;* 8/24/2015)

Indeed, in their view, this lack of market for any of their produce also impeded the extension of agriculture by the individual farmers. Without a reliable market, there was simply no incentive to increase the production of any crop beyond the needs of subsistence:

"Another challenge is the lack of market, because, the people are growing a little bit. They might like to produce more, but with this market, it is troublesome, for the indi-

vidual. If we had a reliable market, with good prices, then the people would go ahead, even privately."
Member of Umoja Group (m), Litowa (*GI 6; 8/24/2015*)

It needs to be added, that farmers from this same Umoja group also saw a lack in local facilities for crop storage, making it even more difficult to produce for the market, as it was virtually impossible to store any surplus produce until market prices indicated profit in selling it. This was seen as another reason for the low production for the market in general (*GI 6; 8/24/2015*).

The lack of reliable markets was also a main theme at the other villages, like Matetereka:

"For me it is the prices for the crops. They are not very good. So, for us as farmers it is hard to get enough for our children. There is no reliable market."
Farmers' Group Member (f), Matetereka C (*GI 9; 9/3/2015*)

Apart from this general complaint, there were also views which would indicate that a better internal organization of the villages' peasantry might increase their changes for achieving better market access:

"Maybe, the main issue is the market. For us in Matetereka (A) we are 500 (people) and everybody is growing maize, beans, groundnuts, a little bit of this, a little bit of that... Therefore, there is no market. If you grow maize, you have nowhere to sell. We cannot, it is too little. But if we could organize better, one can grow maize, one maharage, one ginger... Everybody more of one, then it would be better to access the market. Like we do it now, it is only for subsistence. A little bit of everything. But to sell it, it is too little, that is an issue. We need to tackle that challenge. If you would grow like two crops, but a lot of them, that would be better, and then contribute. We would go ahead."
Member of Tangawizi Group (m), Matetereka A (*GI 7; 9/2/2015*)

Even if the farmers cooperated as groups, in order to go to the market together, however, the small size of the market itself proved to be challenging, as this statement from Mbingamharule illustrates:

"We can cultivate well, but there is no reliable market. So, they are cultivating, with their capital, but for selling, there is no place. Not for the group, and not for the individual person. That is the problem. If the market was good, the life would be better."
Farmers' Group Member (m), Mbingamharule (*GI 14; 9/10/2015*)

With regards to the individuals who completed the questionnaires in the case study villages, the issue of the lack of market access, or a reliable market in general, also appeared as one of the major challenges. However, there were considerable differences between the three villages: Matetereka had by far the highest number of respondents naming the market as one of their major challenges in life – 26 in total (23.9% of respondents; multiple answers possible). In Litowa and Mbingamharule, only 7.0 and 5.9 percent named "market" as one of their major challenges, respectively. Some reason for this apparent difference in the difficulties of finding a market for their harvest might be found in the more central location of the latter two villages within the region.

Indeed, it appears that apart from initiatives like the Soya ni Pesa program and other cash crop promoting activities by various NGOs, there is virtually only one final buyer for the region's main agricultural produce: The National Food Reserve Agency (NFRA) in Songea, who is buying maize from all over the region for storage in their compound. This agency's main task is to secure the food security all over the country, by storing enough food crops to bridge any droughts or other shortcomings in food production that might occur. Their facility in Songea is one out of seven zonal centers of this kind throughout the country. All of them are placed in Regions with relatively high production of food crops. The produce is then stored between one and three years, and released, if necessary, to regions with food shortage, usually the bigger urban agglomerations or the arid parts of Tanzania (GBE 13; 3/13/2015).

The manager of NFRA in Songea, Morgan Mwaipyana, explained that the main challenge of his organization was the low reliability of central government funding, which impeded the agency's ability to pay the farmers in time. Collection of maize for NFRA is usually facilitated through village and ward authorities and then handled by one of the 20 procurement centers of the agency. In the 2014 growing season, NFRA had bought around 75,000 tons of maize in Ruvuma and a total of 132,000 tons were stored in the facility at the time of visit. In the manager's view, NFRA is the only large-scale buyer of maize in Ruvuma, as even most of the private buyers and middlemen, who are buying from the local farmers, would resell their stock to NFRA. According to his view, the bad infrastructure and the general remoteness of Ruvuma makes the market unattractive to private companies. And with the combination of a limited amount of maize NFRA needs every year and the difficulties of on time payment to the farmers induced by the unsecure funding, the challenge for the local peasantry to find a reliable market for their crops become even more understandable (GBE 13; 3/13/2015).

Capital

The overall issue with market access induces a constant shortage of cash income for the peasantry, which in turn is unable to build an own stock of capital for investing in their agriculture. As evidence from this research shows, at least some of the recipients from the local peasantry are very aware of this fact, as the challenge of mtaji (capital, plural: mitaji) was regularly named throughout the interviews:

> "The main problem is money, capital (pesa, mtaji). We don't have capital. So, this means that they have no machines, like a tiller. Really, this is the main problem."
> Member of Mtakuja Tangine Group (m), Litowa (GI 2; 8/24/2015)

Indeed, the shortage of private capital and the lack of access to bank accounts or credits for individual peasants is one of the key reasons for the inception of the vikundi which were interviewed during the field visits. Mutual saving and lending schemes are the "bread and butter" of these groups, regardless of other economic activities (see the activities of the vikundi in chapter 6.2.3).

> "So, there is no capital, so without capital there is no development. So, our group has made a bank account to get credit, that makes it easier. So, with credit, we can get a little capital."
> Farmers' Group Member (m), Matetereka C (*GI 9*; 9/3/2015)

The general shortage of money was also very much apparent with the respondents of the questionnaires, although some differences between the villages emerged in the way those individuals framed their challenges: In Matetereka, 52 out of 109 respondents named the outright shortage of capital (mtaji) as one of their major issues, while only one person in Litowa and 19 (out of 95) in Mbingamharule choose to describe their challenges in the same fashion. On the other hand, 20 individuals in Litowa named "small income" (kipato kidogo) as a central challenge, and another 24 added "poverty" (umaskini) to the list. In Mbingamharule, there was also the theme of "small economy/business" (uchumi mdogo), mentioned by 8 out of 95 respondents. Some people in Matetereka also used terms like these to describe one common issue: The lack of financial resources, which would enable them to invest in their agriculture, or otherwise improve their living conditions. If all the aforementioned categories (no capital/ small income/ poverty/ small economy) are combined, this challenge would be included in the description of challenges of 53.2% of the respondents in Matetereka, 45.0% in Litowa, and 36.8% in Mbingamharule – thus underlining the high importance which the lack of financial resources of any kind (be it income or capital) has in the perception of challenges by the citizens of these three villages.

Farm inputs

This shortage of capital, as well as cash in the first place, leads to another one of the most common challenges named by the local peasantry: Pembejeo – farm inputs. The term usually refers to any kind of necessary inputs, but most often was elaborated as including the two main issues of fertilizer (mbolea) and seeds (mbegu) for annual crops. Compared to the very low prizes the farmers can achieve with the sale of their harvest, the prizes for fertilizers are perceived as being too high for the individual farmers, and even the vikundi as a whole:

> "I think the challenge for the kikundi, is right now the question of inputs, because the prices are very high. So, it is a question of inputs. So, if you had at least one or two bags of fertilizer, that would be a great help for agriculture. But yet, in general we don't have as a group."
> Member of Mshikamano Group (m), Litowa (*GI 4*; 8/24/2015)

The lack of fertilizer as a result of these high prices leads to underperformance in their agriculture, especially in cash crop projects, which are actually supposed to

266

increase the cash income of the members and the group, thereby enabling them to access better farm inputs:

> "I think the biggest challenge is to get seeds. I think, everybody could grow one acre of ginger. But there not enough seeds. So, this is the biggest challenge. Ginger seeds, it's a big problem. But if we can produce enough seeds, I think everybody of us, all the fourteen, could cultivate one acre. ...."
> Member of Tangawizi Group (m), Matetereka A (*GI 7*; 9/2/2015)

This perceived underproduction in turn leads to additional problems when trying to go to the market, as the yields which they can achieve without fertilizers result in production quantities which are just not interesting for the buyers:

> "Generally, it is very hard to get farm inputs. It is easy enough to grow here, but for going to the market, you need more, they don't want just a few debe (bushels)."
> Farmers' Group Member (m), Matetereka C (*GI 9*; 9/3/2015)

Yet not only in cash earning projects, but also "In the cultivation of maize, the main issue is pembejeo, like fertilizer and seeds." (Member of Tupo Tayari Group (m), Matetereka B; *GI 10*; 9/3/2015). This indicates a dual issue, as maize is not only the main food crop and, therefore, the base for the farmers' subsistence, but also their main source of cash income in the first place, without which they cannot make the necessary investments for the next season – creating a vicious circle of low production, low income, low investment and again low production:

> "The challenge that there is, when you are doing agriculture, even as a group, is inputs. So, the year before last year, that is why we decided to start the group, to help each other with inputs. And also, when we sell the harvest, the prices are very low. The second challenge is, many people have a problem to save something for the future. You reach the end of the year, there is nothing left. You have your harvest, but where do you sell it, from what do you buy inputs, the prices for them are high. That is a challenge"
> Farmers' Group Member (m), Mbingamharule (*GI 14*; 9/10/2015)

What is adding to this challenge is the fact that, through their low cash reserve, farmers have a hard time to buy input at the right moment, when the prices would be low. As a result of their vulnerable position, with limited reserves and limited market access for inputs in general, prices for inputs tend to rise when they are needed, while prizes for their produce drop when they harvest it. Without any capital or storage facilities to bridge those price fluctuations, the common farmers are stuck:

> "For example, if you want to get fertilizer, you need it this [the right] time, you need seeds, at their time. But, at this time, when we need it, the prices are high, and we have little money. So, that is why for the wananchi, it is very hard to get pembejeo."
> Farmers' Group Member (f), Matetereka C (*GI 9*; 9/3/2015)

Again, data derived from the household questionnaires supports the importance of farm inputs (or lack thereof) for the local understanding of challenges. Yet, while there was a high rate of occurrence for Litowa and Matetereka (22.0 and 19.3 percent of respondents, respectively), the issue was far less mentioned in Mbingamharule, were only 3 out of the 95 respondents included the topic in their response on their challenges in life.

Indeed, the research also provided the possibility to talk about this situation with one of the biggest producers of fertilizer in the country: Yara, a Norwegian-based private fertilizer producer, who operates its Tanzanian headquarters in Dar es Salaam. The visit was facilitated through SNC, who wanted to establish a partnership with Yara in order to provide better access to farm inputs for the NGOs clients on the village level. The company actually is operating a variety of such "development partnerships" throughout the country, which are seen as an opportunity to extend the company's business base in the more remote areas, where there are no large-scale farmers to buy their fertilizers. Indeed, Yara's representative was seeing the lack of reliable cash income of the small-scale farmers as the main reason for their inability to buy his company's products an – by extend – for their lack of economic development. The lack of a reliable market for agricultural produce from these small-scale farmers was cited as the number one issue preventing them from achieving higher incomes and, therefore, increasing their ability to invest in farm inputs. Hence, Yara was increasingly looking into opportunities to cooperate with local NGOs and government institutions to facilitate the sale of fertilizers to rural smallholders. Apart from the issue of the peasants' financial capacities, there would also be a general lack of knowledge in the application of fertilizers, as well as the issue of "fake products" sold by illegitimate resellers in the villages (GBE 14; 3/18/2015).

"with our hands, only"

As even the access to basic farm inputs represents a recurring seasonal struggle for most of the farmers interviewed, there is hardly any possibility for investment in any kind of modern agricultural tools. Virtually all of the farmers from the case study villages are working their fields in the same way as their ancestors did before independence: With the jembe, or hand hoe in English. This makes daily life especially hard:

> "Ok, they are saying life is so difficult. For what they produce, they use the hand hoe, for instance. And through it they don't see any success. They keep on coming down." Members of Kanyanga Twende Group, Litowa. Interpreted by Dennis Mpazagade (GI 1; 8/22/2015)

And with these rudimentary farming techniques, even the most ambitious of farmers' groups do not see any possibility for an extension of their area under cultivation:

> "Another challenge is the power we have. We cannot cultivate three or more acres with only our hands. We don't have a plough with ox, or whatever. No machine of any kind.

So, each person can only cultivate something like one acre, for both the food and the market. That is another challenge."
Member of Umoja Group (f), Litowa (*GI 6; 8/24/2015*)

Interestingly enough, most groups were seeing a tractor or power tiller as a necessity for the expansion of acreage, only few were also seeing the possibility of keeping cattle with the specific aim of using them for ox-plough cultivation:

"Well, the second challenge for us as a group is that there is a lack of machinery, like a tractor or a tiller, so this an issue. So, we only have our own power, that is a general challenge."
Farmers' Group Member (m), Matetereka B (*GI 10; 9/3/2015*)

In any case, lack of capital was cited as the number one reason for the lack of such farm equipment. Furthermore, the groups from Litowa and Matetereka, which were describing the lack of such machinery, were very aware of the fact that their villages owned a tractor and kept some cattle for these purposes at the times of RDA, and lamented the apparent backward turn in village development. Interestingly enough, only in the village of Matetereka did the issue of machinery, or farm tools in general, appear prominently in the questionnaire results, with 10.1% of respondents mentioning the theme. In both other villages, this shortage of equipment was hardly mentioned (three respondents in Mbingamharule, only two in Litowa). This might imply that the lack of machinery might constitute a secondary issue for most peasants and only emerges for those already active in a farmers' group or a more imminent background of widespread cooperative organization (as in the case of Matetereka).

Lack of knowledge and cooperation

Another theme of challenges, which was not directly connected to the lack of market, but contributing to the low productivity in the eyes of the peasants, was the lack of knowledge in the field of agriculture, since they felt that "to get good information on crops is difficult" (Member of Juhudi (2) Group, Litowa; *GI 5; 8/24/2015*). Furthermore, some of the group members were seeing insufficient knowledge on markets and the economy in general as a major challenge for their development:

"I think one of the biggest challenges to development is education. And the knowledge of business. It is hardly taught at school. So, there is a need for better education to go forward."
Member of Tangawizi Group (m), Matetereka A (*GI 7; 9/2/2015*)

Apparently, while many groups identified their own lack of business know-how as a limitation to their possible success, they experienced problems to access this kind of knowledge, as "there is nobody helping with education. There is a challenge of knowledge. On how to do a project, or to develop, to do business, etc. We don't have." (Farmers' Group Member (f), Matetereka C; *GI 9; 9/3/2015*). Some of the group members had the feeling that this lack of education was actually a result of the reduced willingness to cooperate and share knowledge in Tanzania in general:

> "I think, we could have better development, if the ordinary people would contribute their minds, to send what they need, really, we need to contribute in solidarity. In Tanzania, in general, that is dead. Few people are making a lot of profit. All over the country.... We are also losing in Tanzania, and only a very few people are winning. That is bad."
> Farmers' Group Member (m), Mbingamharule (*GI 14*; 9/10/2015)

Overall, the issue of insufficient (cooperative) knowledge was seen as one of the few challenges in development which was not directly related to a lack of money or capital resulting from low productivity and unsatisfactory market access. Yet, in the eyes of the peasants, it contributed to their perceived low productivity and their low economic success – both individually and as a group.

Concerning the questionnaires, the issue of education, in general, did not rank as high in the frequency of mentioning as the aforementioned categories, but was included in quite a few responses in Matetereka (16.5%). Most of those were referring to school quality, however, and a lack of knowledge in farming was rarely cited as a major challenge. In the two other villages, education was hardly mentioned at all.

Other challenges

Regarding other challenges perceived by the peasants of the case study villages, there were apparent differences within the data derived from the questionnaires. While the answers in Matetereka were commonly relatively long and detailed, many respondents in the other two villages simply stated "hardships of life" or "hard life" as their major challenge (22.1% in Mbingamharule and 17.0% in Litowa), an answer hardly occurring in Matetereka. The latter village also was exceptional concerning the high rate of answers including the lack of social services like health care, care for the elderly and the insufficient water supply (37.6% of respondents in Matetereka). Water supply was categorized as a social service, rather than as infrastructure, as many respondents, as well as participants of group discussions included water supply in this manner. The issue of transport (or lack thereof) was also predominantly found at Matetereka (5.5% of respondents, as opposed to 3.2% in Mbingamharule and none at Litowa.), although this issue was also mentioned by Umoja Group in Litowa, as a contributing factor to the problems regarding market access (*GI 6*; 8/24/2015; *GI 5*; 8/24/2015).

Matetereka was also the only village where more than one respondent mentioned changing weather or climate patterns and the resulting decline in the reliability of rainfall as a challenge to daily life. Shortage of employment opportunities was regarded a bigger issue in Litowa and Matetereka (7 and 5 respondents, respectively) than in Mbingamharule, where it was only named once. Mbingamharule was the village with the highest percentage of respondents stating that they faced no challenges or were generally contempt with their life (10.5%), as well as the highest rate of respondents not replying to the question at all (11.6%). Notable one or two time mentions per village included the challenge of incompetent or corrupt leadership from Litowa and Matetereka, the failure of development projects, and, in three cases in Matetereka, also the shortage of land, which was cited as a reason for not being able to obtain an own shamba by these three individuals. Diseases of animals and crop pests were also mentioned in some cases throughout the questionnaires, as they had been by some of the vikundi during the group discussions (Mshikamano Group, Litowa (*GI 4*; 8/24/2015), Umoja Group, Litowa (*GI 6*; 8/24/2015) and Siliki Group, Mbingamharule (*GI 14*; 9/10/2015)).

The issue of electricity received no mentioning by the respondents in Litowa and Mbingamharule, but was stated by one of those from Matetereka, as it had been the case with the vikundi of Matetereka C (*GI 9*; 9/3/2015). Overall, this topic appears to have lower importance to the villagers themselves than it had for the political actors in Ruvuma at the time of research.

Challenges for the Youth

One of the reasons to include two group interviews with young villagers in the field visits was the question of whether there would be specific challenges for the youth in the village environment – as well as the question how they assessed the opportunities for their future within their communities. First of all, both groups shared the main themes of challenges that had been named by the farmers' groups and the respondents of the questionnaires of their villages of Litowa and Matetereka. Indeed, in Litowa the main challenge was seen in farm inputs and tools (*GI 12*; 9/6/2015), while in Matetereka it was capital and funds for getting higher education, or just any kind of development for the village (*GI 8*; 9/2/2015): "I think to reach development, you need hard work... But, without capital, you cannot achieve development" (Member (m) of Semani Youth Group, Matetereka; *GI 8*; 9/2/2015). Yet, in the overall assessment of their situation, both groups agreed that they would face very limited economic perspectives within their villages. When replying to the question whether this would indicate that they might leave their villages to find better opportunities elsewhere, one member of the Matetereka Youth Group explained their rather pragmatic approach to the issue of economically induced migration:

> "So, everybody wants to have a good life. That means the economic situation [you face], is the basic reason when you decide on where to live. Your needs. And that there is the opportunity for development. If this is to be found here, fine. If not, maybe I will go to Songea.... Because the people need certain things, in any place."
> Member (m) of Semani Youth Group, Matetereka (*GI 8*; 9/2/2015)

This was a general idea that was shared by many of his peers. The young farmers of Litowa, as well, were very open on the issue – but also implicated the high price they would have to pay if they decided to leave their village and head for town:

> "Now they are saying, there are those who would prefer to run away from the village. But the concern is: how can they start off? For instance, this says he has this plan, to leave away. But he would have to leave everything, to start a new life in town."
> Young farmers (m) from Litowa: Interpreted by Dennis Mpazagade (*GI 12*; 9/6/2015)

Figure 14: Integrated assessment of challenges to local development

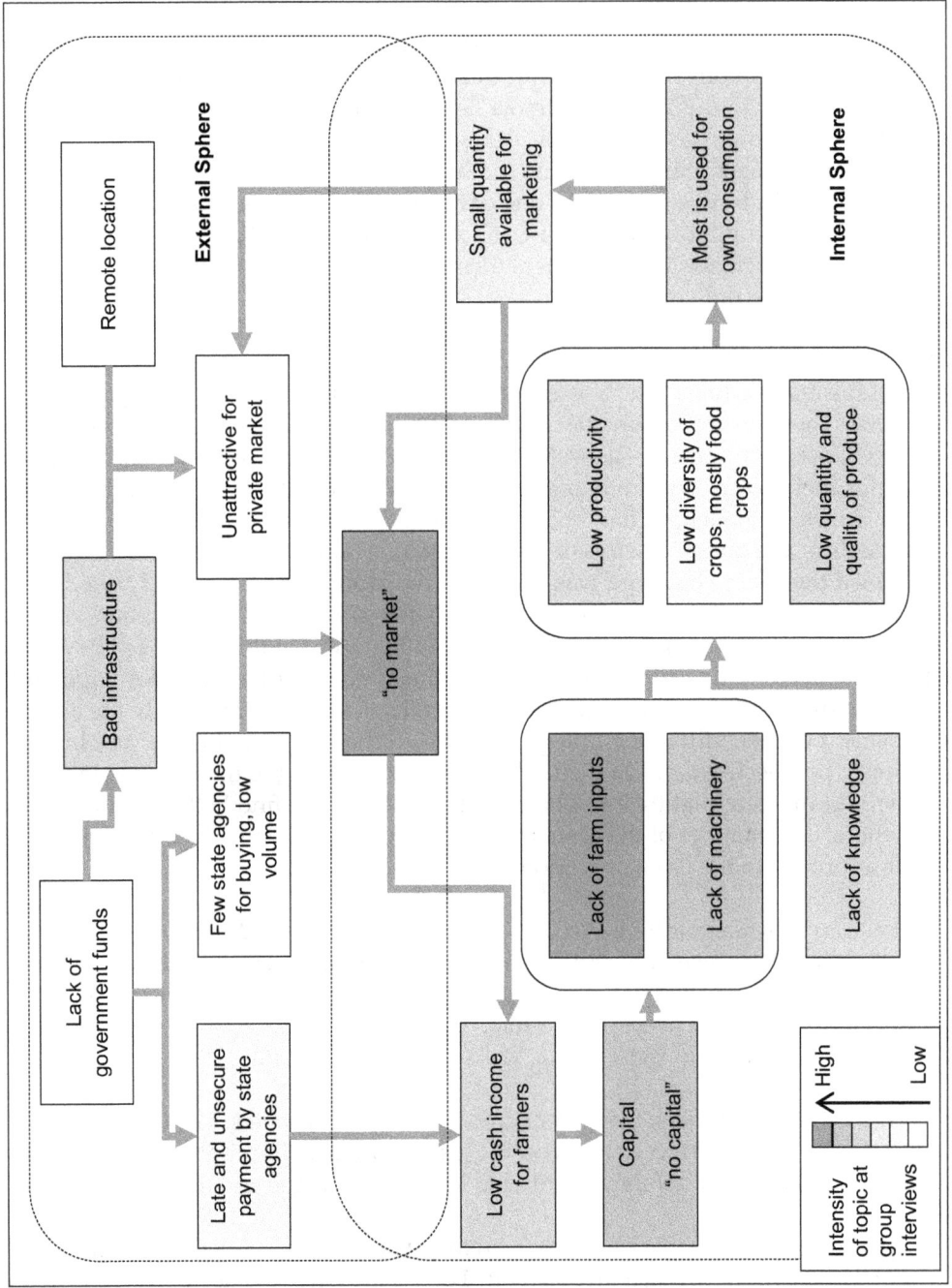

Source: own survey

Integrated assessment of development challenges in Ruvuma

By integrating the challenges to development stated by the different stakeholders from inside and outside the villages, a comprehensive overview was created, which can be seen in Fig. 14. For this illustration, the different challenges were sorted into the "internal sphere", which represents challenges related to agricultural production on the village level, and the "external sphere", which includes challenges that emerge from outside the villages. The central issue, which is that there is "no market" for the peasants' produce was placed in the middle of the illustration, linking both spheres. Indeed, as stated above, the internal challenges can be seen as a vicious circle, in which low income leads to a lack of capital, which in turn leads to a lack of farm inputs and machinery. Because of these shortages, productivity remains low and production remains concentrated on few crops, which are produced in low quantities and unreliable quality. Most of this produce is consumed, so that the remainder is unattractive for the private market, which again leads to low cash income.

Several factors from the "outside sphere" are also contributing to these challenges: The remote location, as well as the bad infrastructure add to the lack of interest from private buyers to engage in the Ruvuma market. Insufficient infrastructure – especially roads – are partly a result of the lack of (central) government funding. This shortage of financial resources of public institutions is also responsible for the shortage of a public market for crops, which could compensate the lack of a private market for the produce of the local peasantry. Furthermore, even those few government agencies that provide a market in Ruvuma (the NFRA, mostly) are suffering from unreliable financial contributions from the government, which in turn leads to late and unreliable payments to the farmers. This is another main factor which leads to their shortage of cash income. The different aspects of this integrated assessment of challenges have been discussed by the local peasantry at different levels of intensity (see above). In order to provide a qualitative illustration of this intensity, different shades of grey have been attributed to the respective topics, with a darker shade implying a higher intensity of discussion.

With regards to the development activities of the different actors approached for this research, it could be said that the vikundi of the case study villages deal with all of the challenges of the internal sphere: Enhancing cash availability through saving and lending schemes, providing mutual advice of agriculture and, in many cases, trying to pool produce in order to access the market together. The introduction of new cash crops has also been one common strategy of those groups (see chapter 6.2.3). Similarly, most NGOs were trying to support or even incept those strategies of farmers' groups and most of their income generating activities aimed at creating a more reliable market to the local peasantry, for instance by organizing market access for a specific crop like soya (see chapter 6.1.2).

6.4 "The smell of Ujamaa is still there" – Aftereffects of the Ujamaa period in the case study area

Following this detailed description of the empirical findings from the field, the next chapters are meant to concretize those findings in the context of the overall research questions of this study. Beginning with the question of what is still remaining from the timers of Ujamaa, this part of the thesis will then continue to discuss the importance of the particular Ujamaa history on the local scale, before addressing the issue of how it affects the local development activities. Last but not least, chapter 6.4.4 will deal with the question of why Ujamaa ended from a local perspective.

6.4.1 What is still there?

Thanks to the results of the empirical research which have been presented above, a clear picture of the different aftereffects of Ujamaa in the case study area has emerged. This enables us to give an overview on what is still there on the ground. First of all, it became clear that none of the original groups, which had founded the first Ujamaa villages in Ruvuma Region in the early 1960s, is still active in its original form. Even the Ujamaa group of Matetereka, which had been described as the last of such groups still active by EDWARDS (1998) in 1998, has finally closed its operations and sold its assets in 2000. There has been no evidence for other Ujamaa groups with continuing operations throughout the research within the case study villages. Furthermore, there are only very few cases of collective agriculture that could be observed during the field visits, and even in those cases, such common cultivation remains limited to relatively small groups of farmers. Even within those groups, all farmers rely on their private fields for subsistence production and any group fields are only used to add additional income to the group members – on top of the production on the private plots -, mostly by cultivating a specific cash crop. In very few cases, there are groups which seem to carry out non-agricultural activities, like building houses together. In neither case, however, is there any form of village wide organization of collective work, nor are there any village shambas left in the case study villages. Taking into account the statements of other stakeholders, like NGOs and regional government, it can be assumed that this is also the case for the rest of the Region. Concerning the aspect of village-wide collective agriculture, Ujamaa therefore appears to be truly over in Ruvuma.

On the other hand, it has also become clear from this study that other elements of Ujamaa still have a considerable effect on the daily life of the villagers in focus. Indeed, the spirit of Ujamaa, and the idea of cooperative development which it entailed, appeared to be very much present at all of the case study sites. The farmers' groups of the present were seen as the heirs of Ujamaa by their members, as well as by other actors, like the village government. There was the omnipresent opinion that this sort of collective development activities was their own new form of Ujamaa. Both the members themselves and the NGOs which supported such groups stated that it was the farmers' own experience in communal work stemming from the times of Ujamaa, which made such group projects much easier to incept. Actually, these remaining ideas of Ujamaa could not only be observed in the former RDA villages of Litowa and Matetereka, but also in Mbingamharule – a village in which, by all available evidence, there has never been any sort of grassroots Ujamaa movement, and where all ideas of Ujamaa had been brought from the outside during villagization.

What is also still there, in all of the villages, is the memory of Ujamaa, which includes a lot of different perceptions by the villagers, depending first of all on the village of residence itself, but also on features like age, gender and field size of the individual. The most detailed local stories of Ujamaa had been shared by the contemporary witnesses, and those narratives also varied between the place of residence. In those villages that had been members of the RDA, the elders were still enthusiastically sharing their stories of a new beginning, and the younger villagers would often regret the fact that the level of development had actually declined since then in their perception.

6.4.2 How important is the Ujamaa history on the local scale?

Nevertheless, it is difficult to arrive at a definite conclusion on the importance of the Ujamaa period in the present-day village environment of Ruvuma. Without a doubt, none of the villages that were visited during the field study would be there in its current form without the development policy of the Ujamaa era: The villages of the RDA had been founded by local peasants, who were inspired by Nyerere's early statements on socialism and nation building, and took their personal conviction to the countryside to start their own interpretation of cooperative development. Their ideas and their success, in turn, inspired Tanzania's first President to change the national development strategy with the Arusha Declaration in 1967 from a centralized idea of modernization through large-scale investment in industry and rural settlement schemes to the concept of Ujamaa villages as the engine for national development. These changes induced the large-scale movement of the peasantry from scattered settlements to nucleated villages during the villagization campaign, and made places like Mbingamharule a village in the first place. While this importance of Ujamaa for the creation of the present-day settlement structure of Tanzania, in general, and Ruvuma, in particular, was once again confirmed by evidence from this research, the importance of the Ujamaa period appears less clear in other aspects.

Since the collection of socio-economic data was not the focus of this study, the question of how the period of Ujamaa and the subsequent changes affected the material wellbeing of individual villagers cannot be answered with absolute certainty. Nevertheless, the qualitative evidence of the different stakeholders' perceptions of the Ujamaa era, as well as the changes after the end of Ujamaa, underlines the perceived importance of Ujamaa, not only for the creation of the different villages, but also for the way in which these stakeholders are trying to develop their villages today.

6.4.3 How does it affect the local activities in development?

Indeed, practically all activities of village development have been connected to the Ujamaa period by the participants of this study in one way or another: For the NGOs in Ruvuma, it was the strong communal thought of the peasantry which, in their perspective, enhanced the effectiveness of their group approach to development. The prevalence of Ujamaa thinking in the villages was therefore mostly seen as an asset to present-day development initiatives and not as an example of backward thinking among their clients. The regional and district government representatives, on the other hand, did not make a clear connection between their own development activities and the Ujamaa history of the area, and were indicating that the idea of cooperative development was somewhat outdated in present-day Tanzania. On the village scale, Ujamaa was seen as an inspiration by practically all of the current farmers' groups, who were seeing themselves as a new form of Ujamaa in most cases. These groups, in turn, were seen as one of the key elements in village development by both the NGOs from the outside and the village governments from the inside.

Furthermore, in the villages of Litowa and Matetereka, the times of Ujamaa were also seen as a period of relatively high development and, therefore, acted as a kind of goal for present-day village development. Even in Mbingamharule, the social achievements of the Ujamaa era were praised by all participants of the research. Nevertheless, in the latter case and in the sub-villages of Matetereka B and C, there was also the common understanding among the farmers' group members that the current situation had significant advantages compared to the times of village-wide Ujamaa organization. They were very keen to underline the importance of individual choice and the sovereignty of their respective groups to decide for themselves, without the intervention of a superior controlling entity like the village government.

6.4.4 Why did Ujamaa end? A local perspective

From the evidence presented in the preceding chapters, it is also possible to add some local perspectives on the question of why Ujamaa ended as a national policy and development strategy in Tanzania. The academic discussion on the national and international perspectives has already been presented in chapter 3. Throughout the field study itself, different perspectives on this issue have emerged for each of the villages. In Mbingamharule, for instance, the question of the end as a national policy was hardly discussed, but in more than one case, participants agreed that the results of communal farming in this village had always been below expectations and work organization for the village shamba was rather seen as a nuisance than as a necessary precondition to village development. Concludingly, respondents from this village did not regret the end of compulsory collective agriculture and saw its termination as the logical consequence of the lack of results they had experienced.

In Litowa, there was a completely different view on the end of Ujamaa, although in most cases, it was not made clear by the respondents if they would refer to the end of the RDA in 1969 or the end of Ujamaa as a national policy in the 1980s. The former event, in any case, appears to have had a greater impact in the memory of the contemporary witnesses and was seen as a very shocking experience. The collective idea of having lost the results of their own work was not only brought forward by those contemporary witnesses, however, but also by members of the farmers' groups and respondents of the questionnaires. Derived from this village narrative of Ujamaa, one can conclude that there was not much development in the village after the end of the RDA, at least in the perception of the villagers themselves. With regards to the reasons for the end of the RDA, there was still a lack of understanding among the contemporary witnesses, although some respondents considered the government's fear to lose control over the peasantry, in general, and the presence of foreigners in the village, in particular, as the main reasons for the end of their organization. The end of Ujamaa as a whole was hardly discussed throughout the field visit in Litowa, although some of the farmers' groups described the difficulties of organizing collective field work on the village level and the village chairman named the continuing drop in motivation to engage in such activities as the reason for the end of collective farming in Litowa.

In comparison to the other villages, the situation in Matetereka appears to be the most complex one. Most participants in this village considered the end of Ujamaa not as something coinciding with the end of the RDA or the end of Nyerere's presidency in 1985, but indeed regarded the end of the original Ujamaa group in 2000 as the end of Ujamaa in that village. Furthermore, key informants like Lukas Mayemba and other members of this original group gave very detailed accounts on the different phases of Ujamaa in the village, as well as their understanding of the reasons for the respective changes. First of all, the end of RDA was seen by the contemporary witnesses as the result of the conflict between different factions inside TANU's Central Committee. The main reason was seen in the behavior of the bureaucrats, who feared both the foreign supporters of RDA and the independence of the peasants, and were therefore challenging Nyerere and his support for the Association. In the end, those bureaucrats won the struggle and were able to destroy the RDA against the will of the President. However, the end of RDA did not mean the end of Ujamaa in the village, as they were able to continue with their organization under the new environment. Even the end of Ujamaa as a national policy could not stop them, in their view.

Yet, what has become evident from this research is that the original Ujamaa group at Matetereka A was never really able to integrate the new villagers, who arrived there during the subsequent period of villagization: While the idealist settlers of Matetereka A were not willing to share the fruits of their labor with the new arrivals, the inhabitants of Matetereka B and C always felt that Ujamaa inside the village was dominated by the interests of those original settlers. These conflicts, which have already been described at length by EDWARDS (1998), could also be observed during field visit for this study. In the end, it seems that there has been an insurmountable gap between the initiators of Matetereka and the majority of the inhabitants of the village, who felt that the founders would share a version of Ujamaa just for themselves, without access for the common villagers. It is reasonable to conclude that this loss of internal support inside the village led to the end of the original Ujamaa group in 2000, and therefore the end of Ujamaa as such.

7 Discussion of findings and implications for the understanding of Ujamaa development

"For the truth is that development means the development of *people*. Roads, buildings, the increase of crop output, and other things of this nature, are not development; they are only tools for development. A new road extends a man's freedom only if he travels upon it. An increase in the number of school buildings is development only if those buildings can be, and are being, used to develop the minds and the understanding of people. An increase in the output of wheat, maize, or beans, is only development only if these things can be sold, and the money used for other things which improve the health, comfort, and understanding of the people."

J.K. Nyerere, *Freedom and Development* (Nyerere 1974a: 26)

With this definitory statement of the late President Nyerere, it is about time to discuss the implications which the empirical findings from the case study sites of Ruvuma have for the wider understanding of the establishment and failure of the Ujamaa development policy in Tanzania, and which lessons might be learned for future attempts to rural development.

On the theoretical side, it has become clear that Nyerere's version of socialist development, in many ways, diverged from the European or Marxist understanding of the term. As it has been shown in chapter 2.2.1, the most basic definition of development in the Marxian sense is a succession of stages of the mode of production. This development is entirely based on humanity's will to forge the resources of nature according to its needs. And as this willpower is shaping the environment of human societies, so is this environment shaping human consciousness and will. Indeed, Ujamaa's concept of history does not deviate much from this historical materialist understanding of human history and human development. However, in contrast to Marx's idea of socialism as the next logical mode of production, following a revolutionary upheaval of the capitalist order which he had analyzed according to the English example, Nyerere imagined African socialism as a social system whose basic elements were deeply rooted within the precolonial past of his continent. In this sense, Ujamaa appeared much less revolutionary than the Marxian version of socialism, especially when it came to the way of establishing it: For Nyerere, socialism was an "attitude of mind", not necessarily a concrete social order of production.

Nevertheless, Ujamaa did ask the question of ownership of the means of production, the question of the appropriate order of state and society, the question of who is controlling the development of a nation, and for whom development is organized. In Nyerere's understanding – as can be seen once again in the citation above – development is synonymous with the development of people. That does not imply, however, that Ujamaa would define development in a non-materialistic way. On the contrary, it did strive for a society of tangible economic development results and their equal distribution among all members of society.

The second pillar of the Ujamaa ideology can be seen in its determination to turn the political independence of the country into economic self-reliance. In this respect, Nyerere's thoughts are closer to Lenin's theory of imperialism than his commitment to non-alignment and his outspoken dissociation to the socialist block of the cold war era might indicate. Indeed, his thinking agreed with the most common idea of imperialist theory, i.e. that the colonization of Africa was driven by capitalism's need for expansion and that this exploitative relation between the global metropolis and the periphery would continue unabated, if the Nations of Africa would not find their own way of non-capitalist development. Indeed, the fear of foreign influence became even more pronounced in the decade following independence and would influence several policies that tried to get all development projects within Tanzania under central control.

As it has been shown throughout chapter 3, however, the concrete development of Ujamaa's ideology and practical implementation was not at all only influenced by the thinking of Nyerere and the actions of the Tanzanian state. From the eve of independence, small grassroots movements, led by politicized farmers, were trying to follow the President's call to build the nation. This thesis has attempted to analyze one of these movements in particular: The Ruvuma Development Association. As much as Nyerere, these young members of TANU Youth League were driven by both their attitude of mind and their wish for a better material future for themselves and their families. Without a lot of resources and further theoretical elaboration, their ad-hoc version of socialist cooperative villages became the true inspiration for Ujamaa's development strategy: Self-organized and self-reliant settlements, based on collective agriculture and participatory, basic-democratic decision making. Many of Nyerere's post-1962 writings implicitly or explicitly refer to this model of development, which was pioneered by these farmers.

During a unique window of opportunity, the fruition of Ujamaa as Tanzania's national ideology was made possible by the coexistence of western capitalism, soviet-style communism and European social-democratic welfare states, and last but not least by the victory of national liberation movements all over Africa. In this international environment, no one was willing to stop the implementation of Nyerere's brand of socialism – on the contrary it received ample support from all sides. The bold statements of the President inspired the creation of the RDA – and the newly gained national independence meant that no old, colonial authority could stop those idealistic farmers to go to the bush and build their own vision for the future. Furthermore, Nyerere's early statements on African socialism attracted support from valuable experts, who were looking for a genuinely new way of development – experts like Ralph Ibbott.

Vice-versa, the success of the RDA, in both political organization and material development enabled Nyerere to refine his broad concept of Ujamaa and to convince the reluctant bureaucratic cadres of TANU to refrain from the classical modernization strategy of the early independence era, in order to embark on a new way of organizing national development: The Arusha Declaration was as much an acknowledgement of the economic restraints Tanzania was facing with its low financial capacities, as it was an appraisal of the success of the RDA's strategy. From then on, the model of the small farmers of Ruvuma was supposed to become the model of the nation. In many ways, the years between 1967 and 1969 were the decisive ones for the fate of Ujamaa.

Yet, in this moment, in which both the national ideology and the successful example set on local scale appeared to converge into the new development strategy of Tanzania, the bureaucratic and centralist notions of the developmental state took control. They took control in the form of a threatened party hierarchy and colonially educated administrators, who feared that these farmers would take their seats in parliament and party. They took over in the form of the fear of foreign influence and foreign agents, who would instigate those small-scale farmers. And they took over in the form of a central state, which conceived itself as a benevolent patron, who had to develop those ignorant and backward peasants – not enable them to continue with their own version of development.

In theory, Ujamaa tried to give freedom and development to the people by enabling them to share. The RDA and its villages embodied and shaped that concept for a short moment, as long as it was allowed to do so. The abolishment of the RDA smashed back any form of agency and empowerment the people had gained. It denied them of their own achievements and moved control back to the central state. On this basis, the "new" centralized version of Ujamaa was doomed to produce passive recipients of a state patron, rather than active citizens working for the development of their country. The farmers of Ruvuma had worked hard for their own community, but after 1969, the community they lived in was not theirs any more: The tractors were gone, the school was closed and the mill in Songea expropriated. After the RDA, the TANU (and later CCM) elite in Dodoma and Dar es Salaam was never able to create a movement even remotely similar to the RDA or other grassroots collectives, not because people wouldn't work for each other, but because they wouldn't work for the others.

If the history of the RDA demonstrates anything, then it is that a socialist idea of collective development has to be based on local initiative and communal ownership – not only in a legal, but also in a sociological sense. A short moment in history gave the peasants of Litowa and Matetereka the chance to take complete control on their own development. The idealistic concept of Ujamaa framed by Nyerere for the development of their newly independent country gave them the spirit of idealism. At the same time, it presented the legal possibility to go to the uncultivated bush of Ruvuma to create their own villages out of nothing. Based on their own understanding of how life should be led and work should be organized – collectively. At the right time, they got the support of solidary organizations with the only means they needed on top of their hard work and their idealism: Access to capital and technical advice, provided by Western NGOs and true idealists like Ralph Ibbott.

Geographically, Ruvuma was remote enough and its infrastructure poor enough to shed those small blooming seeds of socialism from the influence of a bureaucratic bourgeoisie, and the benevolent eyes of Mwalimu Nyerere provided additional coverage. Only when their model, tested more or less by chance by the founders of the RDA, was so successful that the President wanted to make it a national model, when the peasants themselves achieved a state of class consciousness through which they could very well have gained enough knowledge and support to take over the positions of power in postcolonial Tanzania – and some were indeed already members of the Central Committee of the party -, only then the RDA became a real threat to the bureaucratic bourgeoisie.

This class of bureaucrats were in no mood to give up the positions of power they had controlled since independence. Fair enough: Nyerere could hold socialist speeches all day long, as long as those peasants, he so dearly appealed to in the struggle for national development and self-reliance, knew their place in society and worked happily for the advancement of the country – which apparently was not identical with their own advancement, in the eyes of the TANU apparatus. Peasants working by themselves, for themselves and controlled by themselves – that was the true spirit of Ujamaa. And had the RDA not been abandoned by fearful technocrats in the center, the periphery might have continued to develop itself and eventually would have stopped to be the periphery.

That did not happen though: The abolishment of the RDA and all similar organizations in 1969 put agency and power firmly back to the center. From then on, Ujamaa would be a venture of this center to develop the periphery, not a self-controlled effort by the periphery and its people. This approach eventually failed in every way imaginable: The forced movement of millions of peasants during villagization, the supply crisis of 1974-76 and the slow death of collectivism and Ujamaa itself afterwards may – to an outstanding proportion – very well be attributed to this seizure of control by the central bureaucracy.

At the end of the 1970s, the central developmental state, which so firmly had taken control over the development of the peasantry, was itself made inviable through the changing international environment. As the internal economic difficulties increased, Tanzania ran out of options to gain support from any other block than the West – and had to give in to the new leading idea of a small state and an open market economy: The age of neoliberalism had arrived. Under these new circumstances, political structures were liberalized, and ongoing decentralization technically put more power back into the hands of the local farmers. However, if they had once lacked the political power to challenge the central bureaucracy, they now lack the capital and the market access to actually have control over their own development. Or, to put it in NYERERE's (1974a: 26) words again: "A new road extends a man's freedom only if he travels upon it".

As this study has shown, the history of Ujamaa in Tanzania was thoroughly influenced by the interaction between the local and the national scale. During the empirical phase of the research, valuable insights on the local perception of this history could be gathered. First of all, the narratives of the various contemporary witnesses of the Ujamaa era in Ruvuma shed new light on their motivation to engage in this particular form of cooperative development. In fact, it was a combination of both idealist spirit and concrete material benefits, which made these individual farmers join the movement that would become the RDA. Indeed, this was true for the original settlers, which were interviewed at Matetereka, as well as for contemporary witnesses from Litowa and Liweta, who had joined these villages shortly after their inception. On the site of non-RDA villages, only the wazee of Namatuhi stated a strong level of skepticism against this new movement. In Mbingamharule, even the times of centrally organized villagization were evaluated as having some positive effects for village life. However, only in Matetereka, there have been farmers who would continue with their own version of Ujamaa after the end of the RDA. In Litowa, shock and incomprehension were still very vividly felt by those contemporary witnesses – and while all of the stakeholders approached in "Tanzania's first Ujamaa village" were still praising the achievements of those times, no organization of their own survived the end of the Association, let alone the end of the Ujamaa policy in Tanzania.

What has remained, apart from this pride, was called by the present-day farmers' groups "the smell of Ujamaa" – the collective memory of cooperative local development and the general idea that, in working together, every individual is better off in the end. In fact, this sort of spirit could be observed in all of the vikundi in the three case study villages of Litowa, Matetereka and Mbingamharule, and it was also underlined by many of the different NGOs approached in this research. With regards to motivating people to join a collective effort and organize common activities, the particular local history was seen as a big asset by all of the stakeholders involved. Nevertheless, just like during the formative period of the RDA, intrinsic motivation has to be followed up by tangible results. Otherwise many of these groups will not survive their own anniversary.

Indeed, it have been the farmers' groups, which carried the spirit of Ujamaa in the most concrete way. On the other hand, their members' accounts also provided an insight into the general issues of cooperative development: Save for the remaining idealist village founders of Matetereka A, all of them preferred the small extent of their operation, because it granted them with a more direct control over their activities and the fruits of their labor than it had been the case in the times of village-wide collective farming. Especially in Matetereka, the accounts made by vikundi members, as well as by the respondents of the village questionnaires, underlined the issues of cooperative development even on the village scale: The politicized leaders of the original Ujamaa group were able to continue their activities after the end of the RDA, but they were never able to integrate the majority of new inhabitants arriving during villagization into this system. Therefore, even without the external influence of a strong central state, their model of development was bound to fail, eventually.

This lesson, just as much as the negative perception of compulsory collective work from Mbingamharule, and the decline of Litowa after the RDA, lead to the conclusion, that the basic principle of Ujamaa as a basic-democratic approach to cooperative village development is working only if all of the individuals involved perceive to have full direct control over their contribution and can make sense of the necessity of group activities. Neither a central state directive, nor the leadership of convinced local socialists can replace their own commitment towards a common project. That this lack of conviction is not the result of a general opposition to any kind of group engagement has been demonstrated by the vikundi members of Matetereka C and Mbingamharule.

Even given the aforementioned reservations concerning the practical implementation of Ujamaa in the respective villages, the overall assessment of this period remained mostly positive, at least according to the results of the village questionnaires. However, there have been significant differences between the villages, as well as between categories like age, gender, and the farm size of the recipient. Overall, the contingency between an individual's opinion on Ujamaa and his or her place of living was higher than the one between the opinion and any other of the categories. The observed tendency of individuals with bigger field sizes to have a more positive opinion on Ujamaa may imply the need for further study regarding the material results of this era and its perception by the farmers.

Regarding the perception and the definition of development as such, the term was most commonly defined as a succession of steps, illustrated by material possessions and economic progress. From that perspective, the development status of the case study villages was mostly perceived as lacking many basic requirements and the speed of development as being too slow. In some cases, especially in Litowa and Matetereka, the status of development was actually seen as regressing after the end of Ujamaa. In all three case study villages, cooperation, hard work and group activities were seen as one possible way of improving this situation.

So, while all of the results from the case studies and the additional interviews do imply that "the smell of Ujamaa" is still there – in Ruvuma at least – the findings also indicate that the smallholders of the Region face severe challenges under the current economic environment of Tanzania. While in the times of Ujamaa, the central state was taking away the control over their own development, it is now their lack of capital, which impedes even the most ambitious of farmers' groups to make big steps in their economic development. This lack of capital is seen as the result of a lack of income, which in turn is attributed to the lack of market access for their produce. Additional factors, like the lack of inputs and the lack of machinery, which limit the productivity of agriculture, are also perceived to be a result of the lack of cash income. In fact, the multitude of farmers' groups in all of the case study villages can be seen as a manifestation of the developmental spirit of their inhabitants, who are seeking for concrete ways to overcome these limitations and escape this vicious circle of stagnating development in their villages.

8 Conclusions

Overall, the analysis of Ujamaa's ideological development has shown considerable interlinkages between Nyerere's idea of national development and its interpretation by local small-scale farmers within the case study area. Indeed, for a short period of time throughout the 1960s, there appears to have been a very fruitful interaction between this local model of community development and the conceptualization of the Ujamaa idea on the national scale. This model was not based on an isolationist idea of completely self-reliant villages, without connections to the outside world, but was thriving on inter-village cooperation and financial and ideological support from both the national and international level. However, due to the prevalence of bureaucratic and centralist notions within the positions of power in postcolonial Tanzania, and the general fear of external influence, the move to implement this model all over the country after the Arusha Declaration was bound to fail, as it took control away from the small-scale farmers and tried to align any sort of development initiative under the supremacy of the central state and its ruling party.

Yet, even if the policy of *Ujamaa vijijini* has failed to reproduce this sort of local initiative embodied by the villages of the RDA, and its internal and external contradictions made the whole development model inviable from the 1980s onwards, there is still much to be learned from those days, and still some remainders to be build on. "The smell of Ujamaa" is still there, and vividly represented by the communal spirit of the current farmers' group members of those villages. If their challenges regarding market access and lack of capital for investment are addressed, there is a high potential for cooperative development, still sleeping within these communities. In the perceptions of the stakeholders of this research, their lesson from the times of Ujamaa is clear: We can achieve development for ourselves if we work together and have direct control on our activities – if we are given the necessary assets.

The strong and positive perception of local stakeholders towards Ujamaa and cooperative development, in general, has been exemplified by the various farmers' groups interviewed during this research. While there is already considerable development initiative based on their motivation to work together, and several international and national NGOs are trying to improve the material situation of Ruvuma's small-scale farmers based on this group approach, the insights into the assessment of the development situation by the villagers, and the vicious circle of challenges to economic progress, are also illustrating the need for a bigger involvement of the international development community into these inspiring local initiatives. It has become clear throughout this study that the developmental spirit and the eagerness of the common villagers to take the resources of their own cooperative history and turn them into a better future for themselves and their families cannot create sustainable development without the access to markets and capital.

With the continuing growth of both population and regional economic disparities after the end of the Ujamaa period in Tanzania, it is also necessary to take the voices of the youth seriously, who have stated that their first and foremost desire is to pursue a life that offers them economic opportunities and tangible progress. It is about time, then, to increase the support for the developmental spirit embodied by the vikundi of Ruvuma and nourish it by material endorsement. Otherwise, their villages will continue to be places of stagnation and frustration, and the only option for their future residents might be to move to more prosperous regions – within Tanzania or abroad.

Nevertheless, this explorative study in the villages of Litowa, Matetereka and Mbingamharule has shown that, even if there are not many things remaining from the times of Ujamaa on the first look – no cars, no tractors, no buildings other than deteriorating ruins -, there is still a lot of cooperative spirit left to build on – as well as the pride of those villagers, who still know that they once were the role model for the whole nation. Of course, the limited area of case studies for this thesis means that its results cannot be transferred to other parts of Tanzania, or even Ruvuma, without consideration. However, as there are still many contemporary witnesses of the Ujamaa period – and the subsequent changes – alive all over the country, there is still a lot of more stories to be heard, more narratives to be written down and more perceptions to be learned from. And, since the development of Ujamaa has been a particularly differentiated affair in different areas of the country, there might be plenty of valuable insights to be gathered into the opportunities and challenges of cooperative rural development in general. Just as the late Julius K. NYERERE once said:

> "Different are the lives of modern Africans from those of our grandparents, still we and our ancestors are linked together indissolubly. Our present day attitudes and reactions cannot be properly understood without reference to the economy, social organization, and religious basis of the society of fifty years ago; and so on back through time." (NYERERE 1968c: 81)

It is the conviction of the author of this study that these words hold truth until today, and that it is upon us, who are searching for new answers to the challenges of future human development, to seek for these lessons of the past. Therefore, it would be a worthwhile task for forthcoming research, to take this inquiry on the history of Ujamaa to other villages and other regions of Tanzania, and to find out if there, as well, are still small-scale farmers who share the idea that "in unity, there is strength".

Bibliography

ABRAHAM, P., ROBINSON, F. (1974): *Rural development in Tanzania* (Studies in employment and rural development, 14). Washington, DC.

AMIN, S. (2015): "Long Road to Socialism". In: Soyinka, W., Amin, S., Selassie, B. H., Mugo, M. G., Mkandawire, T. (Ed.): *Reimagining Pan-Africanism. Distinguished Mwalimu Nyerere Lecture Series 2009-2013.* Dar es Salaam, 55–111.

ARONSON, J. (1995): "A Pragmatic View of Thematic Analysis". In: *The Qualitative Report* 2 (1), 1-3.

BAKULA, B. B. (1971): "The Effect of Traditionalism on Rural Development: The Omurunazi Ujamaa Village, Bukoba". In: Proctor, J. H. (Ed.): *Building Ujamaa Villages in Tanzania* (University of Dar es Salaam Studies in Political Science, 2). Dar es Salaam, 15–32.

BALDUS, R. D. (1976): *Zur operationalen Effizienz der Ujamaa Kooperative Tansanias* (Marburger Schriften zum Genossenschaftswesen, Reihe B / Band 13). Göttingen.

BARAN, P. A., SWEEZY, P. M. (1968): *Monopoly capital. An essay on the American economic and social order* (Modern reader paperbacks, PB-73). New York.

BEBBINGTON, A. (2005): "Global networks and local developments: Agendas for development geography". In: Nijenhuis, G., Broekhuis, A., van Westen, G. (Ed.): *Space and place in development geography. Geographical perspectives on development in the 21st century.* Amsterdam, 15–30.

BENSON, J. S. (2001): "The impact of privatization on access in Tanzania". In: *Social Science & Medicine* 52 (12), 1903–1915.

BERGOLD, J., THOMAS, S. (2012): "Participatory Research Methods: A Methodological Approach in Motion". In: *Forum: Qualitative Sozialforschung / Forum: Qualitative Social Research* 13 (1), Art. 30.

BERNSTEIN, H. (1981): "Concepts for the Analysis of Contemporary Peasantries". In: Galli, R. (Ed.): *The Political economy of rural development. Peasants, international capital, and the state: case studies in Colombia, Mexico, Tanzania, and Bangladesh.* Albany, 3–24.

BHENGU, M. J. (2011): *African Economic Humanism. The Rise of an African Economic Philosophy.* Aldershot.

BIENEN, H. (1972): "An Ideology for Africa". In: Cliffe, L., Saul, J. S. (Ed.): *Socialism in Tanzania. Volume 1: Politics.* Dar es Salaam, 178–179.

BJERK, P. K. (2010): "Sovereignity and Socialism in Tanzania: The Historiography of an African State". In: *History in Africa* 37, 275–319.

BLAUT, J. M. (1977): "The Theory of Development". In: Peet, R. (Ed.): *Radical geography. Alternative viewpoints on contemporary social issues.* Chicago, 309–314.

BOESEN, J., STORGAARD MADSEN, B., MOODY, T. (1977): *Ujamaa – Socialism from Above.* Uppsala.

BRAIN, J. L. (1977): "Is Transformation Possible? Styles of Settlement in Post-Independence Tanzania". In: *African Affairs* 76 (303), 231–245.

BRIGGS, J. (1979): "Villagisation and the 1974–6 Economic Crisis in Tanzania". In: *The Journal of Modern African Studies* 17 (04), 695.

BRYCESON, D. F. (2010): "Agrarian Fundamentalism or Foresight? Revisiting Nyerere's Vision for Rural Tanzania". In: Havnevik, K., Isinika, A. C. (Ed.): *Tanzania in Transition: From Nyerere to Mkapa*. Dar es Salaam, 71–98.

BUGENGO, J., MUTANGIRA, J. P. B., RWELENGERA, J. B. K. (1976): *The Nyarubanja System and Ujamaa Villages Development in West Lake Region* (Economic Research Bureau (E.R.B.) Paper, 76.1). Dar es Salaam.

BUNTZEL, R. (1976): *Entwicklung kleinbäuerlicher Exportproduktion in Tansania. Zur Entwicklung der Unterentwicklung und zur Agrarpolitik des Ujamaa-Ansatzes* (Sozialökonomische Schriften zur Agrarentwicklung, 15). Saarbrücken.

BUTZMANN, E., PAESLER, F., JOB, H. (2008): „Tansania – Von der deutschen Kolonie zum tropischen Ferienparadies". In: Brogiato, H. P. (Ed.): *Meyers Universum. Zum 150. Geburtstag des Leipziger Verlegers und Geographen Hans Meyer (1858-1929)*. Leipzig, 51–66.

CABRAL, A. (1968): „Grundlagen und Ziele der nationalen Befreiung in Bezug auf die Sozialstruktur". In: Cabral, A. (Ed.): *Die Theorie als Waffe. Der revolutionäre Befreiungskampf in den portugiesischen Kolonien Afrikas* (Kleine Revolutionäre Bibliothek, 4). Berlin, 16–40.

CABRAL, A. (1970): *National Liberation and Culture* (The Program of Eastern African Studies. Occasional Paper, 57). Syracuse, NY.

CARDOSO, F. H. (1982): "Dependency and Development in Latin America". In: Alavi, H., Shanin, T. (Ed.): *Introduction to the Sociology of "Developing Societies"*. London, 112–127.

CEDILLO, V. G. (1973): *Rural Development through Ujamaa – A Tanzania Case Report* (Vienna Institute for Development. Occassional Paper, 73/11). Vienna.

CHAMBERS, R. (1981): "Rapid rural appraisal: Rationale and repertoire.". In: *Public Administration and Development* 1 (2), 95–106.

CHAMBERS, R. (1992): *Rural Appraisal: Rapid, Relaxed and Participatory* (IDS Discussion Paper, 311). Brighton.

CHAMBERS, R. (2007a): *From PRA to PLA and Pluralism: Practice and Theory* (IDS Working Paper, 286). Brighton.

CHAMBERS, R. (2007b): *Participatory Workshops: A Sourcebook of 21 Sets of Ideas and Activities*. London.

CHAMBERS, R. (2008): *Revolutions in Development Inquiry*. London.

CHAMBERS, R., CONWAY, G. R. (1992): *Sustainable rural livelihoods: practical concepts for the 21st century* (IDS Discussion Paper, 296). Sussex.

CHANT, S., MCILWAINE, C. (2009): *Geographies of Development in the 21st Century. An Introduction to the Global South*. Cheltenham.

CLIFFE, L. (1965): "Tanzania: Myth and Reality". In: *Current History* 48 (284), 219–223.

CLIFFE, L. (1967a): "The Impact of the Elections". In: Cliffe, L. (Ed.): *Selections from One Party Democracy. The 1965 Tanzania General Elections*. Nairobi, 88–115.

CLIFFE, L. (1967b): "The Political System". In: Cliffe, L. (Ed.): *Selections from One Party Democracy. The 1965 Tanzania General Elections*. Nairobi, 1–17.

CLIFFE, L. (1971): "Tanzania – Socialist Transformation and Party Development". In: *African Review* 1 (1), 119–135.

CLIFFE, L. (1972): "Democracy in a One-Party State: The Tanzanian Experience". In: Cliffe, L., Saul, J. S. (Ed.): *Socialism in Tanzania. Volume 1: Politics*. Dar es Salaam, 241–247.

COHEN, R. (1972): "Class in Africa: Analytical Problems and Perspectives". In: *Socialist Register 1972* (9), 231–255.

COLLIER, P., RADWAN, S., WANGWE, S. (1986): *Labour and Poverty in Rural Tanzania. Ujamaa and Rural Development in the United Republic of Tanzania*. Oxford.

CORNWALL, A., MUSYOKI, S., PRATT, G. (2001): *In Search of a New Impetus: Practitioners Reflections on PRA and Participation in Kenya* (IDS Working Paper, 131). Brighton.

COULSON, A. (1976): "Who Controls Tanzania's Economy. An Outline Political Economy of Tanzania". In: Karl, M. (Ed.): *Ujamaa and Self-Reliance: Building Socialism in Tanzania* (The Future of the Missionary Enterprise, 19). Rome, 20–27.

COULSON, A. (1982): *Tanzania. A political economy*. Oxford.

DARAJA, A. W. M. (1971): "The Tanzanian Pattern of Rural Development: Some Administrative Problems". In: Proctor, J. H. (Ed.): *Building Ujamaa Villages in Tanzania* (University of Dar es Salaam Studies in Political Science, 2). Dar es Salaam, 48–54.

DARLING, F. (2016): "Outsider Indigenous Research: Dancing the Tightrope Between Etic and Emic Perspectives". In: *Forum: Qualitative Sozialforschung / Forum: Qualitative Social Research* 17 (3), Art. 6.

DATOO, B. A. (1977): "Peasant Agricultural Production in East Africa: The Nature and Consequences of Dependence". In: *Antipode* 9 (1), 70–78.

DICKENSON, J., GOULD, B., CLARKE, C., MATHER, S., PROTHERO, M., SIDDLE, D., SMITH, C., THOMAS-HOPE, E. (1995): *A Geography of the Third World. Second Edition*. London, New York.

DONNER-REICHLE, C. (1988): *Ujamaadörfer in Tansania. Politik und Reaktionen der Bäuerinnen*. (Arbeiten aus dem Institut für Afrika-Kunde, 58). Hamburg.

DOS SANTOS, T. (1970): „The Structure of Dependence". In: *The American Economic Review* 60 (2), 231–236.

ECKERT, A. (2007): *Herrschen und Verwalten. Afrikanische Bürokraten, staatliche Ordnung und Politik in Tanzania, 1920-1970* (Studien zur Internationalen Geschichte, 16). Munich.

EDWARDS, D. M. (1998): *Matetereka: Tanzania's last Ujamaa Village* (Occasional Papers-Edinburgh University. Centre of African Studies, 77). Edinburgh.

EDWARDS, D. M. (2003): *Settlement, livelihoods and identity in Southern Tanzania: A comparative history of the Ngoni and Ndendeuli*. Edinburgh.

ELLMAN, A. O. (1970): *Progress, Problems and Prospects in Ujamaa Development in Tanzania* (Economic Research Bureau (E.R.B.) Paper, 70.18). Dar es Salaam.

ENGELHARD, K. (1994): *Tansania* (Perthes-Länderprofile). Gotha.

ENTRALGO, A. (1986): *De Berlin a las independencias: antecedentes, desenvolvimento y limites de lo particular africano* (Enfoques (CEAMO), 9). Havanna.

ERGAS, Z. (1980): "Why Did the Ujamaa Village Policy Fail? – Towards a Global Analysis". In: *The Journal of Modern African Studies* 18 (3), 387–410.

FAN, S., NYANGE, D., RAO, N. (2005): *Public investment and poverty reduction in Tanzania: Evidence from household survey data* (DSGD Discussion Paper, No. 18). Washington, DC.

FANON, F. (1966): *Die Verdammten dieser Erde*. Frankfurt am Main.

FANON, F. (1972): *Für eine afrikanische Revolution. Politische Schrifften*. Frankfurt am Main.

FLINT, C., SHELLEY, F. M. (1996): "Structure, Agency, and Context. The Contributions of Geography to World-Systems Analysis". In: *Sociological Inquiry* 66 (4), 496–508.

FOUÉRÉ, M.-A. (2014): "Julius Nyerere, Ujamaa, and Political Morality in Contemporary Tanzania". In: *African Studies Review* 57 (01), 1–24.

FRANK, A. G. (1966): "The development of underdevelopment". In: *Monthly Review* 18, 17–31.

FRANK, A. G. (1979): *Dependent accumulation and underdevelopment*. New York.

FREYHOLD, K. von (1975): "The Role of Agricultural Extension in Ujamaa Village Development". In: Hänsel, H., De Vries, J., Ndeya, P. C. (Ed.): *Agricultural Extension in Ujamaa Village Development. Papers and Proceedings of a Workshop*. Dar es Salaam, 84–93.

FREYHOLD, M. v. (1979): *Ujamaa Villages in Tanzania*. New York.

FRIESE, S. (2011): "Using ATLAS.ti for Analyzing the Financial Crisis Data". In: *Forum: Qualitative Sozialforschung / Forum: Qualitative Social Research* 12 (1), Art. 39.

FURTADO, C. (1968): *The economic growth of Brazil. A survey from colonial to modern times*. Berkeley.

GAMA, L. M. (1989): *Die Rolle der Partei bei der Umgestaltung auf dem Lande in Tansania. Erfahrungen der Ruvuma-Region*. Berlin.

GONDWE, Z. S. (1986): "Agricultural policy in Tanzania at the crossroads". In: *Land Use Policy* 3 (1), 31–36.

HARVEY, D. (1998): "The Geography of Class Power". In: *Socialist Register* 1998 (34), 49–74.

HAVNEVIK, K. (2010): "Postscript: Transition in Tanzania – Summary and Trends 2005-2010". In: Havnevik, K., Isinika, A. C. (Ed.): *Tanzania in Transition: From Nyerere to Mkapa*. Dar es Salaam, 265–277.

HEDLUND, S., LUNDAHL, M. (1989): *Ideology as a Determinant of Economic Systems: Nyerere and Ujamaa in Tanzania* (The Scandinavian Institute for African Studies. Research Report, 84). Uppsala.

HEGEL, G. W. F. (2013a): *Grundlinien der Philosophie des Rechts*. Berlin.

HEGEL, G. W. F. (2013b): *Phänomenologie des Geistes*. Berlin.

HEGEL, G. W. F. (2013c): *Vorlesungen über die Geschichte der Philosophie. Erster Teil*. Berlin.

HEGEL, G. W. F. (2014): *Enzyklopädie der philosophischen Wissenschaften im Grundrisse*. Berlin.

HEWITT, T. (1999): "Institutional tensions and private sector promotion in Tanzania: whose agenda?". In: *Technovation* 19 (6–7), 383–391.

HILFERDING, R. (1955): *Das Finanzkapital. Eine Studie über die jüngste Entwicklung des Kapitalismus*. Berlin.

HIRJI, K. F. (1976): "Tanu Youth League". In: Karl, M. (Ed.): *Ujamaa and Self-Reliance: Building Socialism in Tanzania* (The Future of the Missionary Enterprise, 19). Rome, 41–48.

HIRJI, K. F. (1982): "The "Marxism-Leninism" of Professor D. Wadada Nabudere". In: Tandon, Y. (Ed.): *The Debate. Debate on Class, State & Imperialism*. Dar es Salaam, 68–76.

HOBSON, J. A. (1902): *Imperialism. A Study*. New York.

HUIZER, G. (1973): "The Ujamaa Village Program in Tanzania: New Forms of Rural Development". In: *Studies in Comparative International Development* 8 (2), 183–207.

HYDÉN, G. (1980): *Beyond Ujamaa in Tanzania. Underdevelopment and an Uncaptured Peasantry*. London.

HYDÉN, G., KARLSTROM, B. (1993): "Structural adjustment as a policy process: The case of Tanzania". In: *World Development* 21 (9), 1395–1404.

IBBOTT, R. (1969): *The disbanding of the Ruvuna Development Association, Tanzania*. Dar es Salaam.

IBBOTT, R. (1970): *History of the Ruvuma Development Association, Tanzania*. Dar es Salaam.

IBBOTT, R. (2014): *Ujamaa. The hidden story of Tanzania's socialist villages*. London.

IBBOTT, R., MILLINGA, N. (1964a): *Ruvuma Development Association Tanganyika – Newsletter, March 1964*. Ed. by Ruvuma Development Association. Songea.

IBBOTT, R., MILLINGA, N. (1964b): *Ruvuma Development Association Tanganyika – Newsletter, September 1964*. Ed. by Ruvuma Development Association. Songea.

IBBOTT, R., MILLINGA, N. (1964c): *Ruvuma Development Association Tanzania – Newsletter, December 1964*. Ed. by Ruvuma Development Association. Songea.

IBBOTT, R., MILLINGA, N. (1965a): *Ruvuma Development Association Tanzania – Newsletter, June 1965*. Ed. by Ruvuma Development Association. Songea.

IBBOTT, R., MILLINGA, N. (1965b): *Ruvuma Development Association Tanzania – Newsletter, March 1965*. Ed. by Ruvuma Development Association. Songea.

IBBOTT, R., MILLINGA, N. (1966): *Ruvuma Development Association Tanzania – Newsletter, March 1966*. Ed. by Ruvuma Development Association. Songea.

IBHAWOH, B., DIBUA, J. I. (2003): "Deconstructing Ujamaa: The Legacy of Julius Nyerere in the Quest for Social and Economic Development in Africa". In: *African Journal of Political Science* 8 (1), 59–83.

ILIFFE, J. (1969a): *Tanganyika under German Rule. 1905-1912*. London.

ILIFFE, J. (1969b): "The Age of Improvement and Differentiation (1907-1945)". In: Kimambo, I. M., Temu, A. J. (Ed.): *A History of Tanzania*. Nairobi, 123–160.

INSTITUT FÜR SOZIALFORSCHUNG (IfS) (Ed.) (1970): *Transformation oder Mobilisierung als Anreiz zur Veränderung der Produktionsweisen am Beispiel von „Settlements" und „Ujamaa-Dörfern" in Tansania*. Frankfurt am Main.

INTERVIEW WITH E. NDONDE (1975): "Litowa". In: Cliffe, L., Lawrence, P., Luttrell, W. L., Migot-Adhola, S. E., Saul, J. S. (Ed.): *Rural Cooperation in Tanzania*. Dar es Salaam, 360–369.

JENNINGS, M. (2002): "'Almost an Oxfam in Itself': Oxfam, Ujamaa and Development in Tanzania". In: *African Affairs* 101 (405), 509–530.

JENNINGS, M. (2003): "'We Must Run while Others Walk': Popular Participation and Development Crisis in Tanzania, 1961-9". In: *The Journal of Modern African Studies* 41 (2), 163–187.

JENNINGS, M. (2007): "'A Very Real War': Popular Participation in Development in Tanzania During the 1950s". In: *The International Journal of African Historical Studies* 40 (1), 71–95.

JENNINGS, M. (2008): *Surrogates of the State. NGOs, Development and Ujamaa in Tanzania*. Bloomfield.

JOB, H. (2017): „Ostafrika als touristische Destination". In: Eberth, A., Kaiser, A. (Ed.): *Ostafrika*. Darmstadt, 126–142.

JOB, H., METZLER, D. (2003): „Tourismusentwicklung und Toursimuspolitik in Ostafrika". In: *Geographische Rundschau* 55 (7/8), 10-17.

JOB, H., WEIZENEGGER, S. (2003): „Tourismus in Entwicklungsländern". In: Becker, C., Hopfinger, H., Steinecke, A. (Ed.): *Geographie der Freizeit und des Tourismus: Bilanz und Ausblick*. Munich, 629–640.

JUMA, R. S. (1976): "Ujamaa Development in Tanzania". In: Karl, M. (Ed.): *Ujamaa and Self-Reliance: Building Socialism in Tanzania* (The Future of the Missionary Enterprise, 19). Rome, 36–37.

KAMAT, V. (2008): "This Is Not Our Culture! Discourse of Nostalgia and Narratives of Health Concerns in Post-Socialist Tanzania". In: *Africa: Journal of the International African Institute* 78 (3), 359–383.

KANIKI, M. H. Y. (1974): "TANU: The Party of Independence and National Consolidation". In: Ruhumbika, G. (Ed.): *Towards Ujamaa. Twenty Years of TANU Leadership*. Dar es Salaam, 1–30.

KAUTSKY, K. (1914): „Der Imperialismus". In: *Die Neue Zeit* 32-II (21), 908–922.

KOPOKA, P. A. (2002): "Health Service Delivery in Tanzania in the 21st Century". In: Mbelle, A. V., Mjema, G. D., Kilindo, A. A. (Ed.): *The Nyerere Legacy and Economic Policy Making in Tanzania*. Dar es Salaam, 193–211.

KOPONEN, J. (1995): *Development for Exploitation. German colonial policies in Mainland Tanzania, 1884-1914*. Helsinki, Hamburg.

KUMAR, S. (2002): *Methods for Community Participation. A Complete Guide for Practitioners*. Bourton on Dunsmore.

KÜRSCHNER, F. (1975): „Das Konzept der Ujamaa-Dörfer: Eine Kritische Bestandsaufnahme". In: *Africa Spectrum* 10 (3), 245–262.

LAL, P. (2012): "Self-Reliance and the State: The Multiple Meanings of Development in early Post-Colonial Tanzania". In: *Africa* 82 (02), 212–234.

LAL, P. (2015): *African socialism in postcolonial Tanzania. Between the village and the world*. New York.

LAURIEN, I. (1995): "'That Homa Homa was worse, child!' Berichte afrikanischer Zeitzeugen über den Maji-Maji Aufstand in Deutsch-Ostafrika". In: Heine, P., van der Heyden, U. (Ed.): *Studien zur Geschichte des deutschen Kolonialismus in Afrika. Festschrift zum 60. Geburtstag von Peter Sebald*. Pfaffenweiler, 350–367.

LAWI, Y. Q. (2007): "Tanzania's Operation Vijiji and Local Ecological Consciousness: The Case of Eastern Iraqwland, 1974-1976". In: *The Journal of African History* 48 (1), 69–93.

LENIN, W. I. (1971): „Kleinbürgerlicher und Proletarischer Sozialismus". In: Lenin, W. I. (Ed.): *Werke, Band 9*. Berlin, 441–449.

LENIN, W. I. (1972): „Der Imperialismus als höchstes Stadium des Kapitalismus. Gemeinverständlicher Abriß". In: Lenin, W. I. (Ed.): *Werke, Band 22*. Berlin, 189–309.

LETT, J. (1990): "Emics and etics: Notes on the epistemology of anthropology". In: Headland, T. N., Pike, K. L., Harris, M. (Ed.): *Emics and etics: The insider/outsider debate*. Thousand Oaks, CA, 127–144.

LEVINE, K. (1972): "The TANU ten-house cell system". In: Cliffe, L., Saul, J. S. (Ed.): *Socialism in Tanzania. Volume 1: Politics*. Dar es Salaam, 329–337.

LEWIN, R. (1973): "Matetereka". In: Cliffe, L., Saul, J. S. (Ed.): *Socialism in Tanzania. Volume 2: Policies*. Dar es Salaam, 189–194.

LEYARO, V., MORRISEY, O., OWENS, T. (2010): *Food Price Changes and Consumer Welfare in Tanzania 1991-2007* (CREDIT Research Paper, 10/01). Nottingham.

LIMBU, F. L., MASHINDANO, O. J. (2002): "Agricultural Sector and Poverty in Tanzania". In: Mbelle, A. V., Mjema, G. D., Kilindo, A. A. (Ed.): *The Nyerere Legacy and Economic Policy Making in Tanzania*. Dar es Salaam, 41–71.

LINDNER, K. (2011): „Eurozentrismus bei Marx". In: Bonefeld, W., Heinrich, M. (Ed.): *Kapital & Kritik. Nach der "neuen" Marx-Lektüre*. Hamburg, 93–129.

LOFCHIE, M. F. (1978): "Agrarian Crisis and Economic Liberalisation in Tanzania". In: *The Journal for Modern African Studies* 16 (3), 451–475.

LOPES, C. (1988): "The erosion of a socialist ideal in African national movements". In: Lopes, C., Rudenbeck, L. (Ed.): *The socialist ideal in Africa: A debate* (The Scandinavian Institute for African Studies. Research Report, 81). Uppsala, 7–19.

LUXEMBURG, R. (1921): *Die Akkumulation des Kapitals. Ein Beitrag zur ökonomischen Erklärung des Imperialismus*. Leipzig.

LYIMO, F. F. (2012): *Rural Coopertation in the Cooperative Movement in Tanzania*. Dar es Salaam.

MABELE, R. B. (1975): "Extension Programme Development and Agricultural Production Planning". In: Hänsel, H., De Vries, J., Ndeya, P. C. (Ed.): *Agricultural Extension in Ujamaa Village Development. Papers and Proceedings of a Workshop*. Dar es Salaam, 107–132.

MAGHIMBI, S. (1995): "The conflict between the state and grassroots-based institutions in Tanzania's rural development". In: Forster, P. G., Maghimbi, S. (Ed.): *The Tanzanian Peasantry: Further Studies*. Aldershot, 37–50.

MAIR, S. (1996): *Politischer Wandel in Ostafrika. Kenia, Tansania und Uganda auf dem Weg zur Demokratie?* Ebenhausen.

MALEMA, B. A. (2006): *Soya Bean Production and Utilization in Tanzania*. Dar es Salaam.

MAMDANI, M., BHAGAT, H. (1982): "A Critique of Issa Shivji's Book Class Struggles in Tanzania". In: Tandon, Y. (Ed.): *The Debate. Debate on Class, State & Imperialism*. Dar es Salaam, 36–40.

MAPOLU, H. (1973): *The Social and Economic Organisation of Ujamaa Villages*. Dar es Salaam.

MARX, K. (1960a): „Die britische Herrschaft in Indien". In: Marx, K., Engels, F. (Ed.): *Werke, Band 9. MEW 9*. Berlin, 127–133.

Marx, K. (1960b): „Die künftigen Ergebnisse der britischen Herrschaft in Indien". In: Marx, K., Engels, F. (Ed.): *Werke, Band 9. MEW 9*. Berlin, 220–226.

Marx, K. (1964): „Zur Kritik der Hegelschen Rechtsphilosophie. Einleitung". In: Marx, K., Engels, F. (Ed.): *Werke, Band 1. MEW 1*. Berlin, 378–391.

Marx, K. (1972a): „Das Kapital. Kritik der politischen Ökonomie. Dritter Band". In: Marx, K., Engels, F. (Ed.): *Werke, Band 25. MEW 25*. Berlin, 32–919.

Marx, K. (1972b): „Das Kapital. Kritik der politischen Ökonomie. Erster Band". In: Marx, K., Engels, F. (Ed.): *Werke, Band 23. MEW 23*. Berlin, 49–802.

Marx, K. (1972c): „Das Kapital. Kritik der politischen Ökonomie. Zweiter Band". In: Marx, K., Engels, F. (Ed.): *Werke, Band 24. MEW 24*. Berlin, 31–518.

Marx, K. (1982): „Grundrisse der Kritik der politischen Ökonomie". In: Marx, K., Engels, F. (Ed.): *Werke, Band 42. MEW 42*. Berlin, 19–875.

Marx, K., Engels, F. (1960a): „Manifest der Kommunistischen Partei". In: Marx, K., Engels, F. (Ed.): *Werke, Band 4. MEW 4*. Berlin, 459–493.

Marx, K., Engels, F. (Ed.) (1960b): *Werke, Band 9. MEW 9*. Berlin.

Marx, K., Engels, F. (1962): „Die deutsche Ideologie. Kritik der neuesten deutschen Philosophie in ihren Repräsentanten Feuerbach, B. Bauer und Stirner, und des deutschen Sozialismus in seinen verschiedenen Propheten". In: Marx, K., Engels, F. (Ed.): *Werke, Band 3. MEW 3*. Berlin, 9–530.

Massaro, R. J. (1998): "The Political Economy of Spatial Rationalization and Integration Policies in Tanzania". In: Silberfein, M. (Ed.): *Rural settlement structure and African development*. Boulder, CO, 273–307.

Mayring, P. (2000): „Qualitative Inhaltsanalyse". In: *Forum: Qualitative Sozialforschung / Forum: Qualitative Social Research* 1 (2), Art. 20.

Mayring, P. (2010): *Qualitative Inhaltsanalyse. Grundlagen und Techniken*. Weinheim, Basel.

Mbelle, A. V., Kilindo, A. A., Mjema, G. D. (2002a): "Poverty and the Nyerere Legacy". In: Mbelle, A. V., Mjema, G. D., Kilindo, A. A. (Ed.): *The Nyerere Legacy and Economic Policy Making in Tanzania*. Dar es Salaam, 11–22.

Mbelle, A. V., Mjema, G. D., Kilindo, A. A. (Ed.) (2002b): *The Nyerere Legacy and Economic Policy Making in Tanzania*. Dar es Salaam.

Mboya, T. (1963): "African Socialism". In: *Transition* (8), 17–19.

Mboya, T. (1972): "Tensions in African Development. Address at Conference on Tensions in Development New College, Oxford, 1961". In: Mboya, T. (Ed.): *The Challenge of Nationhood. A Collection of Speeches and Writings*. London, 23–33.

McHenry, D. E. (1979): *Tanzania's ujamaa villages. The implementation of a rural development strategy* (Research series – Institute of International Studies, University of California, Berkeley, no. 39). Berkeley.

Meier Kruker, V., Rauh, J. (2005): *Arbeitsmethoden der Humangeographie*. Darmstadt.

Meyns, P. (1977): *Nationale Unabhängigkeit und ländliche Entwicklung in der 3. Welt. Das Beispiel Tansania*. Berlin.

Meyns, P. (1982): "Tanzania – The Struggle for National Independence and Socialism. Comments on Issa Shivji's essay "Tanzania: The Class Struggle Continues"". In: Tandon, Y. (Ed.): *The Debate. Debate on Class, State & Imperialism*. Dar es Salaam, 16–35.

MISHILI, F. J., TEMU, A. A., FULTON, J., LOWENBERG-DeBOER, J. (2009): *Consumer Preferences as Drivers of Common Bean Trade in Tanzania: A Marketing Perspective*. West Lafayette.

MOHAN, J. (1966): "Varieties of African Socialism". In: *Socialist Register* 1966 (3), 220–266.

MOHIDDIN, A. (1972): "Ujamaa na Kujitegemea". In: Cliffe, L., Saul, J. S. (Ed.): *Socialism in Tanzania. Volume 1: Politics*. Dar es Salaam, 165–177.

MORSE, Y. L. (2013): "Party matters. The institutional origins of competitive hegemony in Tanzania". In: *Democratization* 21 (4), 655–677.

MPANGALA, G. P. (2004): "Transition to Democracy in Tanzania". In: Mushi, S. S., Mukandala, R., Yahya-Othman, S. (Ed.): *Democracy and Social Transformation in East Africa*, 3–15.

MUELLER, S. D. (1980): "Retarded Capitalism in Tanzania". In: *Socialist Register* 1980 (17), 203–226.

MUSHI, S. S. (2004): "Tanzania's Political Culture". In: Mushi, S. S., Mukandala, R., Yahya-Othman, S. (Ed.): *Democracy and Social Transformation in East Africa*, 45–57.

MUSTAFA, K. (1990): "The Pastoralist Question". In: O'Neill, N., Mustafa, K. (Ed.): *Capitalism, socialism and the development crisis in Tanzania*. Aldershot, Brookfield, VT, 101–124.

MUSTI DE GENNARO, B. (1981): "Ujamaa: The Aggrandizement of the State". In: Galli, R. (Ed.): *The Political economy of rural development. Peasants, international capital, and the state: case studies in Colombia, Mexico, Tanzania, and Bangladesh*. Albany, 111–155.

NABUDERE, D. W. (1982): "Imperialism, State, Class and Race. A Critique of Issa Shivji's Class Struggles in Tanzania". In: Tandon, Y. (Ed.): *The Debate. Debate on Class, State & Imperialism*. Dar es Salaam, 55–67.

NATIONAL BUREAU OF STATISTICS (NBS) (Ed.) (2012): *Population Distribution of Tanzania Regions by District, Ward and Village/Mtaa*. Unpublished.

NELLIS, J. R. (1972): *A Theory of Ideology. The Tanzanian Example*. Nairobi.

NGAIZA, R. S. (2012): *Kilimo Kwanza. The Declaration of Tanzania's Agricultural Transformation* (FAO-University of Nairobi -Regional Workshop on an Integrated Policy Approach to Commercializing Smallholder Maize Production. Nairobi, 6/6/2012). URL: http://www.tanzania.go.tz/egov_uploads/documents/Kilimo_Kwanza_Tanzania_en.pdf (Date of last Retrieval: 2/15/2017).

NGEZE, P. B. N. M. (1975): "On Staff Constraints in Planning - A Comment". In: Hänsel, H., De Vries, J., Ndeya, P. C. (Ed.): *Agricultural Extension in Ujamaa Village Development. Papers and Proceedings of a Workshop*. Dar es Salaam, 133–139.

NKRUMAH, K. (1963): *Africa Must Unite*. New York.

NKRUMAH, K. (1965): *Neo-Colonialism, the Last Stage of Imperialism*. London.

NURSEY-BRAY, P. F. (1980): "Tanzania: The Development Debate". In: *African Affairs* 79 (314), 55–78.

NYERERE, J. K. (1962a): *The Second Scramble*. Dar es Salaam.

NYERERE, J. K. (1962b): *Ujamaa. The Basis of African Socialism*. Dar es Salaam.

NYERERE, J. K. (1967a): *Education for Self-Reliance*. Dar es Salaam.

NYERERE, J. K. (1967b): *The Arusha Declaration*. Dar es Salaam.

NYERERE, J. K. (1968a): "After the Arusha Declaration. Presidential Address to the TANU National Conference, 17 October 1967". In: Nyerere, J. K. (Ed.): *Ujamaa. Essays on Socialism*. Dar es Salaam, 145–177.

NYERERE, J. K. (1968b): "Agriculture is the Basis of Development". In: Nyerere, J. K. (Ed.): *Freedom and Socialism. Uhuru na Ujamaa*. Dar es Salaam, 104–106.

NYERERE, J. K. (1968c): "Congress on African History". In: Nyerere, J. K. (Ed.): *Freedom and Socialism. Uhuru na Ujamaa*. Dar es Salaam, 80–85.

NYERERE, J. K. (Ed.) (1968d): *Freedom and Socialism. Uhuru na Ujamaa*. Dar es Salaam.

NYERERE, J. K. (1968e): "Progress in the Rural Areas". In: Nyerere, J. K. (Ed.): *Ujamaa. Essays on Socialism*. Dar es Salaam, 178–186.

NYERERE, J. K. (1968f): "Socialism and Rural Development". In: Nyerere, J. K. (Ed.): *Ujamaa. Essays on Socialism*. Dar es Salaam, 106–144.

NYERERE, J. K. (1968g): "The Purpose is Man". In: Nyerere, J. K. (Ed.): *Ujamaa. Essays on Socialism*. Dar es Salaam, 90–105.

NYERERE, J. K. (1968h): "The Varied Paths to Socialism". In: Nyerere, J. K. (Ed.): *Ujamaa. Essays on Socialism*. Dar es Salaam, 76–90.

NYERERE, J. K. (1970): *Non-alignment in the 1970s*. Dar es Salaam.

NYERERE, J. K. (1974a): "Freedom and Development". In: Nyerere, J. K. (Ed.): *Man and Development*. Dar es Salaam, 25–41.

NYERERE, J. K. (1974b): "The Church and Society". In: Nyerere, J. K. (Ed.): *Man and Development*. Dar es Salaam, 82–101.

NYERERE, J. K. (1974c): "The Rational Choice". In: Nyerere, J. K. (Ed.): *Man and Development*. Dar es Salaam, 111–125.

NYERERE, J. K. (1975): "Presidential Circular No. 1 of 1969". In: Cliffe, L., Lawrence, P., Luttrell, W. L., Migot-Adhola, S. E., Saul, J. S. (Ed.): *Rural Cooperation in Tanzania*. Dar es Salaam, 27–34.

NYERERE, J. K. (1977a): *The Arusha Declaration. Ten Years After*. Dar es Salaam.

NYERERE, J. K. (1977b): *The Plea of the Poor*. Dar es Salaam.

NYERERE, J. K. (1978): *Tanzania Rejects Western Domination of Africa*. Dar es Salaam.

OBIOHA, U. P. (2014): "Radical Communitarian Idea of the Human Person in African Philosophical Thought: A Critique". In: *The Western Journal of Black Studies* 38 (1), 13–23.

OKOKO, K. A. B. (1987): *Socialism and self-reliance in Tanzania*. London, New York.

OLIECH, K. C. (1975): "Comprehensive, Integrated Village Planning and the Role of Adult Education – A Comment". In: Hänsel, H., De Vries, J., Ndeya, P. C. (Ed.): *Agricultural Extension in Ujamaa Village Development. Papers and Proceedings of a Workshop*. Dar es Salaam, 142–150.

O'NEILL, N., MUSTAFA, K. (Ed.) (1990): *Capitalism, socialism and the development crisis in Tanzania*. Aldershot, Brookfield, VT.

OWEN, R. (1817): "Essay First". In: Owen, R. (Ed.): *A New View of Society. Or Essays on the Principle of the Formation of the Human Character, Preparatory to the Development of a Plan for Gradually Ameliorating the Condition of Mankind*. London, 15–30.

PAESLER, F. (2015): *Regionalentwicklung und Mensch-Umwelt-Interaktion. Zwei Fallbeispiele aus Kenia und der Demokratischen Republik Kongo* (Würzburger Geographische Arbeiten, 113). Würzburg.

PEET, R., HARTWICK, E. (2009): *Theories of Development. Contentions, Arguments, Alternatives.* London.

PESEK, M. (2005): *Koloniale Herrschaft in Deutsch-Ostafrika. Expeditionen, Militär und Verwaltung seit 1880.* Frankfurt am Main.

PONTE, S. (2000): "From Social Negotiation to Contract: Shifting Strategies of Farm Labor Recruitment in Tanzania Under Market Liberalization". In: *World Development* 28 (6), 1017–1030.

PONTI, M. (2012): "Uncovering Causality in Narratives of Collaboration: Actor-Network Theory and Event Structure Analysis". In: *Forum: Qualitative Sozialforschung / Forum: Qualitative Social Research* 13 (1), Art. 11.

PRATT, C. (1978): *The Critical Phase in Tanzania. 1945-1968. Nyerere and the emergence of a socialist strategy.* Nairobi.

PREWITT, K., HYDÉN, G. (1967): "Voters Look at the Elections". In: Cliffe, L. (Ed.): *Selections from One Party Democracy. The 1965 Tanzania General Elections.* Nairobi, 67–87.

PUTTERMAN, L. (1985): "Extrinsic versus Intrinsic Problems of Agricultural Cooperation: Anti-incentivism in Tanzania and China.". In: *Journal of Development Studies* 21 (2), 175–204.

PUTTERMAN, L. (1986): *Peasants, Collectives, and Choice. Economic Theory and Tanzania's Villages* (Contemporary Studies in Economic and Financial Analysis, 57). Greenwich, CO, London.

PUTTERMAN, L. (1995): "Economic reform and smallholder agriculture in Tanzania: A discussion of recent market liberalization, road rehabilitation, and technology dissemination efforts". In: *World Development* 23 (2), 311–326.

RAIKES, P. L. (1975): "Ujamaa and Rural Socialism". In: *Review of African Political Economy* (3), 33–52.

RAUCH, T., ALFF, U. (1997): „Jenseits von Ujamaa-Sozialismus und neoliberaler Strukturanpassungspolitik: Entwurf einer neuen Strategie der ländlichen Entwicklung in Tanzania". In: *Africa Spectrum* 32 (2), 151–172.

REUBER, P. (2012): *Politische Geographie.* Paderborn.

ROBERT, D., SHENHAV, S. (2014): "Fundamental Assumptions in Narrative Analysis: Mapping the Field". In: *The Qualitative Report* 19 (38), 1–17.

ROBERTS, B. (2004): "Political Activism and Narrative Analysis: The Biographical Template and the Meat Pot". In: *Forum: Qualitative Sozialforschung / Forum: Qualitative Social Research* 5 (3), Art. 10.

RODNEY, W. (1972): "Tanzanian Ujamaa and Scientific Socialism". In: *African Review* 1 (4), 61–76.

RODNEY, W. (2012): *How Europe underdeveloped Africa.* Cape Town.

RODNEY, W., BOTCHWERY, K. (1976): "Why the first Development Decade failed in Tanzania. The African Development Experience of the Sixties". In: Karl, M. (Ed.): *Ujamaa and Self-Reliance: Building Socialism in Tanzania* (The Future of the Missionary Enterprise, 19). Rome, 30–34.

Ronner, E., Baijukya, F. P., Giller, K. E. (2013): *Opportunities for N2Africa in Tanzania*. Ed. by N2Africa. URL: http://www.n2africa.org/sites/n2africa.org/files/images/images/N2Africa_Opportunities%20for%20N2Africa%20in%20Tanzania.pdf (Date of last Retrieval: 4/15/2017).

Ronner, E., Giller, K. E. (2013): *Background information on agronomy, farming systems and ongoing projects on grain legumes in Tanzania*. Ed. by N2Africa. URL: http://www.n2africa.org/sites/n2africa.org/files/N2Africa_Characterization%20Tanzania%20final.pdf (Date of last Retrieval: 4/15/2017).

Rostow, W. W. (1956): "The Take-Off Into Self-Sustained Growth". In: *The Economic Journal* 66 (261), 25–48.

Rostow, W. W. (1959): "The Stages of Economic Growth". In: *The Economic History Review* 12 (1), 1–16.

Rostow, W. W. (1971): *The stages of economic growth. A non-communist manifesto*. Cambridge, UK.

Rudenbeck, L. (1988): "Erosion – and conditions of regeneration. Comments on Carlos Lopes' text". In: Lopes, C., Rudenbeck, L. (Ed.): *The socialist ideal in Africa: A debate* (The Scandinavian Institute for African Studies. Research Report, 81). Uppsala, 21–25.

Rugumamu, S. M. (1997): *Lethal aid. The illusion of socialism and self-reliance in Tanzania*. Trenton, NJ.

Rweyemamu, J. F. (1973): *Underdevelopment and industrialization in Tanzania. A study of perverse capitalist industrial development*. Nairobi, New York.

Samoff, J. (1981): "Crises and Socialism in Tanzania". In: *The Journal of Modern African Studies* 19 (02), 279.

Santos, M. (1974): "Geography, Marxism and Underdevelopment". In: *Antipode* 6 (3), 1–9.

Saul, J. S. (1972a): "Background to the Tanzania Election 1970". In: Cliffe, L., Saul, J. S. (Ed.): *Socialism in Tanzania. Volume 1: Politics*. Dar es Salaam, 277–299.

Saul, J. S. (1972b): "Class and Penetration in Tanzania". In: Cliffe, L., Saul, J. S. (Ed.): *Socialism in Tanzania. Volume 1: Politics*. Dar es Salaam, 118–126.

Saul, J. S. (1972c): "Nyerere on Socialism: a review". In: Cliffe, L., Saul, J. S. (Ed.): *Socialism in Tanzania. Volume 1: Politics*. Dar es Salaam, 180–182.

Saul, J. S. (1973a): "Radicalism and the Hill". In: Cliffe, L., Saul, J. S. (Ed.): *Socialism in Tanzania. Volume 2: Policies*. Dar es Salaam, 289–292.

Saul, J. S. (1973b): "Who is the Immediate Enemy?". In: Cliffe, L., Saul, J. S. (Ed.): *Socialism in Tanzania. Volume 2: Policies*. Dar es Salaam, 354–358.

Saul, J. S. (1974): "The State in Post-Colonial Societies: Tanzania". In: *Socialist Register* 1974 (11), 349–372.

Saul, J. S., Woods, R. (1969): "African Peasantries". In: Council for the Social Sciences in East Africa (Ed.): *Annual Social Science Conference 1969 – Proceedings Volume 3. University of Dar Es Salaam 8.-12.12.1969*. Dar es Salaam, 1250–1257.

Schicho, W. (2009): „Ujamaa: Sozialismus und/oder Entwicklung". In: Becker, J., Weissenbacher, R. (Ed.): *Sozialismen. Entwicklungsmodelle von Lenin bis Nyerere* (Historische Sozialkunde/internationale Entwicklung, 28). Vienna, 175–188.

SCHMID, L., JOB, H. (2011): "‚Serengeti darf nicht sterben!' – 50 Jahre integriertes Nationalparkmanagement in Tansania". In: *Natur und Landschaft* 86 (2), 52–58.

SCHMIED, D. (1989): *Subsistence cultivation, market production, and agricultural development in Ruvuma Region, Southern Tanzania* (Bayreuth African studies series, 15). Bayreuth.

SCHNEIDER, L. (2004): "Freedom and Unfreedom in Rural Development: Julius Nyerere, Ujamaa Vijijini, and Villagization". In: *Canadian Journal of African Studies* 38 (2), 344–392.

SCHNEIDER, L. (2014): *Government of Development. Peasants and Politicians in Postcolonial Tanzania*. Bloomington, Indianapolis.

SCHOLZ, F. (2004): *Geographische Entwicklungsforschung. Methoden und Theorien*. Berlin, Stuttgart.

SCHÖNBORN, M. (1973): *Die Entwicklung Tansanias zum Einparteienstaat* (ifo Forschungsberichte der Afrika-Studienstelle, 44). Munich.

SCHULTHEIS, M. J., SESHAMANI, L. (1982): *Rural Development and Incentives: A Comperative Study of Village Development in the Southern Highland Regions of Tanzania*. Dar es Salaam.

SCHUMPETER, J. A. (1919): *Zur Soziologie der Imperialismen*. Tübingen.

SEMBOJA, J., THERKILDSEN, O. (1994): "Decentralization, participation and spatial equity in rural tanzania: A comment". In: *World Development* 22 (5), 807–810.

SHERIDAN, M. T. (2004): "The Environmental Consequences of Independence and Socialism in North Pare, Tanzania, 1961-88". In: *The Journal of African History* 45 (1), 81–102.

SHITUNDU, J. (2002): "Industrialisation and the Nyerere Legacy". In: Mbelle, A. V., Mjema, G. D., Kilindo, A. A. (Ed.): *The Nyerere Legacy and Economic Policy Making in Tanzania*. Dar es Salaam, 134–149.

SHIVJI, I. G. (1973): "Tanzania – The Silent Class Struggle". In: Cliffe, L., Saul, J. S. (Ed.): *Socialism in Tanzania. Volume 2: Policies*. Dar es Salaam, 304–330.

SHIVJI, I. G. (1976): *Class Struggles in Tanzania*. Dar es Salaam.

SHIVJI, I. G. (1982): "The State in the Dominated Social Formations of Africa: Some Theoretical Issues". In: Tandon, Y. (Ed.): *The Debate. Debate on Class, State & Imperialism*. Dar es Salaam, 172–181.

SHIVJI, I. G. (1998): *Not yet democracy. Reforming land tenure in Tanzania*. Dar es Salaam.

SHIVJI, I. G. (2006): *Let the people speak. Tanzania down the road to neo-liberalism* (Codesria book series). Dakar.

SHIVJI, I. G. (2009): *Where is Uhuru? Reflections on the Struggle for Democracy in Africa*. Dar es Salaam.

SIPPEL, H. (1995): „Recht und Herrschaft in kolonialer Frühzeit: Die Rechtsverhältnisse in den Schutzgebieten der Deutsch-Ostafrikanischen Gesellschaft (1885-1890)". In: Heine, P., van der Heyden, U. (Ed.): *Studien zur Geschichte des deutschen Kolonialismus in Afrika. Festschrift zum 60. Geburtstag von Peter Sebald*. Pfaffenweiler, 466–493.

SKARSTEIN, R. (2010): „Smallholder Agriculture in Tanzania: Can Economic Liberalisation Keep its Promises". In: Havnevik, K., Isinika, A. C. (Ed.): *Tanzania in Transition: From Nyerere to Mkapa*. Dar es Salaam, 99–130.

Smith, C. D. (1989): *Did Colonialism Capture the Peasantry? A Case Study of Kagera District, Tanzania* (The Scandinavian Institute for African Studies. Research Report, 83). Uppsala.

Songea District Council (SDC) (Ed.) (2012): *Mpango wa Matumizi Bora ya Ardhi wa Kijiji cha Mbingamhalule kata ya Mbingamhalule Tarafa ya Muhukuru*. Songea.

Songea District Council (SDC) (Ed.) (2013): *Songea District Council Profile*. Songea.

Southern Agricultural Growth Corridor of Tanzania (SAGCOT) (Ed.) (2015): *What is SAGCOT?* URL: http://www.sagcot.com/who-we-are/what-is-sagcot/ (Date of last Retrieval: 2/16/2017).

Soya ni Pesa Project (SnP) (Ed.) (2015): *Newsletter. November 2015. Issue 4*. Dar es Salaam.

Soya ni Pesa Project (SnP) (Ed.) (2017): *Overview*. URL: http://soyanipesaproject intanzania.weebly.com/ (Date of last Retrieval: 2/10/2017).

Spalding, N. (1996): "The Tanzanian Peasant and Ujamaa: A Study in Contradictions". In: *Third World Quarterly* 17 (1), 89–108.

Sunkel, O. (1972): "Big Business and "Dependencia". A Latin American View". In: *Foreign Affairs* 50 (3), 517–531.

Tandon, Y. (Ed.) (1982a): *The Debate. Debate on Class, State & Imperialism*. Dar es Salaam.

Tandon, Y. (1982b): "Who is the Ruling Class in the Semi-Colony?". In: Tandon, Y. (Ed.): *The Debate. Debate on Class, State & Imperialism*. Dar es Salaam, 50–54.

Tanzanian Markets-PAN (Ed.) (2013): *Assessment of Adherence to Recommended Weights and Measures in Grain Value Chain and Implication on Transaction Costs* (Policy Brief, 2-ENG/ 2013). URL: https://agriknowledge.org/downloads/6108vb31r (Date of last Retrieval: 1/8/2017).

Taylor, P. J. (2003): "Radical Political Geographies". In: Agnew, J., Mitchell, K., Toal, G. (Ed.): *A Companion to Political Geography* (Blackwell Companions to Geography, 3). Malden, MA, 47–58.

Tellis, W. M. (1997): "Application of a Case Study Methodology". In: *The Qualitative Report* 3 (3), 1-19.

Tetzlaff, R. (1970): *Koloniale Entwicklung und Ausbeutung. Wirtschafts- und Sozialgeschichte Deutsch-Ostafrikas 1885-1914* (Schriften zur Wirtschafts- und Sozialgeschichte, 17). Berlin.

The Presidential Commission on the Establishment of a Democratic One Party State (Presidential Commission) (Ed.) (1967): "Extracts from the Presidential Commission Report". In: Cliffe, L. (Ed.): *Selections from One Party Democracy. The 1965 Tanzania General Elections*. Nairobi, 116–143.

The United Republic of Tanzania (URT) (Ed.) (1997a): *Ruvuma Region Socio-Economic Profile*. Dar es Salaam.

The United Republic of Tanzania (URT) (Ed.) (1997b): *The Regional Administration Act, 1997*. Dar es Salaam.

The United Republic of Tanzania (URT) (Ed.) (1999): *The Tanzania Development Vision 2025*. Dar es Salaam.

The United Republic of Tanzania (URT) (Ed.) (2005a): *Agricultural Sector Development Programme (ASDP). Support through Basket Fund*. Dar es Salaam.

THE UNITED REPUBLIC OF TANZANIA (URT) (Ed.) (2005b): *The Cooperative Reform and Modernization Program. 2005-2015*. Dar es Salaam.

THE UNITED REPUBLIC OF TANZANIA (URT) (Ed.) (2006): *Kilimo Bora cha Zao la Soya. Idara ya Maendeleo ya Mazao. Sehemu ya Uendelezaji wa Mazao*. Morogoro.

THE UNITED REPUBLIC OF TANZANIA (URT) (Ed.) (2008): *Agricultural Marketing Policy*. Dar es Salaam.

THE UNITED REPUBLIC OF TANZANIA (URT) (Ed.) (2011a): *Tanzania Bread-Basket Transformation Project. A Pilot Programs for the Kilombero and Southern Highland Regions*. Dar es Salaam.

THE UNITED REPUBLIC OF TANZANIA (URT) (Ed.) (2011b): *The Tanzania Five Year Development Plan 2011/12-2015/16. Unleashing Tanzania´s Latent Growth Potentials*. Dar es Salaam.

THE UNITED REPUBLIC OF TANZANIA (URT) (Ed.) (2012): *National Sample Census of Agriculture 2007/2008. Volume Vj: Regional Report: Ruvuma Region*. Dar es Salaam.

THE UNITED REPUBLIC OF TANZANIA (URT) (Ed.) (2013a): *2012 Population and Housing Census. Population Distribution by Administrative Areas*. Dar es Salaam.

THE UNITED REPUBLIC OF TANZANIA (URT) (Ed.) (2013b): *National Agriculture Policy*. Dar es Salaam.

THE UNITED REPUBLIC OF TANZANIA (URT) (Ed.) (2016): *Ruvuma Region. Basic Demographic and Socio-Economic Profile*. Dar es Salaam.

THE WORLD BANK (2016): *Report No: PAD345. International Development Association Project Appraisal Document on a Proposed Credit in the Amount Of (Sdr50.8) Million (Us$70 Million Equivalent) to The United Republic of Tanzania for a Southern Agricultural Growth Corridor of Tanzania (SAGCOT) Investment Project*.

TORDOFF, W., MAZRUI, A. (1972): "The left and the super-left in Tanzania". In: *Journal of Modern African Studies* 10 (3), 427–445.

TOROKA, S. (1973): "Education for Self-reliance: The Litowa Experiment". In: Cliffe, L., Saul, J. S. (Ed.): *Socialism in Tanzania. Volume 2: Policies*. Dar es Salaam, 264–271.

TREUHEIT, W. (1971): *Sozialismus in Entwicklungsländern*. Köln.

VAN DER BOM, F. (2013): *Soya ni Pesa. MSc Internship report*. Ed. by N2Africa. URL: http://www.n2africa.org/sites/n2africa.org/files/images/Frederik%20v%20d%20 Bom%20MSc%20Internship%20Report%20final.pdf (Date of last Retrieval: 2/10/2017).

WALLERSTEIN, I. (1974): *The Modern World System. Volume 1*. New York.

WALLERSTEIN, I. (1980): *The Modern World System. Volume 2*. New York.

WALLERSTEIN, I. (1988): *The Modern World System. Volume 3*. New York.

WATZAL, L. (1982): *Ujamaa – the end of a utopia?* Munich.

WEAVER, J. H., KRONEMER, A. (1981): "Tanzanian and African socialism". In: *World Development* 9 (9-10), 839–849.

WENNER, K. (1970): *Shamba Letu*. Boston.

WILSON, R. T. (2015): *The Soybean Value Chain in Tanzania. A report from the Southern Highlands Food Systems Programme*. Ed. by Food and Agricultural Organization of the United Nations (FAO). URL: http://www.fao.org/fileadmin/user_upload/ivc/ PDF/SFVC/Tanzania_soybean.pdf (Date of last Retrieval: 5/15/2017).

WILY, L. A. (2003): *Community-based land tenure management. Questions and answers about Tanzania's new Village Land Act,1999* (IIED Issue paper, no. 120). London.

WINTERS, C. A., CURNEY, S., SULIVAN, T. (2010): "The Evolution of a Coding Schema in a Paced Program of Research". In: *The Qualitative Report* 15 (6), 1415–1430.

WOODS, R. (1975): "Peasants and Peasantries in Tanzania and their Role in Socio-Political Development". In: Cliffe, L., Lawrence, P., Luttrell, W. L., Migot-Adhola, S. E., Saul, J. S. (Ed.): *Rural Cooperation in Tanzania*. Dar es Salaam, 39–50.

Appendix 1: Qualitative Interviews

Guideline-Based Expert Interviews (GBE)									
ID	Date of Interview	Location	Inter-viewee(s)	Organi-zation/ Position	Type of Organi-zation	Language	Interpre-tation by	No. of Guideline used	Duration of interview
GBE 1	02/23/2015	Songea	Welmoed Ryphema; Brito Mgoyo	Caritas Songea	NGO	English	n/a	1	35min
GBE 2	02/23/2015	Songea	Ladislaus Bigambo	RUCODIA	NGO	English	n/a	1	15min
GBE 3	02/24/2015	Songea	Rachel Teri; Dennis Mpaza-gade	MVIWATA	NGO	English	n/a	1	25min
GBE 4	02/24/2015	Songea	Iskata C. Msigwa	PADI	NGO	English	n/a	1	30min
GBE 5	02/24/2015	Songea	Wilbert Matumbi	TMMTF	NGO	English	n/a	1	20min
GBE 6	02/25/2015	Peramiho	Father Fidelis	Prior at Peramiho	Church	English	n/a	3	25min
GBE 7	02/26/2015	Litowa	Michael Komba	Village Chairman, Litowa	Public Admini-stration	Kiswahili	Brother Augustine	4	35min
GBE 8	03/02/2015	Songea	Charles Mihayo	District Planning Officer	Public Admini-stration	Englisch	n/a	2	15min
GBE 9	03/10/2015	Songea	Damas Mbogoro	Former Member of Parliament	Public Admini-stration	English	n/a	n.a.	35min
GBE 10	03/10/2015	Songea	Xaver Komba	Songea Network Center	NGO	German	Daniel Mann	1	25min
GBE 11	03/11/2015	Mbinga-mharule	Omare Kamare; Ernest S. Madau	Village Govern-ment, Mbinga-mharule	Public Admini-stration	Kiswahili	Daniel Mann	5	25min
GBE 12	03/12/2015	Songea	Anthony Nginga	Regional Develop-ment Officer	Public Admini-stration	English	n/a	2	20min
GBE 13	03/13/2015	Songea	Morgan Mwaipya-na	NFRA	National Food Reserve	English	n/a	7	15min
GBE 14	03/18/2015	Dar es Salaam	William Ngeno (YARA); Petro Komba (SNC)	YARA	Private Corpo-ration / NGO	English	n/a	8	35min
GBE 15	08/30/2015	Matete-reka	Remigius W. Njafula	Village Chairman, Matetereka	Public Admini-stration	Kiswahili	Daniel Mann/ Josephat Mwasula-ma	4&5	20min
GBE 16	09/01/2015	Matete-reka	Elias M. Mbawala	Head Teacher	School	English /partly Kiswahili	n/a	10	35min
GBE 17	09/09/2015	Songea	Neema Lutate-nekwa	Caritas Songea (Soya ni Pesa)	NGO	English	n/a	n.a.	15min

Narrative Interviews with Contemporary Witnesses of Ujamaa (NCW)						
ID	Date of Interview	Location	Inter-viewee(s)	Language	Interpretation by	Duration of interview
NCW 1	02/26/2015	Litowa	Joakim M. Sako	Kiswahili	Brother Augustine	40min
NCW 2	02/28/2015	Peramiho	Telesphor Mwenda	English	n/a	20min
NCW 3	03/03/2015	Liweta	Bele Kumasi Nyoni; Lucia Eluka	Kiswahili	Dennis Mpazagade	30min
NCW 4	03/06/2015	Matetereka	Mzee Lukas Mayemba	Kiswahili	Dennis Mpazagade	1h 30min
NCW 5	03/06/2015	Matetereka	Gervas Mkomba	Kiswahili	Dennis Mpazagade	15min
NCW 6	03/11/2015	Mbinga-mharule	Group of Elders	Kiswahili	Daniel Mann	25min
NCW 7	03/11/2015	Namatuhi	Stanislaus Senda	Kiswahili	Xaver Komba	10min
NCW 8	03/11/2015	Namatuhi	Merkiol Senda; Stanislaus Senda	Kiswahili	Xaver Komba	40min
NCW 9	08/24/2015	Litowa	Fabian Kaziulaya Shawa	Kiswahili	Daniel Mann	15min
NCW 10	08/31/2015	Matetereka	Group of Elders/ Former Students of RDA School	Kiswahili	Daniel Mann	2h

Group Interviews (GI)

ID	Date of Interview	Location	Inter-viewees	Type of Group	Langua-ge	Inter-pretation by	No. of Guideline used	Duration of interview
GI 1	08/22/2015	Litowa	Kanyanga Twende Group	Kikundi (Farmers' Group)	Kiswahili	Dennis Mpazagade	9	40min
GI 2	08/24/2015	Litowa	Mtakuja Tangine Group	Kikundi (Farmers' Group)	Kiswahili	Daniel Mann	9	50min
GI 3	08/24/2015	Litowa	Juhudi Group	Kikundi (Farmers' Group)	Kiswahili	Daniel Mann	9	45min
GI 4	08/24/2015	Litowa	Mshikamano Group	Kikundi (Farmers' Group)	Kiswahili	Daniel Mann	9	35min
GI 5	08/24/2015	Litowa	Jahudi (2) Group	Kikundi (Farmers' Group)	Kiswahili	Daniel Mann	9	40min
GI 6	08/24/2015	Litowa	Umoja Group (Madamba B)	Kikundi (Farmers' Group)	Kiswahili	Daniel Mann	9	1h
GI 7	09/02/2015	Matetereka	Tangawizi Group	Kikundi (Farmers' Group)	Kiswahili	Daniel Mann	9	45min
GI 8	09/02/2015	Matetereka	Samani Youth Group	Youth Group	Kiswahili	Josephat Mwasulama	9	35min
GI 9	09/03/2015	Matetereka	3 Farmers' groups of Matetereka C	Kikundi (Farmers' Group)	Kiswahili	Daniel Mann	9	50min
GI 10	09/03/2015	Matetereka	2 Farmers' groups of Matetereka B	Kikundi (Farmers' Group)	Kiswahili	Daniel Mann	9	35min
GI 11	09/03/2015	Matetereka	Kujitegemea Group	Kikundi (Farmers' Group)	Kiswahili	Daniel Mann	9	35min
GI 12	09/06/2015	Litowa	Young Farmers	Youth Group	Kiswahili	Dennis Mpazagade	9	35min
GI 13	09/08/2015	Mbinga-mharule	7 Farmers' groups of Mbinga-mharule	Kikundi (Farmers' Group)	Kiswahili	Daniel Mann	9	40min
GI 14	09/10/2015	Mbinga-mharule	4 Farmers' groups of Mbinga-mharule	Kikundi (Farmers' Group)	Kiswahili	Daniel Mann	9	40min

Guidelines used for qualitative interviews

Guideline 1:

Questions for Songea NGOs
1. What is the main objective of your organization?
2. How long have you been active in Ruvuma?
    Your NGO?
    Yourself?
3. Where are you active?
    Within the region?
    Elsewhere in Tanzania? Comparison?
4. What does development mean for you?
5. What is the biggest challenge in Ruvuma?
6. What kinds of project to you do?
7. What do you know about the history of Ujamaa?
    The RDA?
8. Are there still things remaining from the Ujamaa era?
9. What kind of cooperative movements do you know/ work with?
10. What has changed in the region since…
    1985?
    2000?
    You have been active here? (mostly asked, since people had issues remembering/ addressing the 1985 question)
11. Do you know the villages of Matetereka, Litowa and Liweta? Contacts?
12. Do you have additional data/ information?

Guideline 2:

Questions for Regional and District officers
1. How long have you served in this office?
2. What are your main tasks?
3. What does development mean for you?
4. What is the biggest challenges for development in Ruvuma/ Songea?
5. What do you know about the history of Ujamaa in the region?
    The RDA?
6. What has changed since then?
7. What do you know about the villages of Matetereka, Litowa and Liweta?
    Contacts?
8. Do you have additional data/ information?
    The regional/district budget?

Guideline 3:

Questions for Peramiho Abby
1. How long have you been in Permiho?
   (What are your main tasks?)
2. What does development mean for you?
3. What are the biggest challenges for development in Ruvuma?
4. What kinds of projects are you currently doing? Where?
5. What do you know about the history of Ujamaa in the region?
   The RDA?
6. What has changed since then?
7. Are there still things remaining?
8. What kind of cooperatives do you know? Work with?
9. What do you know about the villages of Matetereka, Litowa and Liweta?
   Contacts?
10. Do you have additional data/ information?

Guideline 4:

Questions for Litowa Village chairman
1. What are your main tasks?
2. How long have you been in this position?
3. What are the main economic activities in this village?
4. What does development mean for you?
5. What are the main challenges?
6. What do you know about the history of Litowa?
   The RDA?
   Villagization?
7. What has changed since then?
8. Are there still things remaining?
   Communal fields?
9. Inquiring the possibilities of coming back. Group discussions, etc.
10. Do you have additional data/ information/ budget/ people to talk with?

Guideline 5:

Ouestions for Mbingamharule Village Government. Maswali kwa mwenyekiti wa kijiji cha Mbingamharule

1. Ni kazi kuu yako nini, kama mwenyekiti?
   (What are your main tasks, as village chairman?)
2. Ulikuwa mwenyekiti wa Mbingamharule lini?
   (Since when are you village chairman of Mbingamharule?)
3. Je, ni shughuli kuu ya kiuchumi ya kijiji?
   (What are the main economic activities of the village?)
4. Je, maendeleo maana nini kwa ajili yenu?
   (What does development mean for you?)
5. Ni changamoto kuu nini?
   (What are the main challenges?)
6. Unajua nini kuhusu historia ya kijiji hiki?
   Historia ya ujamaa hapa?
   (What do you know about the history of this village?
   The local history of Ujamaa?)
7. Nini kimebadilisha tangu wakati huu?
   (What has changed since those times?)
8. Je, kuna bado mambo iliyobaki kutoka nyakati za ujamaa?
   (Are there any things remaining from the times of Ujamaa?)
9. Je, i kuwa kuangalia bajeti ya kijiji?
   (Is it possible to have a look at the village budget?)
10. Una data nyingine yoyote ya kijiji?
    (Do you have any additional data?)

Guideline 6: (unused/ intended for Mbingamharule group of elders – switched to Narrative Interview)

Guideline 7:

Questions for NFRA (National Food Reserve)

1. Where do you buy the maize?
2. How much? Other crops?
3. Where do you sell it?
4. What other organizations are there to buy maize and other crops in Ruvuma?
5. What have been the main changes in the last 15 years?
6. Since when is NFRA in operation?
7. What are the main challenges?
8. You have any data available? Further information?

Guideline 8:

Questions for YARA Dar es Salaam
1. How long have you been working for this company?
2. What are YARA's activities? Since when?
3. What kind of farm inputs do you sell?
   Where?
   How much?
4. How much goes to Songea/ Ruvuma?
5. Which are your main competitors?
6. What's the difference?
7. What are the biggest challenges?
8. What have been the biggest challenges in the last 15/30 years?
9. Can you provide me with data?

Guideline 9:

Questions for Farmers' Groups. Maswali wa kikundi
1. Je, ni shughuli kuu ya kikundi chetu?
   (What are the main activities of your group?)
2. Mnazalisha pamoja, au mnauza vizao pamoja, tu?
   (Are you farming together, or only selling your produce together?)
3. Mlianza lini kwa kikundi hiki?
   (When did you start with this group?)
4. Je, wanachama wenu wanafanya nini kwa ajili ya maisha? Kulima tu?
   (What are your members doing for a living? Only agriculture?)
5. Ni changamoto kuu kile?
   (What are the main challenges?)
6. Je, maendeleo maana nini kwa ajili yenu?
   (What does development mean for you?)
7. Mnafikiri nini kuhusu nyakati za ujamaa?
   (What is your opinion on the times of ujamaa?)
8. Nini kimebadilisha tangu wakati huo? Ilikuwa ni kwa bora au mbaya?
   (What has changed since then? Has it been better or worse?)
9. Ni mipango yenu ya baadaye ni nini?
   (What are your plans fro the future?)
10. Je, una maswali yoyote ajili yangu?
    (Do you have any questions about myself?)

Guideline 10

Questions for Matatereka primary school
1. How long have you been in this position?
2. How many students and teacher does your school have?
3. What are the main challenges for your school?
4. How do you see the development in this area?
5. Which role does ujamaa history have in education here?

Appendix 2: Village Questionnaire

Original version of the questionnaire used in the case study villages (Example from Litowa)

Maswali kwa wakulima wa Litowa

1. a) Umazaliwa hapa Litowa?
   ☐ Ndiyo ☒ Hapana   Kama hapana:
   b) Ulitoka wapi?
   MADABA SONGEA
   c) Kwa nini ulikuja Litowa?
   KUFUKAAZIA MAENDELEO YA KIJIJI

2. Familia yako ni ya watu wangapi?
   Wanaume 2 /Wanawake …
   Watoto 3

3. Shamba lako linaukubwa gani?
   ekari 3

4. Je, unalima mazao gani?
   MAHINDI

5. Unavuna kiasi gani kwa kila msimu?
   GUNIA 45

6. Je, umeagjiin watu katik maeneo yako ya kazi?
   ☐ Ndiyo ☒ Hapana
   Kama ndiyo, Je ni Wangapi?

7. Je, unazalisha kwa ajili ya chakula tu?
   ☐ Ndiyo ☒ Hapana
   Kama unazalishwa kwa ajili ya biashara, kwa kukuango gani?
   CHA KAWAIDA GUNIA 40

8. Je unafuga?
   ☒ Ndiyo ☐ Hapana
   Kama ni ndiyo, je unafuga nini? Na ni kiasi gani cha mifugo?
   KUKU, NGURUWE
   16   11

9. Unachanzo kingine cha mapato zaidi ya shamba?
   ☐ Ndiyo ☒ Hapana
   Kama ni ndiyo ni chanzo gani?

10. Je unakula mara ngapi kwa siku au unapata milo mingapi kwa siku?
    ☐ 1 ☐ 2 ☒ 3

11. Ni wewe ni mwanachama wa kikundi chochote?
    ☐ Ndiyo ☒ Hapana

12. Changamoto ipi unakumbana nayo katika maisha?
    NYINGI KAMA :
    - UKOSEFU WA PEMBEJEO ZA KILIMO, NA GHARAMA
      YAKE NI KUBWA KUZIPATA
    - UKOSEFU WA MIKOPO KWA WAKULIMA
    - UKOSEFU WA MIAMKO YA MAZAO
    - UKOSEFU WA ELIMU YA UZIALO BORA KWA WAKULIMA

13. Unafikiri nini kuhusu maendeleo ya kijiji?
    - VIANZISHWE VIKUNDI KWA WAKULIMA NA
      KAKO PEIPEMF
    - SERIKALI ICHANGIE FEDHA KWA VIFAA ILI
      KUFNDISHA MIRADI YA MAENDELEO VIJIJINI

14. Unafikiri nini kuhusu wakati wa Ujamaa?
    - WANANCHI WALIPOBEA KUPEWA MIRAADA
      NA SASA WAMEATMIRIKA NA ILE HALIYA
      UGAAUAA HILYO KUDIFEBEMEA KWAO
      INAKUWA TABU SANA KWA SASA

15. Jinsia yako
    ☐ Mwanake ☒ Mwanamume

16. Umri wako
    ☐ 14-18 ☐ 19-25 ☐ 26-35 ☒ 36-50 ☐ 51-65 ☐ above 65

English meaning of the items of the village questionnaire

The village questionnaire as presented above was designed in Kiswahili by the author and used in the three villages of Litowa, Matetereka and Mbingmharule in this form, with the respective village name. All questionnaire interviews were conducted in Kiswahili by local research assistants. For the sake of confirmability, the English meaning of each question is provided below:

Questionnaire for the farmers of [-Village-]

1. a) Have you been born here in [-Village-]?

   ☐ Yes ☐ no   If no,
   b) Were did you come from?
   _____
   c) Since when are you living in [-Village-]?
   _____

2. How many members does your family have?

   Men:....../ Women: ....
   Children:..........

3. How big is your field?
   Acre(s)

4. Which crops do you cultivate?

5. How big is your harvest each year?

6. Are you employing additional people for your agriculture?
   ☐ Yes ☐ No
   If yes, how many people? :

7. Are you cultivating for your own food consumption, only?
   ☐ Yes ☐ No
   If you are farming for the market as well, what quantity do you sell?

8. Are you keeping animals?
   ☐ Yes ☐ No
   If yes, which animals do you keep? And how many?

9. Do you have any additional income, apart from your agriculture
   ☐ Yes...☐ No
   If yes, which kind of?

311

10. **How many meals do you usually have each day**
   ☐ 1 ☐ 2 ☐ 3
11. **Are you a member of any kind of farmers' group?**
   ☐ Ndiyo ☐ Hapana
12. **What are the biggest challenges you are facing?**

13. **What do you think about the development of the village?**

14. **What do you think about the times of Ujamaa?**

15. **Your gender**
   ☐ female ☐ male
16. **Your age**
   ☐ 14-18 ☐ 19-25 ☐ 26-35 ☐ 36-50...☐ 51-65 ☐ above 65

Age and Gender Distribution of the village samples

The respective age and gender distribution of the respondents can be seen in Figure 15 through 17. Only in the village of Litowa, more than one respondent under 18 took part in the study. In Litowa and Matetereka, the highest percentage of respondents could be found in the 26 to 35 age group, in Mbingamharule, most came from the 36-50 group. While the interviewers were advised to try to represent both genders equally, in Matetereka there was a considerable excess of male respondents (72 to 36, with one undeclared). This excess was especially pronounced within the 25-35 and the above 51-65 age groups. A graphical representation of the respective age and gender distribution of the village samples can be seen in Figures 15 through 17.

Figure 15: Age and Gender of Respondents to Village questionnaires, Litowa

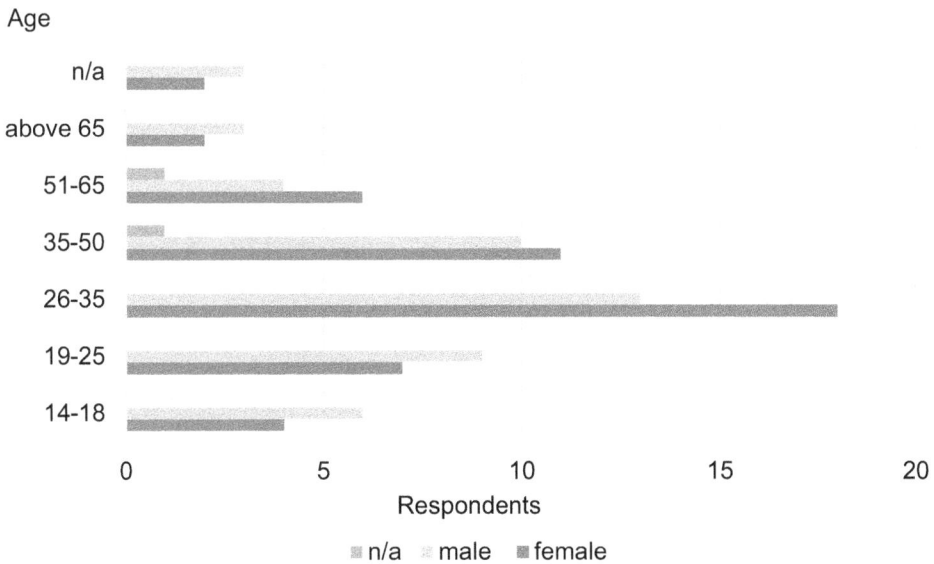

Figure 16: Age and Gender of Respondents to Village questionnaires, Matetereka

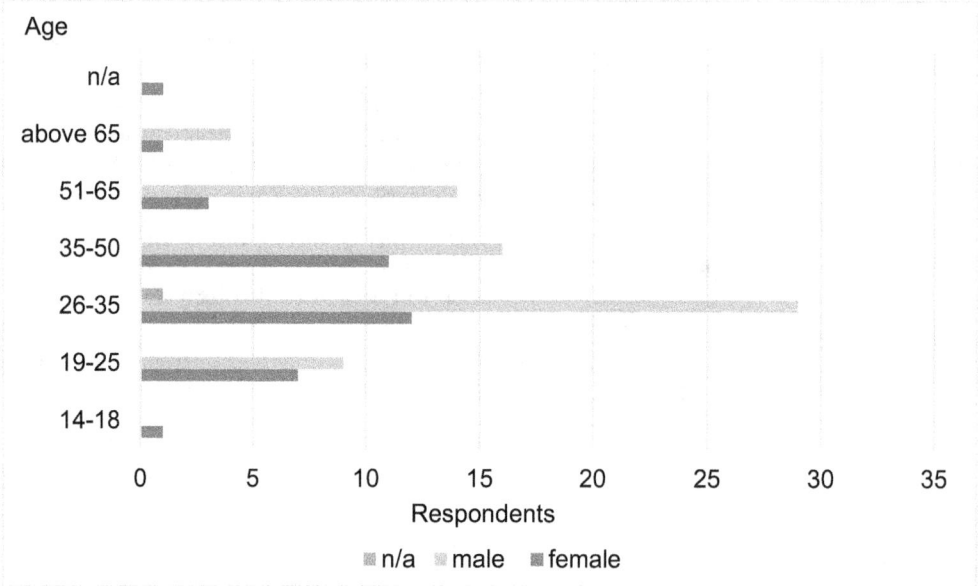

Figure 17: Age and Gender of Respondents to Village questionnaires, Mbingamharule

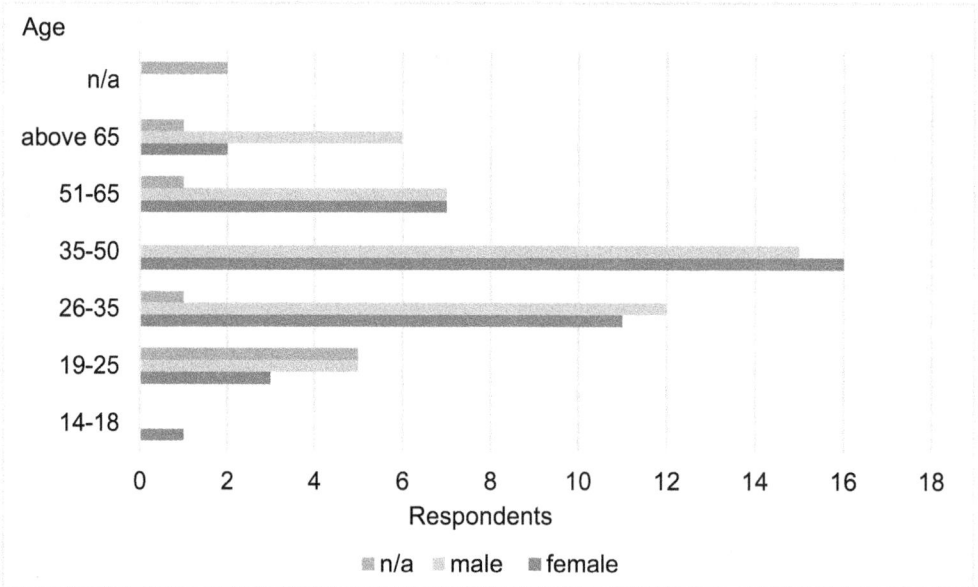

Appendix 3: Impressions from Liweta and Namatuhi

In addition to the empirical research in the three case study villages of Litowa, Ma-tetereka and Mbingamharule, interviews with contemporary witnesses took place in the villages of Liweta and Namatuhi in March 2015. Although these visits took only one day each, a short description of the villages and their history shall be given at this stage, acting as a background for the empirical results presented in the subsequent chapters.

Liweta was one of the best-known villages of the RDA during the heydays of the association, and in many ways acted as a model village of its own - with a history very similar to Litowa and Matetereka. Here, 18 men had started to work in 1963, one year after the establishment of Litowa, but made little progress in their farming, until they got into contact with advisors from the latter village. After that, however, the village made steady progress in establishing a system of collective agriculture and communal organization under the advisory of the SERA. Three years after Liweta's foundation, its inhabitants had 75 acres of land under communal cultivation, and another 80 acres of private plots. Members of Liweta and Litowa, together, built a 15 mile long motorable road connecting the villages, enabling even closer cooperation and eliminating the need for the long detour via Songea town (BRAIN 1977: 240p.).

After the end of the RDA, however, the village fell into a virtual coma, resembling the stagnation of development seen in Litowa. Old RDA structures, like the water tank and the Ujamaa hall fell beyond repair, while the new arrivals of the villagization era were settling south of the original Liweta village, along the road connecting the village to the Songea-Njombe highway. According to local sources, the original sett-lement north of the Liweta river was given up altogether in 1995. As of 2015, nature is slowly taking back all the remains of the original Ujamaa settlement of Liweta, and the entire village is now constituted around 4 km south of that site. In 2012, Liweta village counted 1,118 inhabitants (NBS 2012: 191).

Liweta was also seen as a possible location for an additional case study and vi-sited for that reason the 3rd of March 2015. However, time restrictions during the second field visit in August and September 2015, as well as lack of support by the local authorities impeded further empirical work in this village. Therefore, only the observations described above and one interview with two contemporary witnesses (NCW 3; 3/3/2015) from Liweta have been included in this study.

So, while Liweta shares its particular history as a settlement begun by grassroots activists with the likes of Litowa and Matetereka, even in this time of new villages being founded throughout the region, there were areas where little happened. One of these places was Namatuhi, around 30 km south of Songea town. There had been a school established by the Peramiho missionary in colonial times, and the place became known by the name of the small stream in its vicinity - Namatuhi. In fact, there was no village at this place, only scattered little hamlets in the whole area, and the one closest to the school was the one of the Senda family. Two wazee from this family (Merkiol Senda and Stanislaus Senda) were interviewed during the research (NCW 7; 3/11/2015; NCW 8; 3/11/2015).

The idea of searching for contemporary witnesses of the Ujamaa era in this particular village was brought forward by Xaver Komba, who had also suggested including his hometown of Mbingamharule as an example for a non-RDA village (see chapter 5.4.3.). Apart from his ability to act as a local guide in these parts of Songea district, Namatuhi was in his perception notable for having a large "Ujamaa building" in the center of the village - for him an indicator that it was worth a visit for a researcher interested in this subject. During the visit in Namatuhi on 11th of March 2015, the building was identified, yet local accounts on its former use varied: While most of the locals referred to it as an Ujamaa building, a badge on the entrance to the now abandoned three story structure stated 1989 as the year of construction - well beyond the actual Ujamaa era. Apart from this building, no alleged remains of the Ujamaa era were pointed out by the inhabitants of Namatuhi.

Based on the fact that the data gathered in Mbingamharule were seen as sufficient to illustrate the development of a non-RDA village in Ruvuma, the decision was taken not to return for further research during the second field trip to Ruvuma. Nevertheless, the interviews cited above were included as valuable perspectives on the narrative of Ujamaa development. As of 2015, the village appeared to have a settlement structure similar to that of Mbingamharule, with a small commercial center around the market, a primary school and a church. The 2012 census data stated 2,659 inhabitants for Namatuhi village (NBS 2012: 191).

www.ingramcontent.com/pod-product-compliance
Lightning Source LLC
Chambersburg PA
CBHW081428270326
41932CB00019B/3128